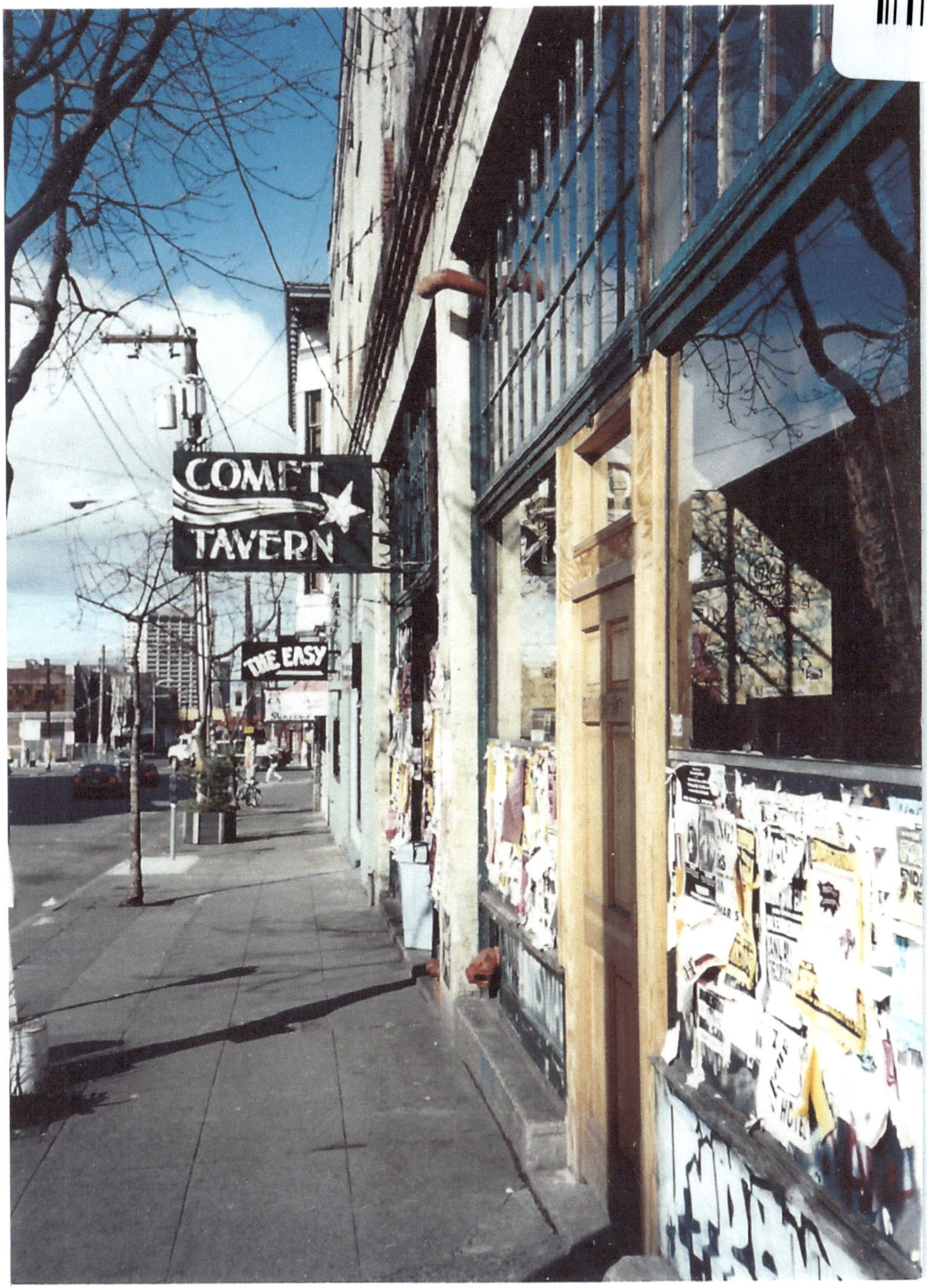

I0753659

COMET
TAVERN
THE EASY

Seattle Street Art

Volume #1

"The Comet Wall"

An Urbansubcultures Production

By Robert "Fritz" Davis

Copyright 2012
ISBN-13: 978-0615616483
ISBN-10: 0615616488

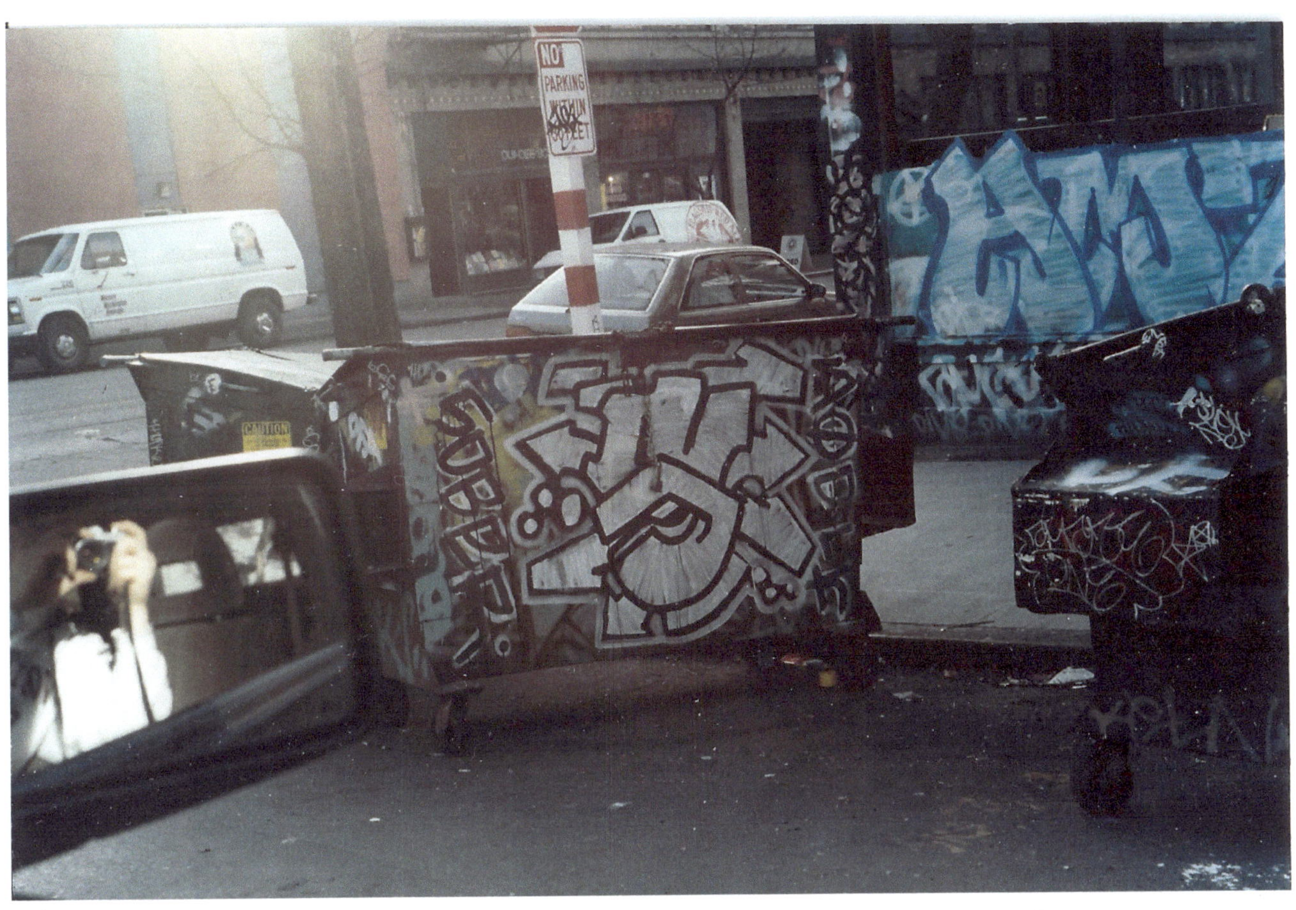
NO
PARKING
WITHIN
CAUTION

This book is dedicated to my beautiful wife, Paige Davis

Special thanks to,

Aaron Larson
Nathan Hivic
Paul Woodard

"Witness the strength of Street Knowledge"

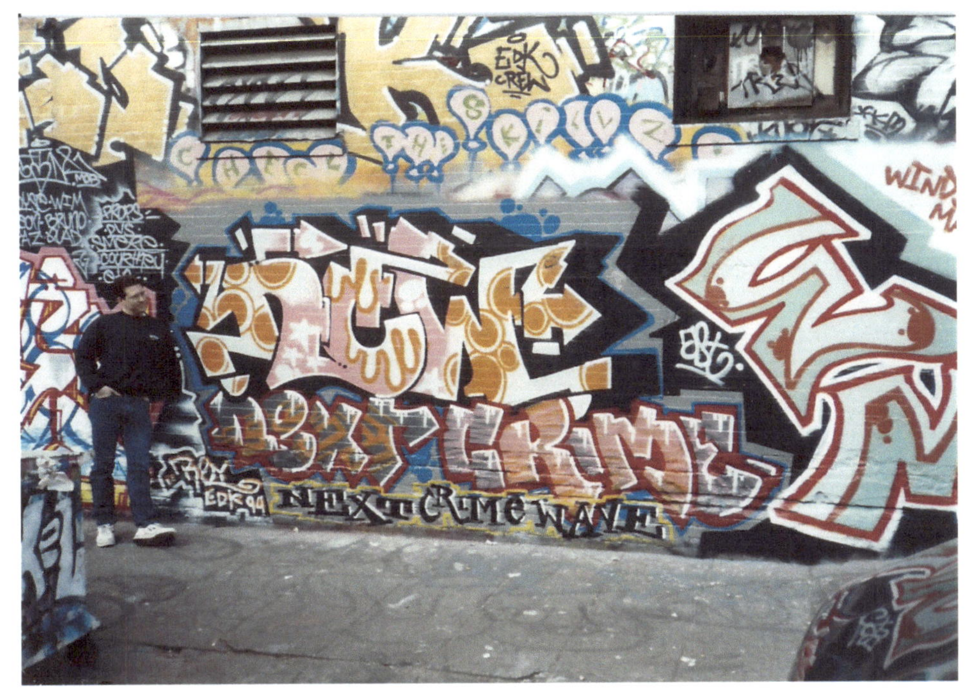

Urbansubcultures.com

"The Comet Wall"

When we take it upon ourselves to create some form of public art, we take a risk, opening the door for criticism and scrutiny from the general public, and pressure from competitive peers. I admire anyone who has the hutzpah to do that.

None of the art contained in this book still exists today. Some is of a very high quality, some, not so much. Either way I think it all has heart.

The Comet Tavern wall on Capitol Hill in Seattle was a hotbed of competitive popular street art for several years. From 1993 through 1996 I took photographs of the ever changing canvas that was the "Comet Wall." The fleeting nature of the medium has always fascinated me. Often the artwork wouldn't even last 24 hours before being painted over, so the pictures are very rare in the sense that the art existed for such a short time. Almost all street art by it's nature exists very temporarily, until it is either painted over, removed or covered up somehow. There are lots of colorful walls encased in concrete, as Downtown buildings are erected literally an inch apart from one another sometimes forming a kind of graffiti art time capsule.

Twenty years ago I was there on Capitol Hill taking these pictures every day. Things have changed a lot in Seattle since then. There is little notable street art in the city anymore, certainly nothing like The Comet or the old Vogue wall down on 1st Ave. There are only a few active spots these days and none of them are as in-your-face prominent. It's too bad really, but I suppose it's like all other art forms, things evolve and styles change. Attitudes and art trends progress with time. Which I might add, makes these photographs even more poignant as they represent an old school style.

After sifting through my collection of photographs depicting this particular wall, I decided on these awesome photos. I give you over two hundred of what I think are the best images, as an overall representation of the paintings and the scene during that time.

There was a lot of activity at the Comet wall in those days. Sometimes groups of people would gather on warm summer nights to watch the painters do their thing. Patrons of the Tavern would come out to see what was going on, and enjoy the art being created right there on the street. Ah, the smell of spray paint and draft micro brew! Seattle was a very amazing place to be in the 1990's with the grunge music scene in full swing and the technology tsunami rolling over the city and surrounding areas. I saw life changing bands and amazing art during those years. But those times are long gone now, so I hope this wonderfully unique collection of photographs will serve as a nostalgic inspiration. And everyone should be able to enjoy the vibrant urban art phenomenon that they represent.

Robert "Fritz" Davis
Seattle, WA 2012

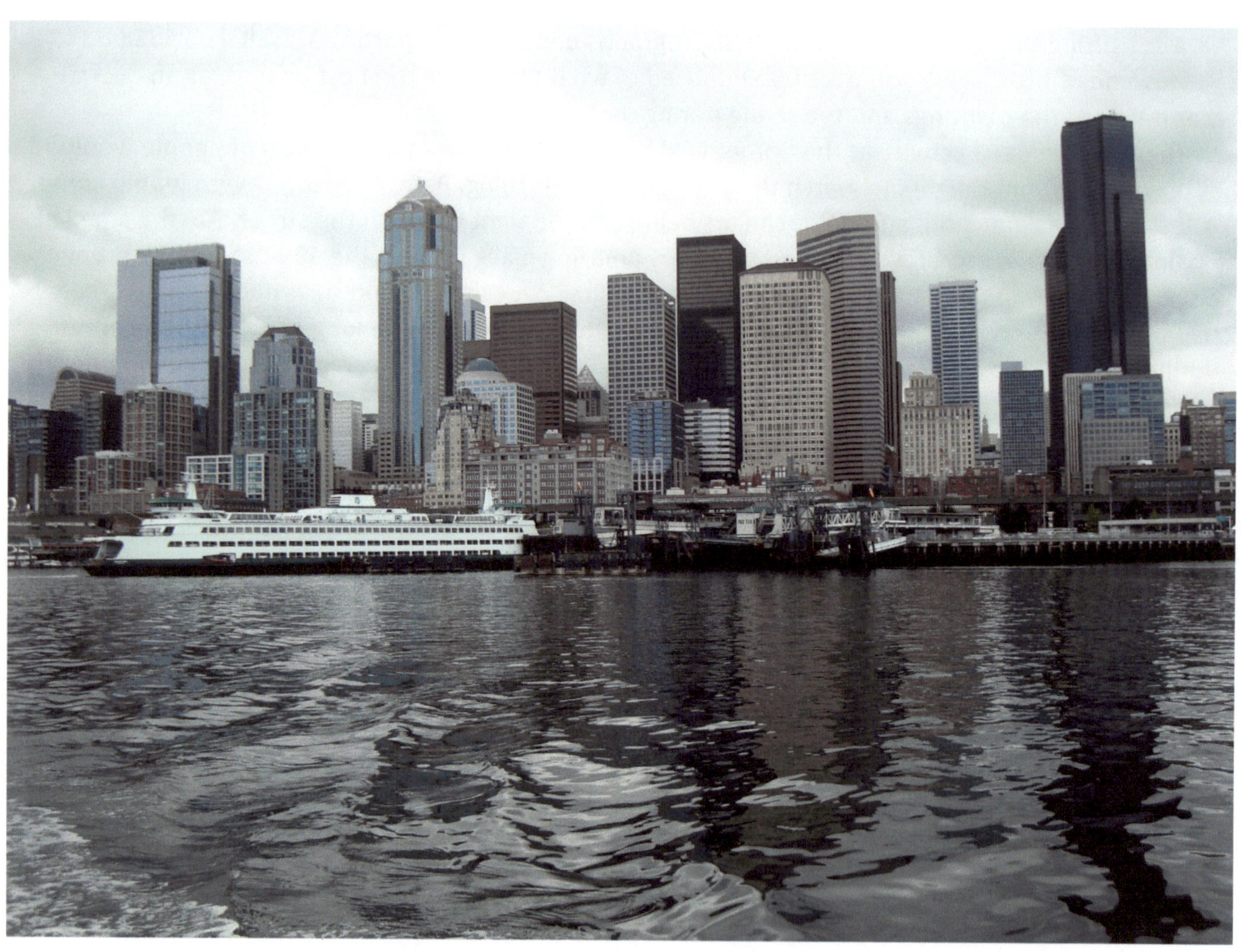

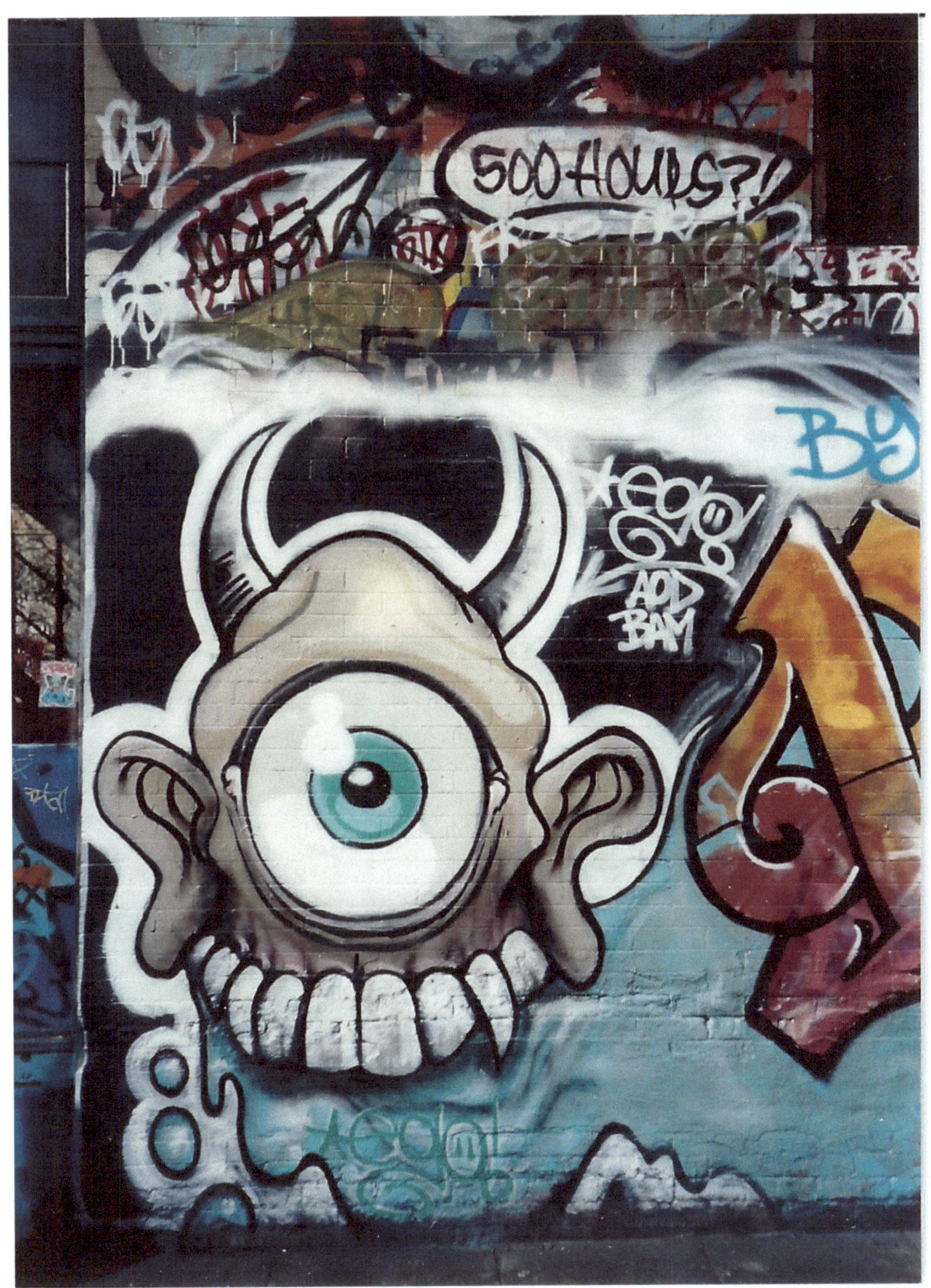
500 HOURS?!
AOD
BAM

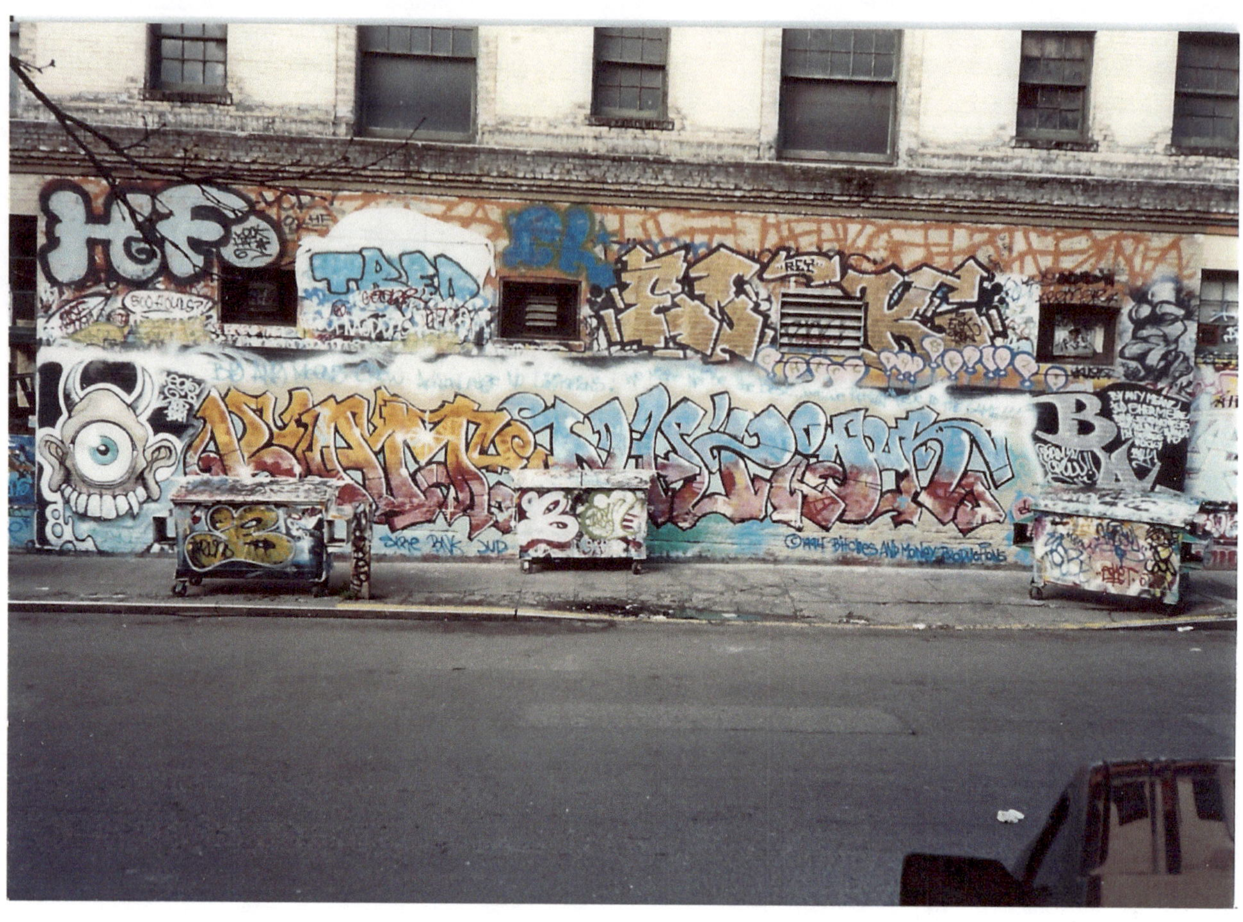

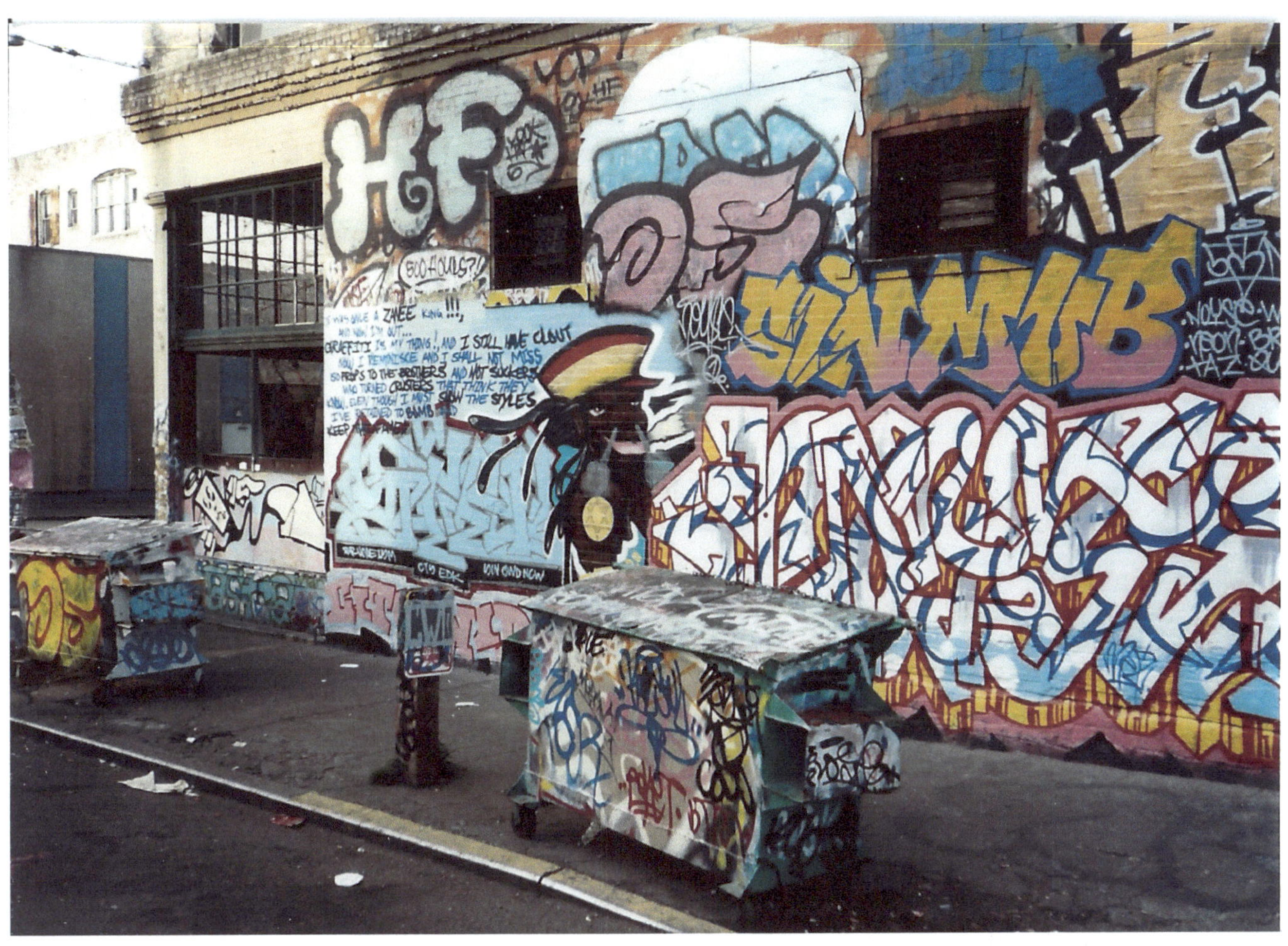
HF
GRAFFITI IS MY THING!, AND I STILL HAVE CLOUT
NOW, I REMINISCE AND I SHALL NOT MISS
SO PROPS TO THE BROTHERS AND NOT SUCKERS
KNOW, EVEN THOUGH I MUST SHOW THE STYLES

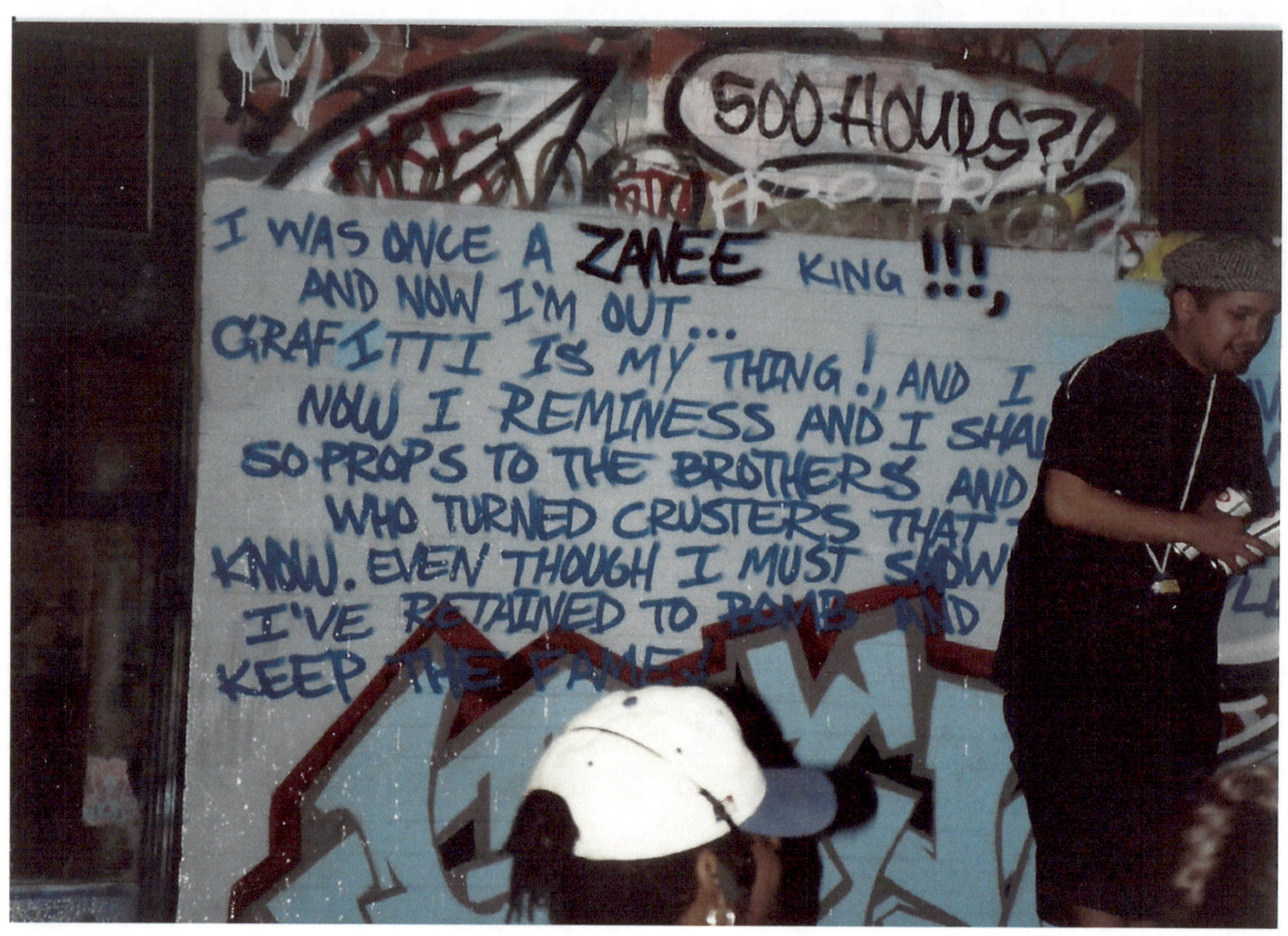

500 HOURS?!
I WAS ONCE A ZANEE KING !!!,
AND NOW I'M OUT...
GRAFITTI IS MY THING !, AND I
NOW I REMINESS AND I
SO PROPS TO THE BROTHERS AND
WHO TURNED CRUSTERS THAT
KNOW. EVEN THOUGH I MUST
I'VE RETAINED TO BOMB AND
KEEP THE FAME!

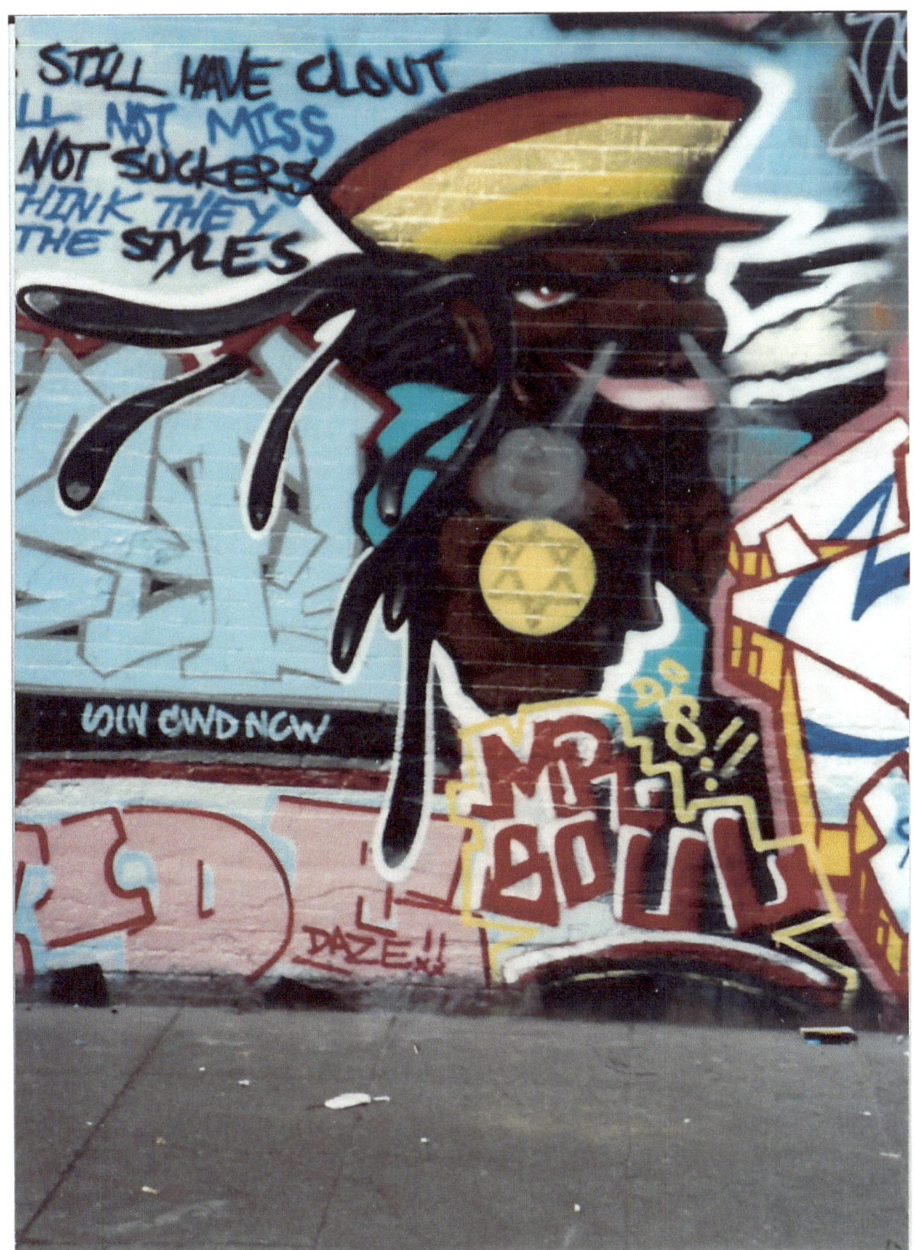
STILL HAVE CLOUT
LL NOT MISS
NOT SUCKERS
HINK THEY
THE STYLES
DAZE!!

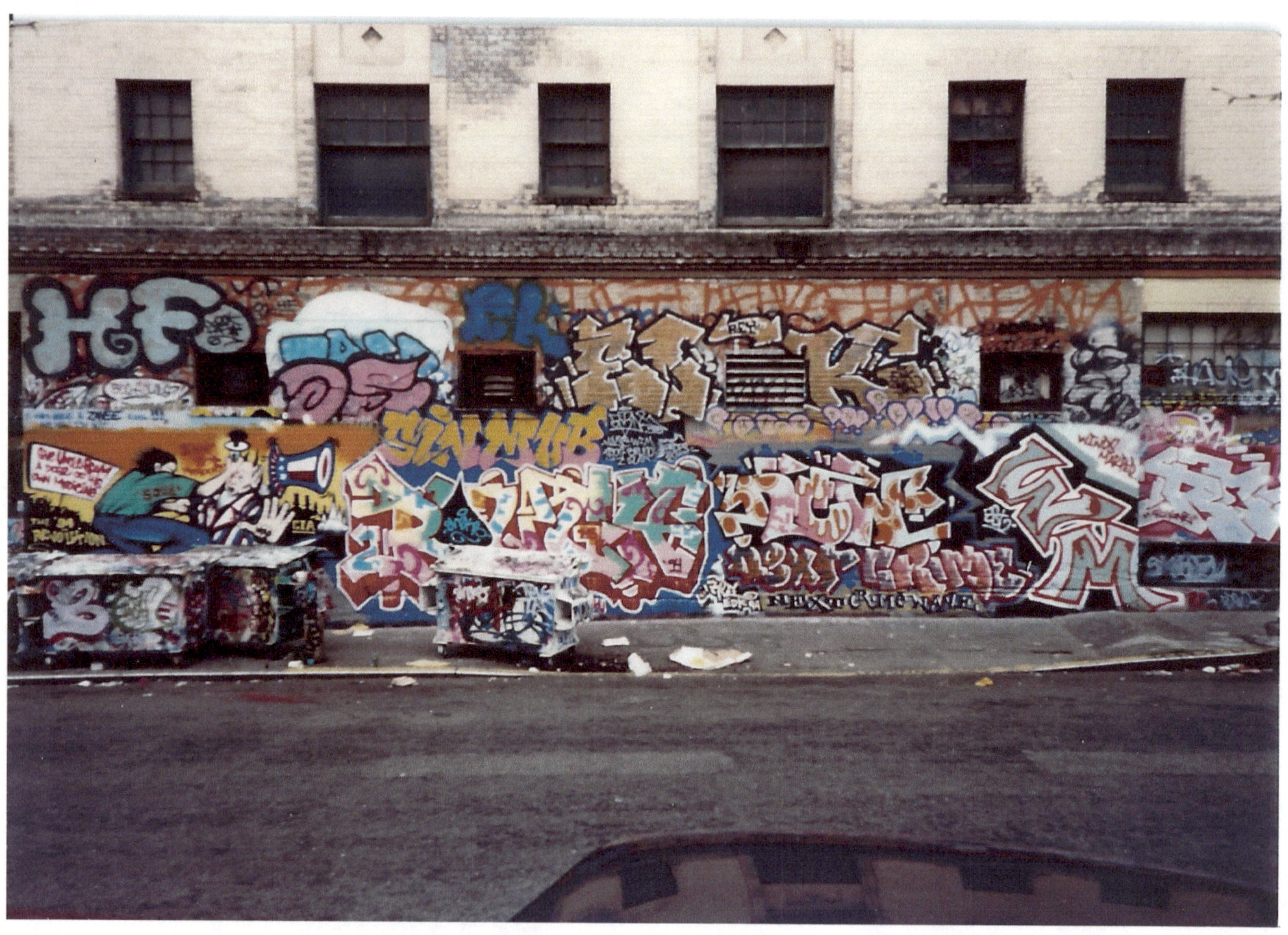

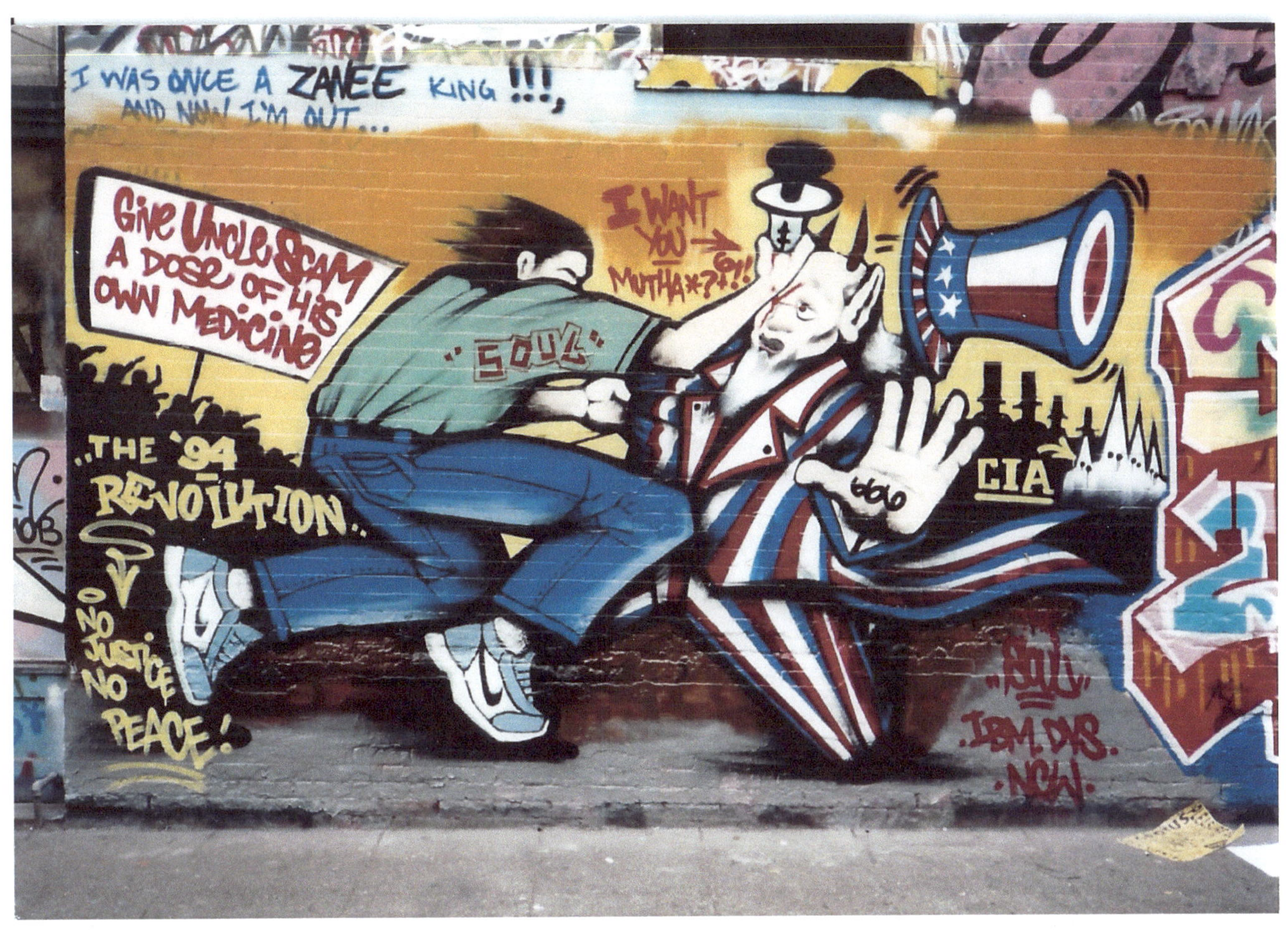
I WAS ONCE A ZANEE KING !!!,
AND NOW I'M OUT...
Give Uncle Scam A DOSE OF HIS OWN MEDICINE
I WANT YOU → MUTHA*?!!
"SOUL"
..THE '94 REVOLUTION..
NO JUSTICE NO PEACE!
CIA
666
"SOUL"
.IBM.DYS.
.NCW.

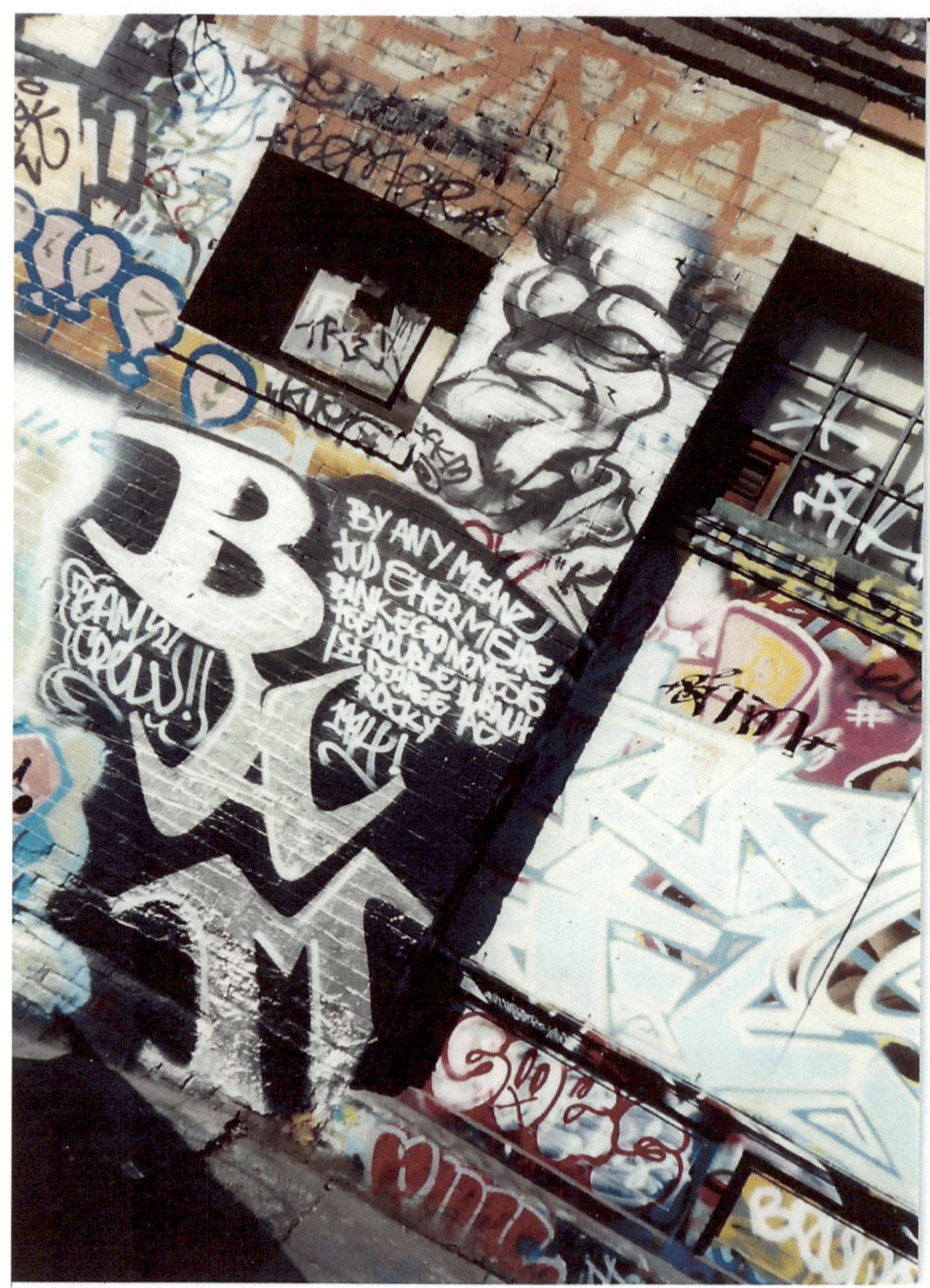
BY ANY MEANZ
ROCKY

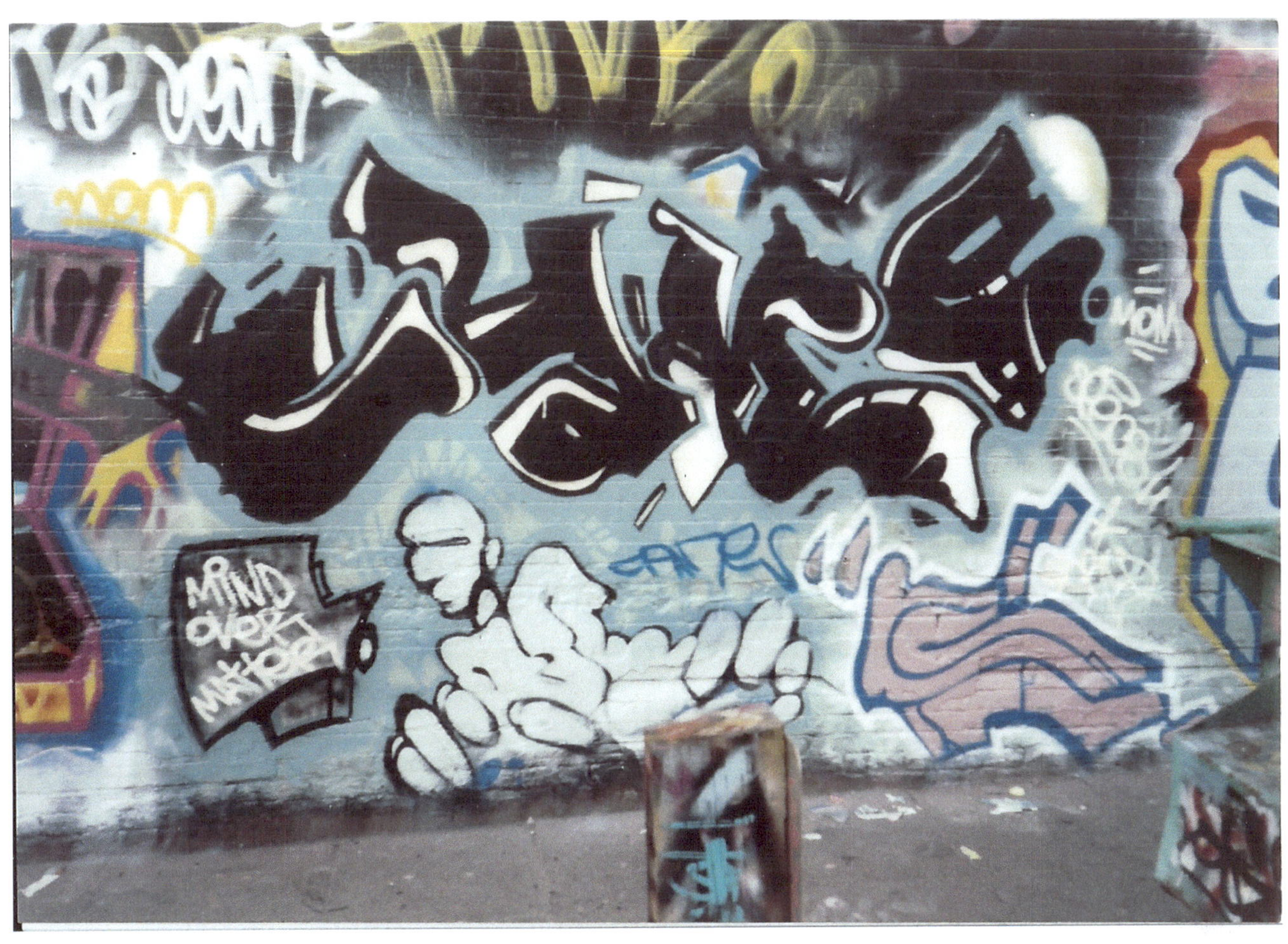
MIND
OVER
MATTER

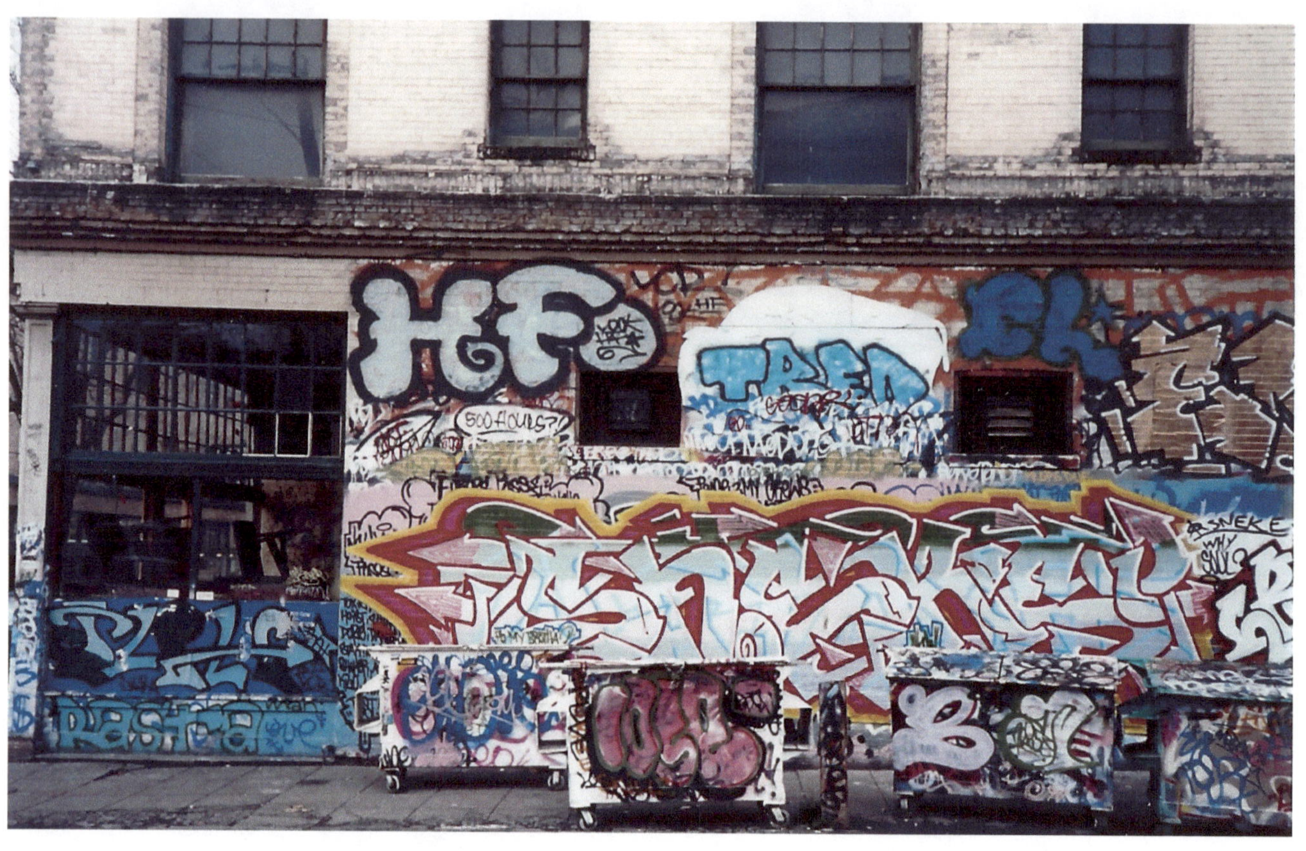
HF
500 HOURS?
SNEKE

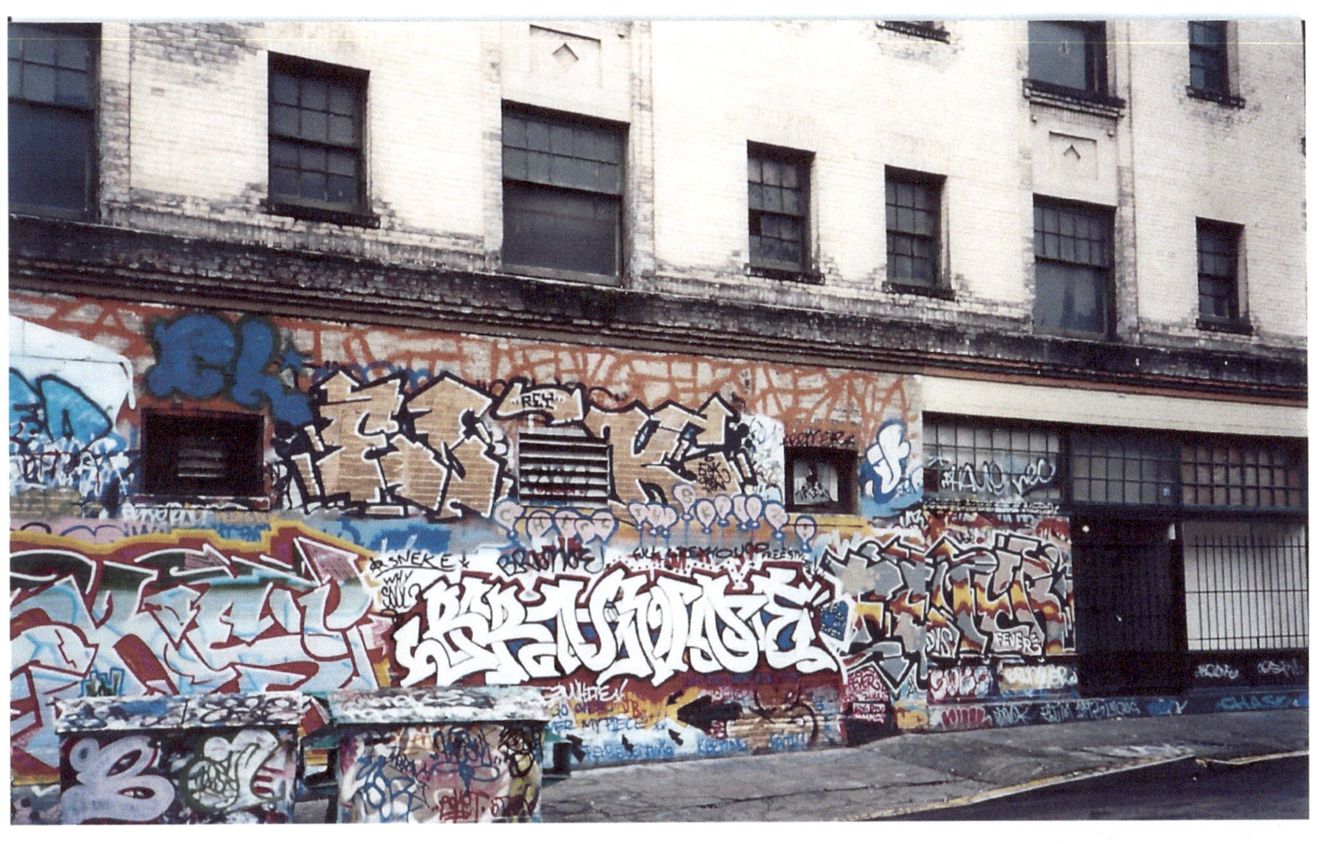

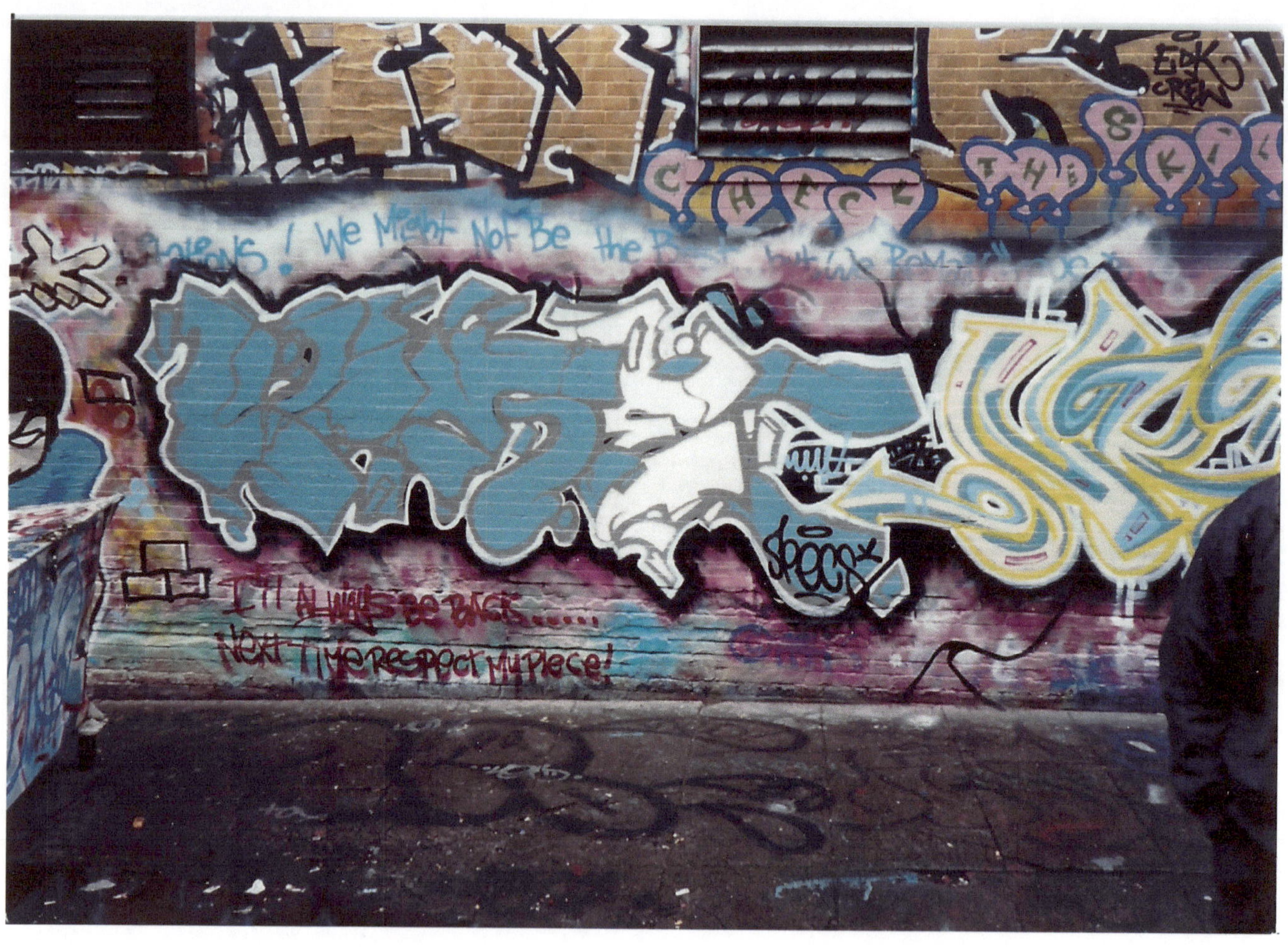

We Might Not Be the
EBK CREW
SPECS
I'll Always Be Back......
Next Time Respect My Piece!

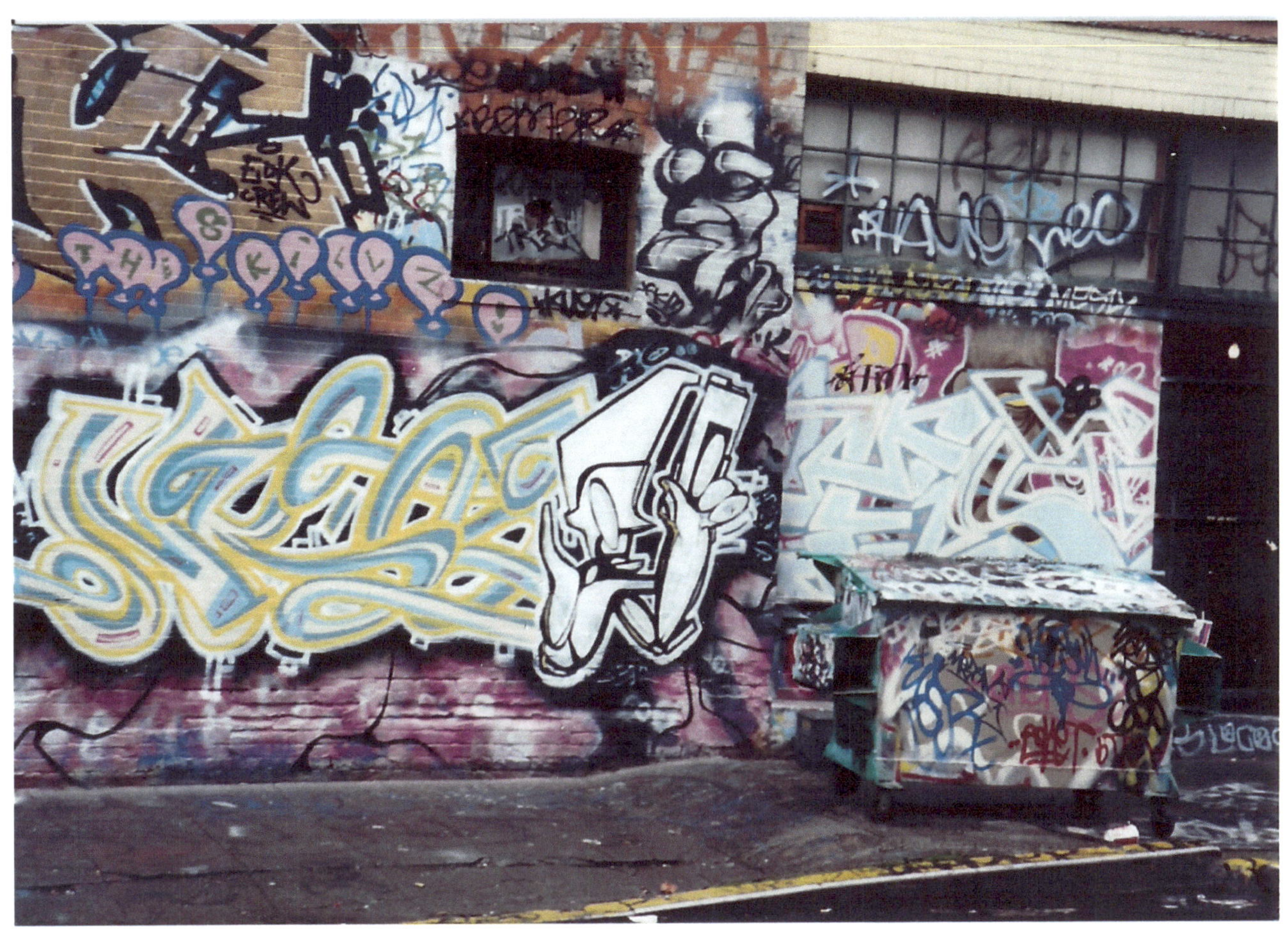

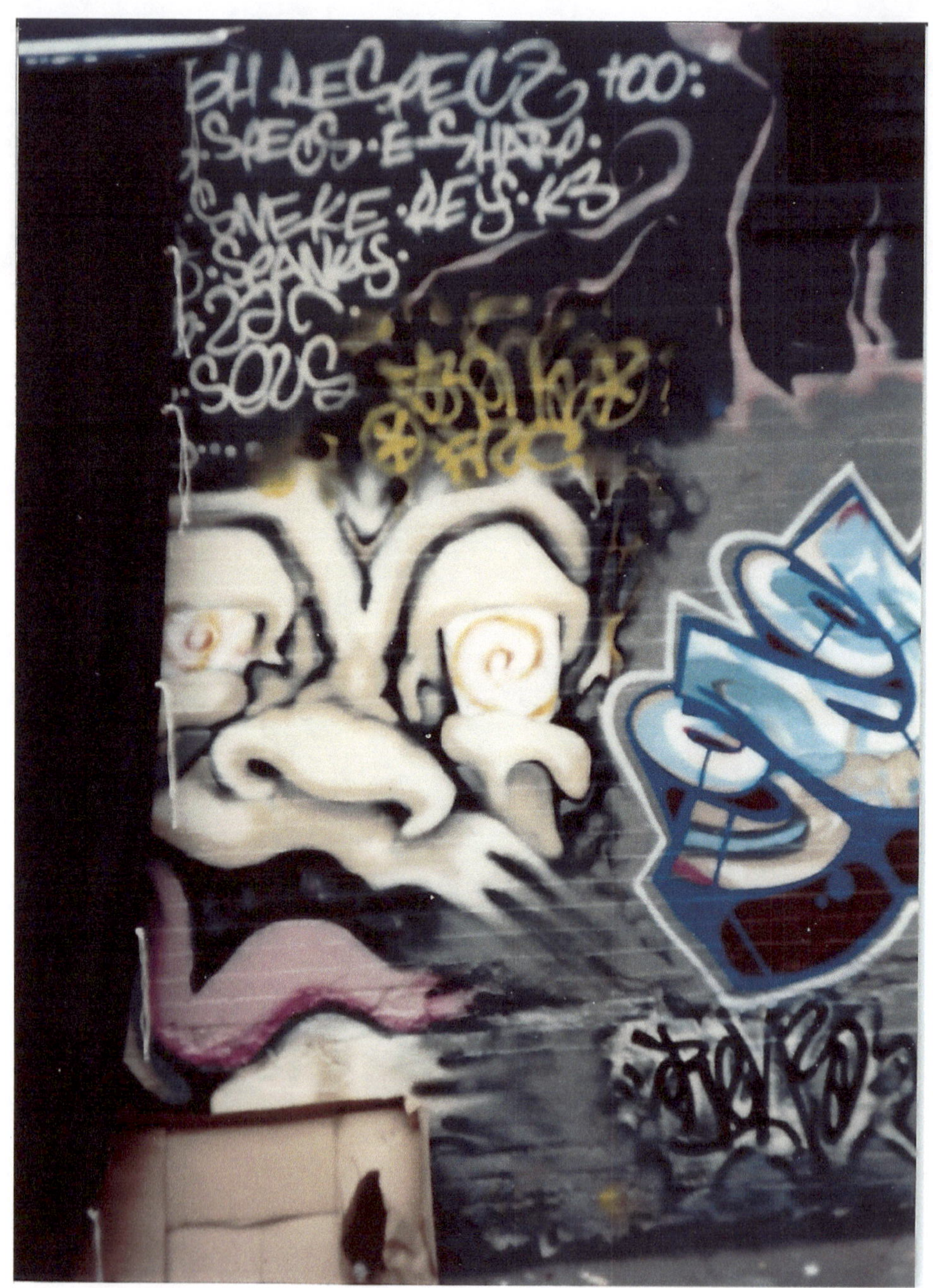

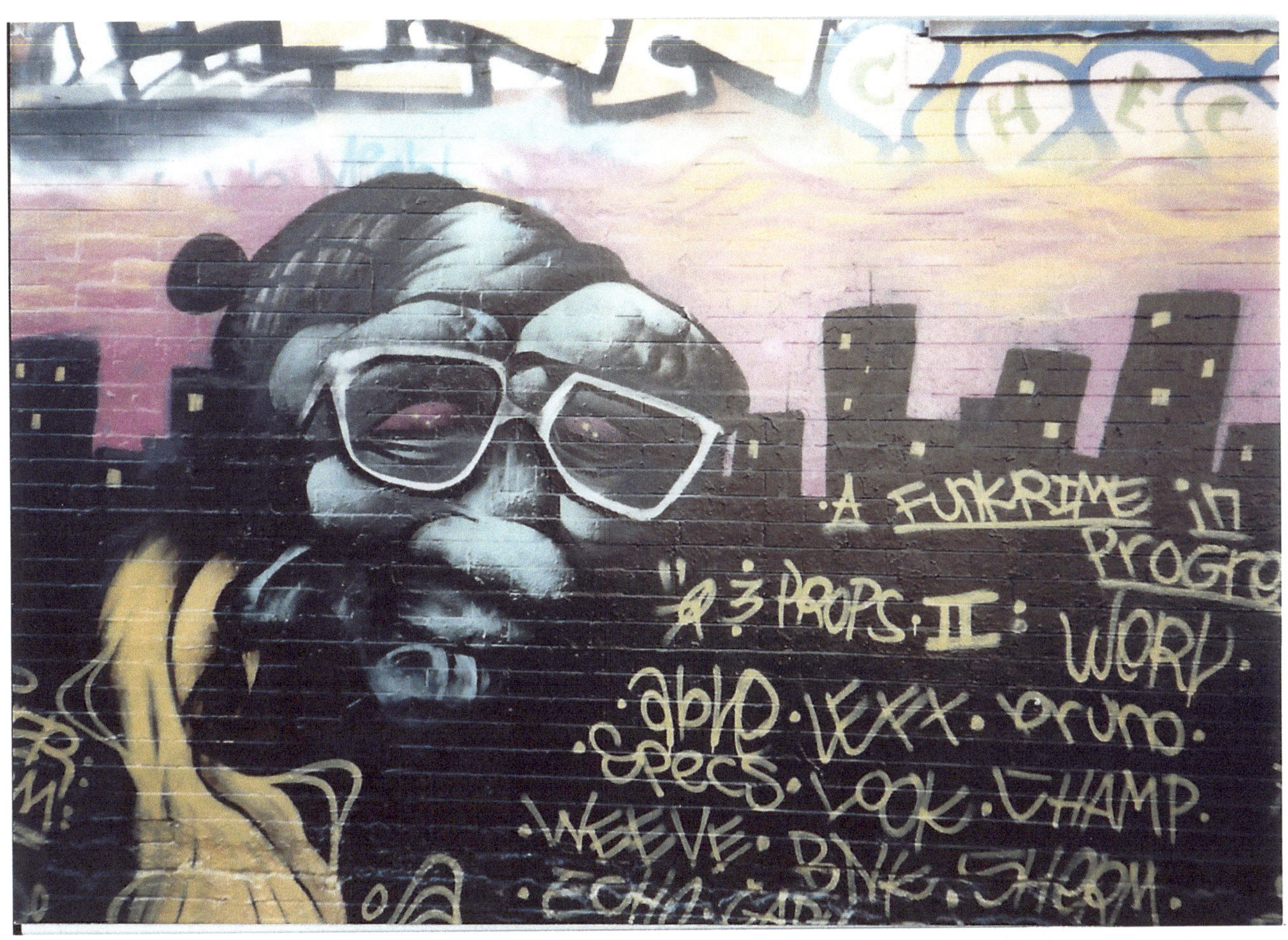
A FUNKRIME in
3 PROPS II
able
bruno
specs
LOOK
CHAMP
WEEVE

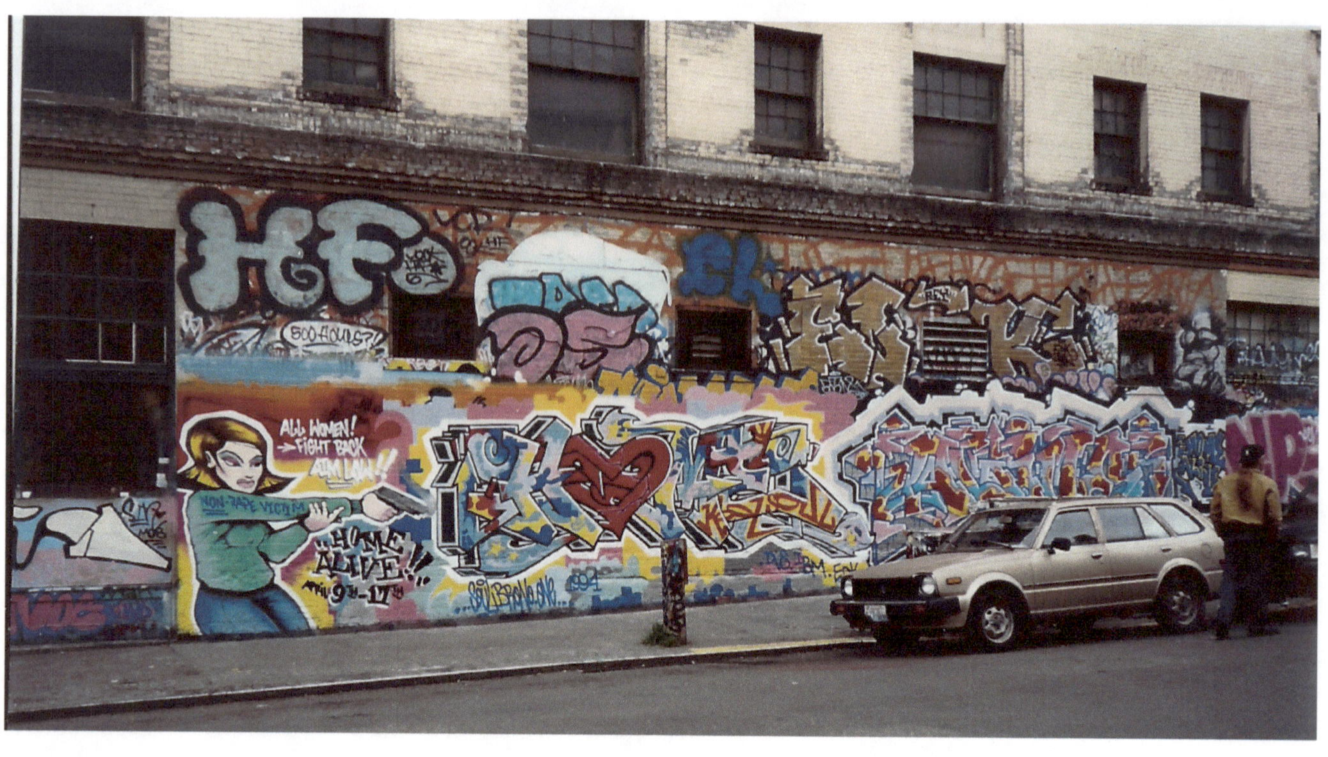
ALL WOMEN!
→ FIGHT BACK
AIM LOW!!
..HOME ALIVE!!..

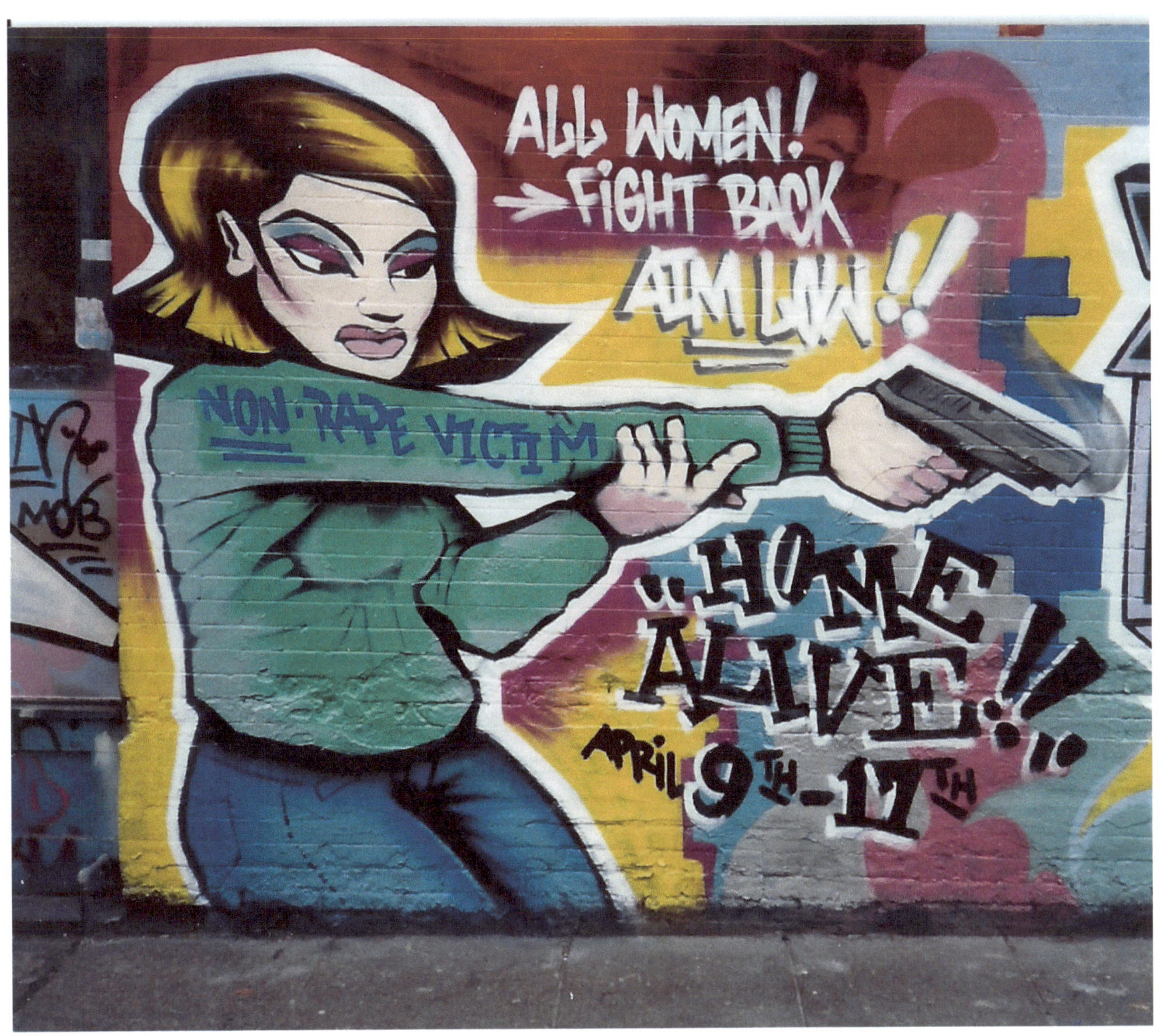
ALL WOMEN!
FIGHT BACK
AIM LOW!!
NON-RAPE VICTIM
..HOME ALIVE!!..
APRIL 9TH-17TH
MOB

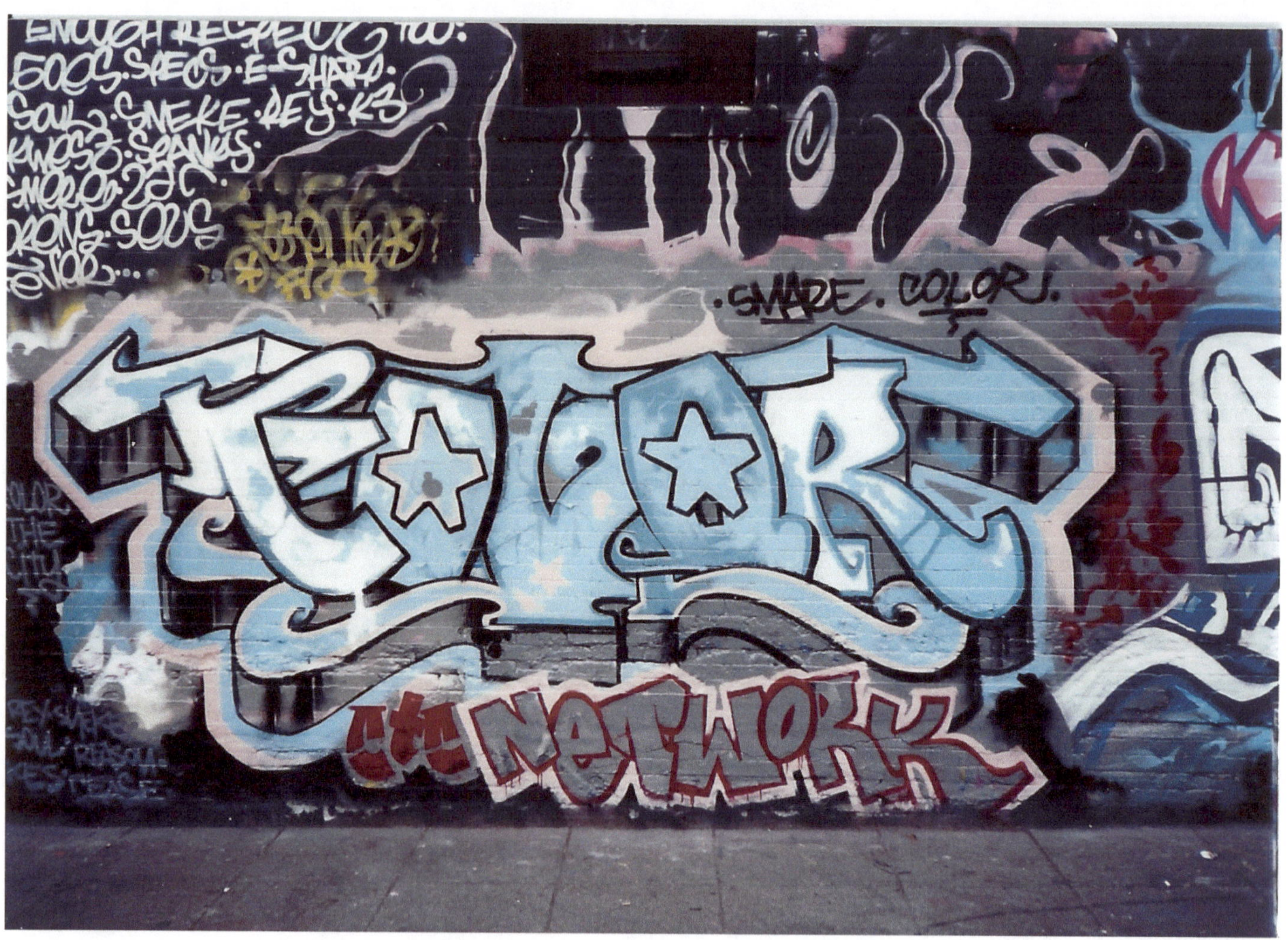
COLOR
NETWORK

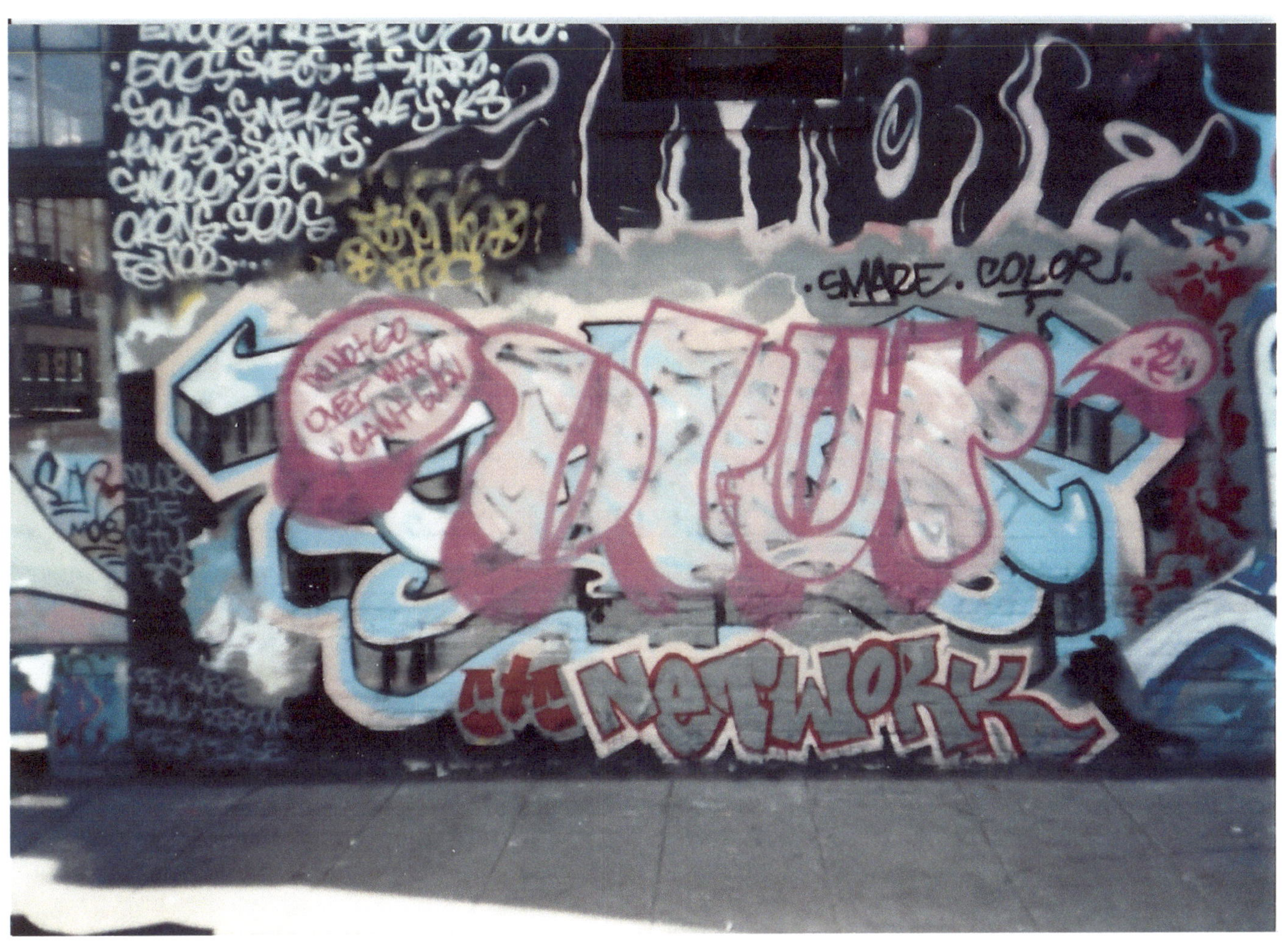
NETWORK

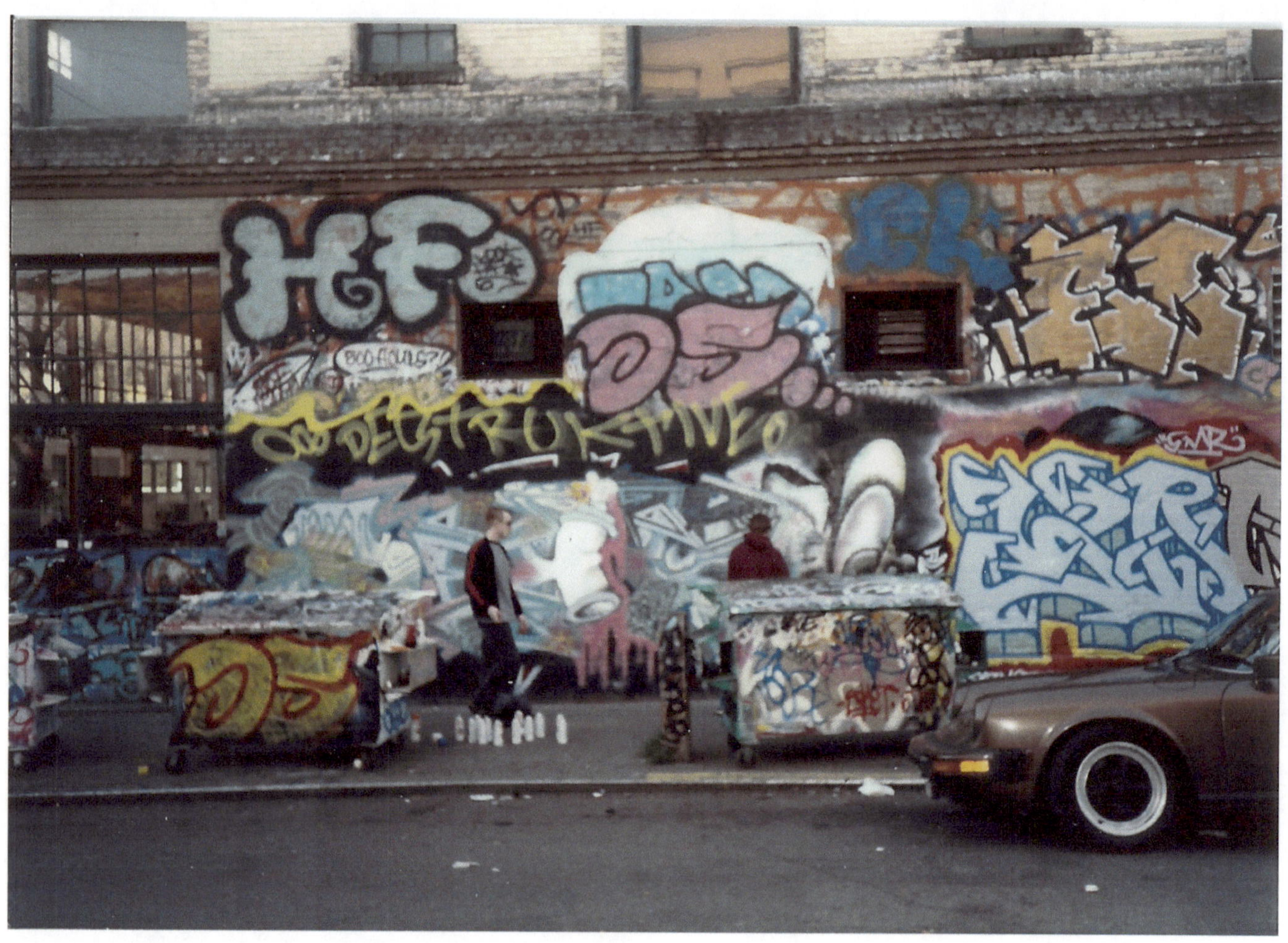
DESTRUKTIVE

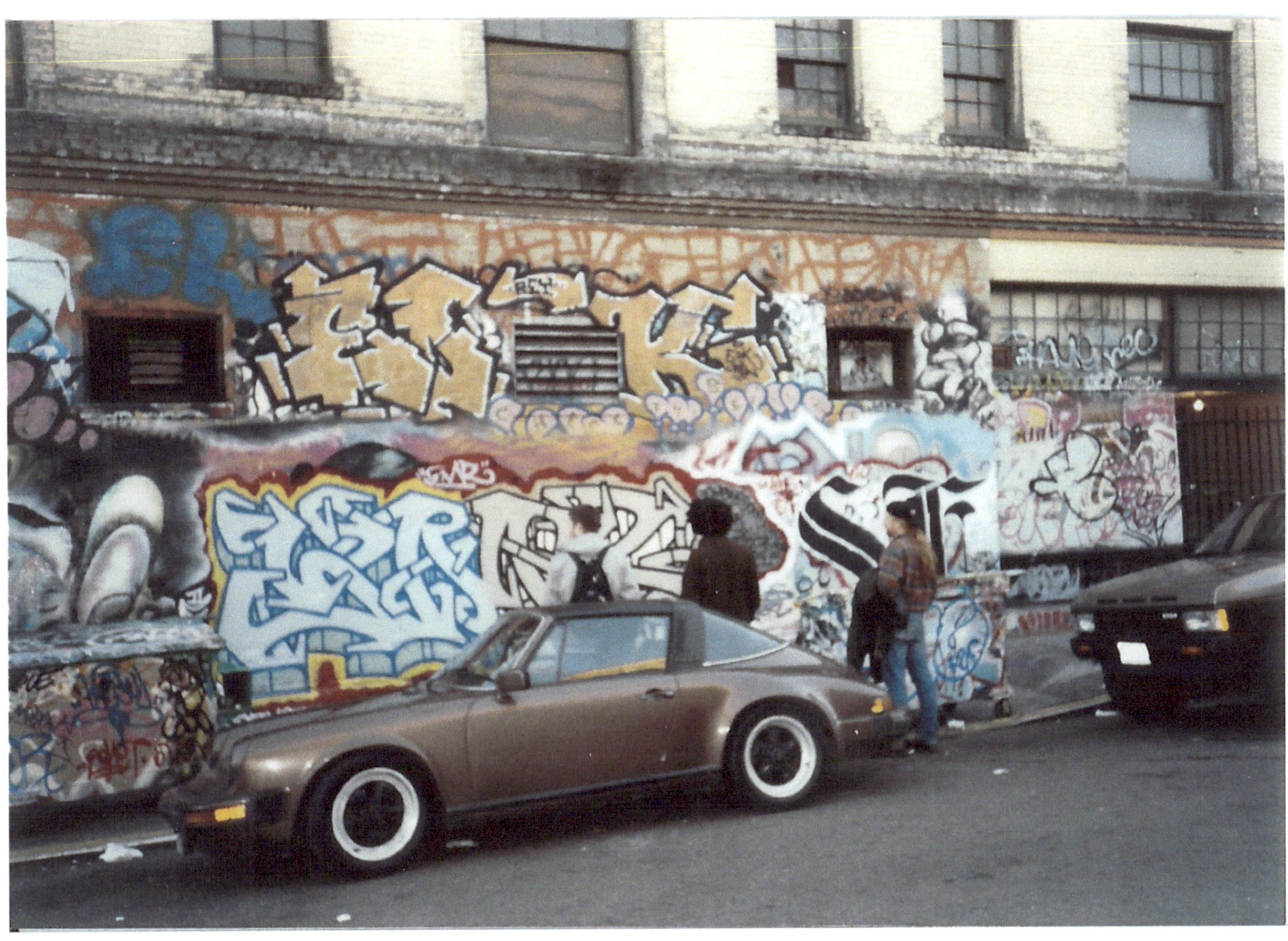

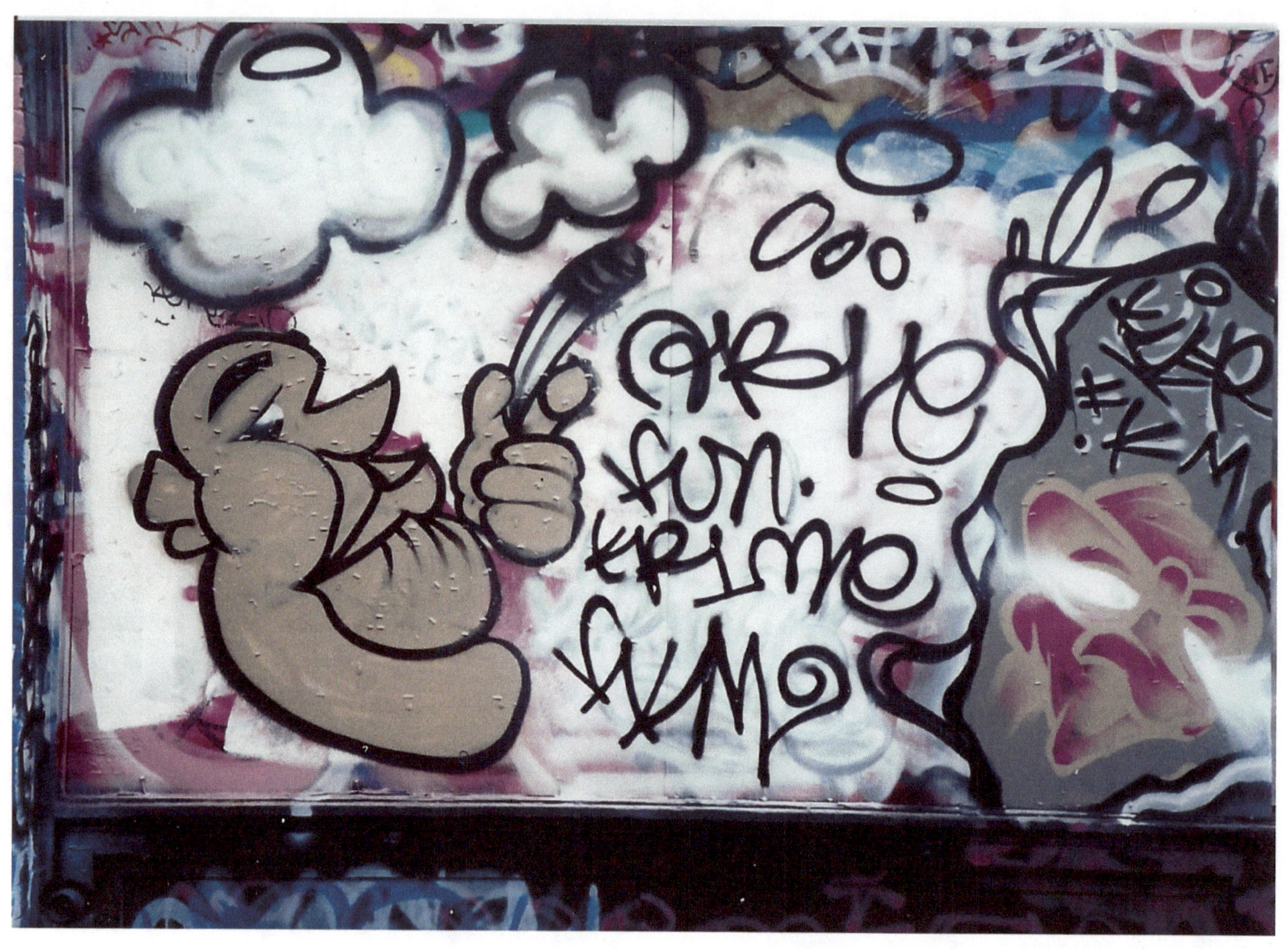

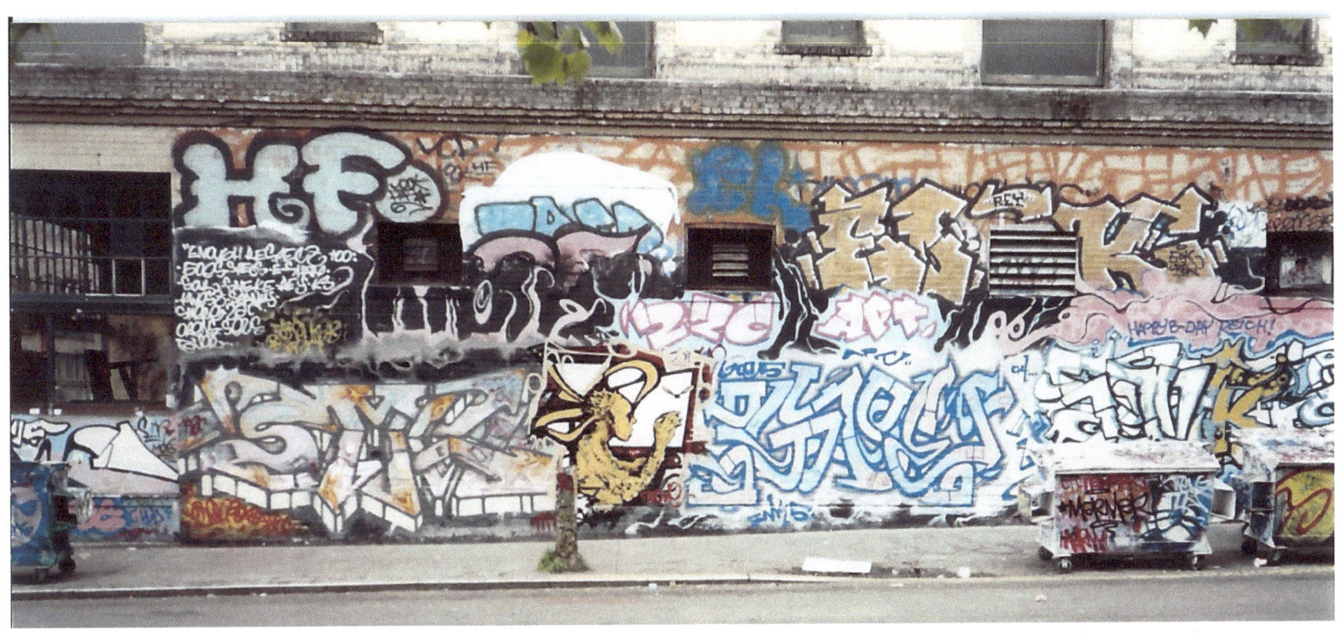
HF
HAPPY B-DAY REICH!

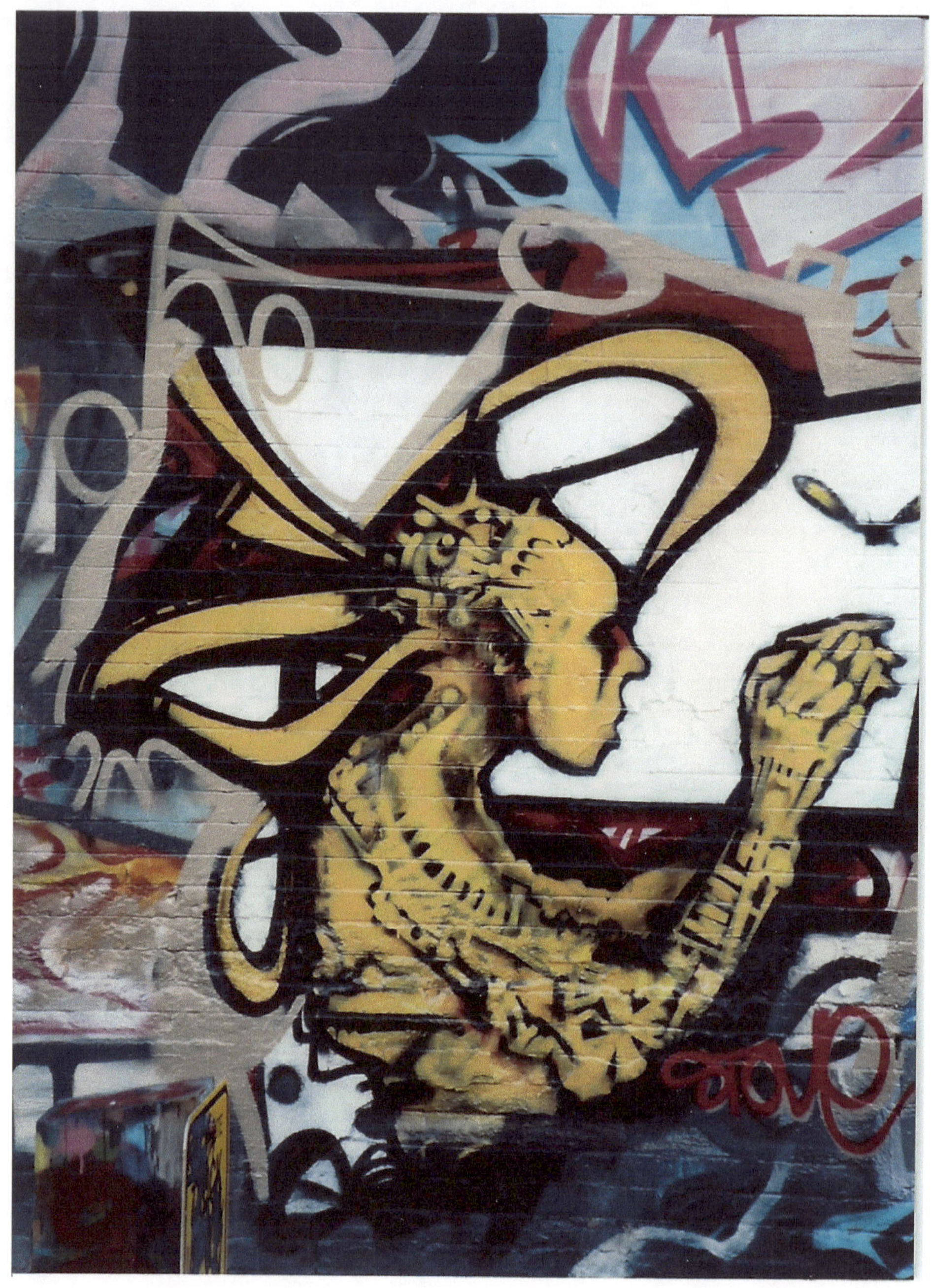

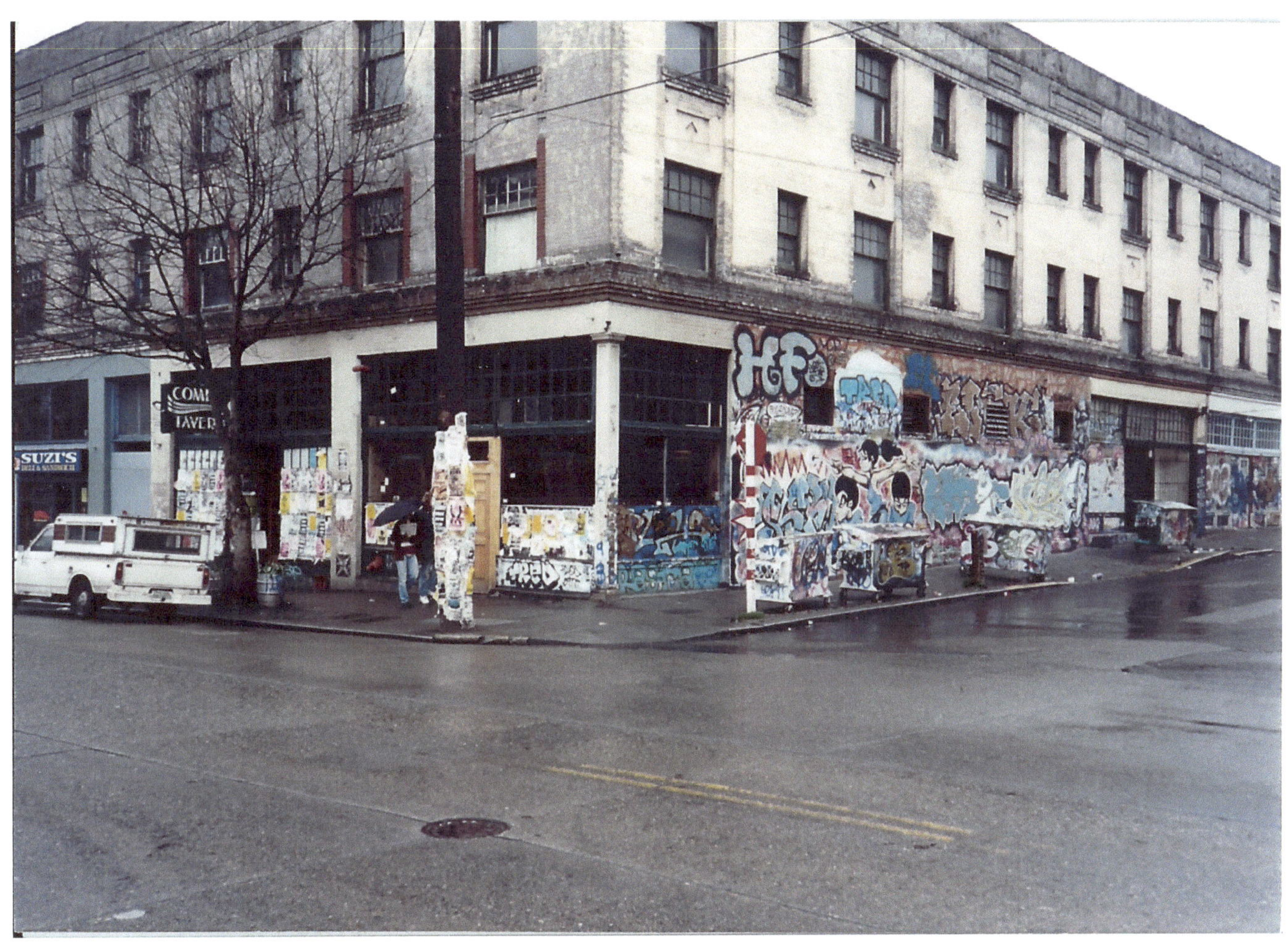
SUZI'S

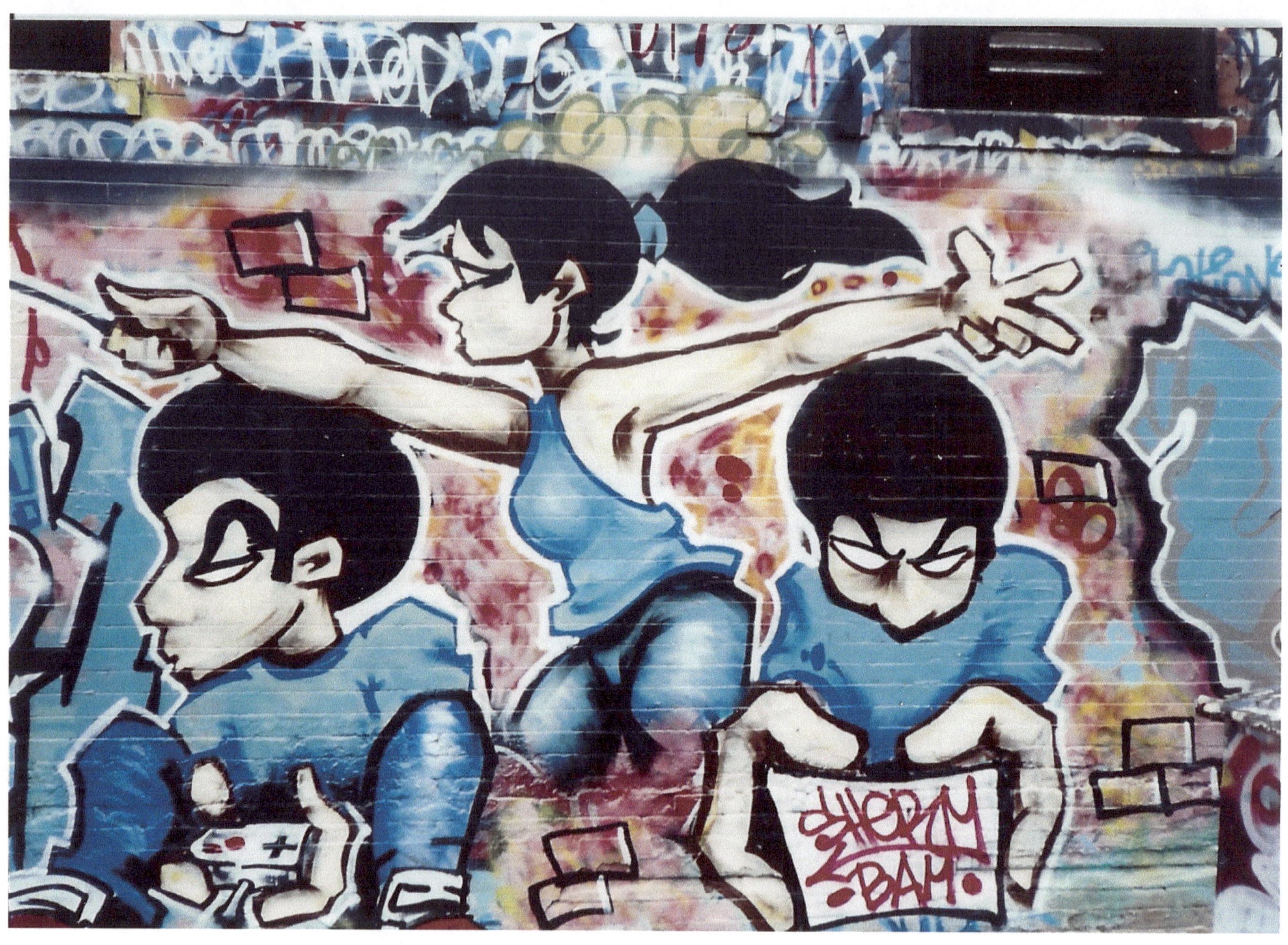

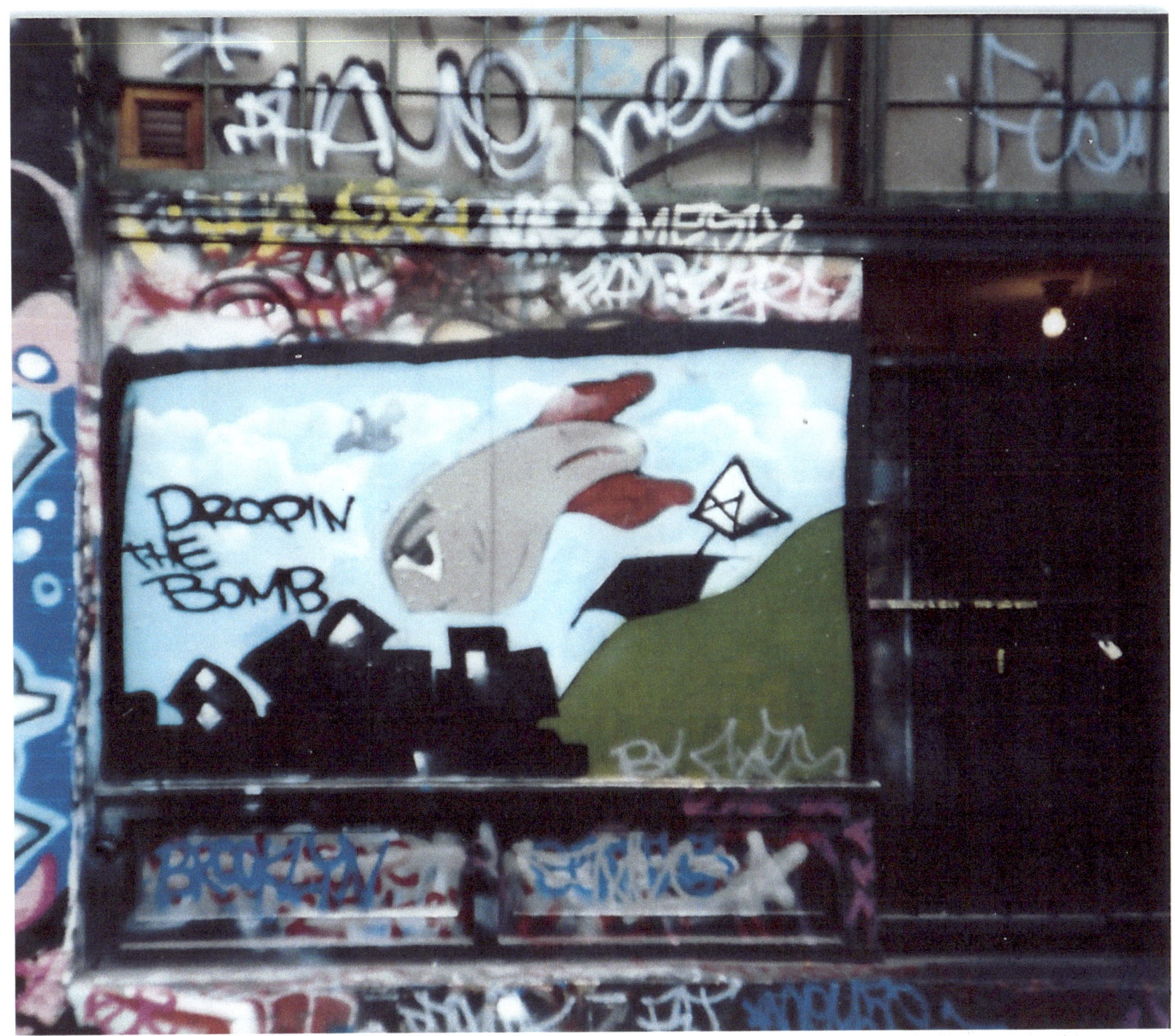
DROPIN
THE
BOMB

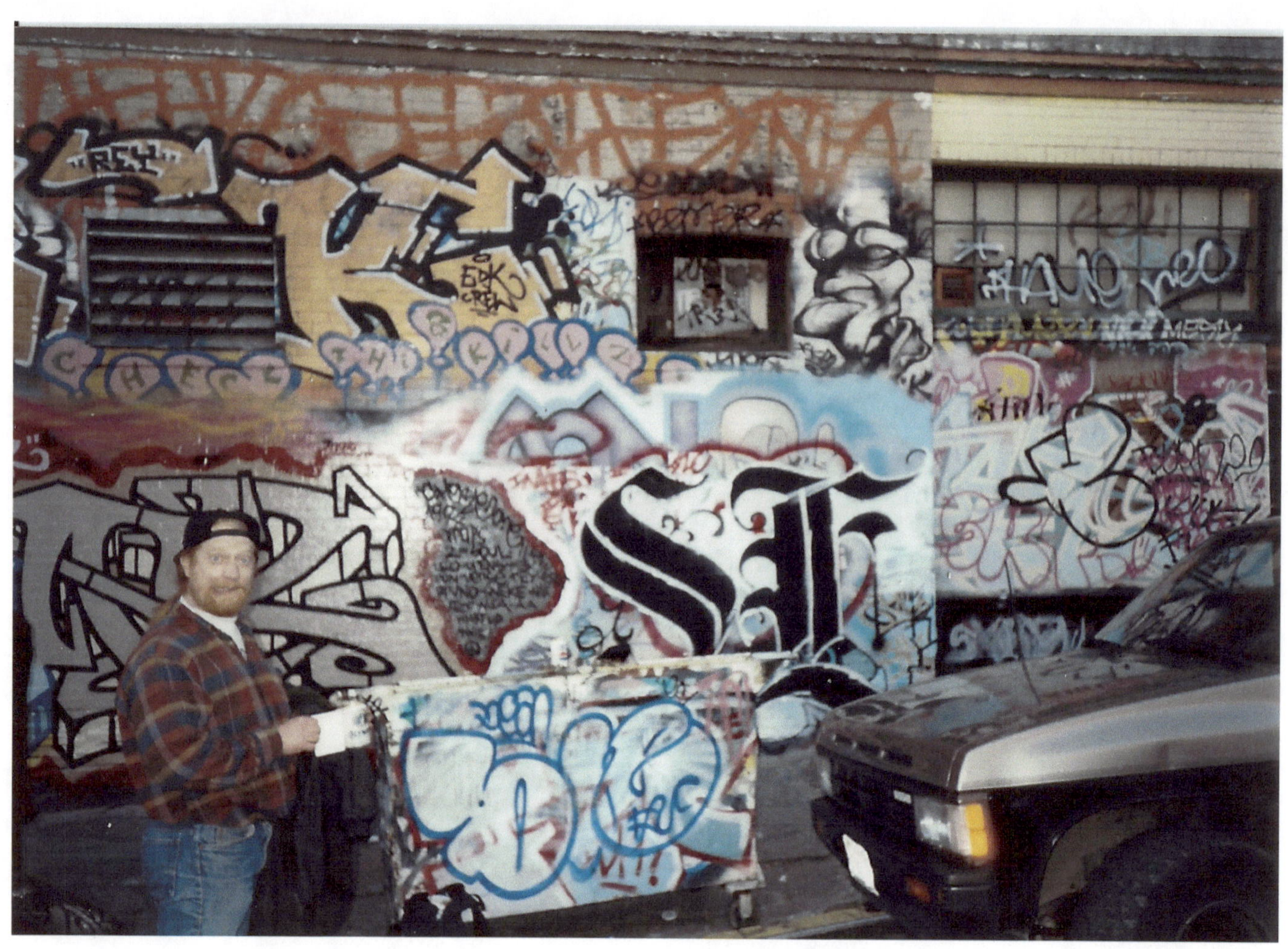

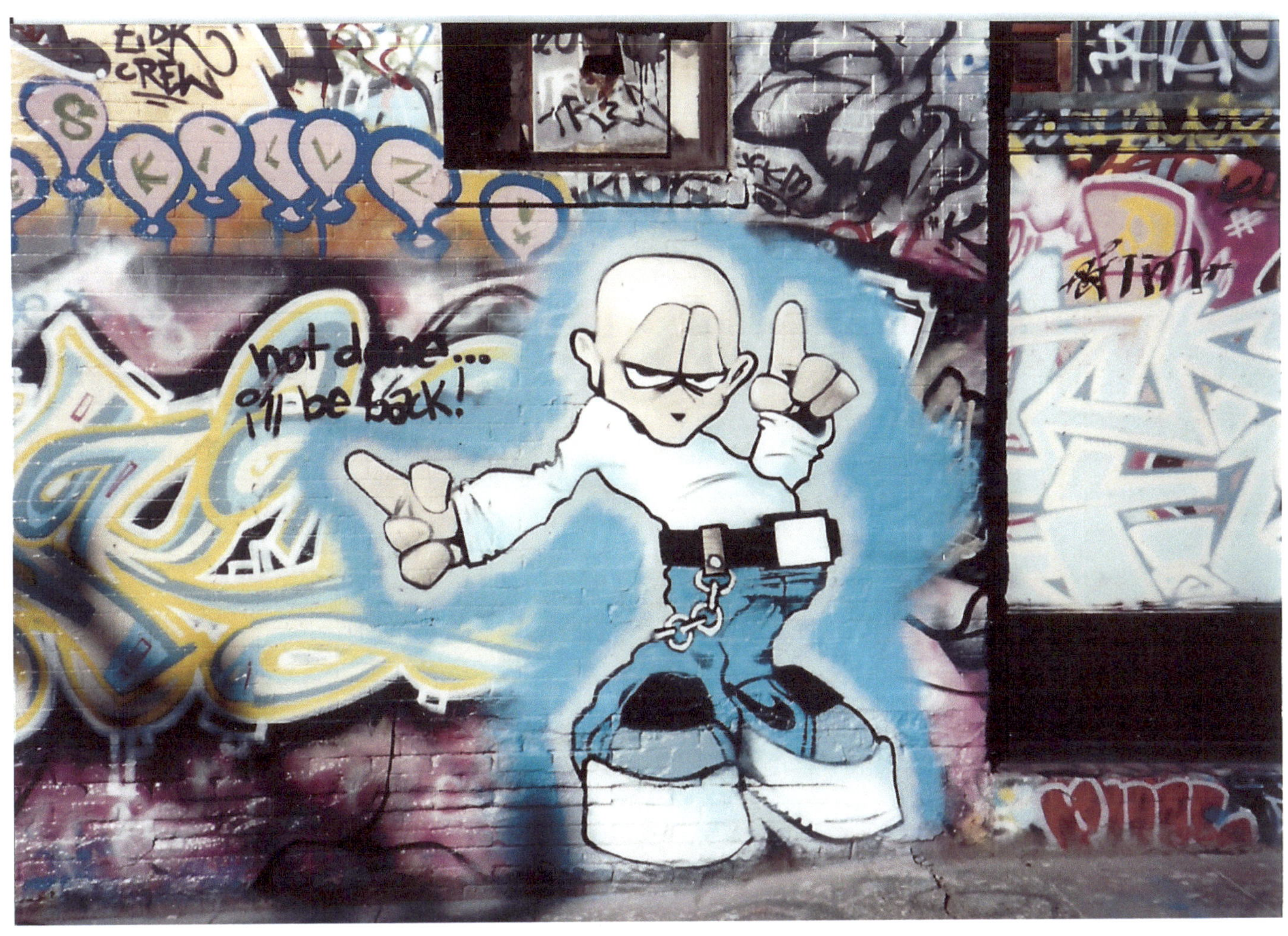
not done...
i'll be back!

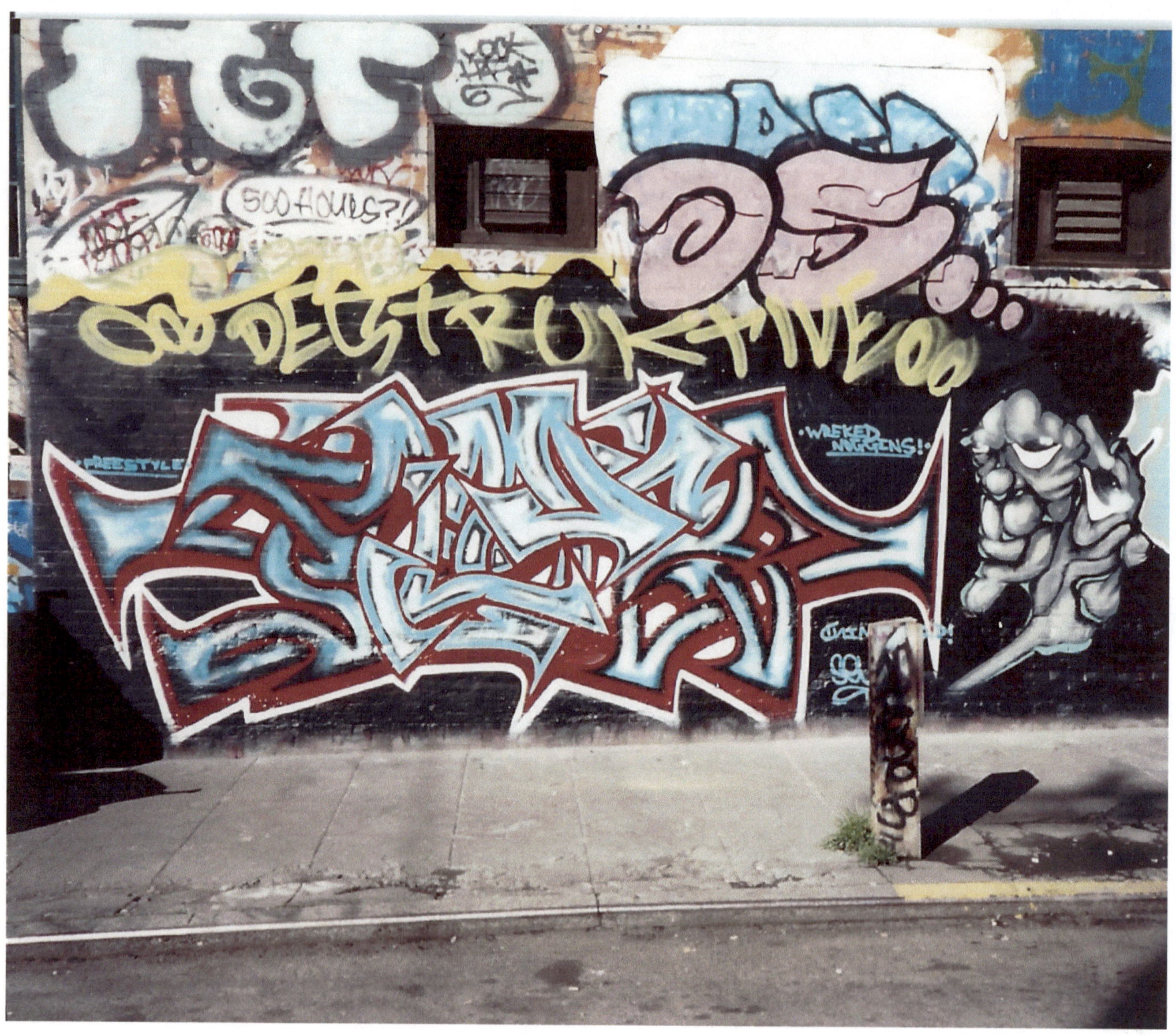
500 HOURS?!
DESTRUKTIVE
FREESTYLE

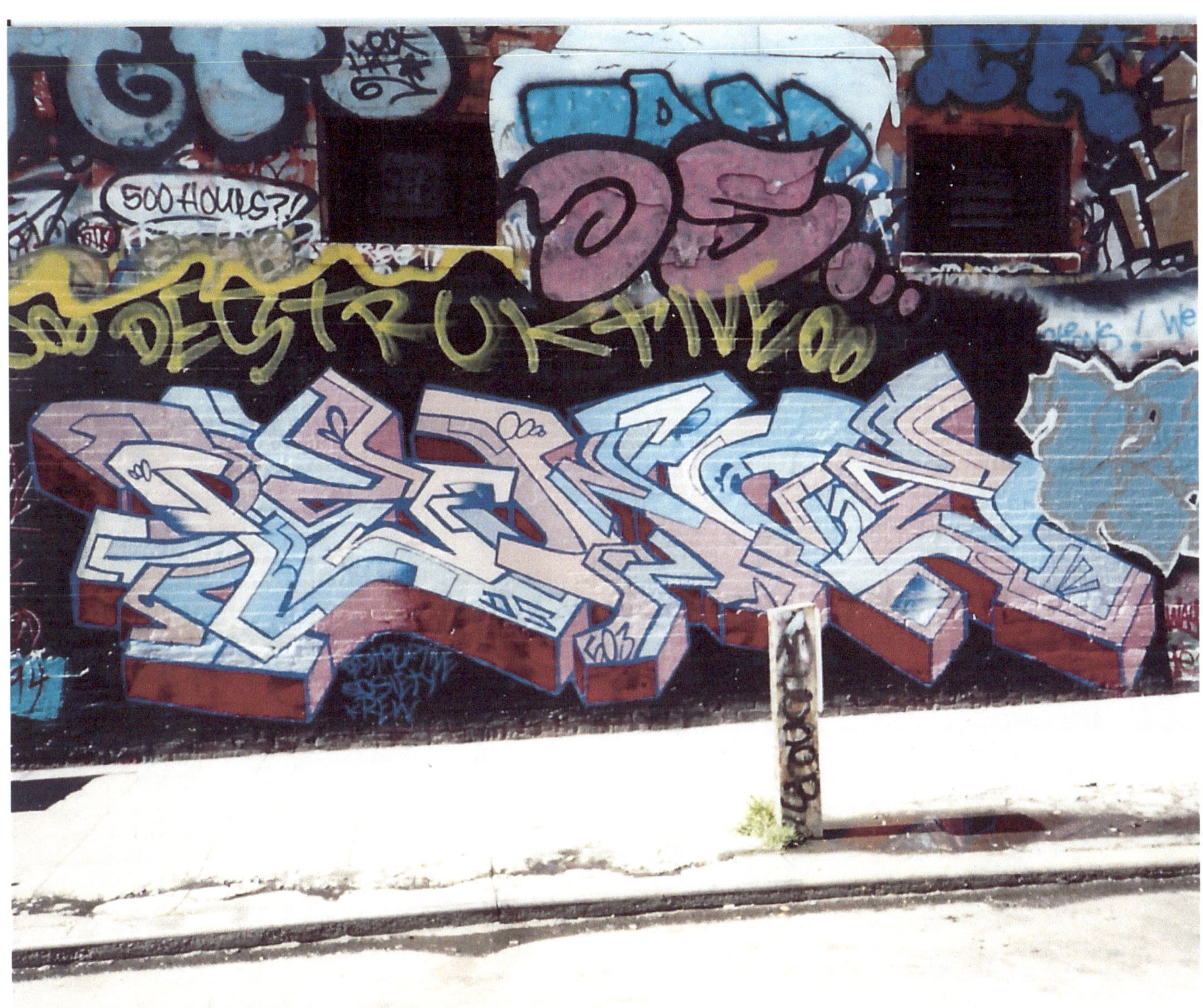
500 HOURS?!

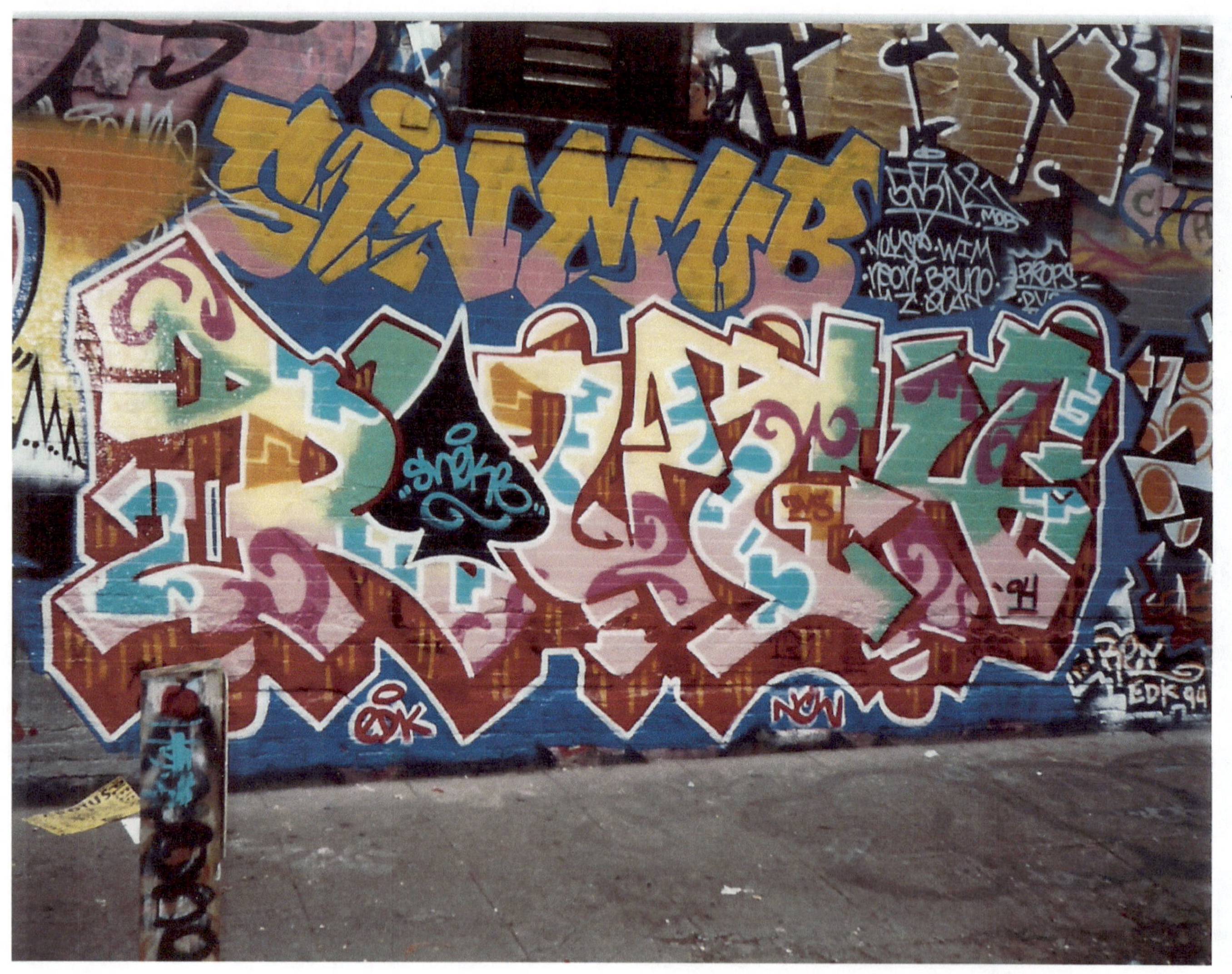

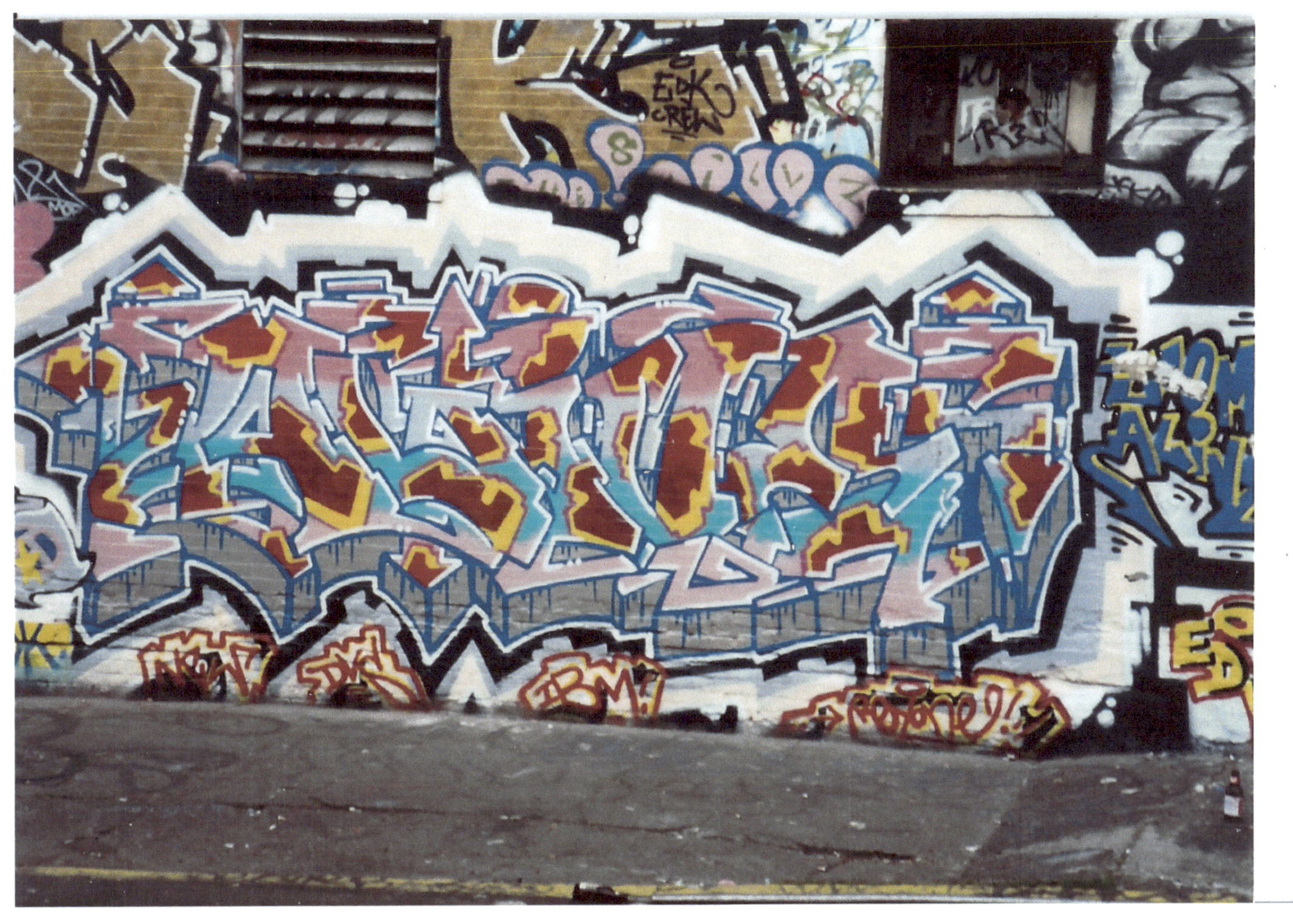
EDK
CREW

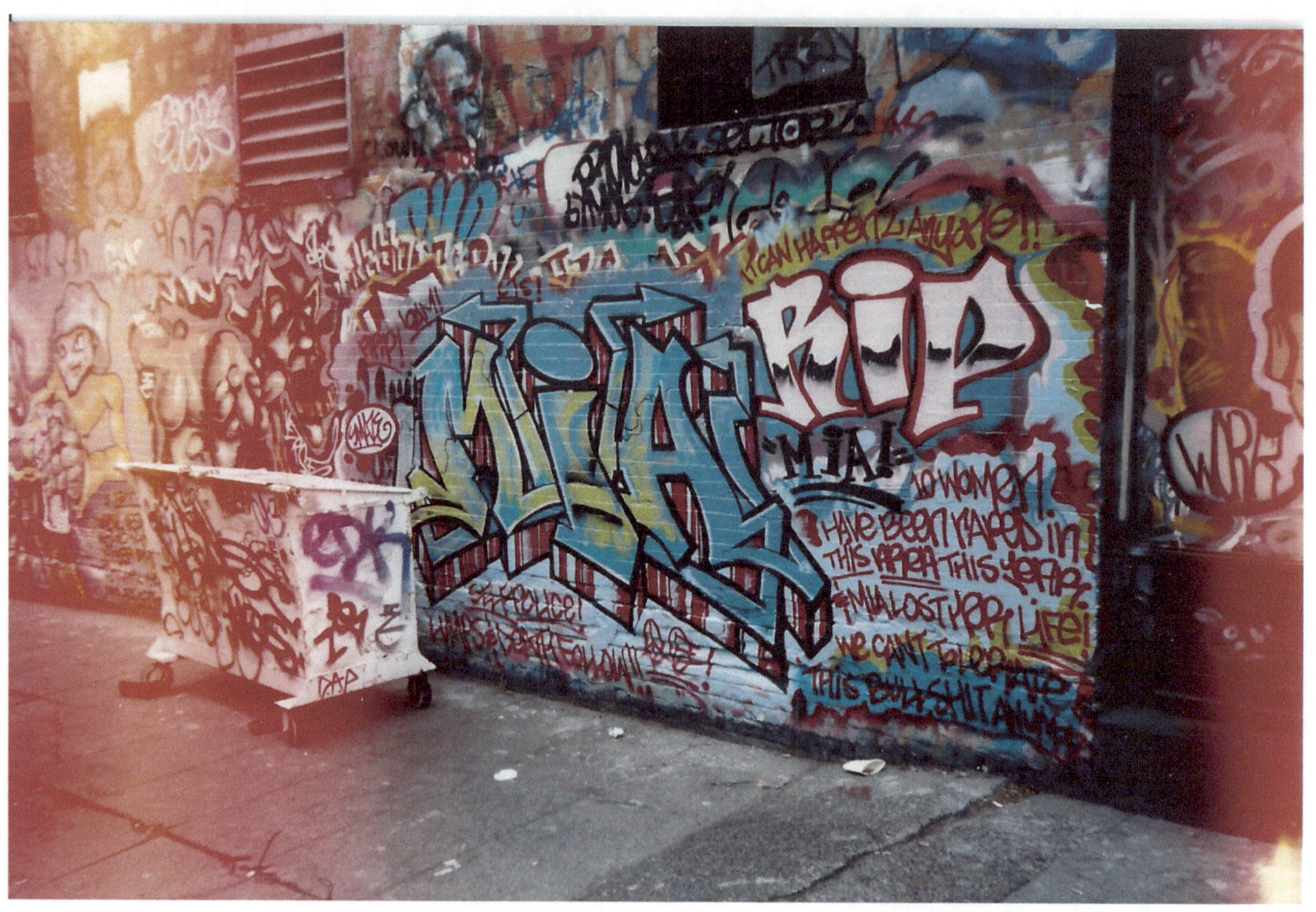
IT CAN HAPPEN 2 ANYONE!!
RIP
MIA
10 WOMEN HAVE BEEN RAPED IN THIS AREA THIS YEAR
& MIA LOST HER LIFE!
WE CAN'T TOLERATE
THIS BULLSHIT

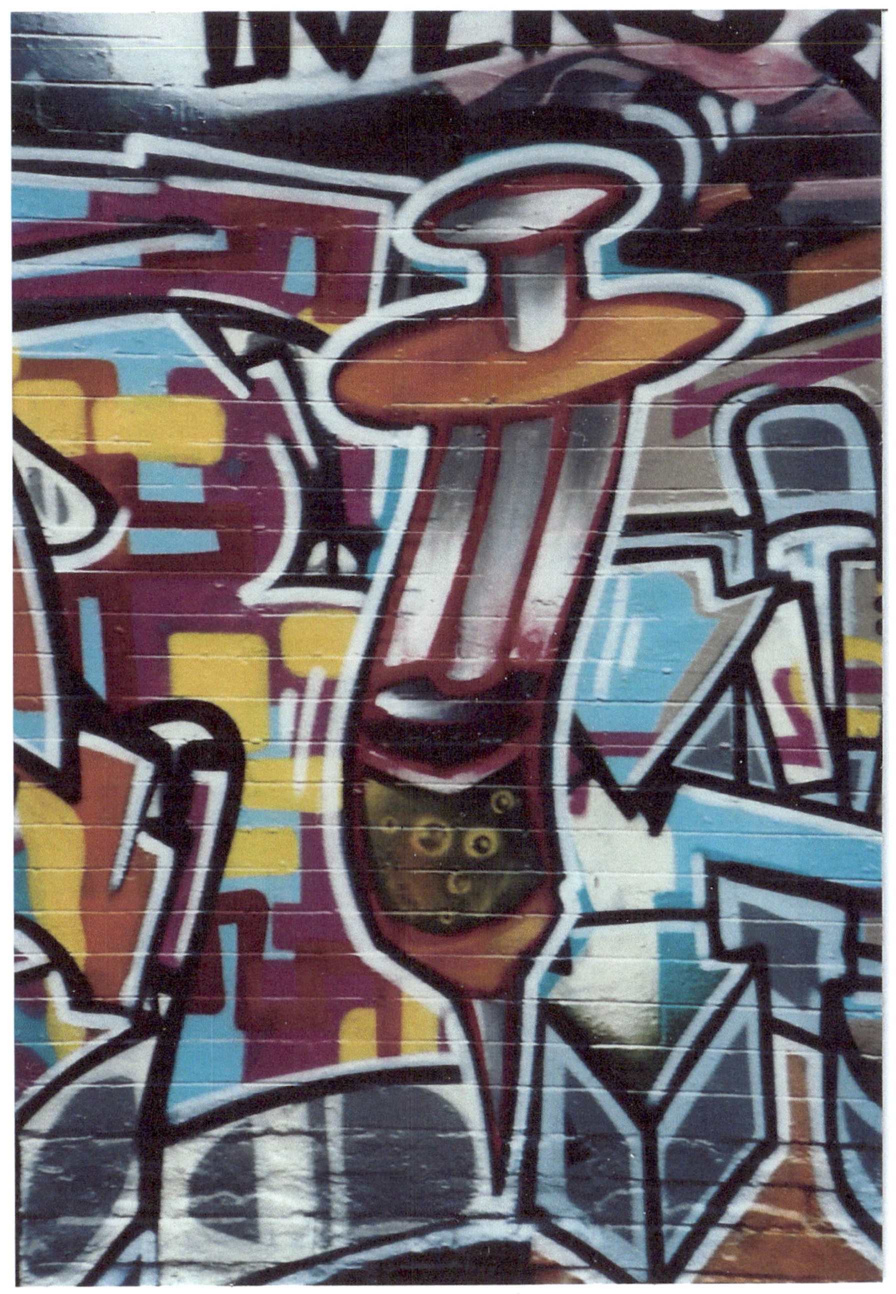

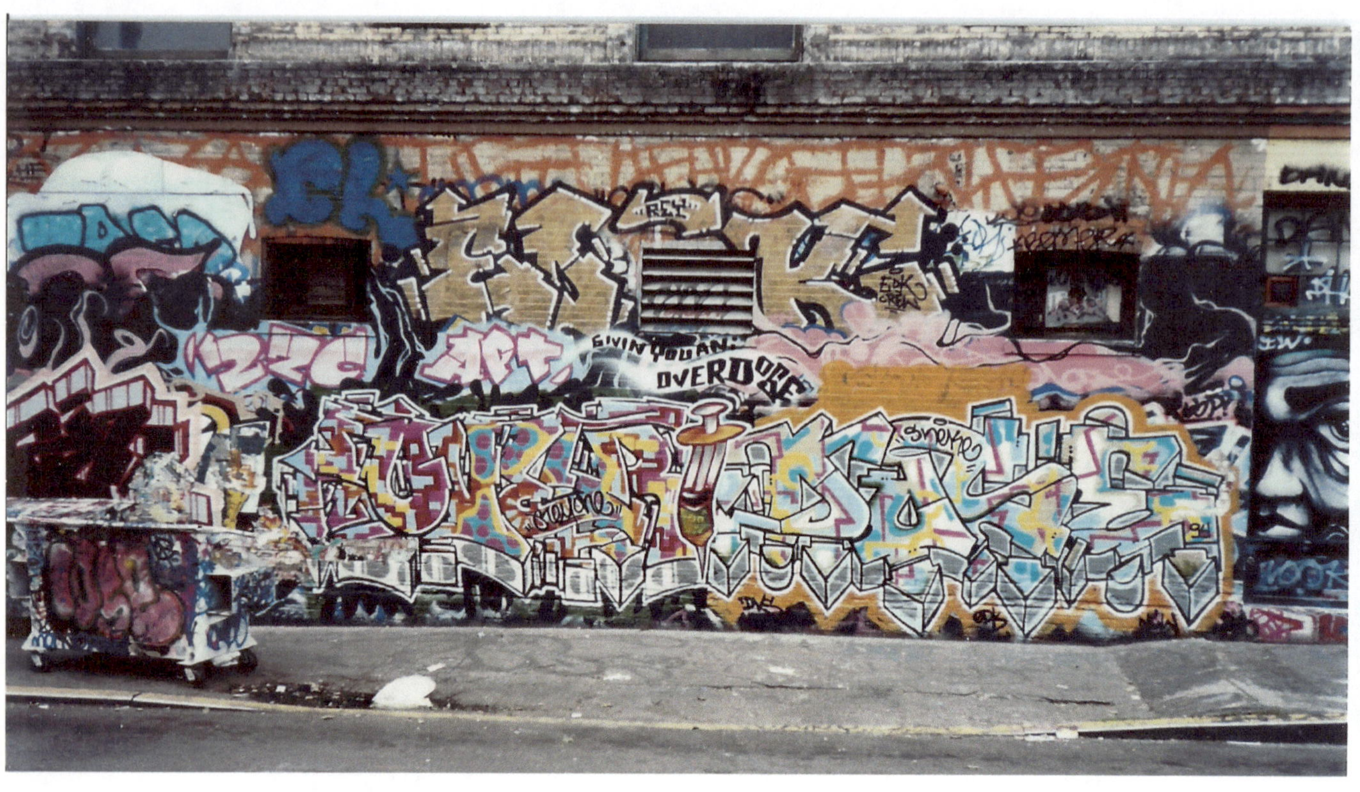
GIVIN YOU AN
OVERDOSE

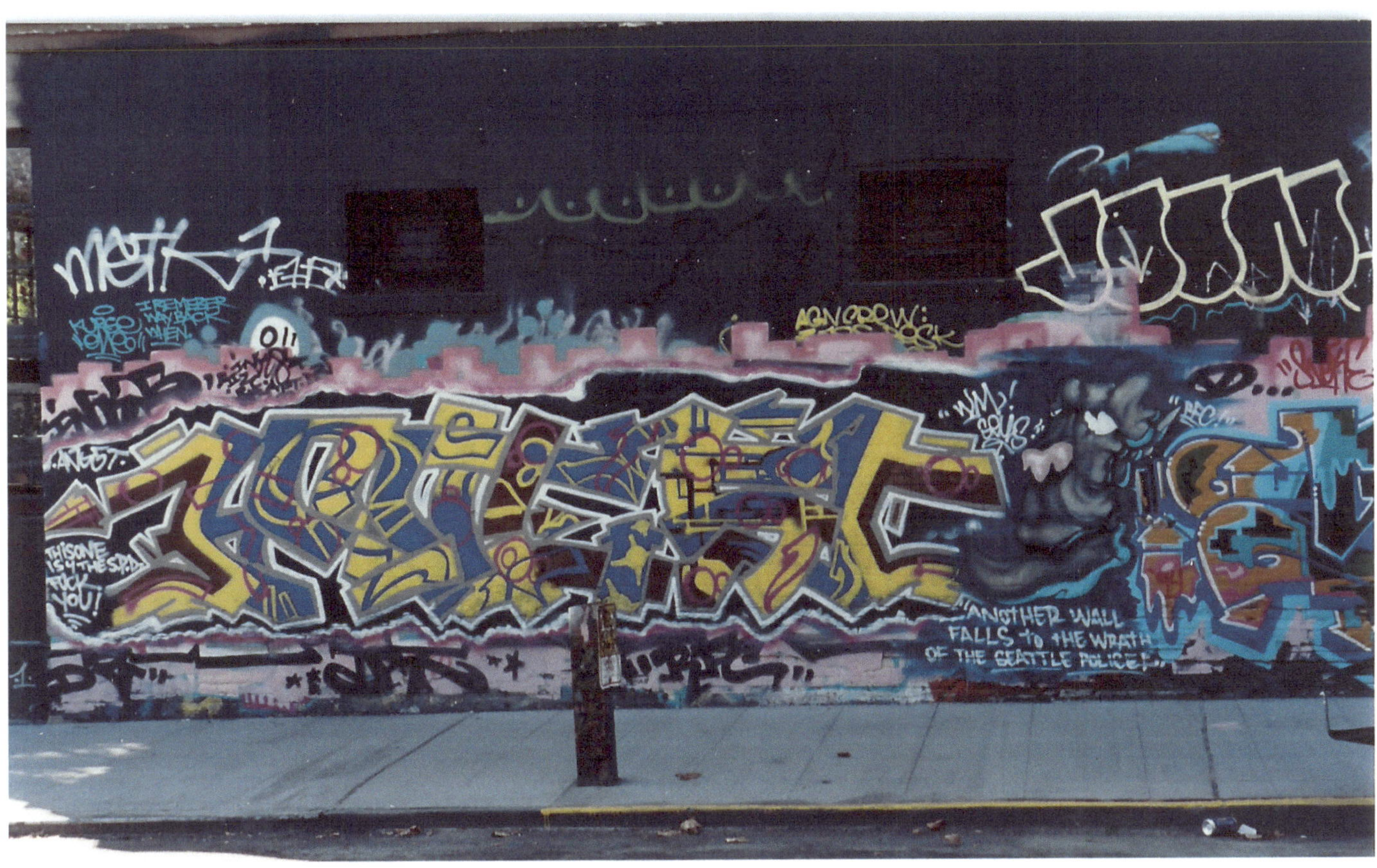
I REMEMBER WAY BACK WHEN
THIS ONE IS 4 THE S.P.D.
FUCK YOU!
ANOTHER WALL FALLS TO THE WRATH OF THE SEATTLE POLICE!

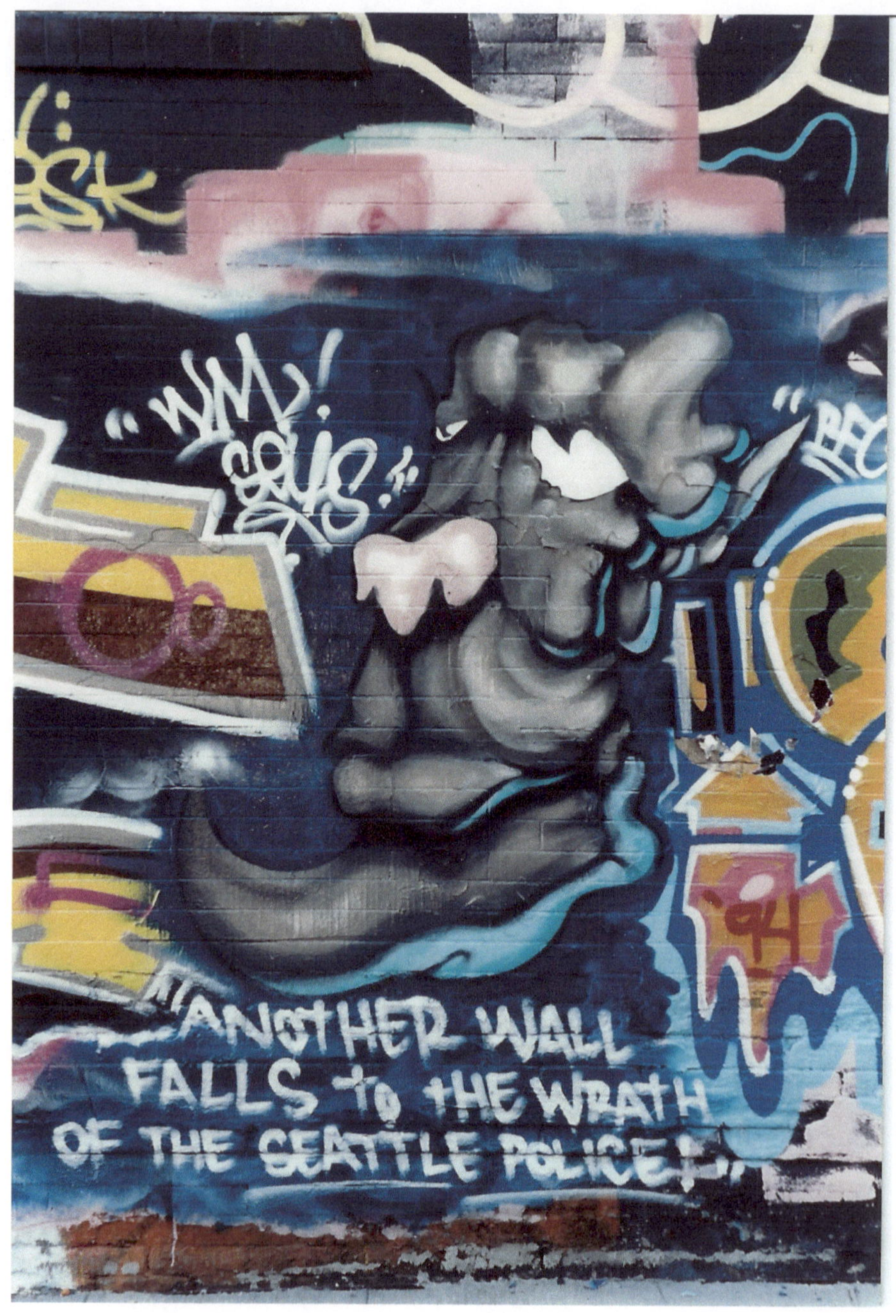
"ANOTHER WALL
FALLS to THE WRATH
OF THE SEATTLE POLICE

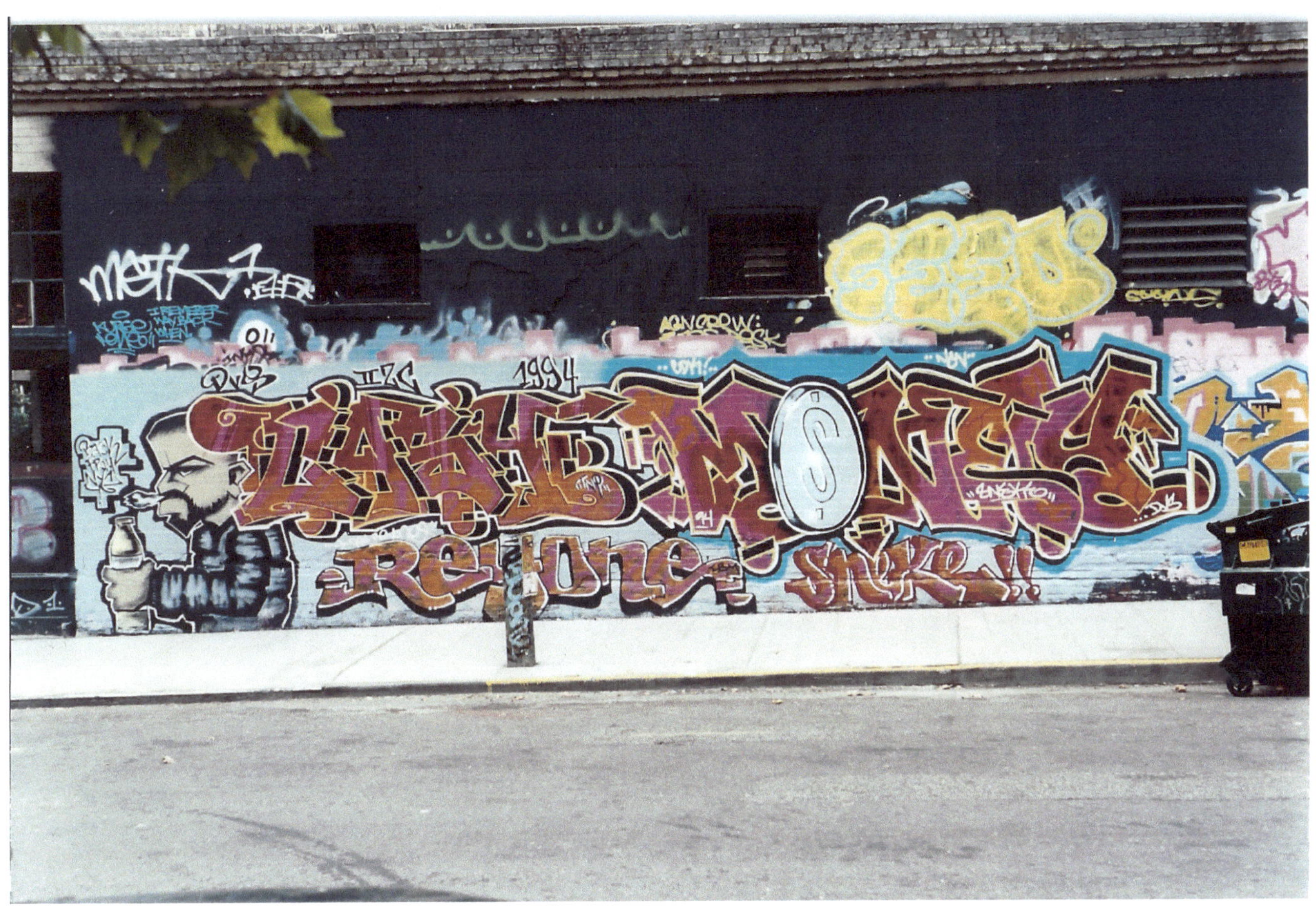
1994

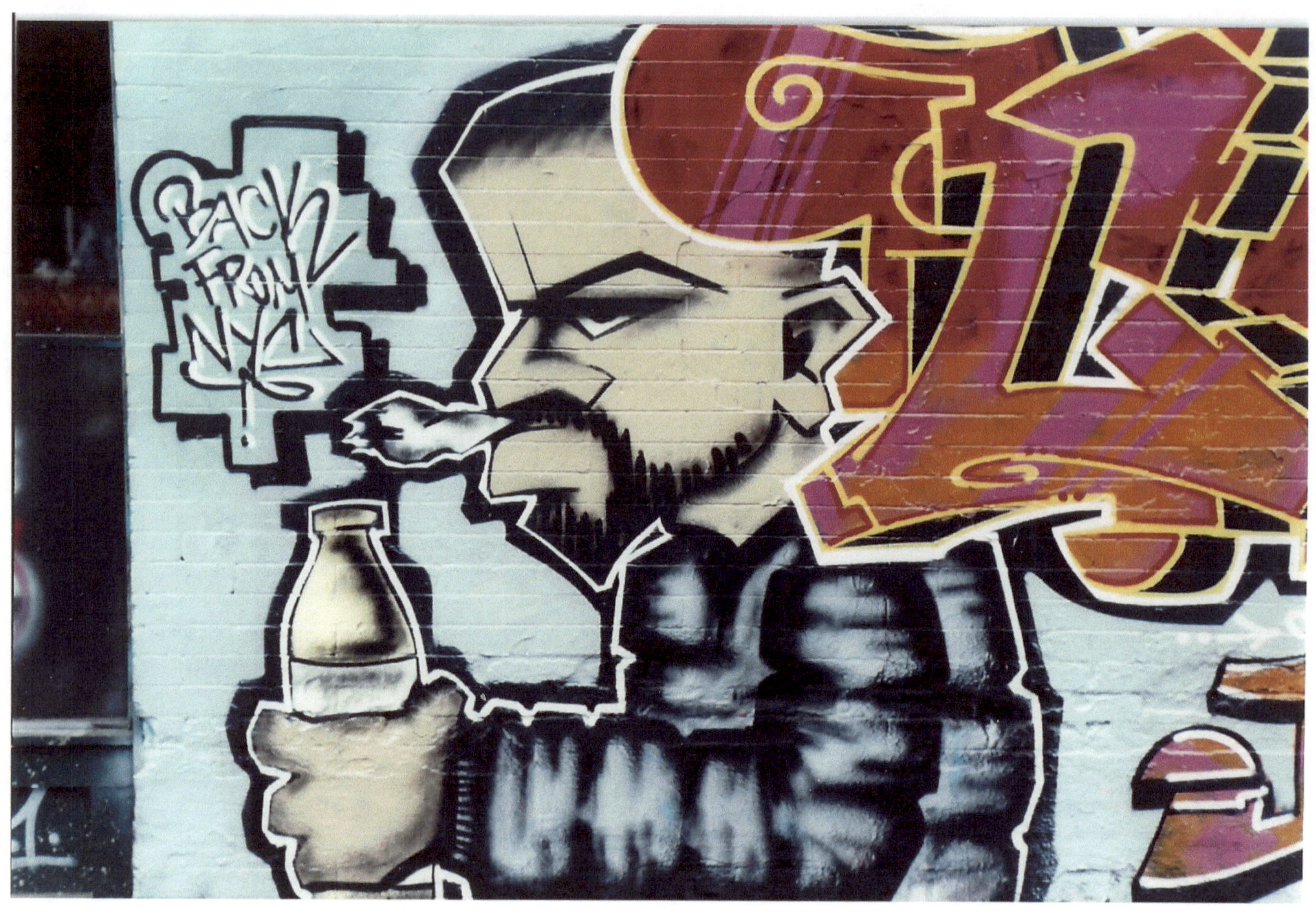
BACK FROM NYC

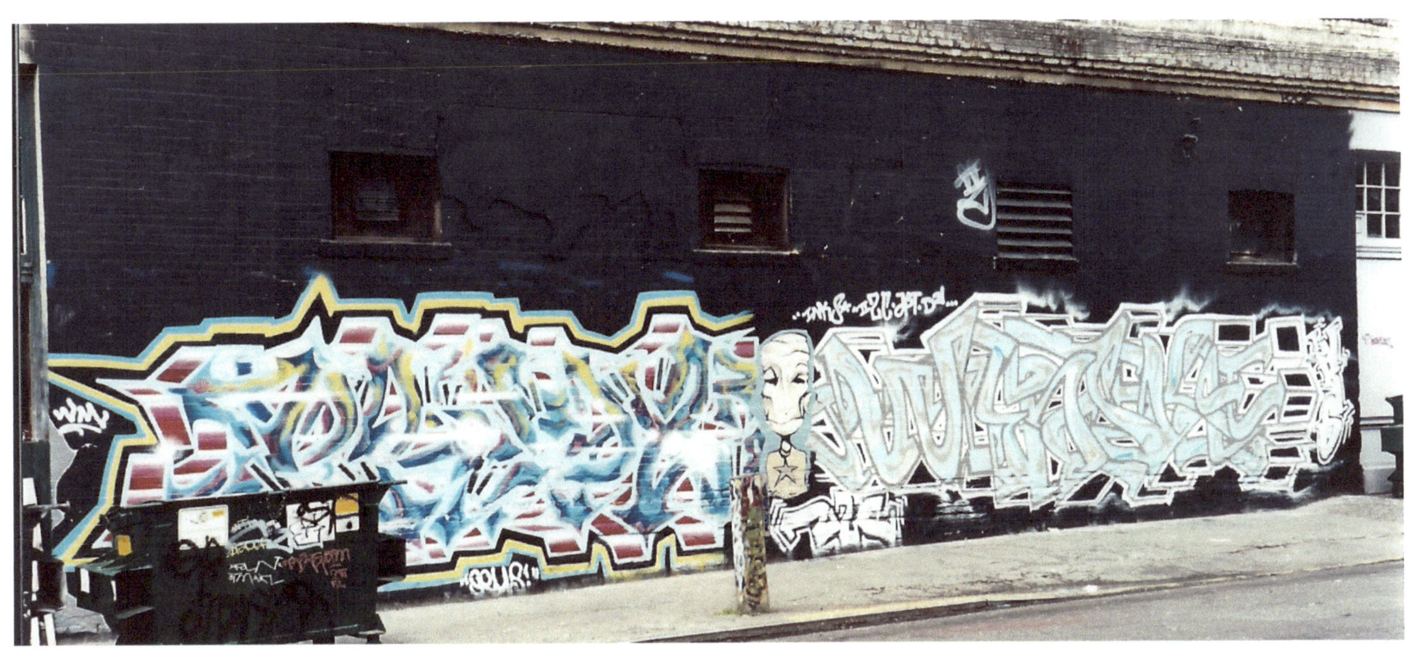

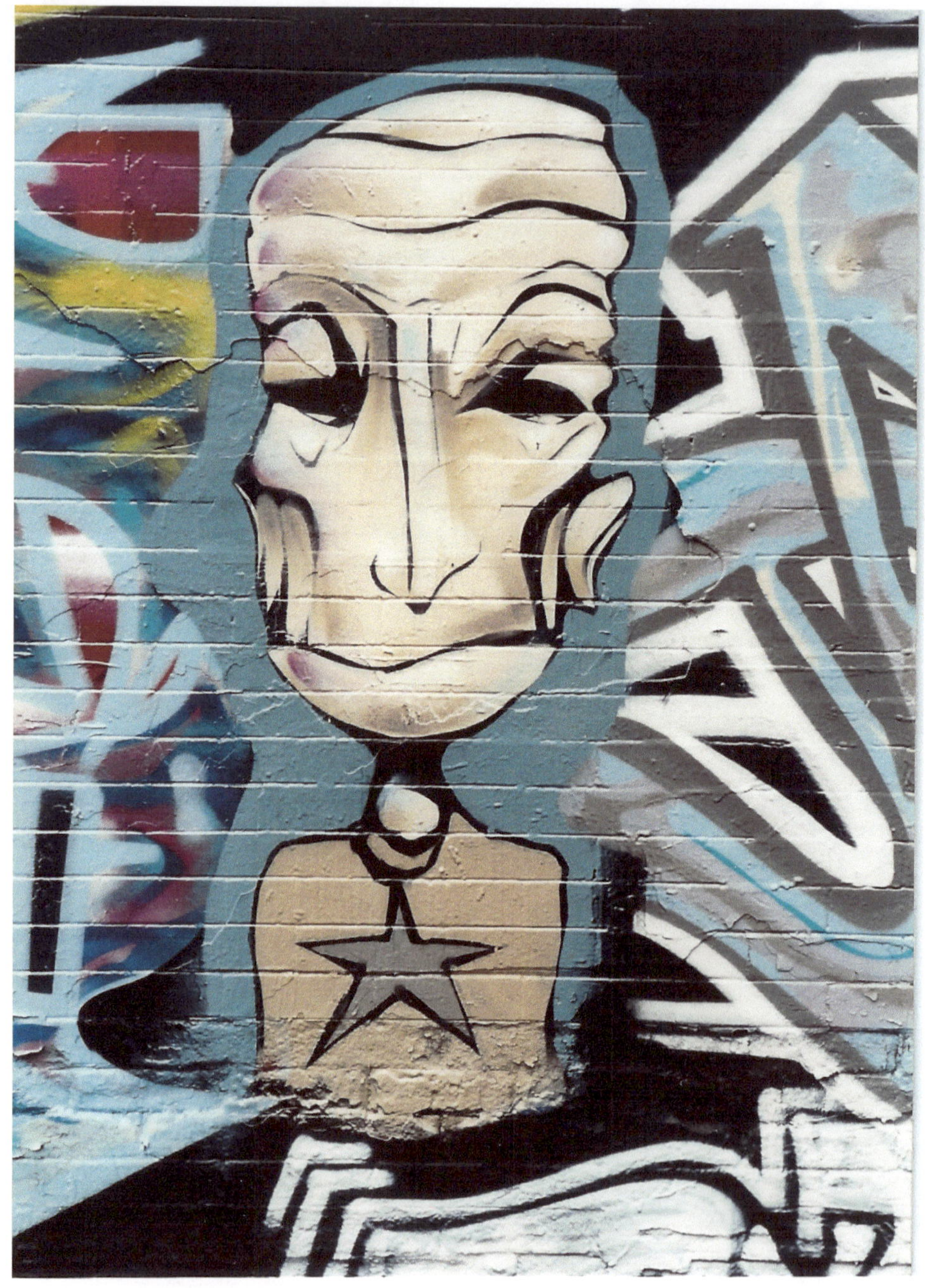

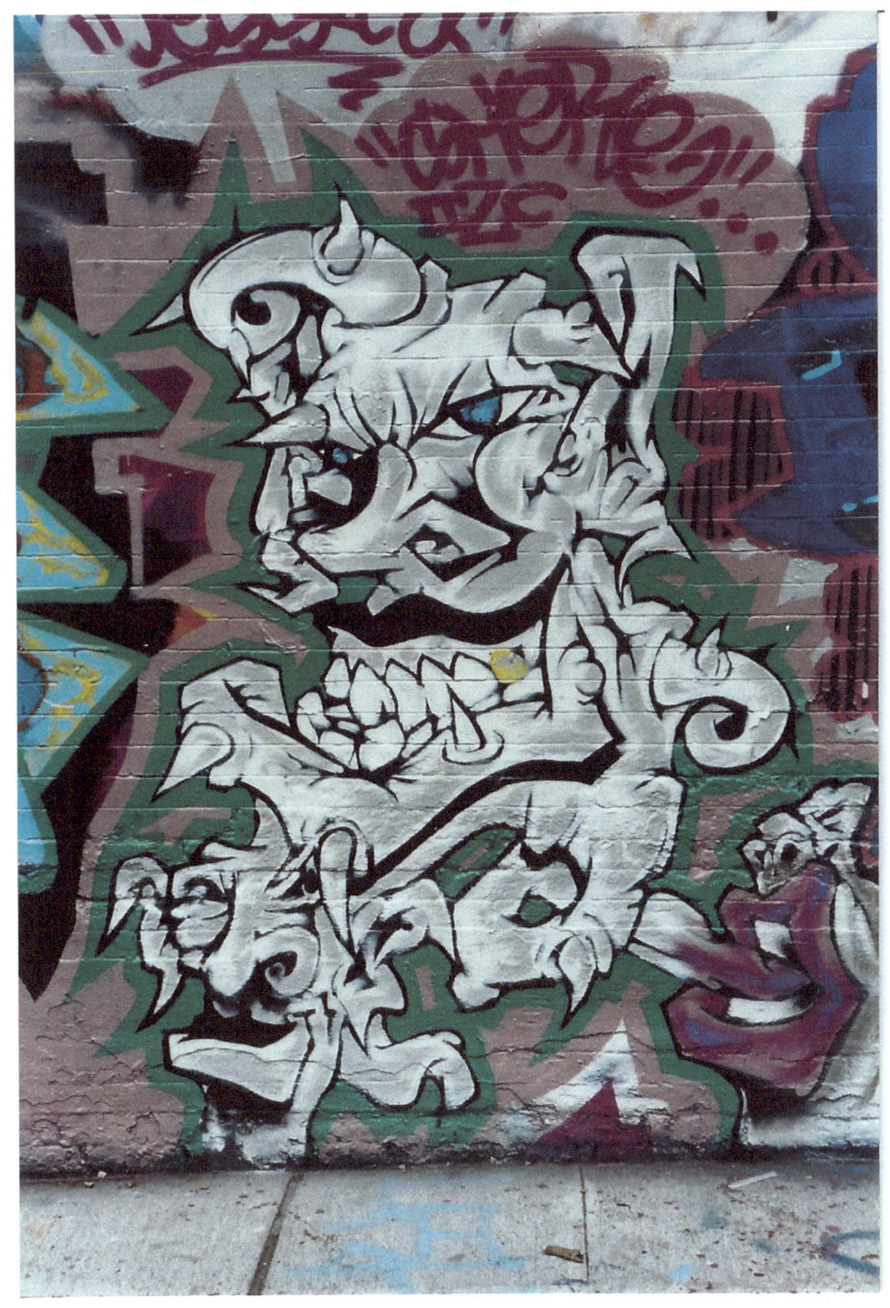

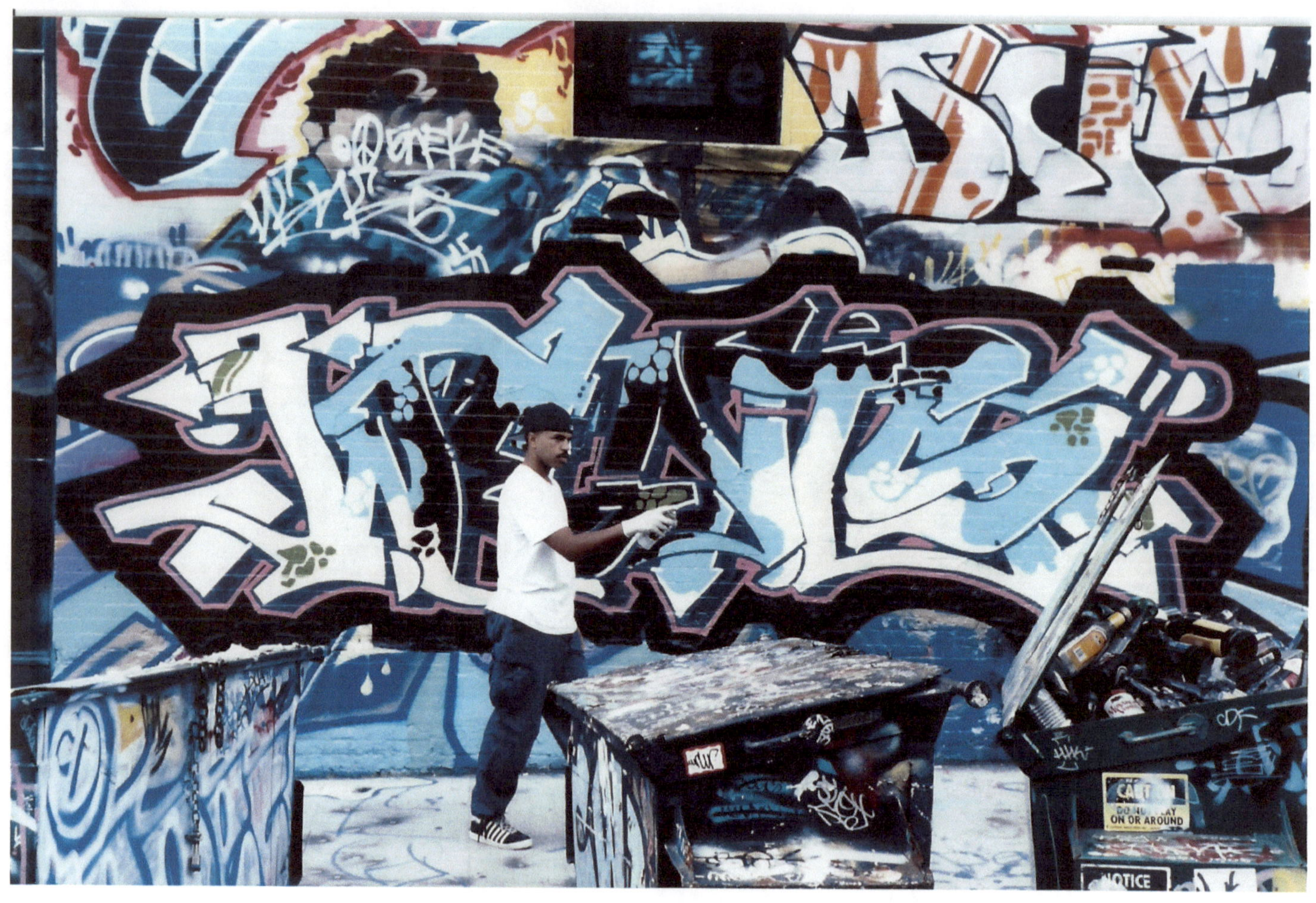
ON OR AROUND
NOTICE

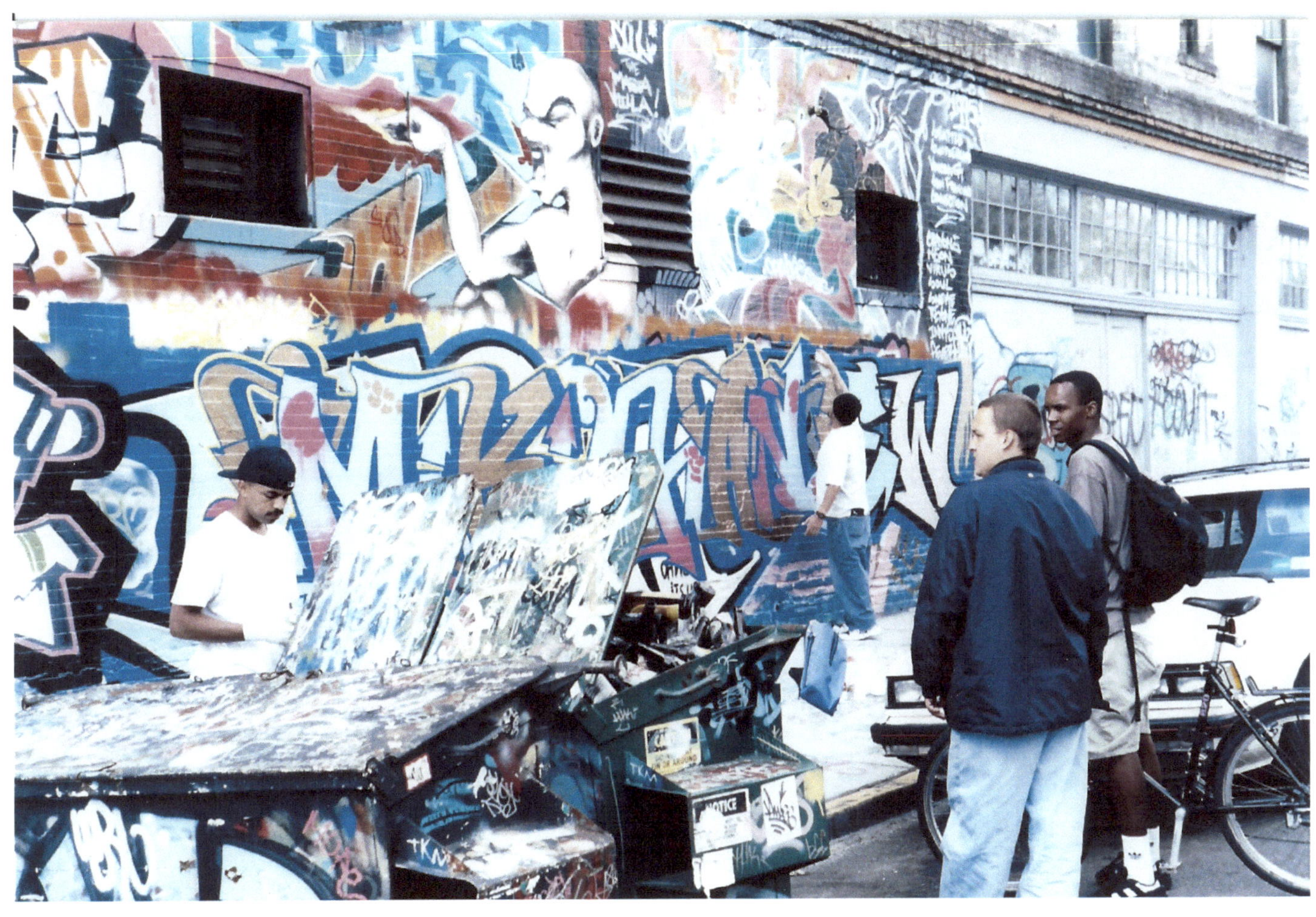
NOTICE

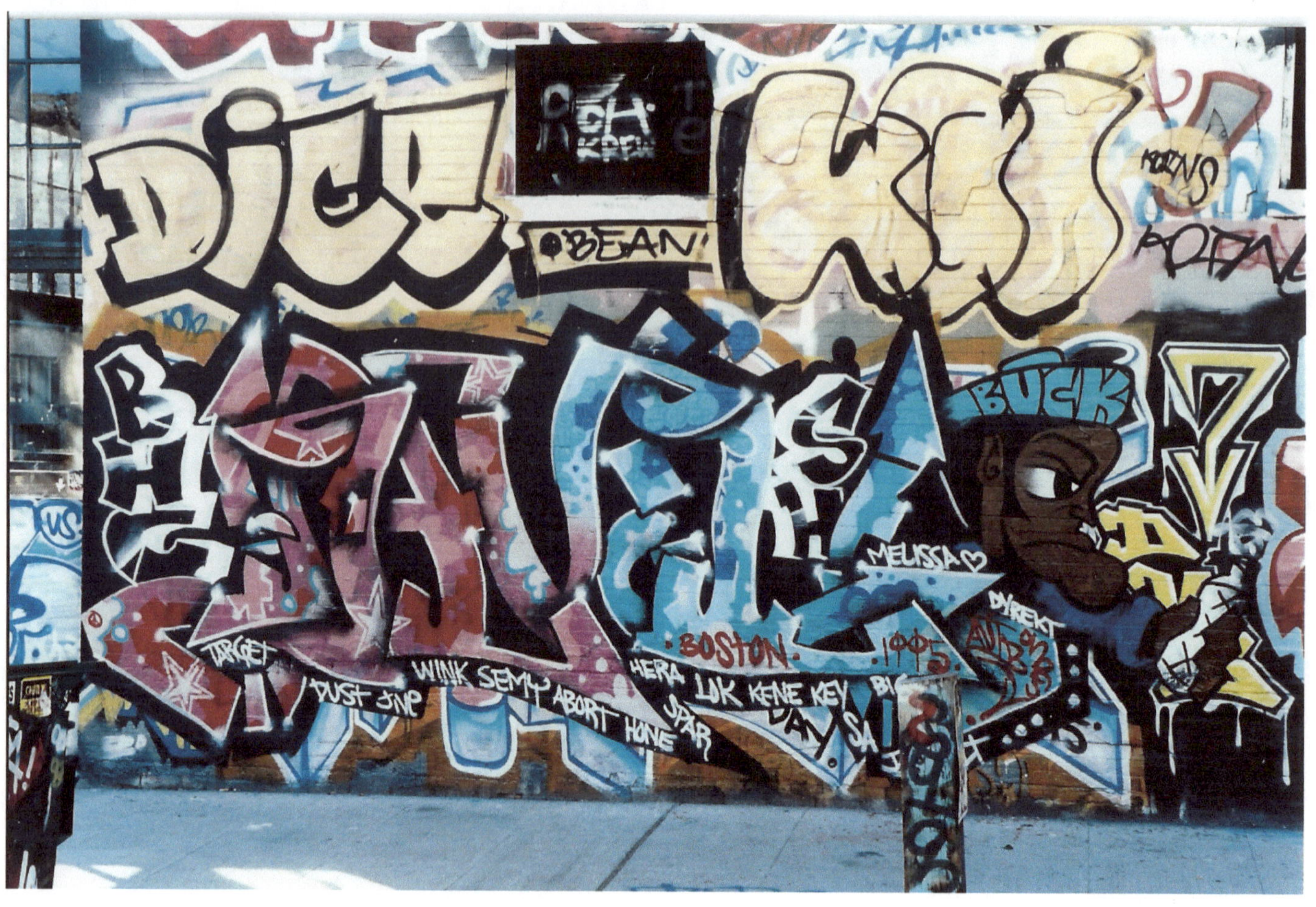
BEAN
BUCK
MELISSA
DYREKT
BOSTON
1995
TARGET
DUST JNP
WINK SEMY ABORT HONE
HERA LUK KENE KEY
SPAR
DAY

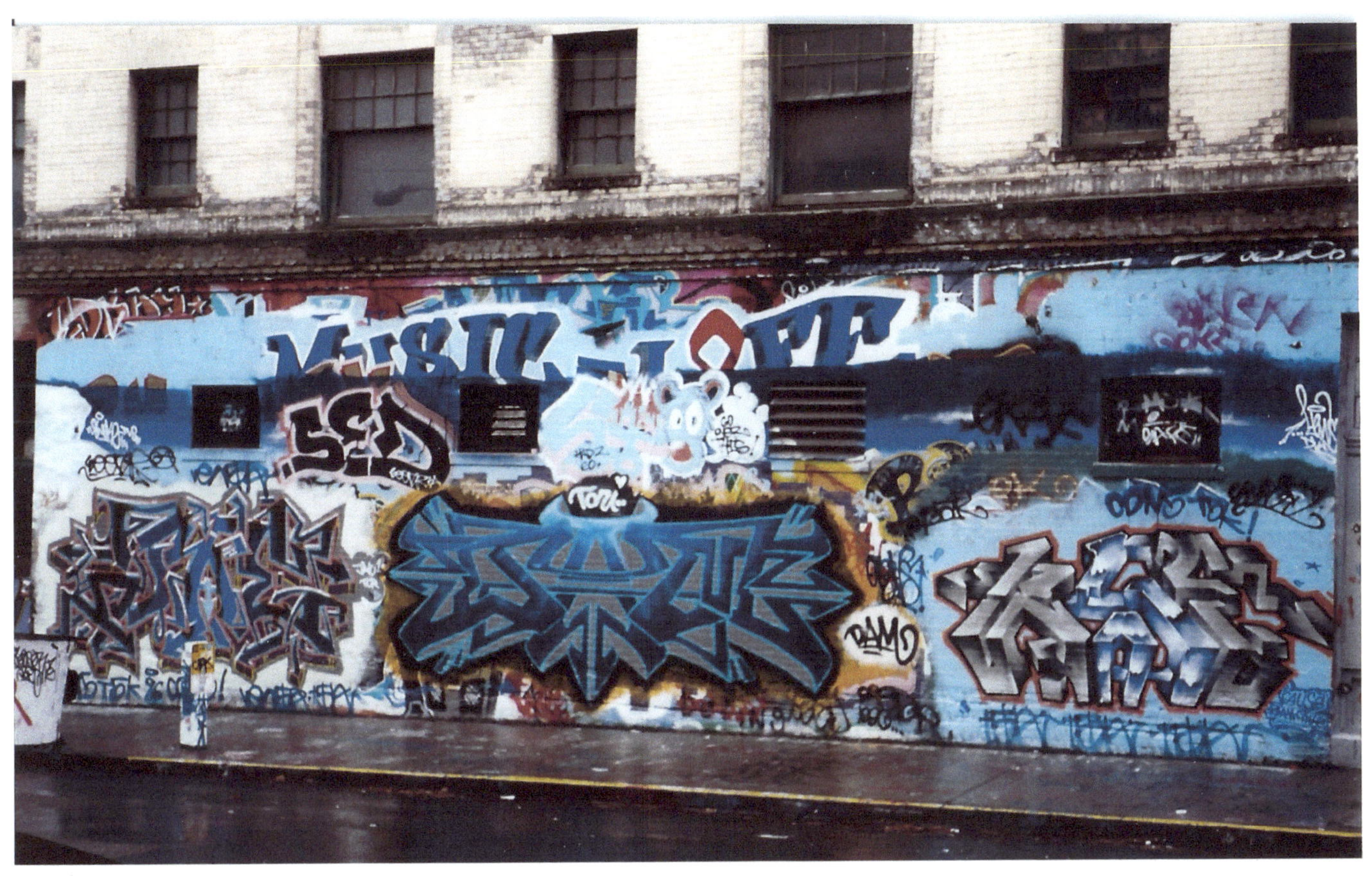
SED
DAMO

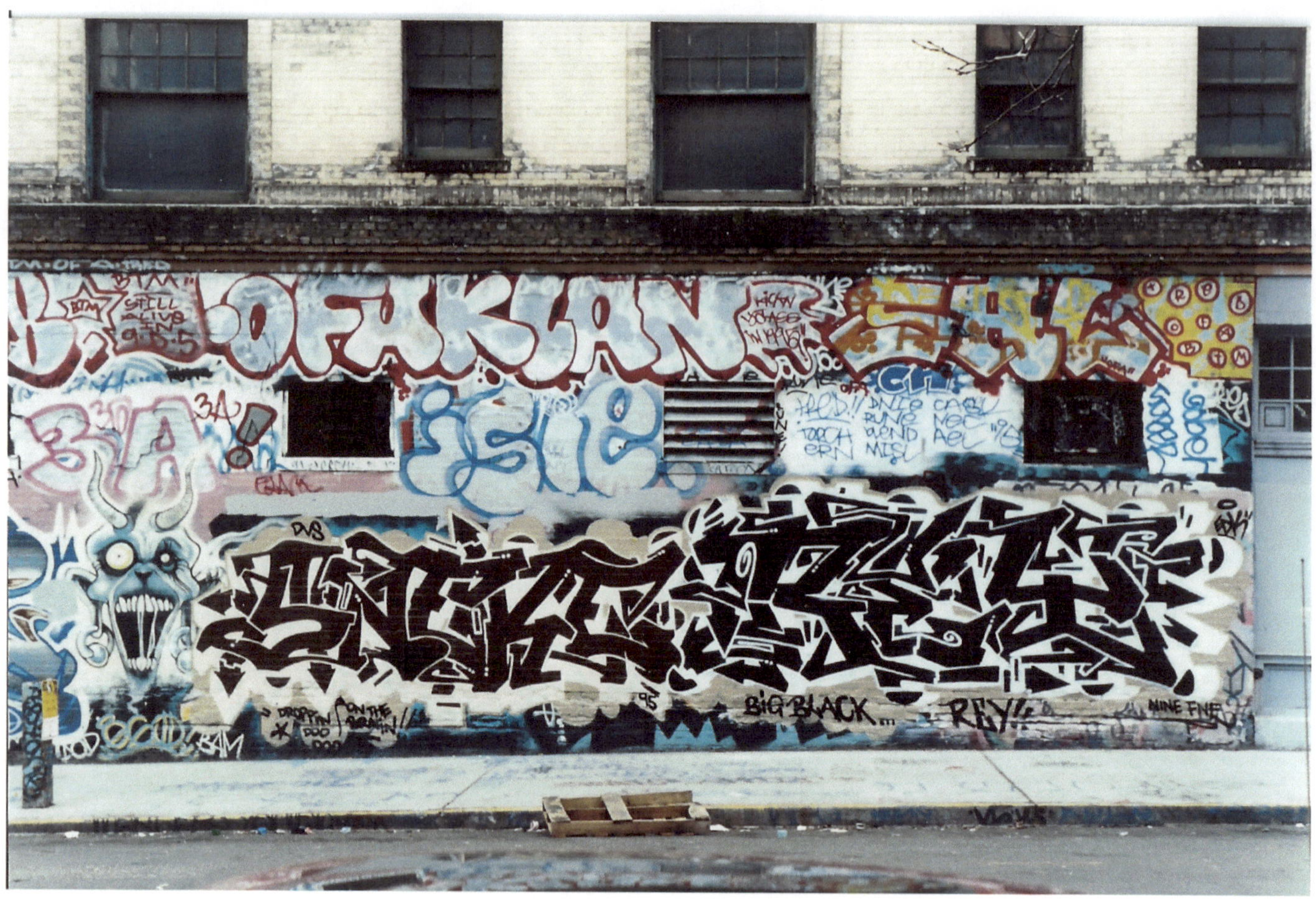
BIG BLACK...
REY!!

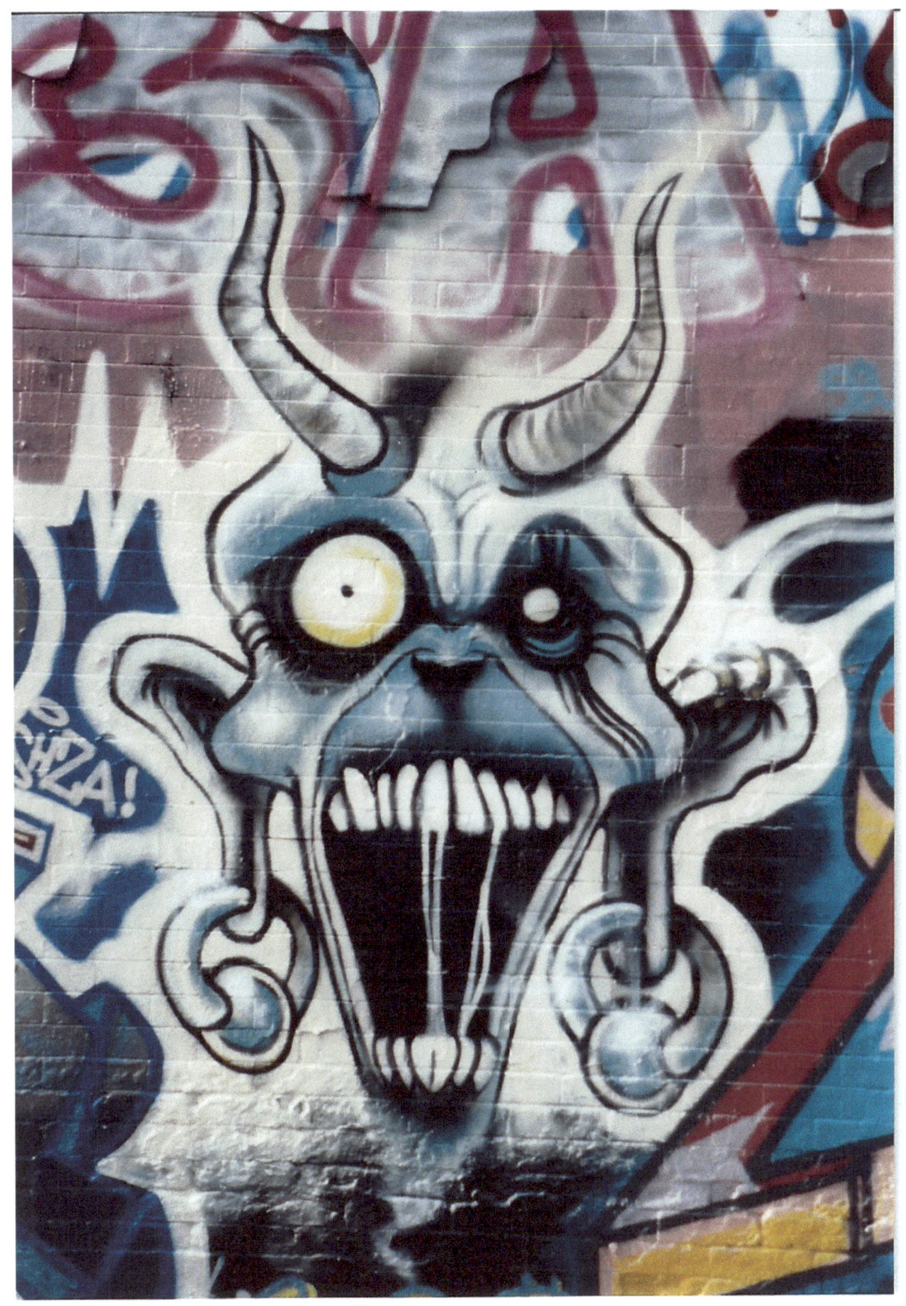

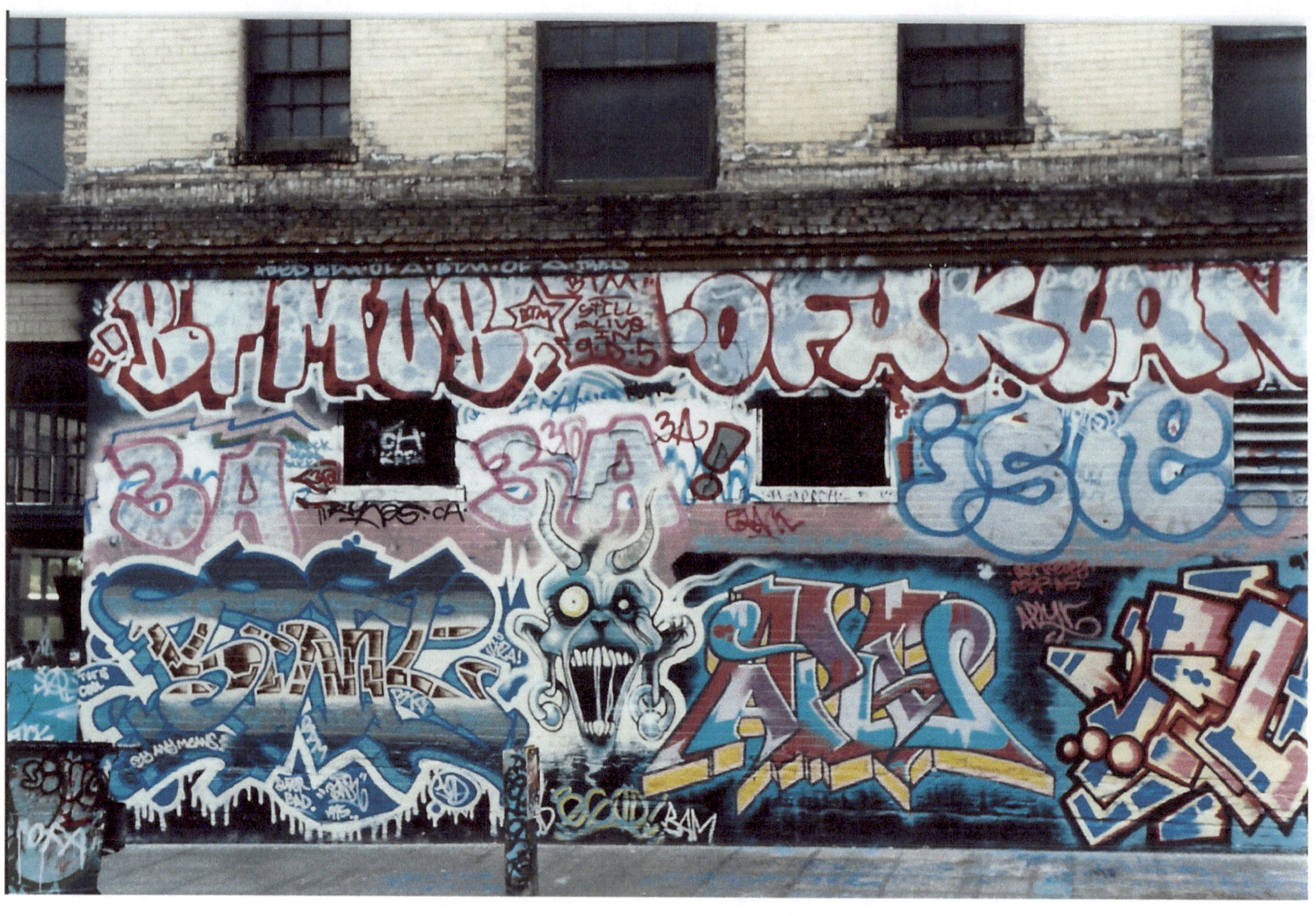

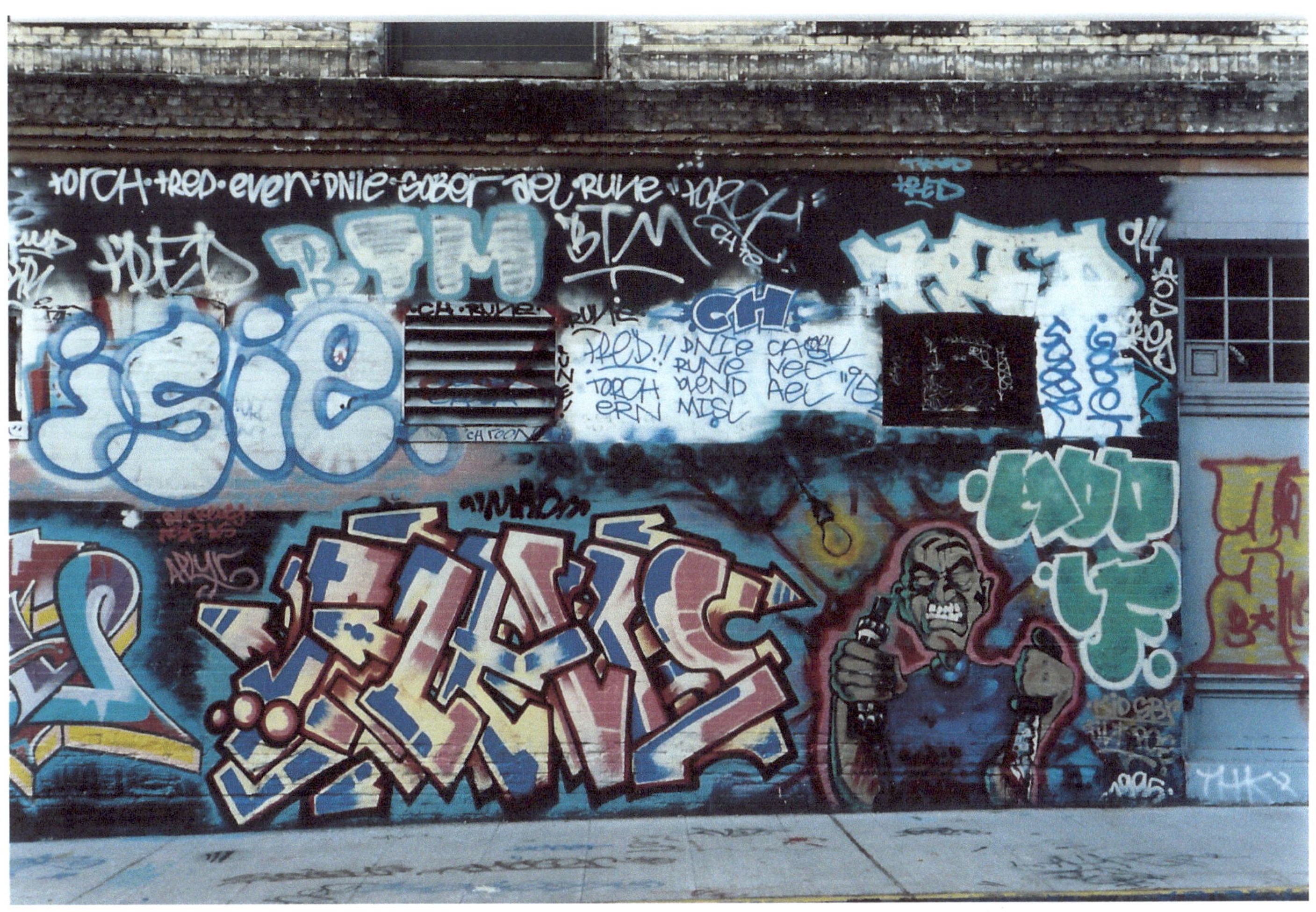

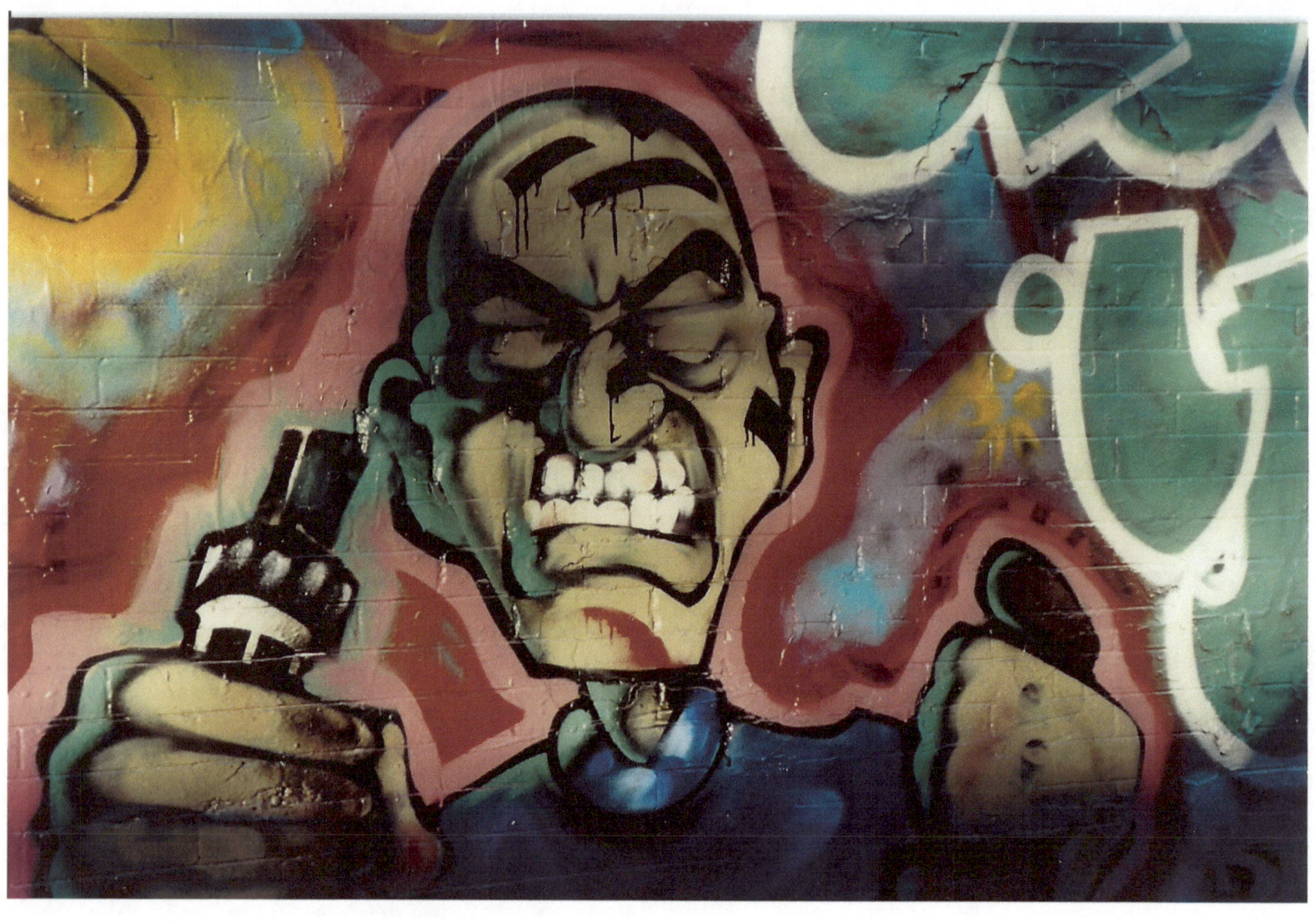

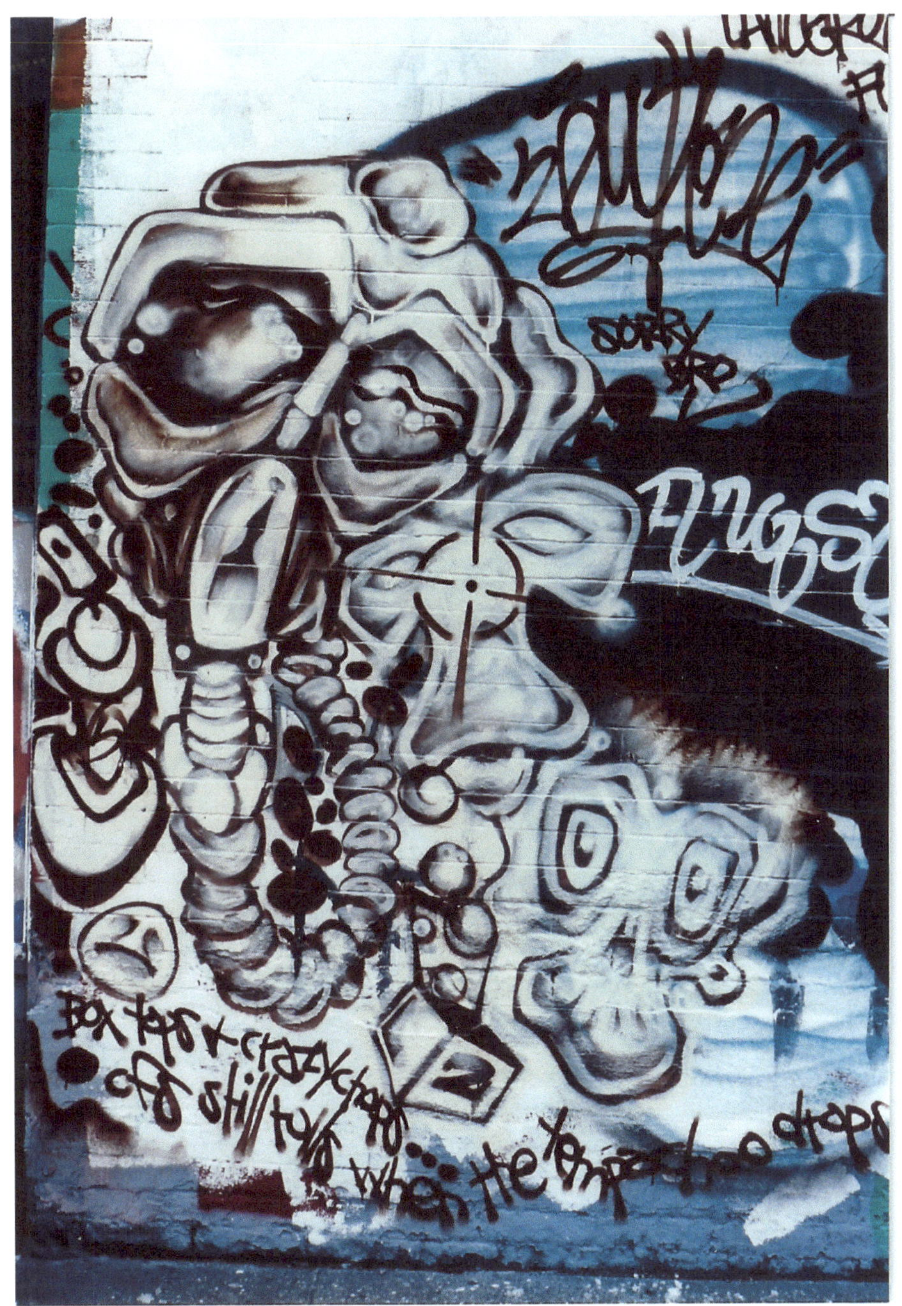

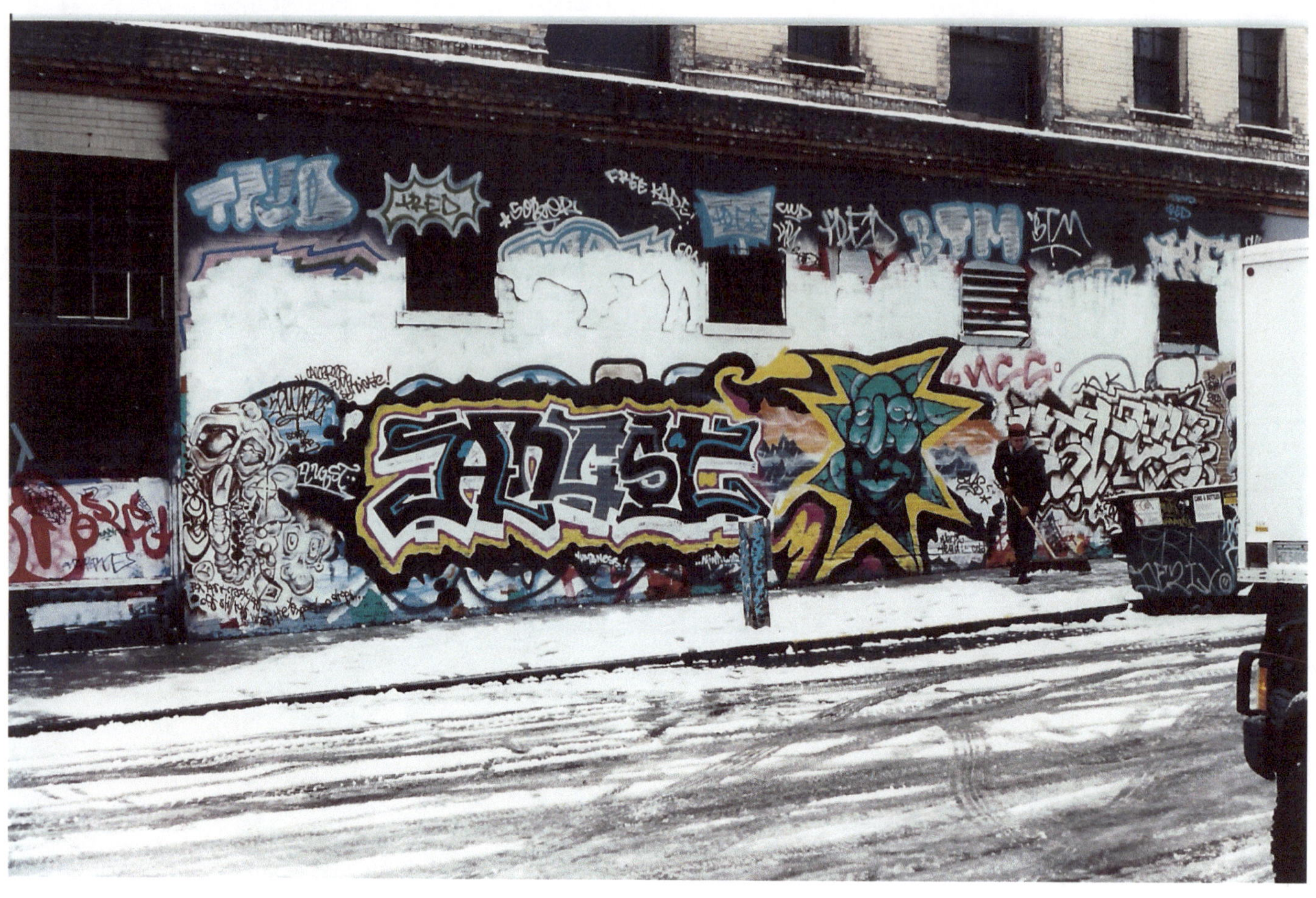
FREE KADE
BTM

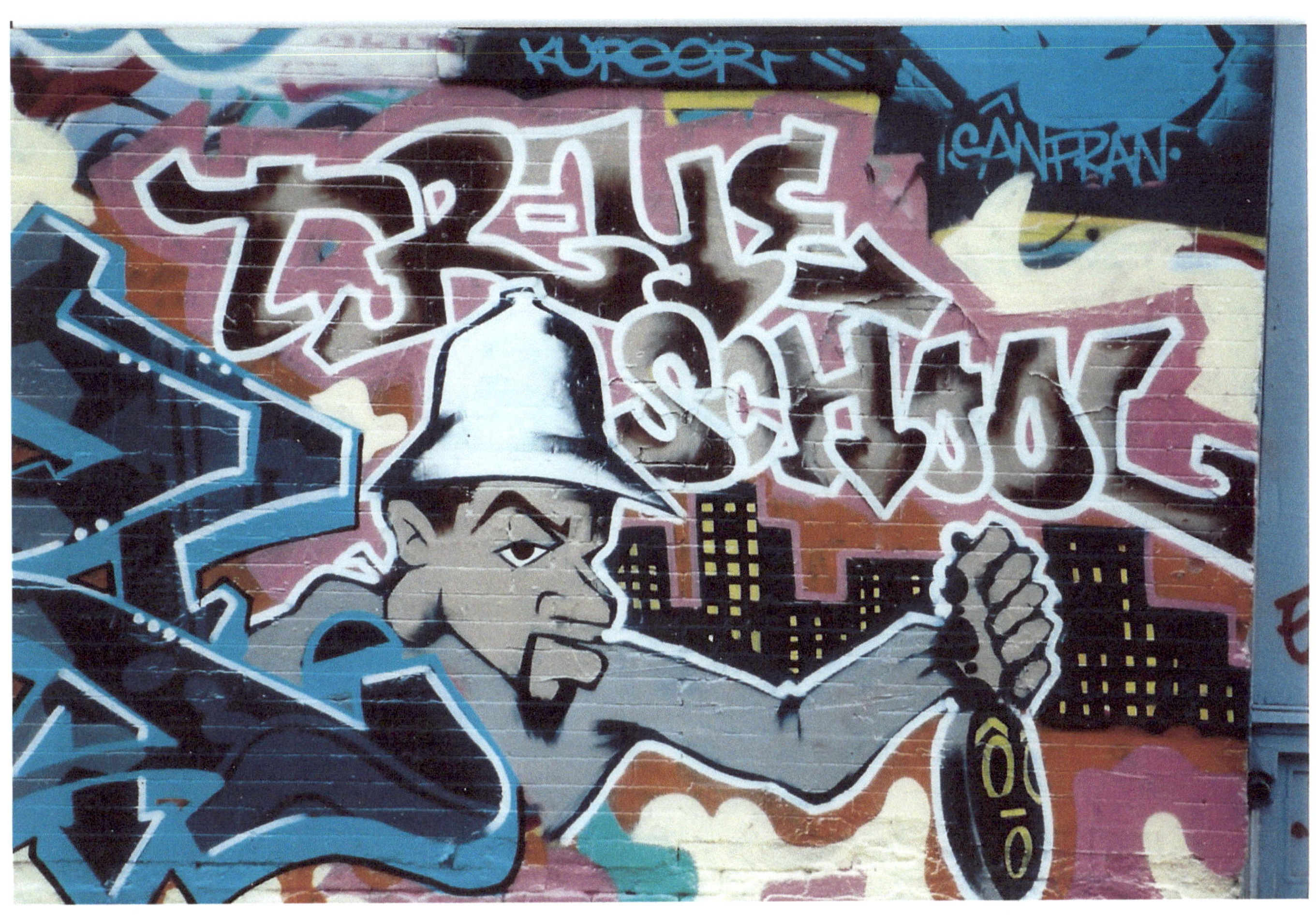
SANFRAN

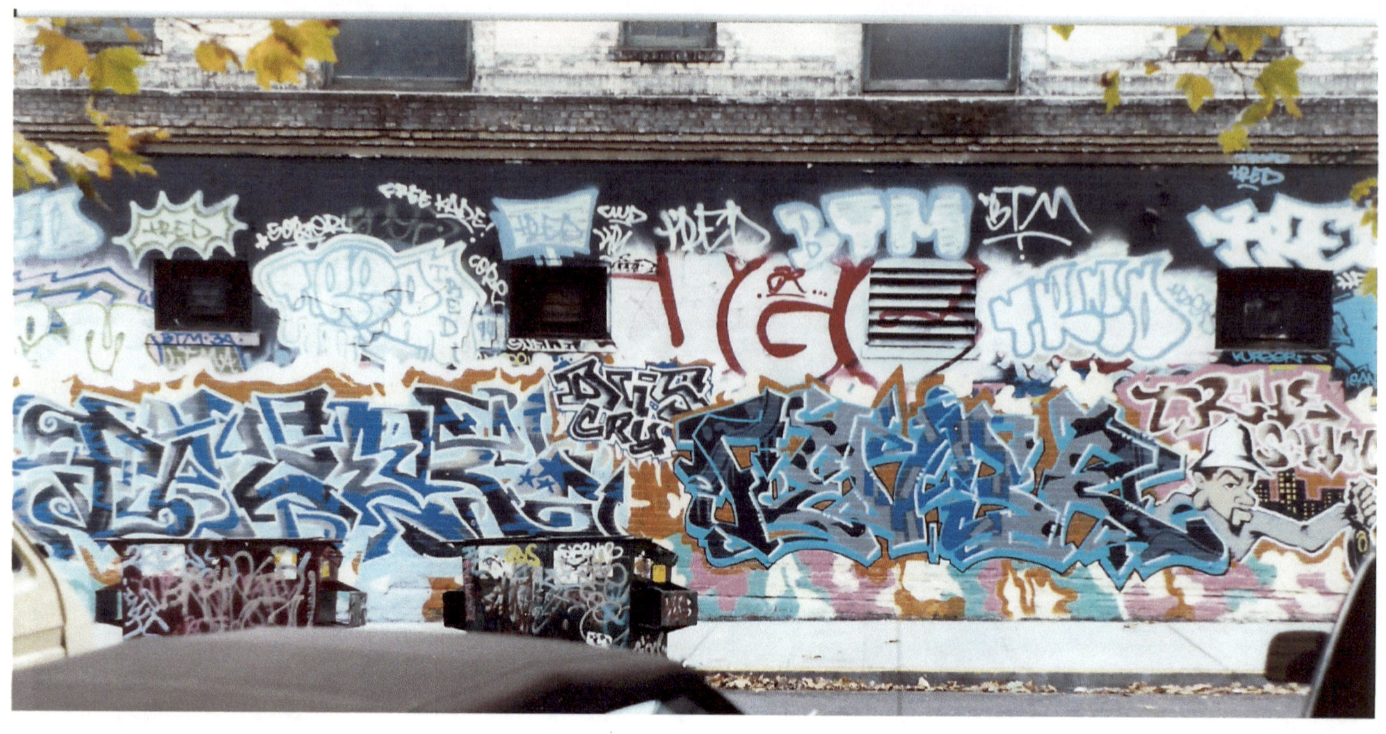
BTM

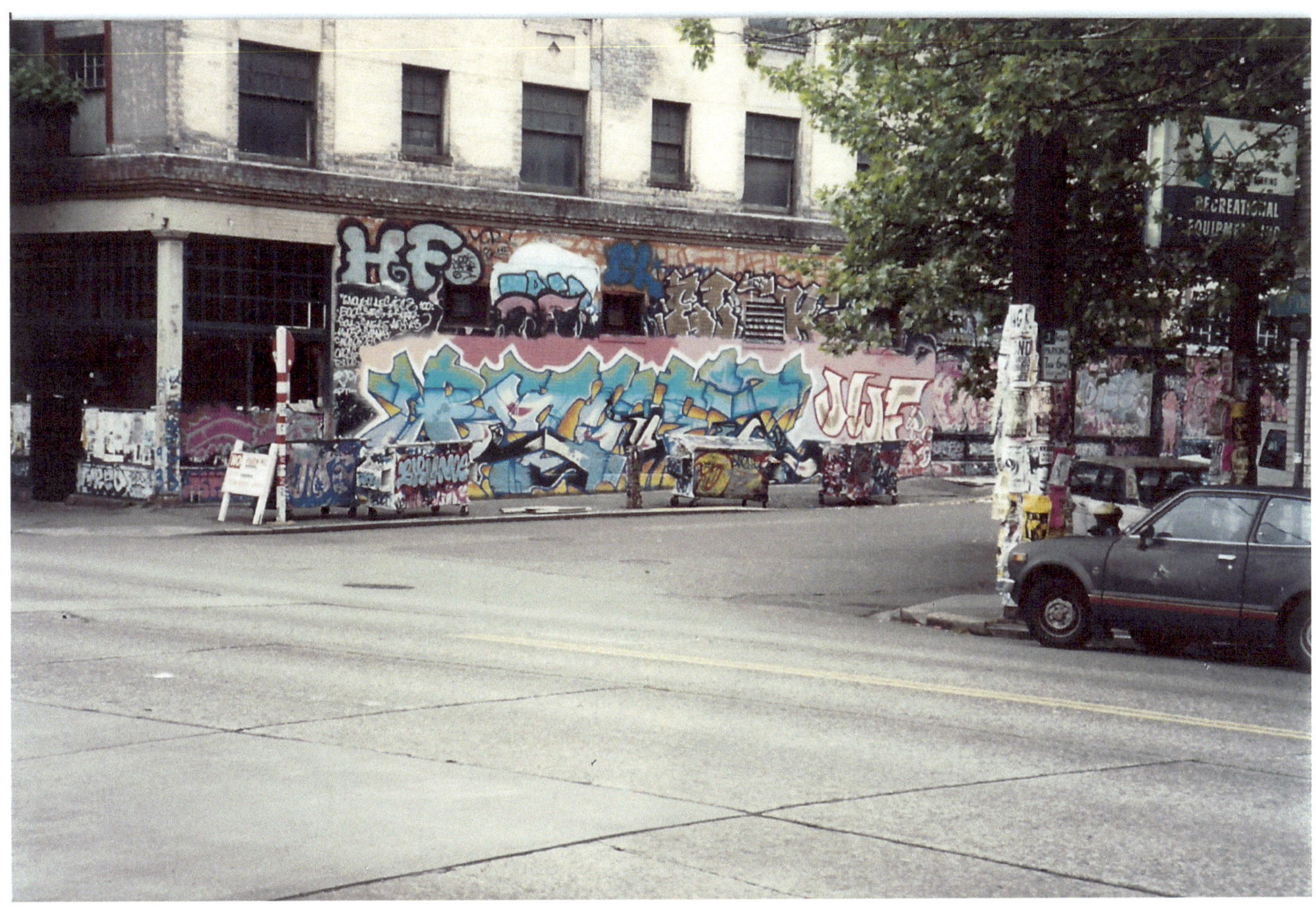
RECREATIONAL

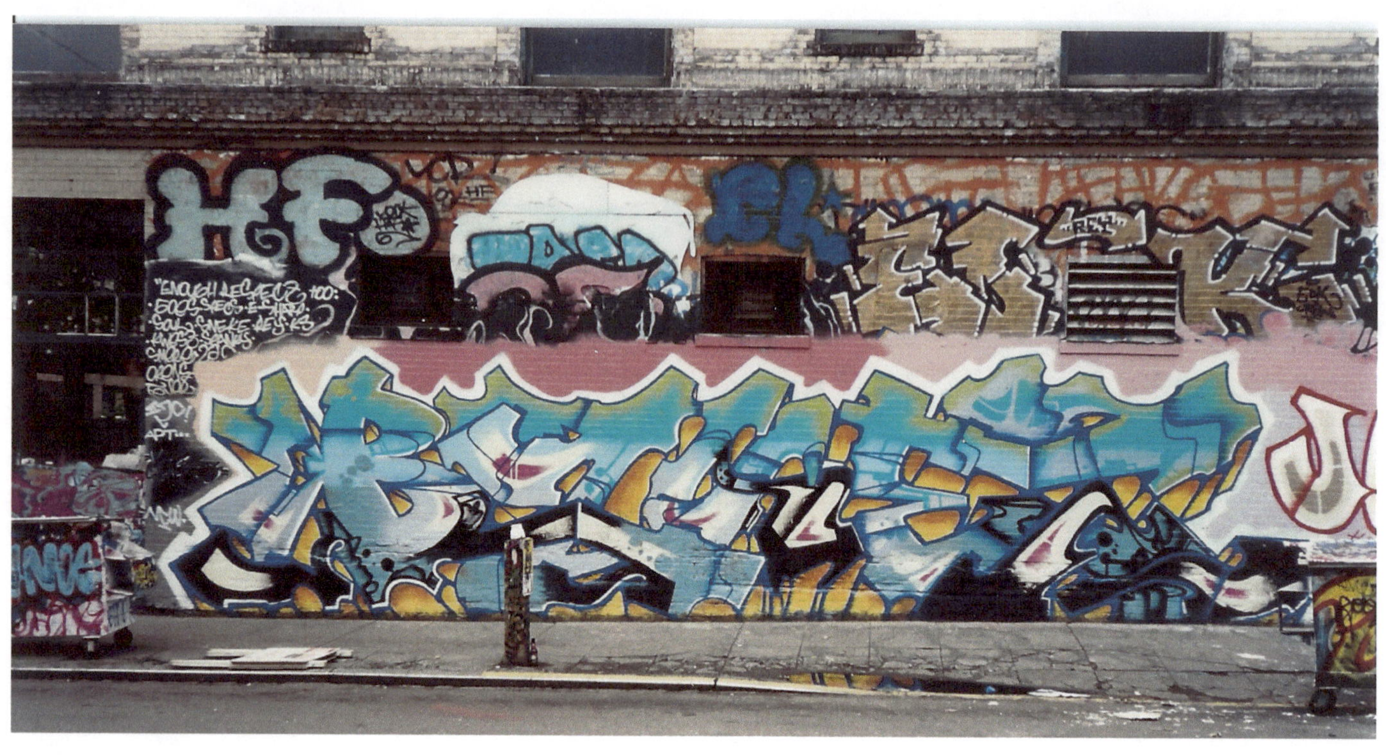

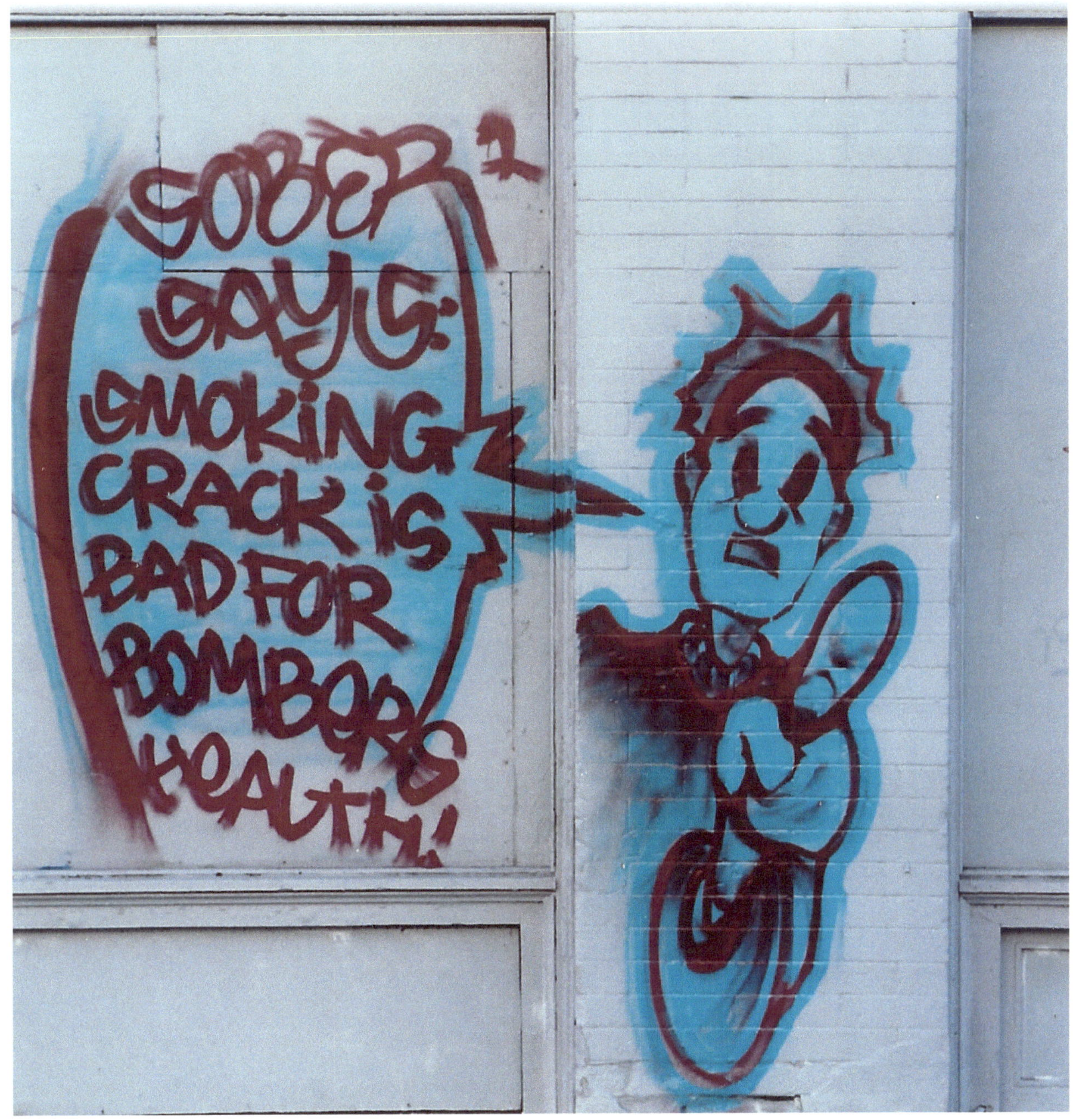
SOBER 1
SAYS:
SMOKING
CRACK IS
BAD FOR
BOMBERS
HEALTH!

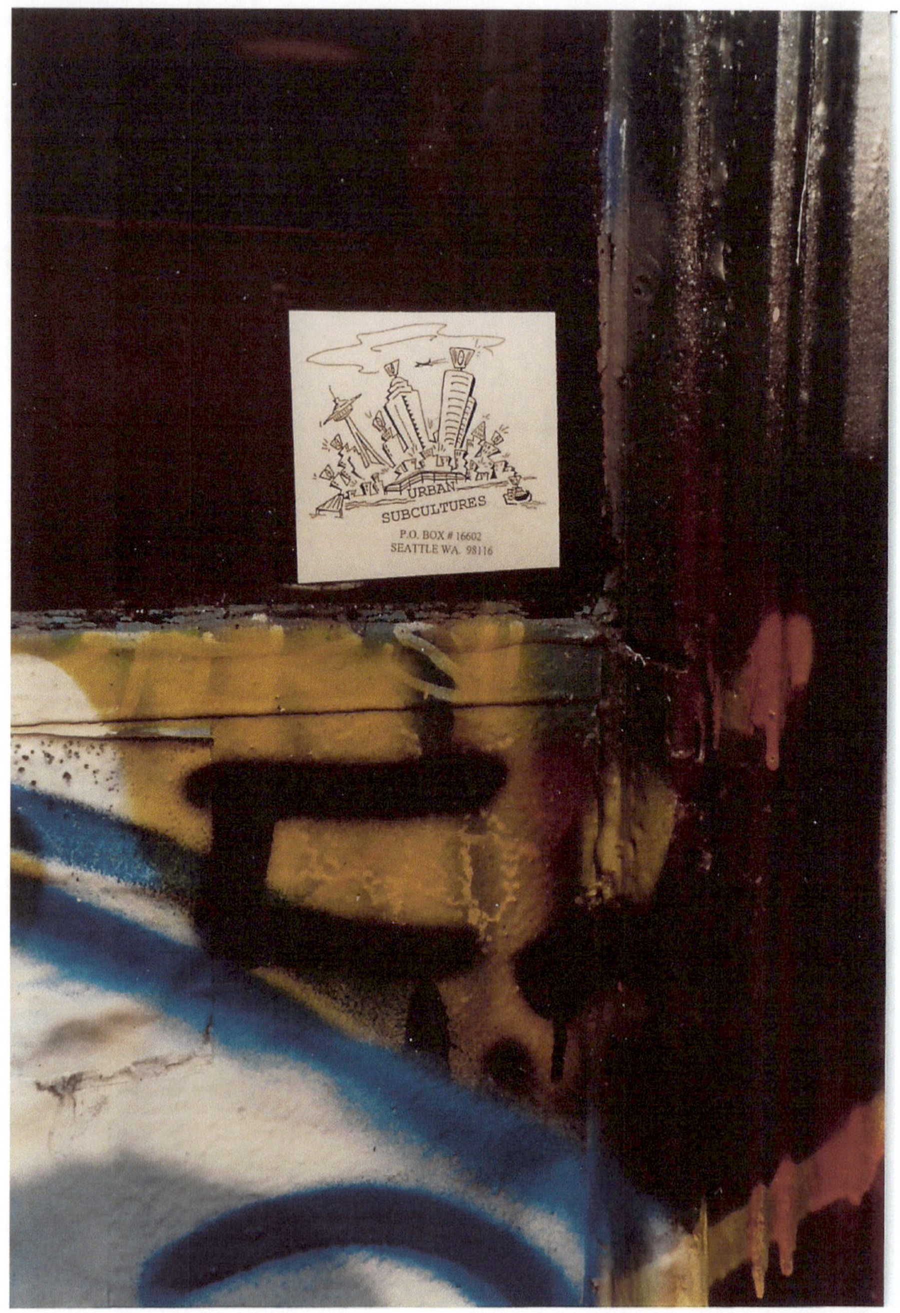
URBAN
SUBCULTURES
P.O. BOX # 16602
SEATTLE WA. 98116

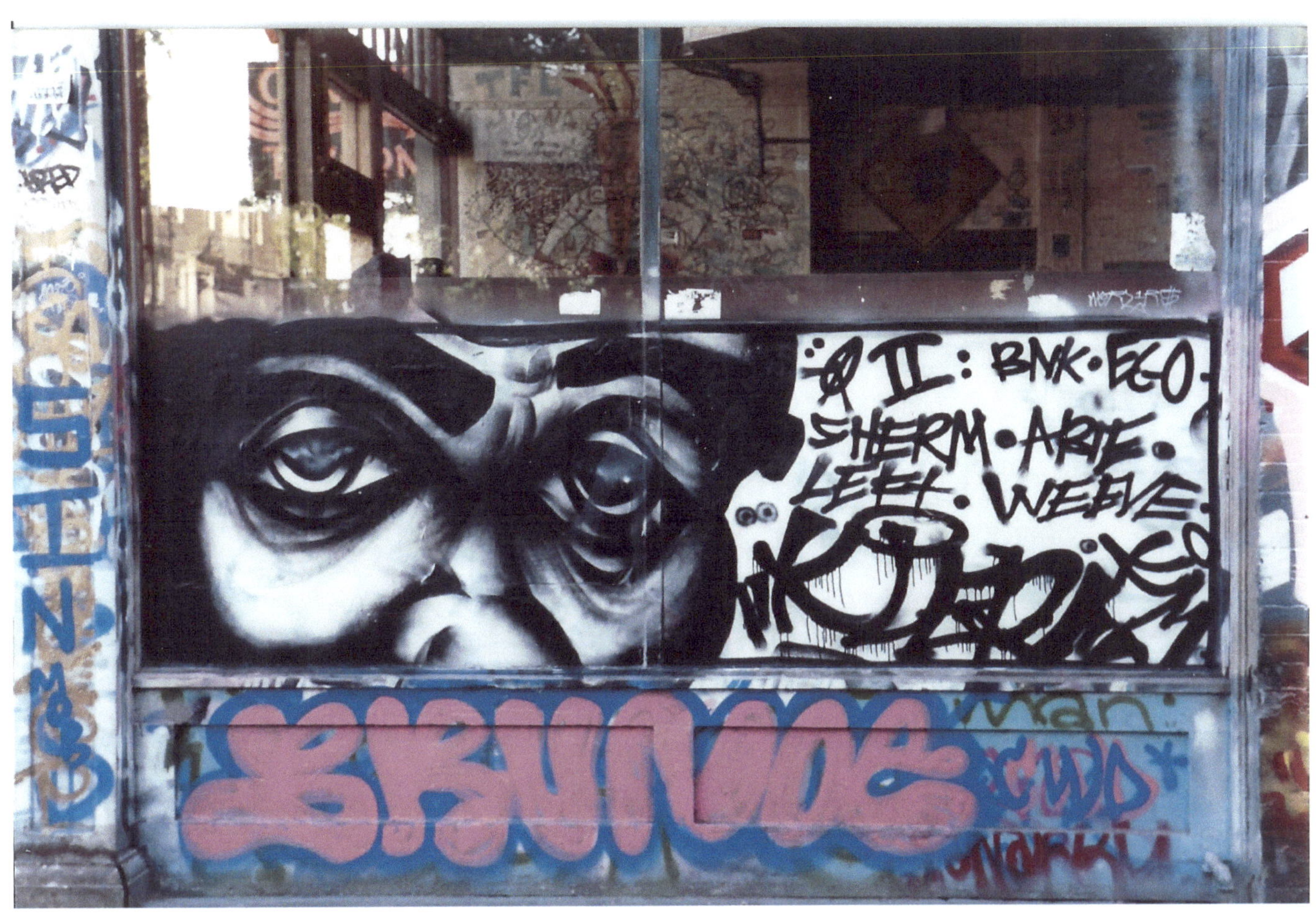

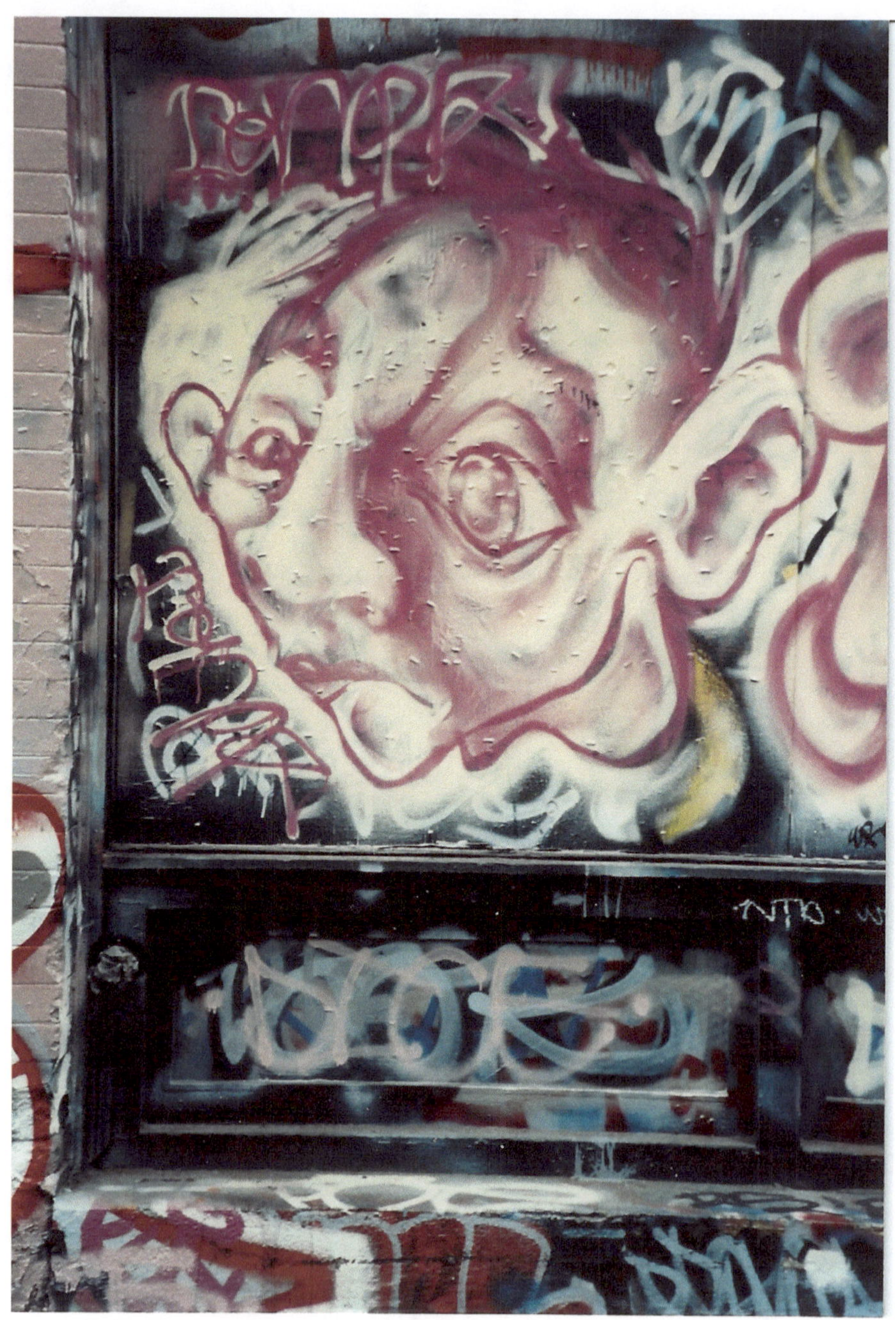

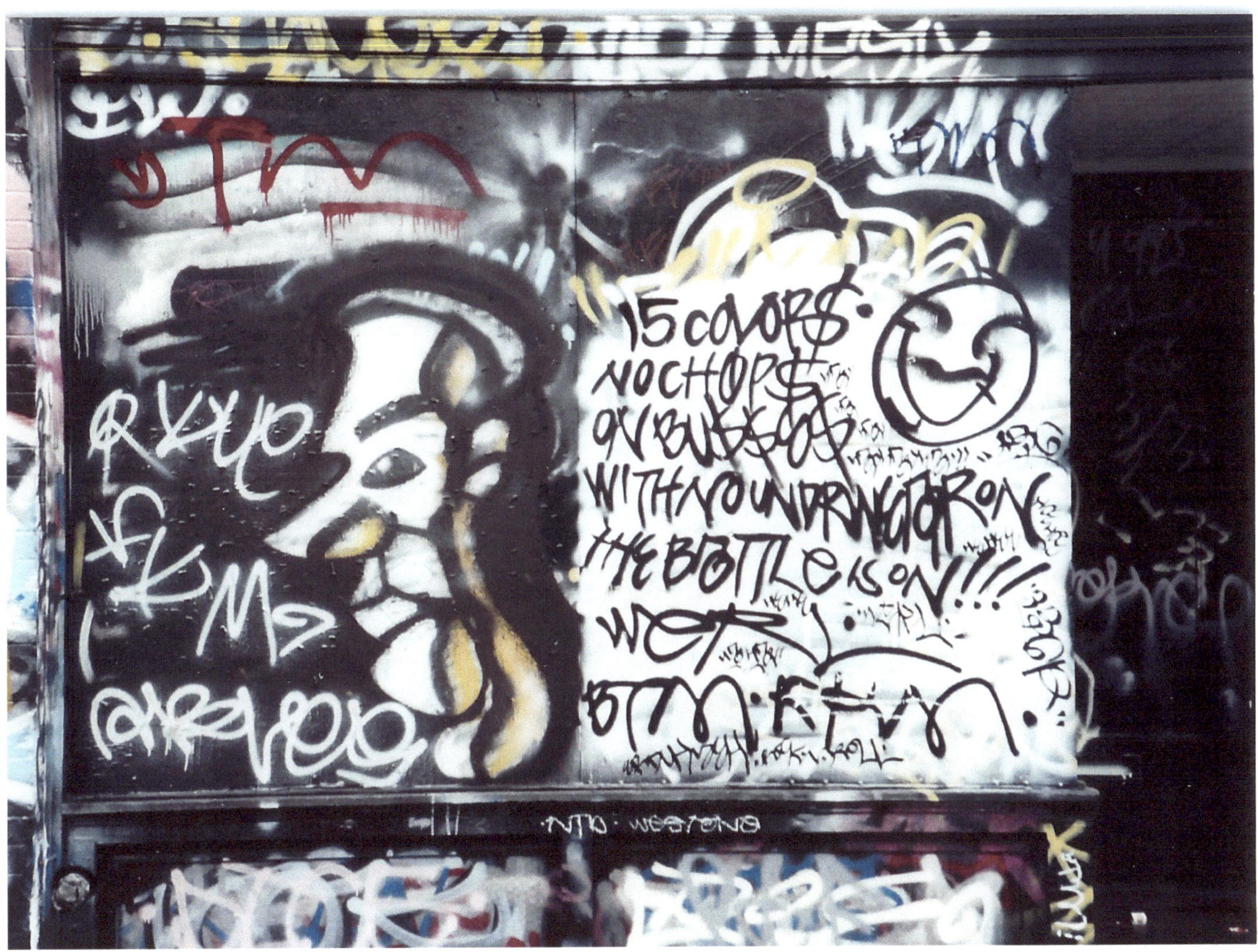
15 COLORS
THE BATTLE IS ON!!!

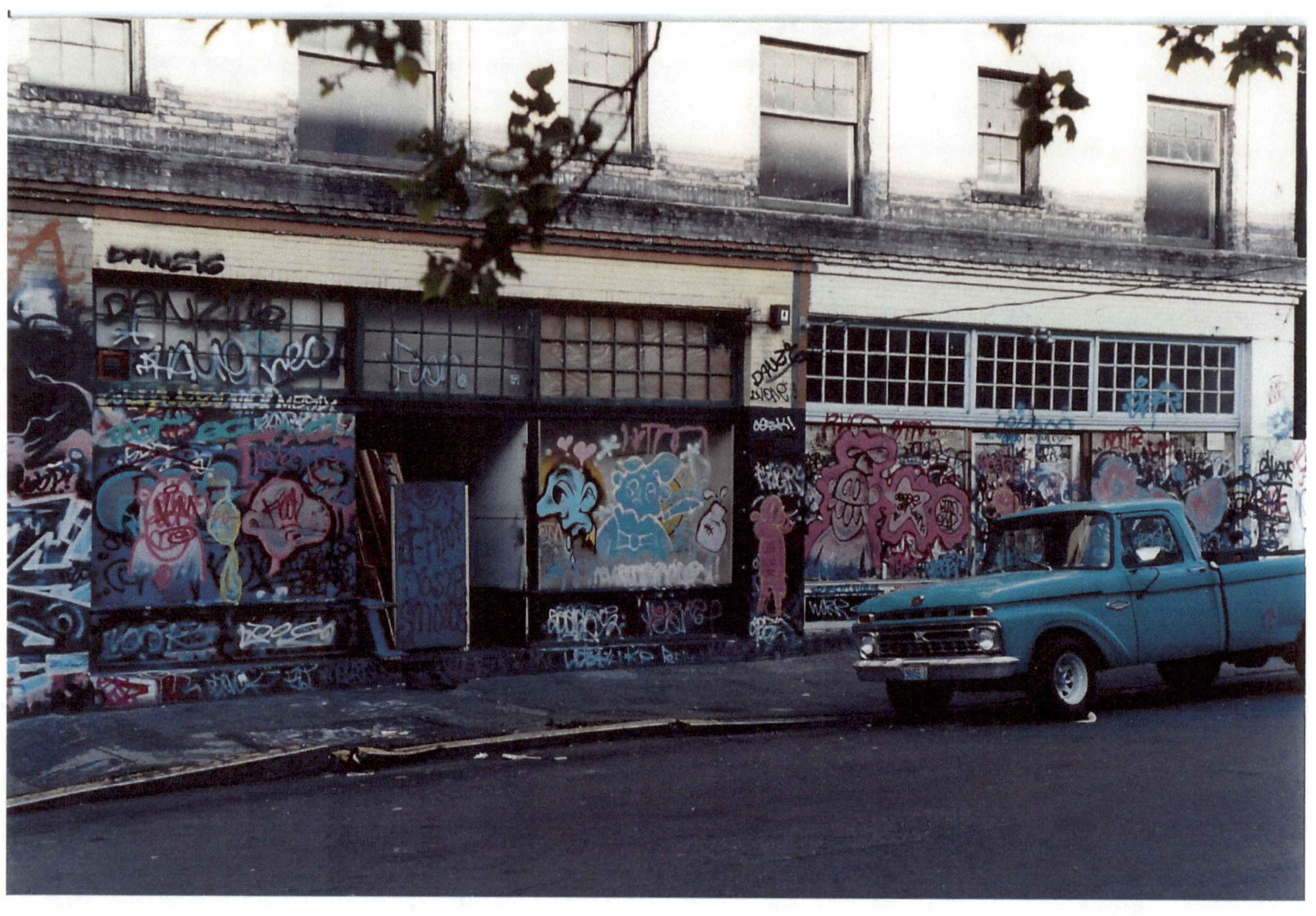

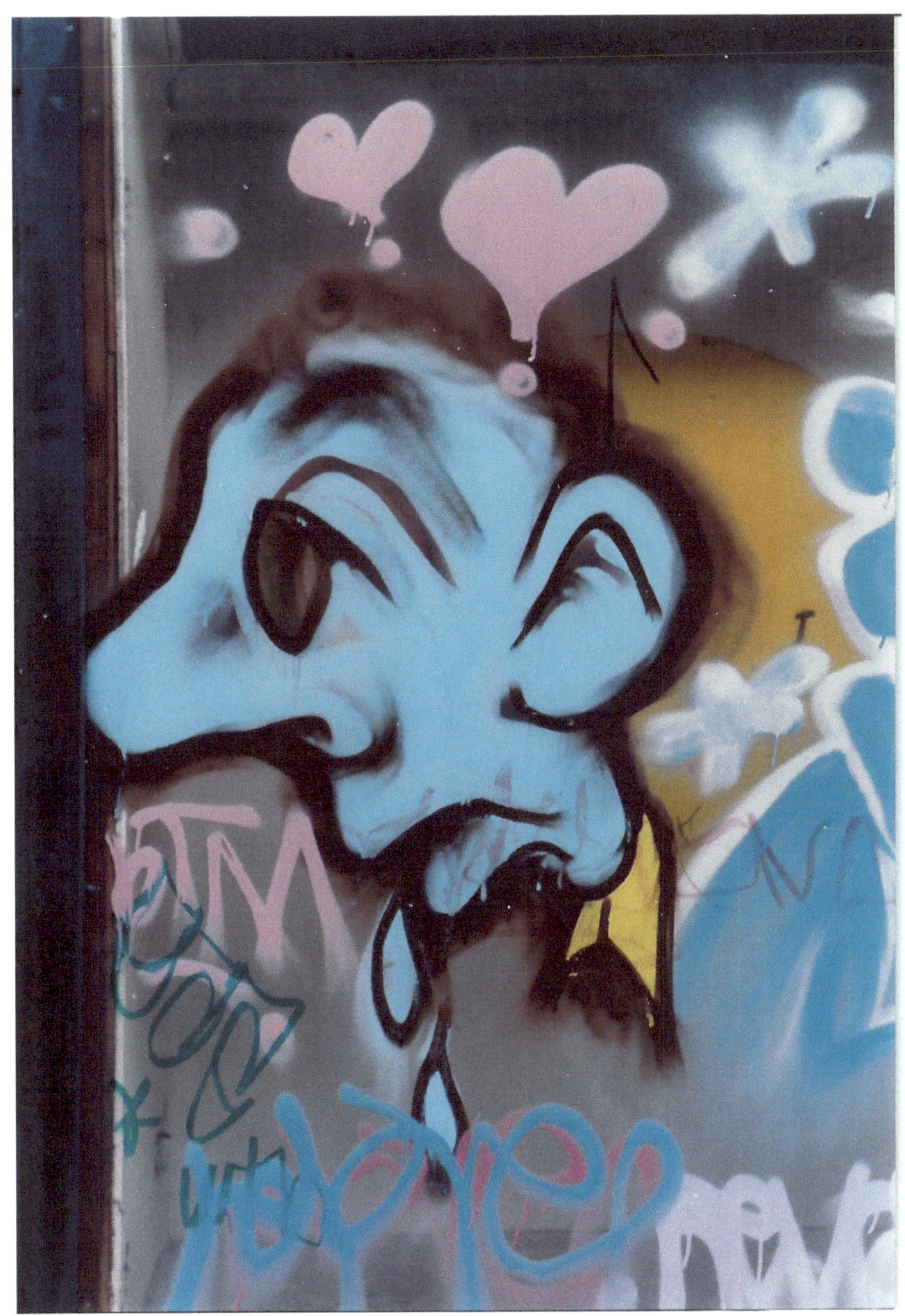

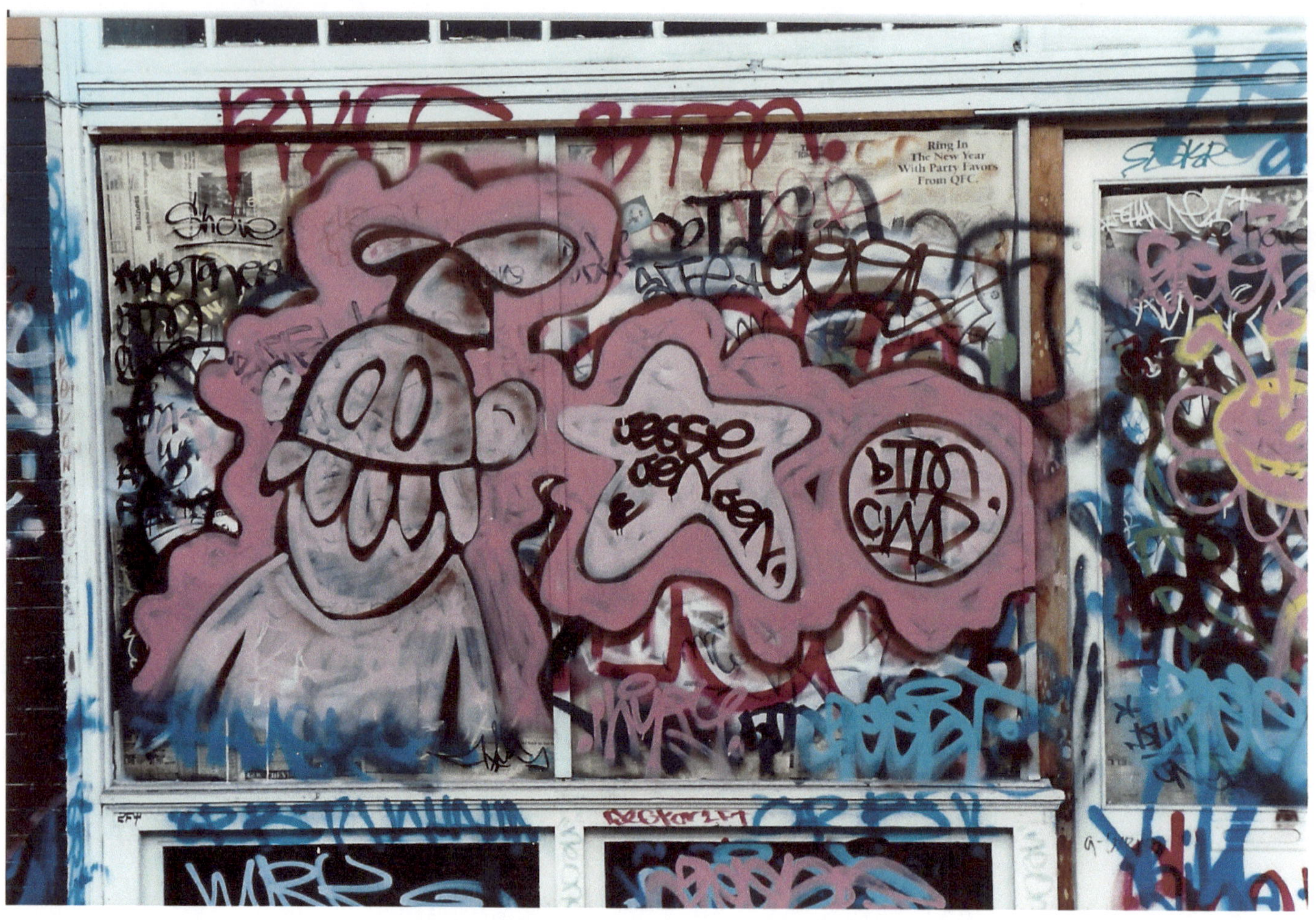
Ring In
The New Year
With Party Favors
From QFC.

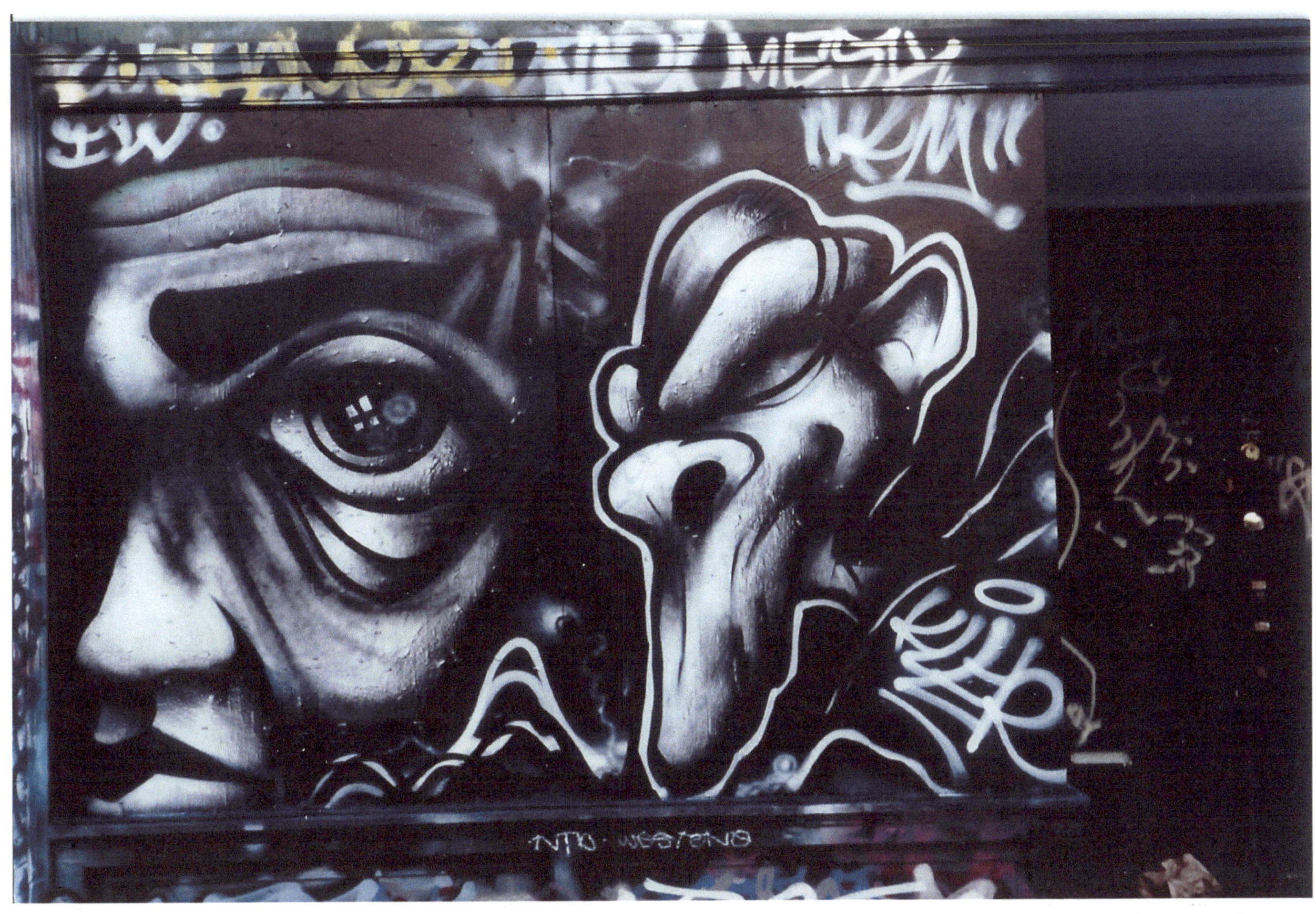

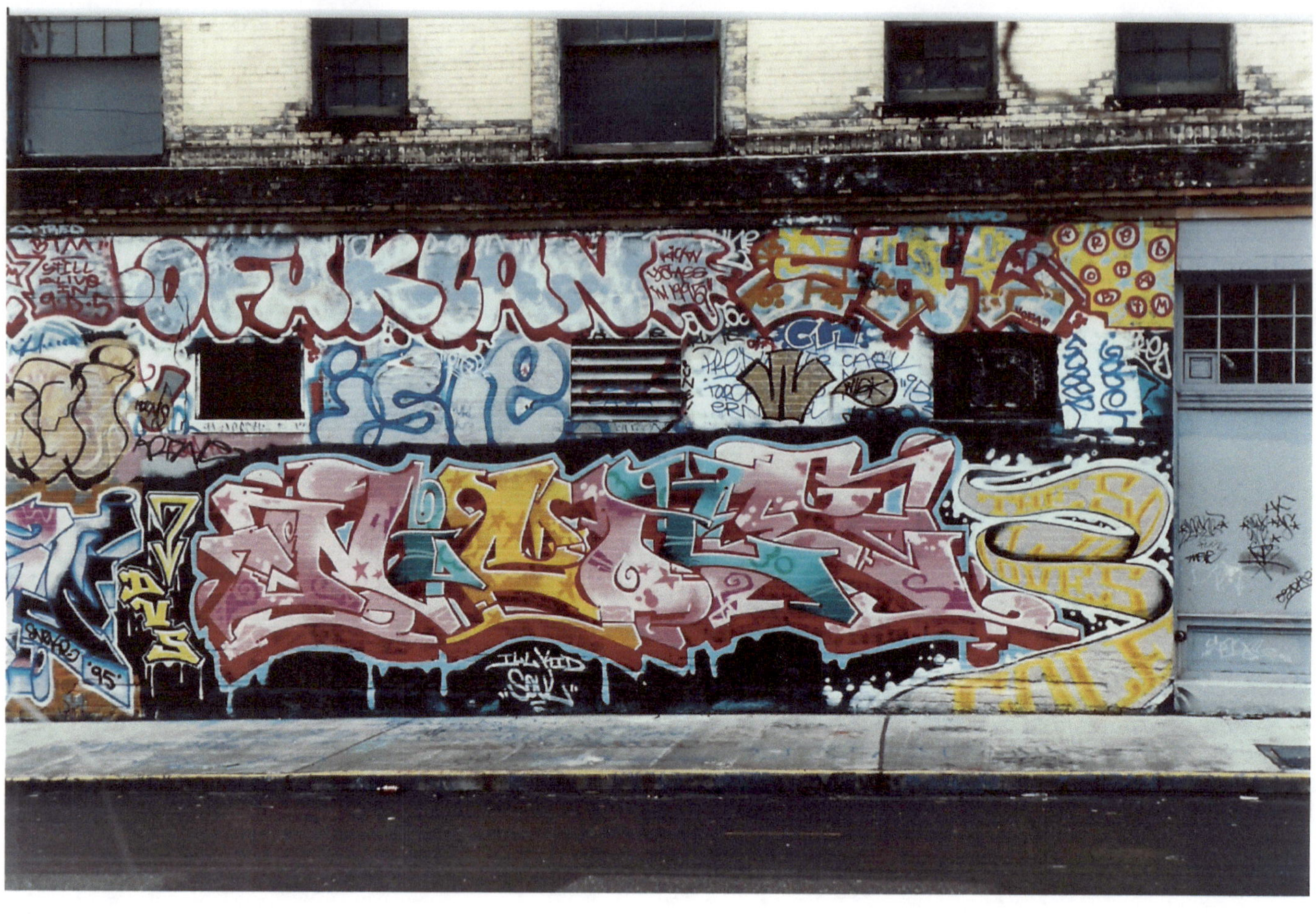

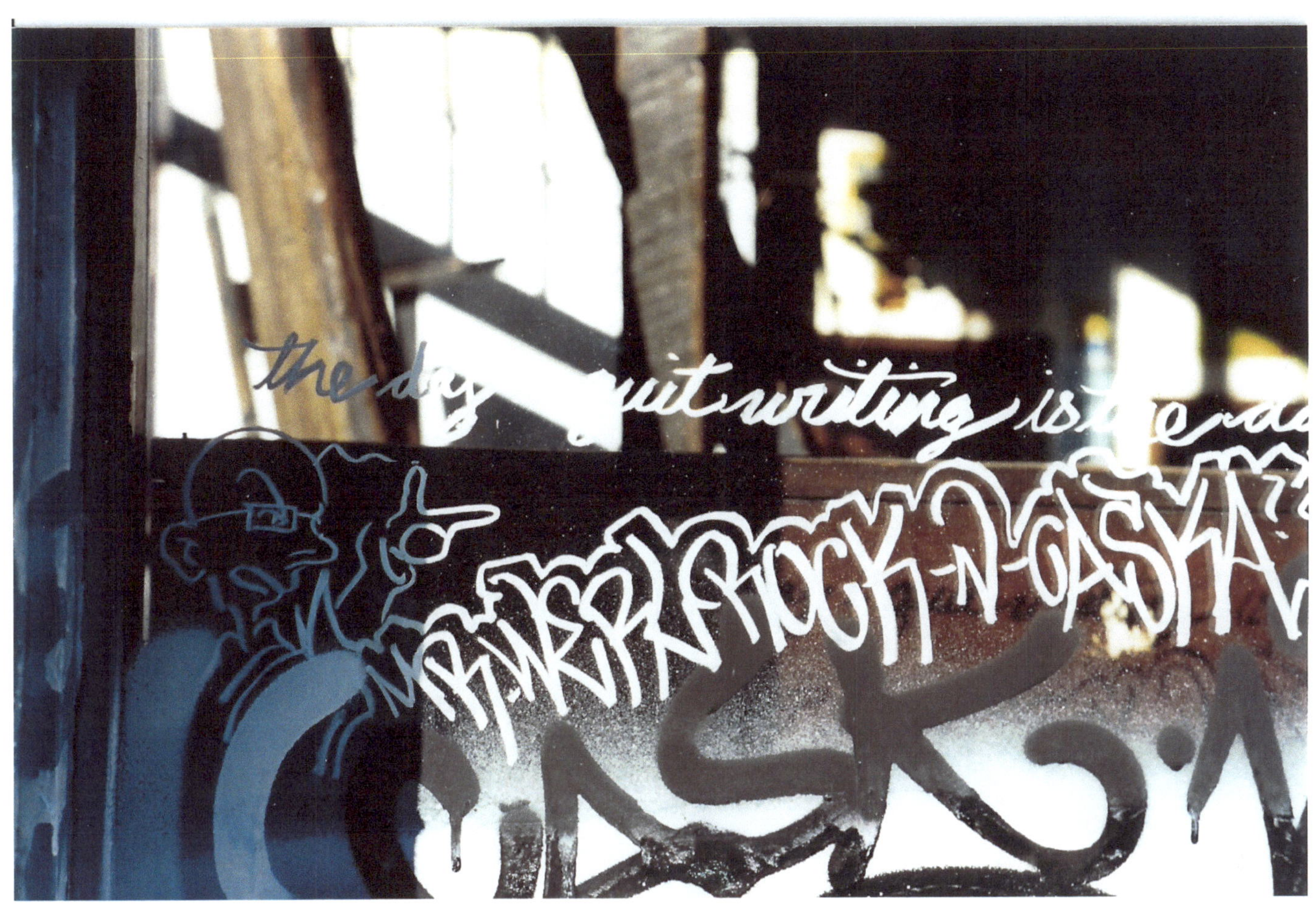
quit writing is

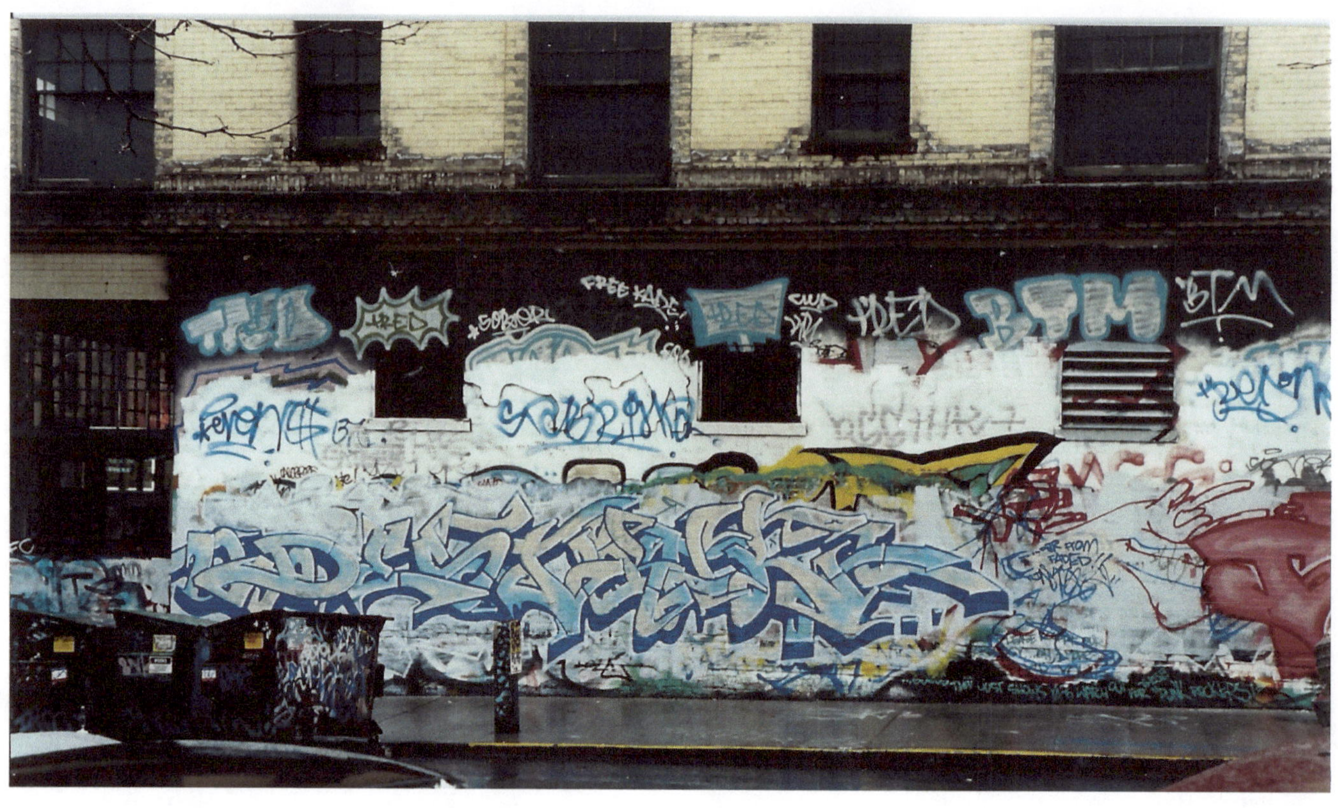
BTM

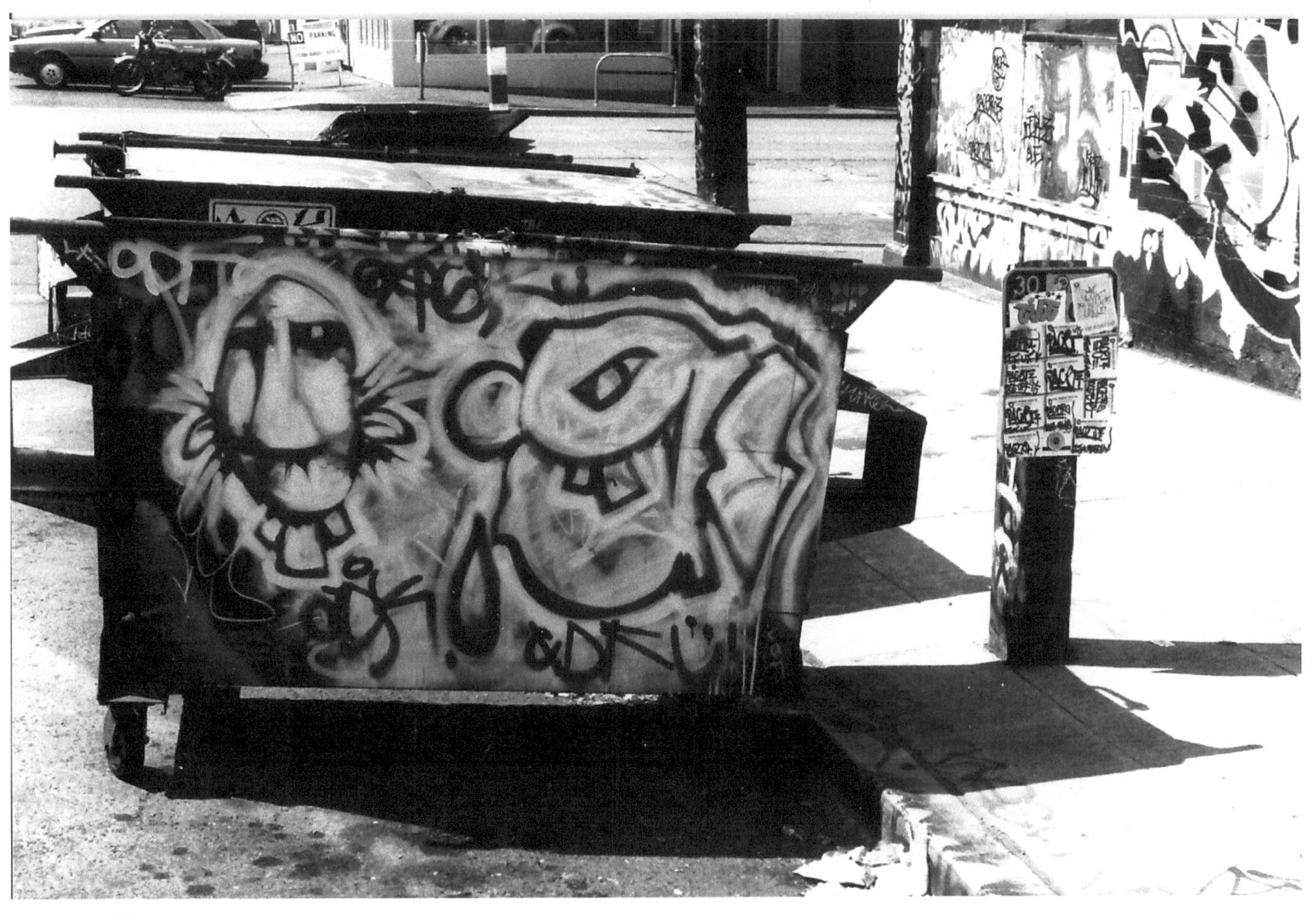

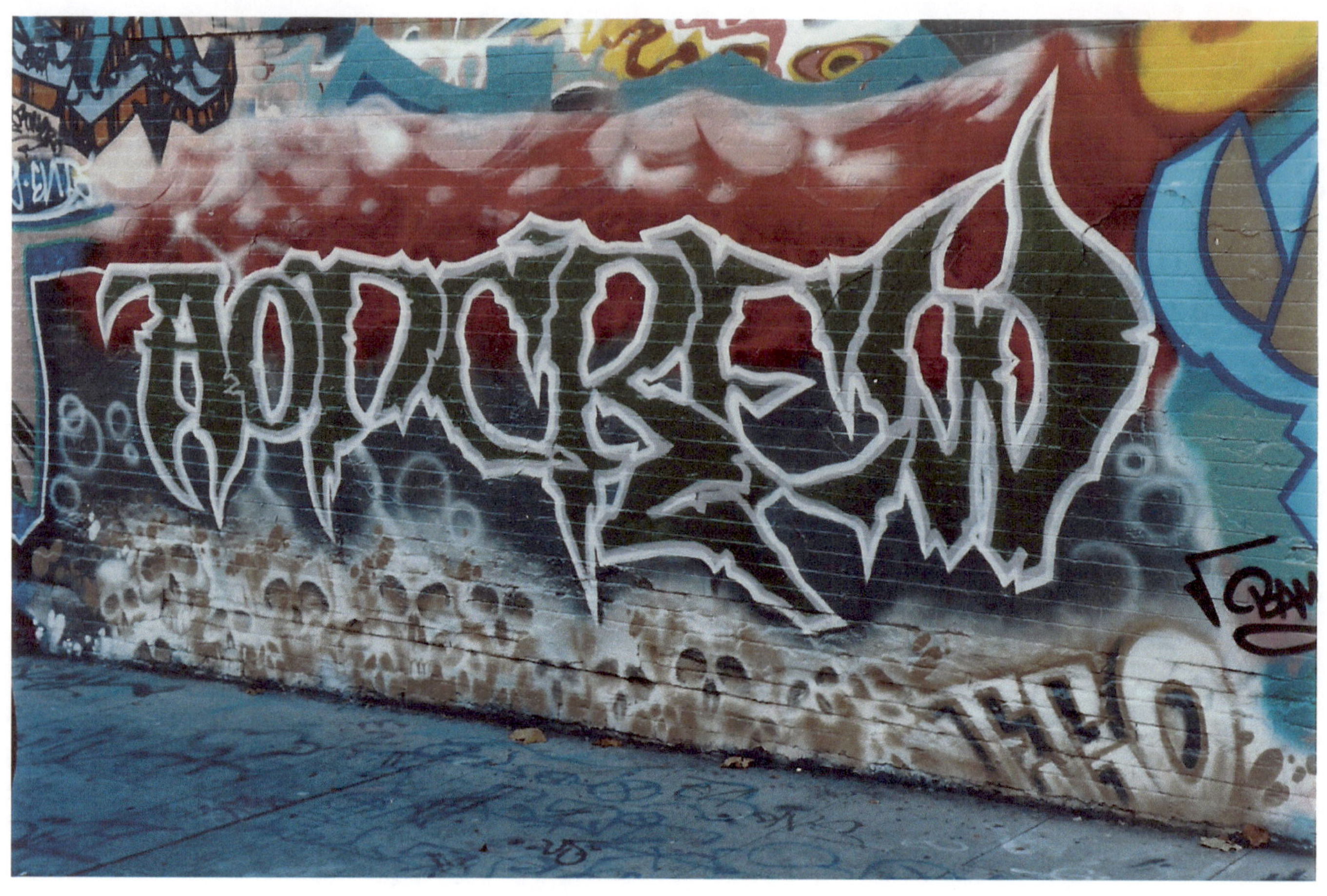

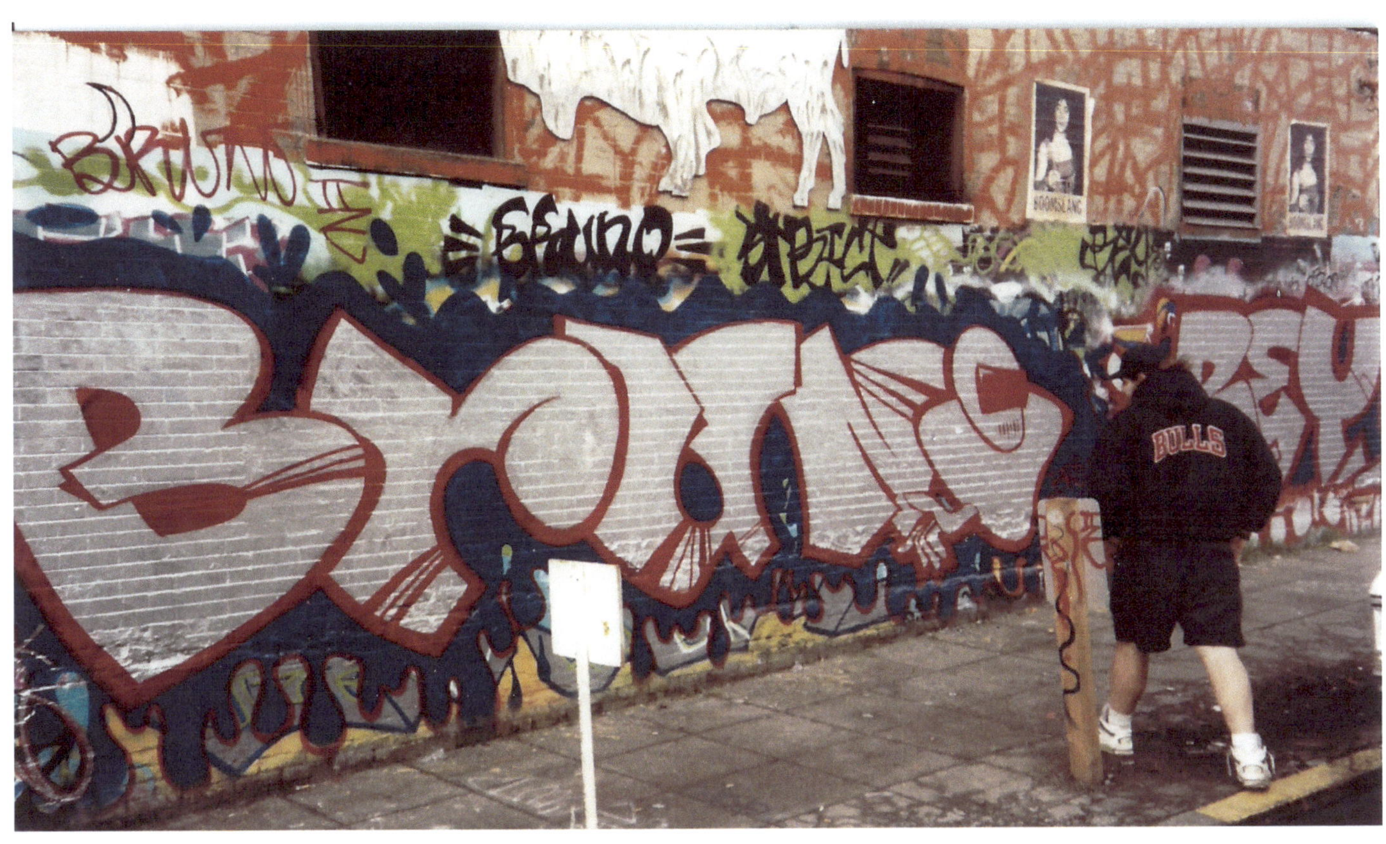
BULLS

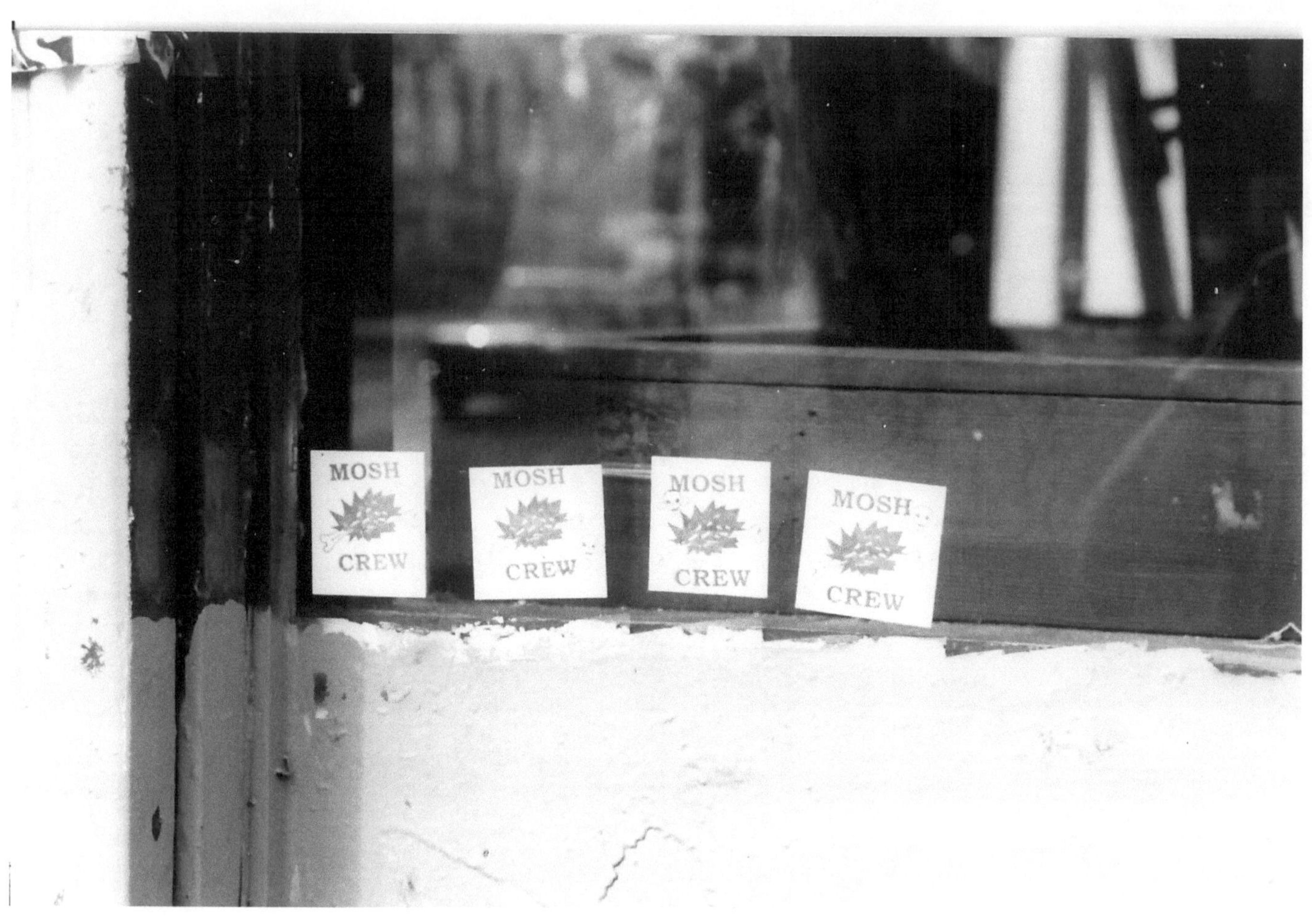
MOSH
CREW
MOSH
CREW
MOSH
CREW
MOSH
CREW

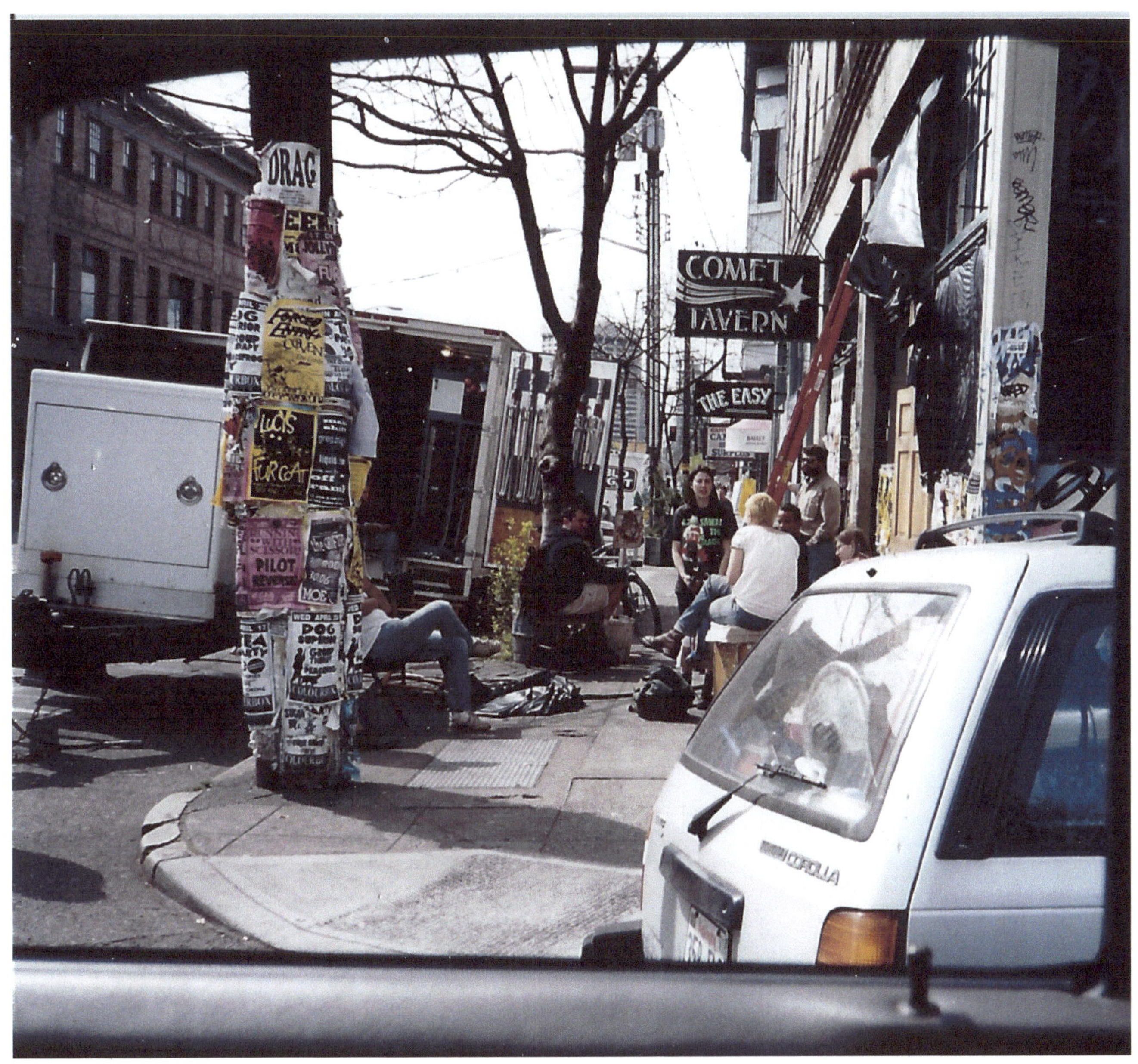
DRAG
COMET
TAVERN
THE EASY
PILOT
COROLLA

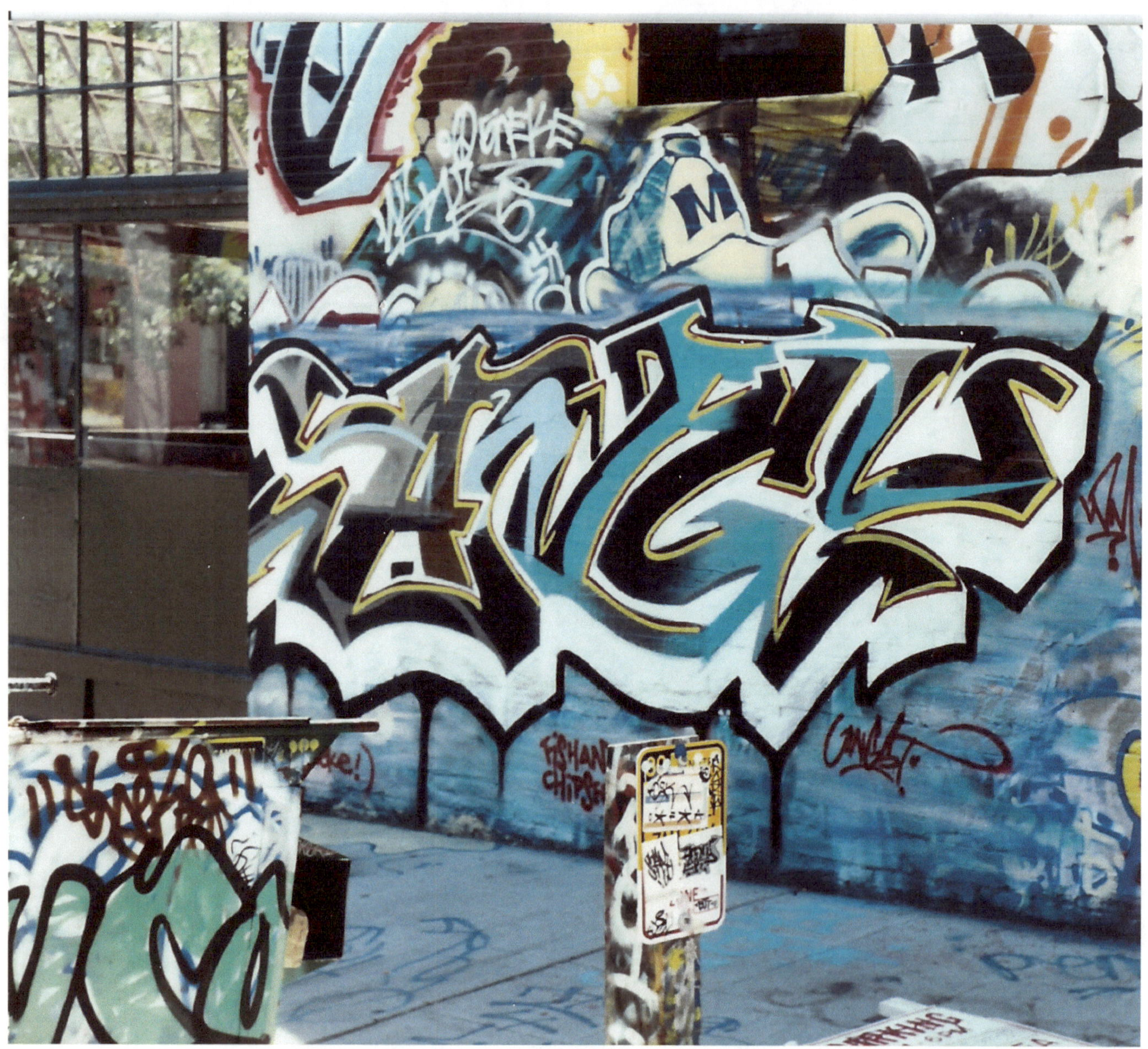

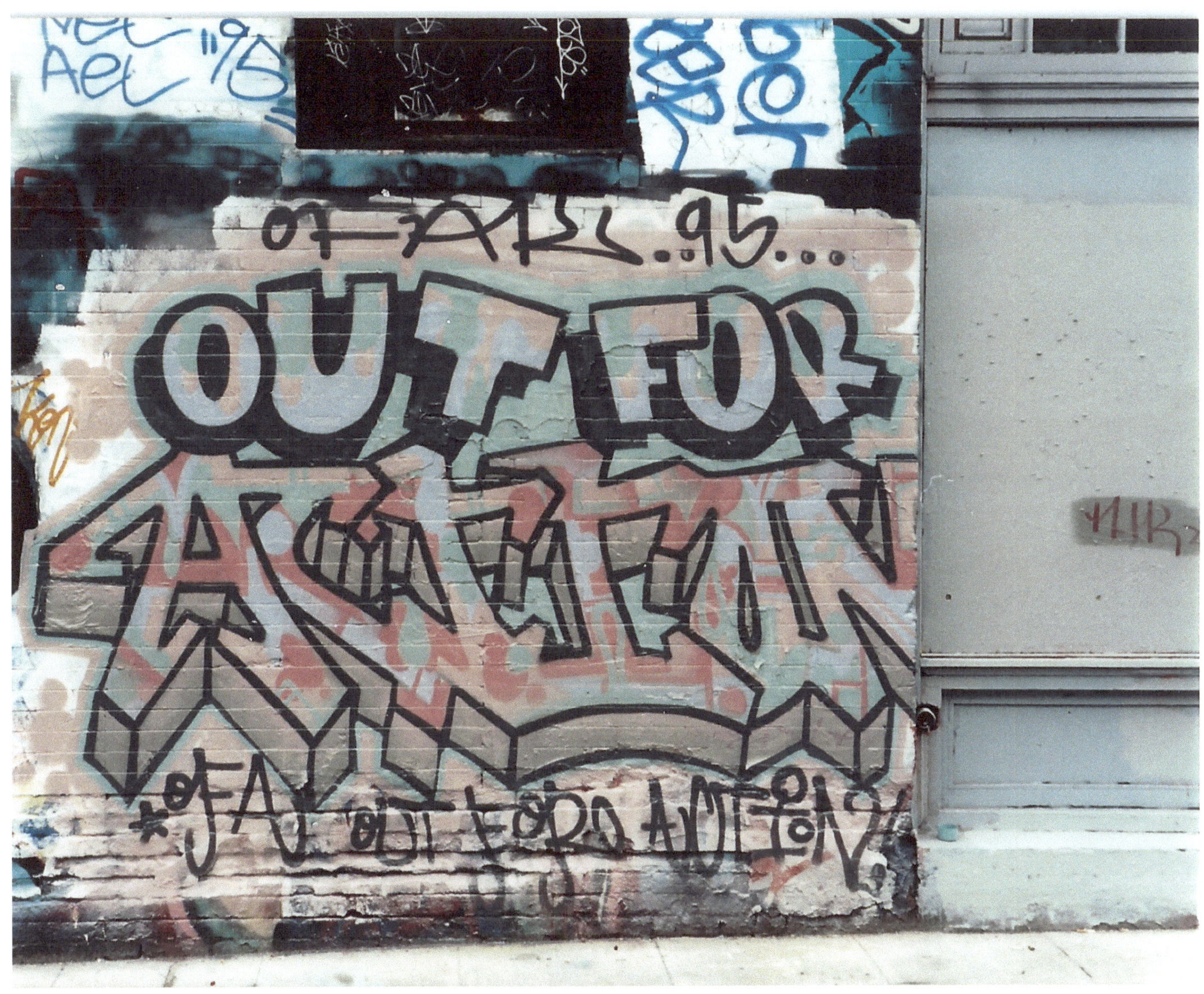
OUT FOR

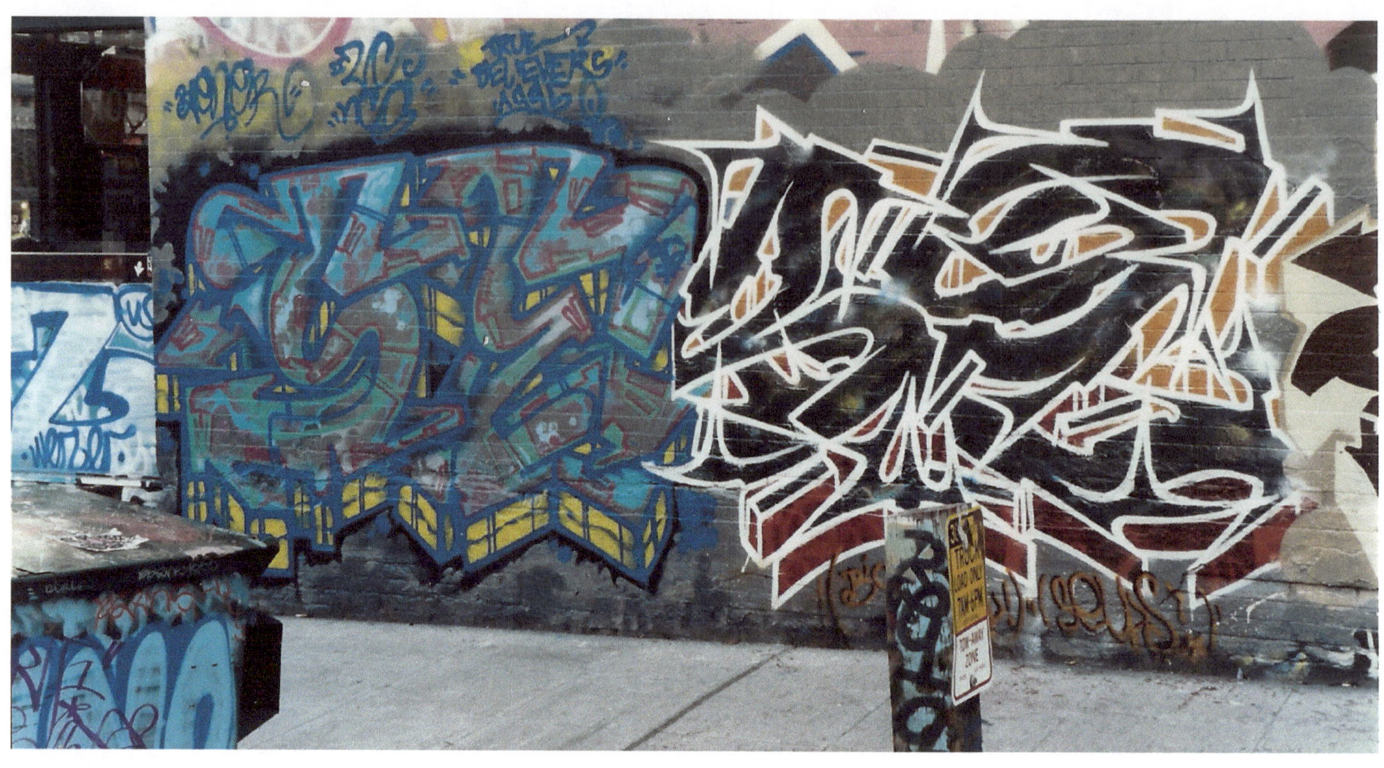

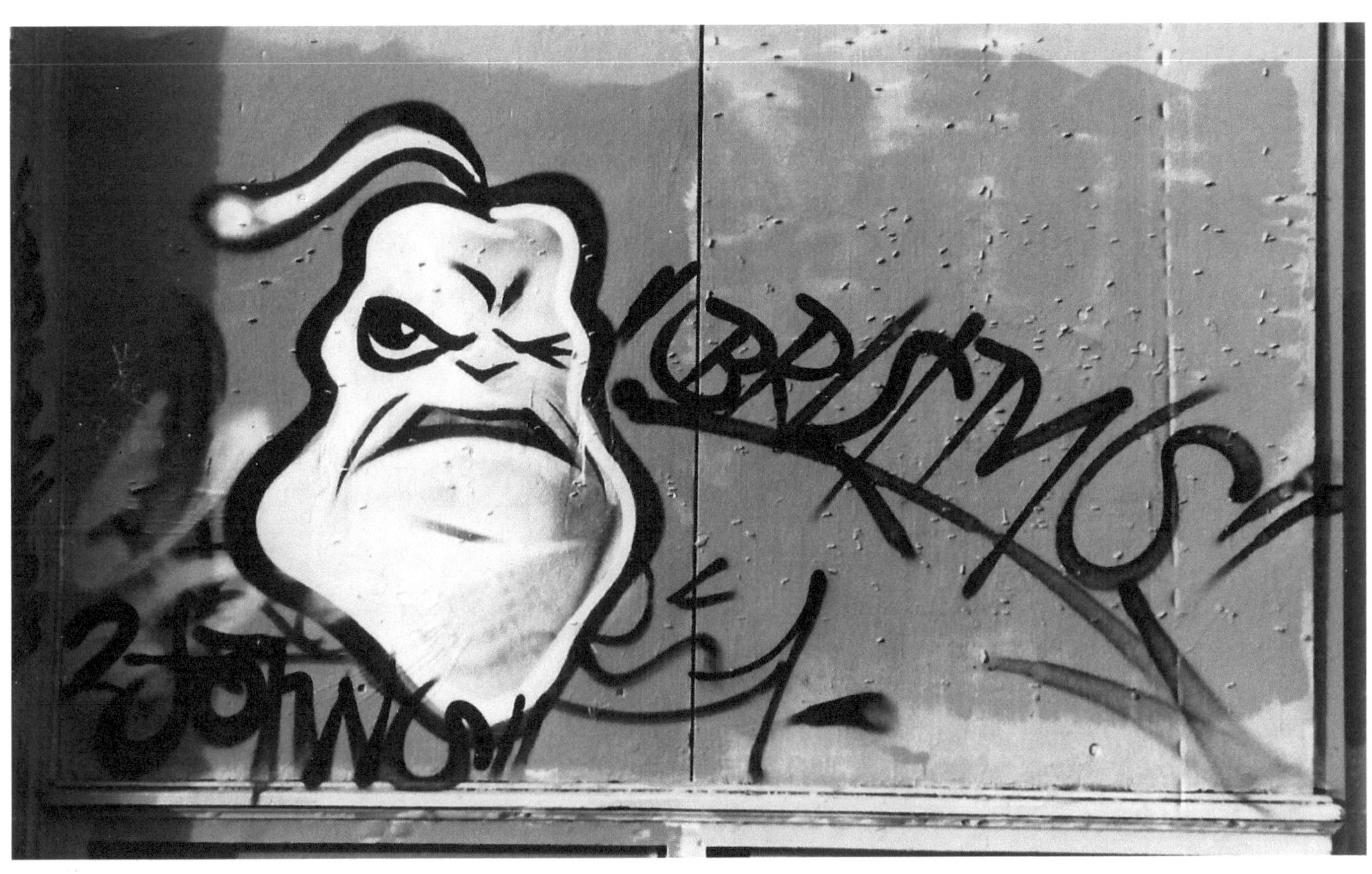

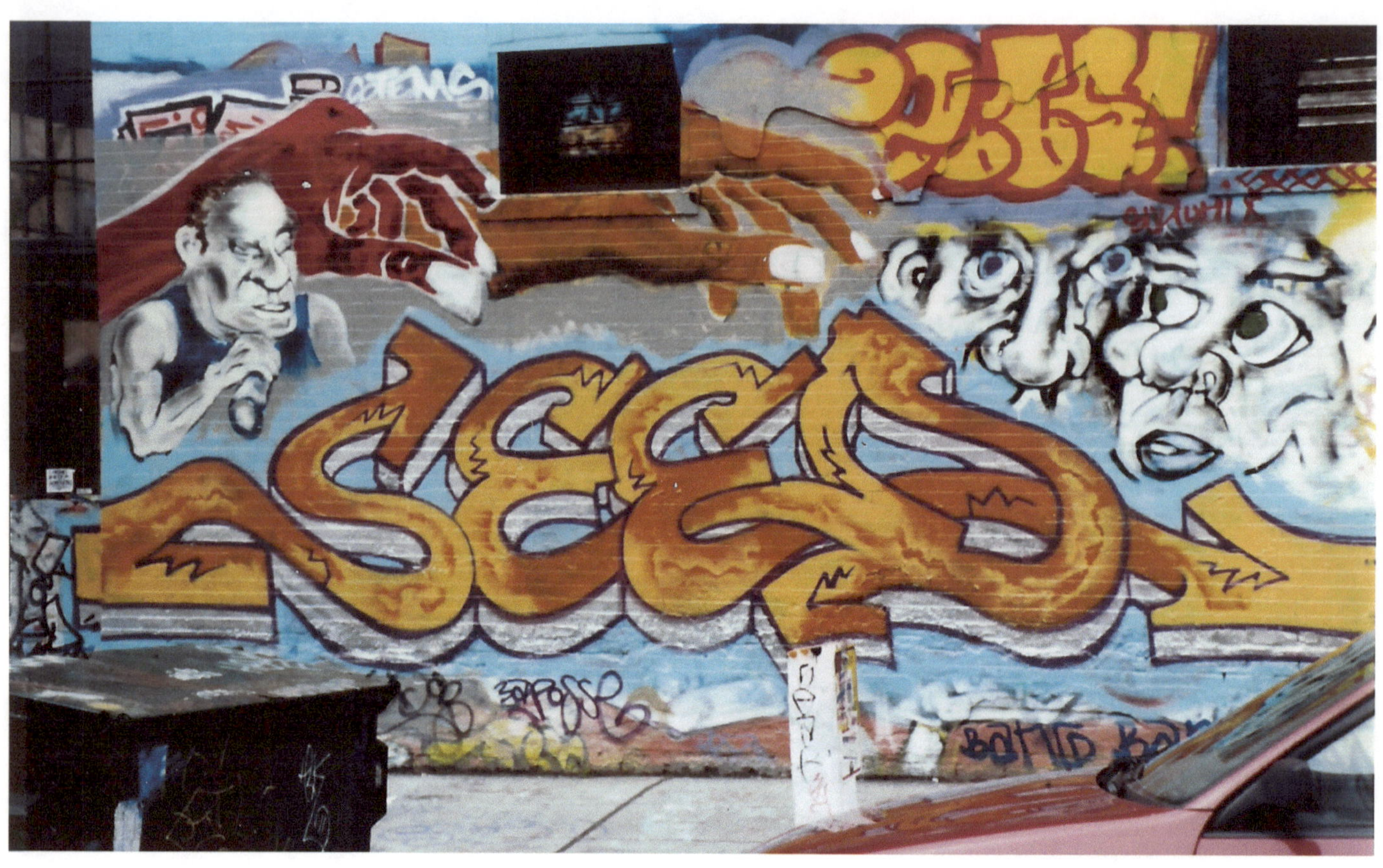

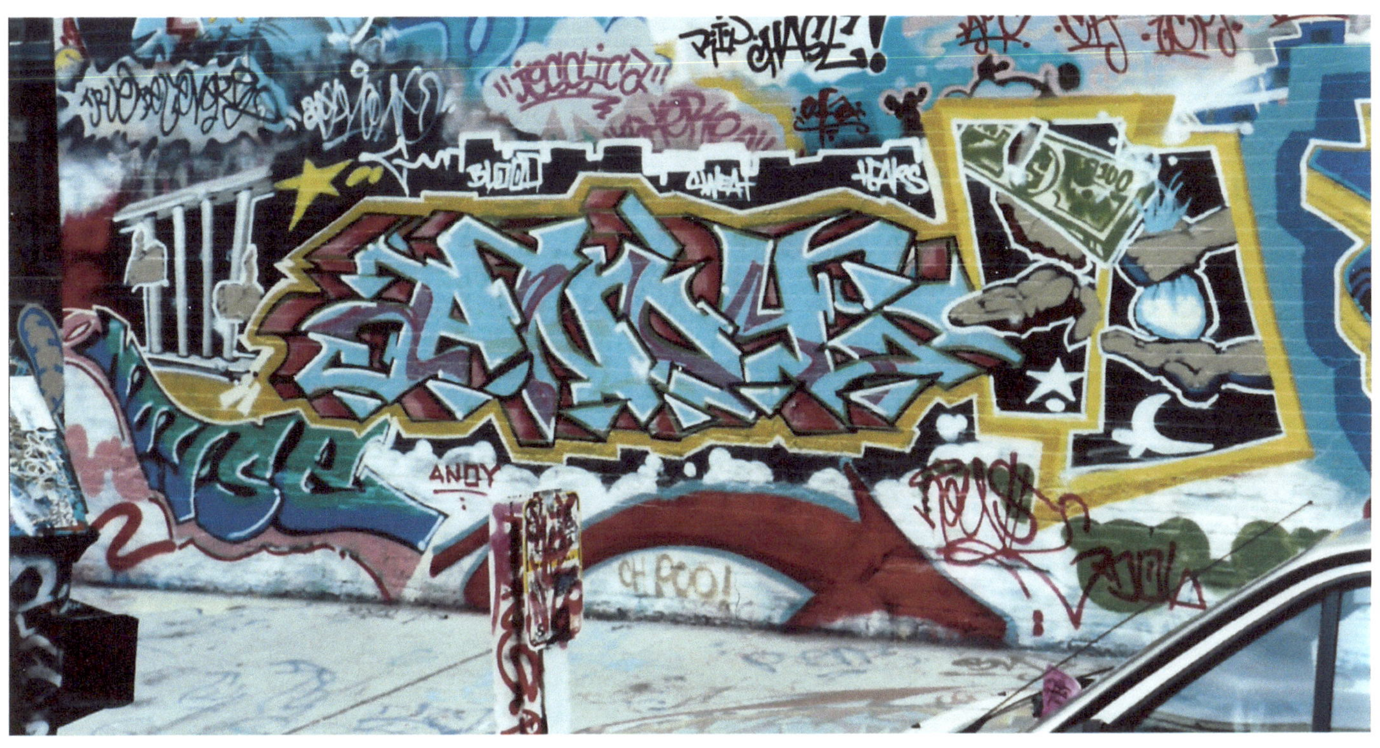
BLOOD
SWEAT
TEARS
ANDY

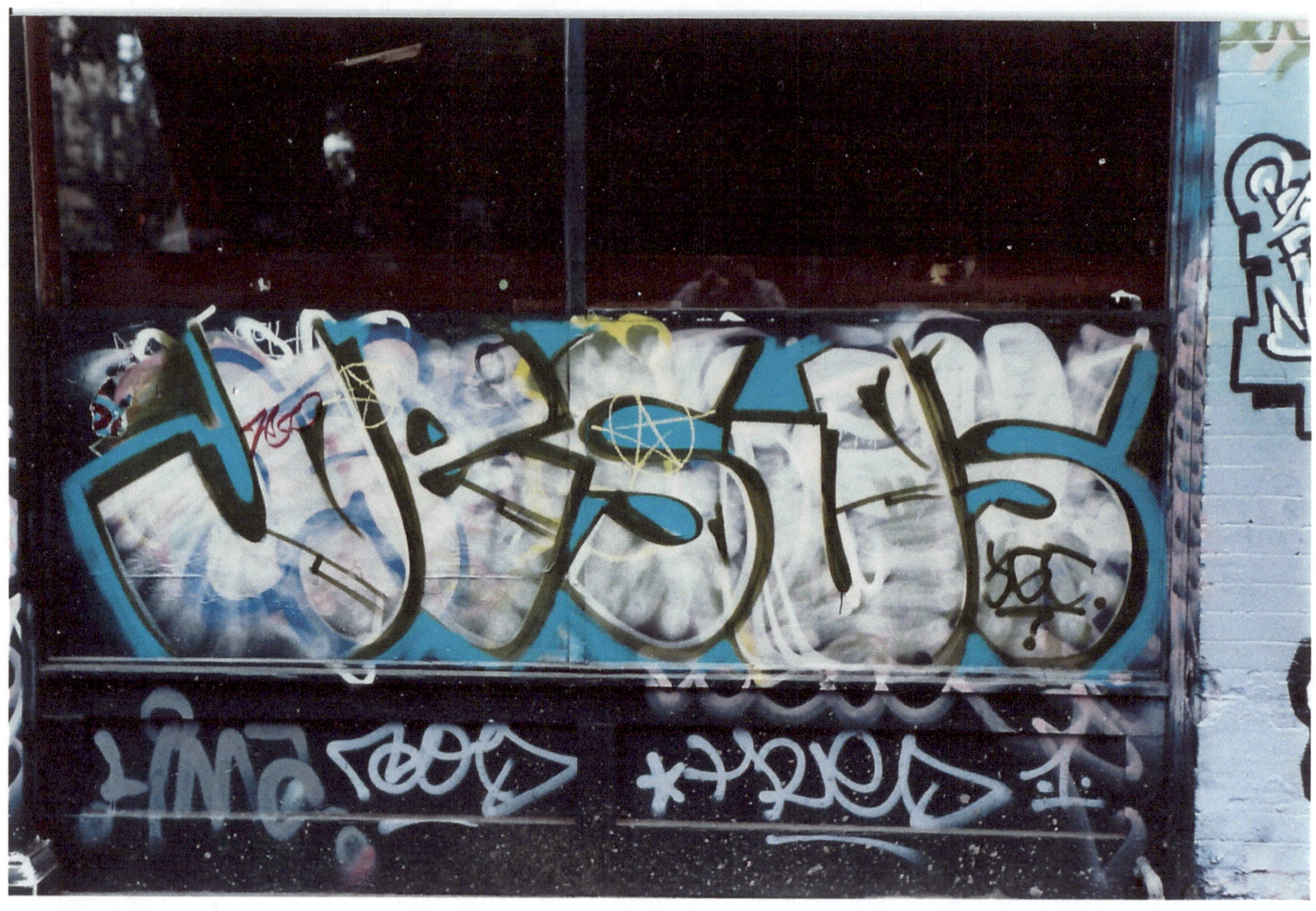

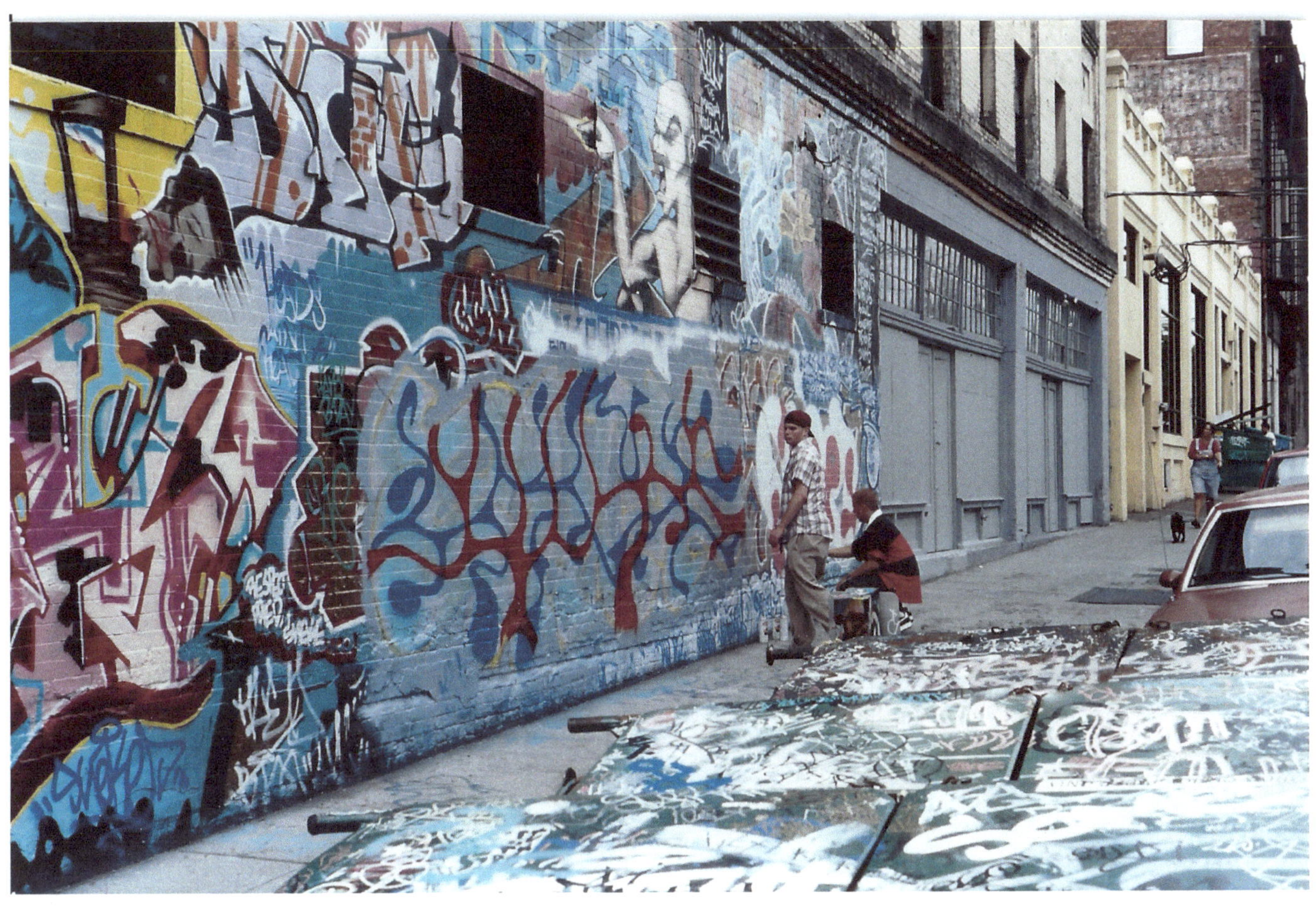

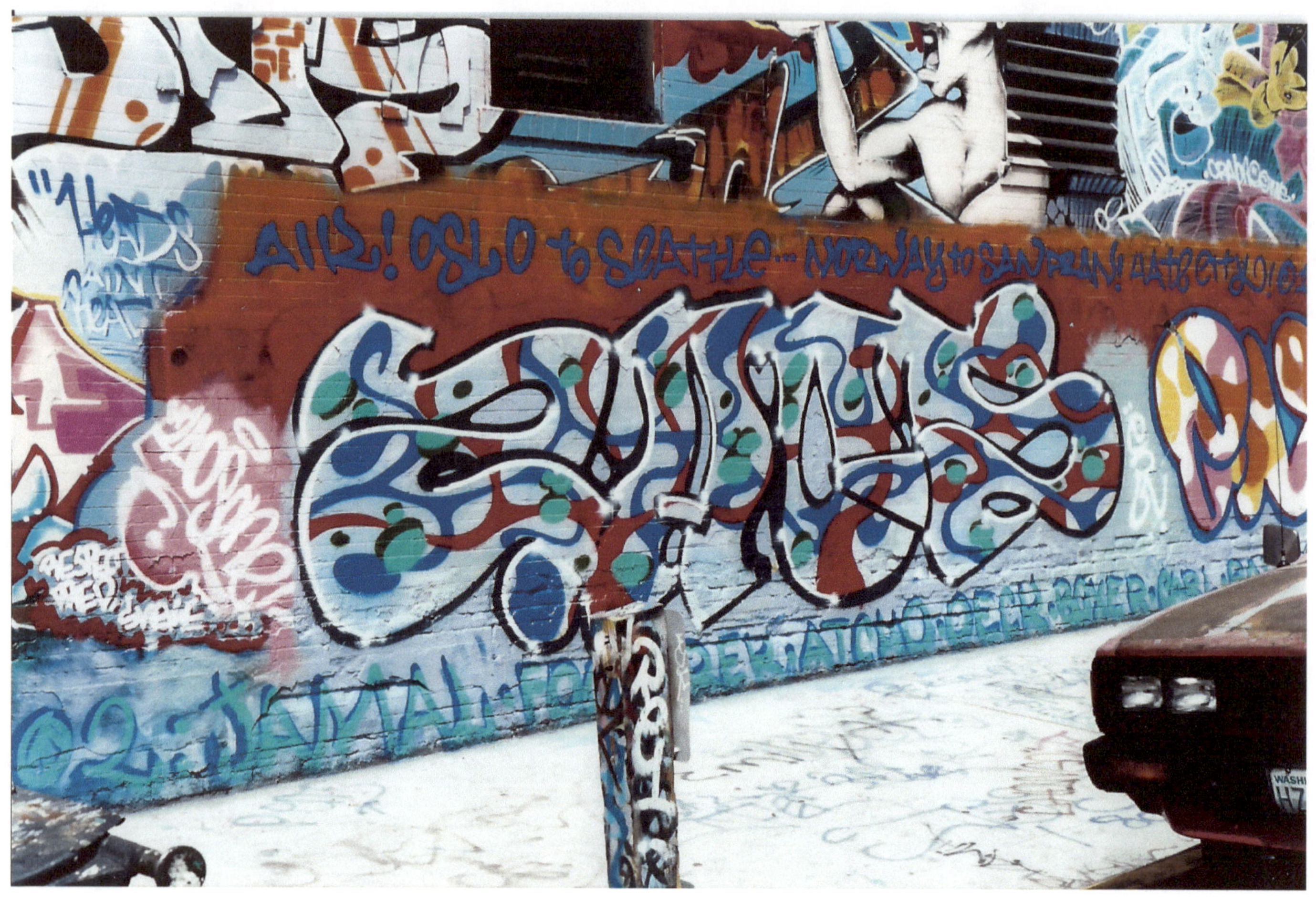
AIR! OSLO to SEATTLE... NORWAY to SAN FRAN!

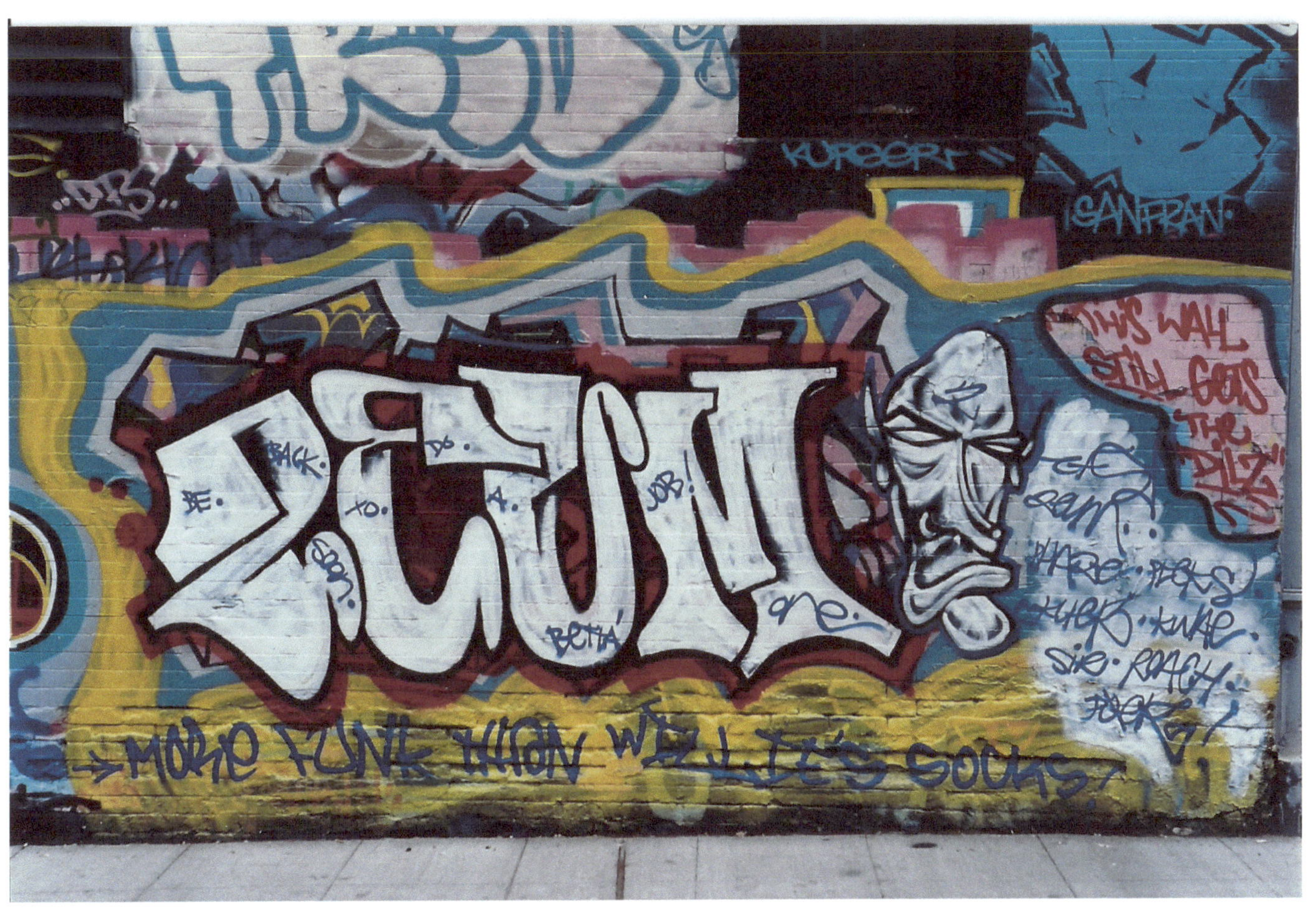
SANFRAN
THIS WALL STILL GETS THE BIZ
BE. BACK. TO. DO. A. JOB!
BETTA
ONE
MORE FUNK THAN

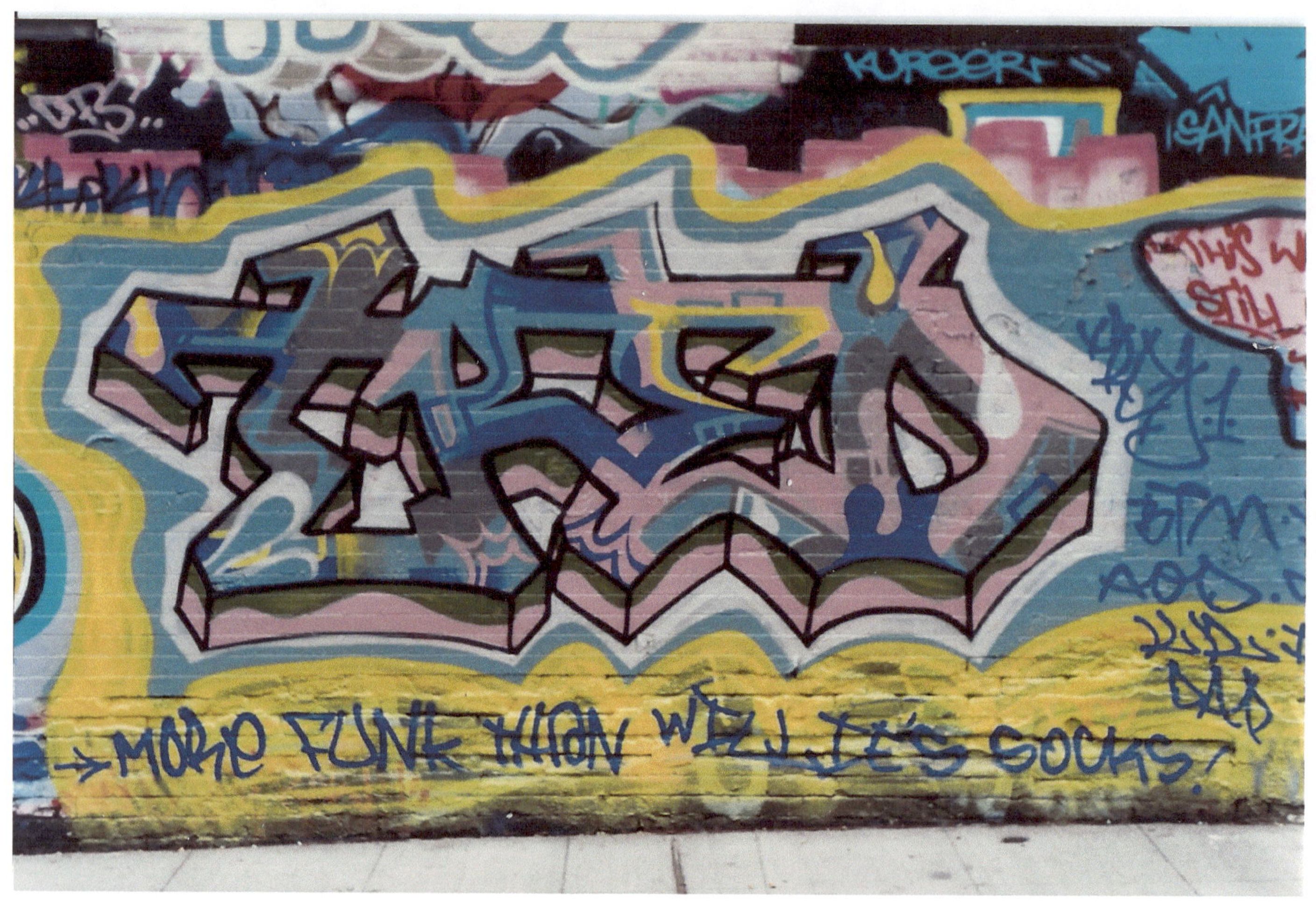
→ MORE FUNK THAN WILLIE'S SOCKS!

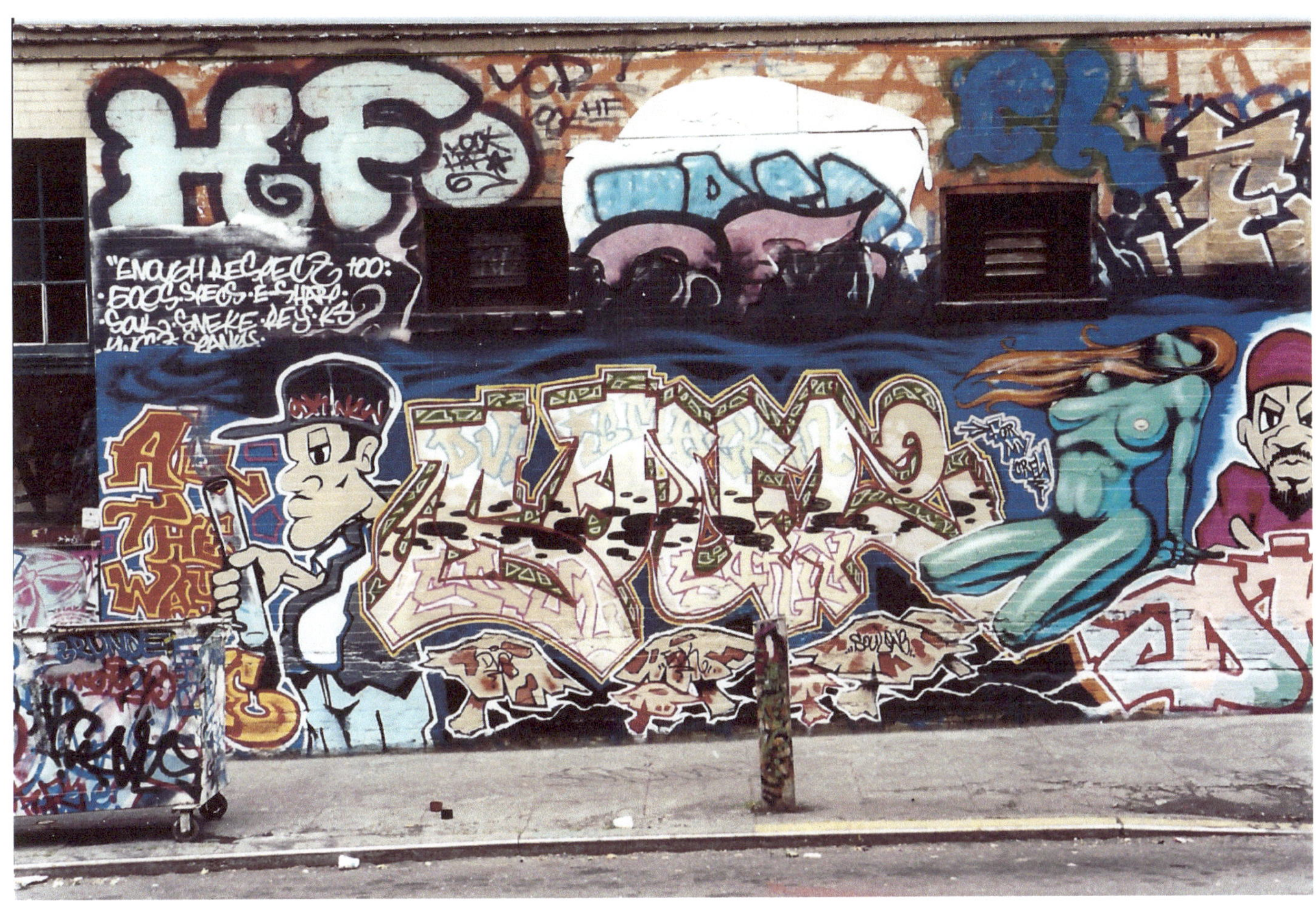
HF

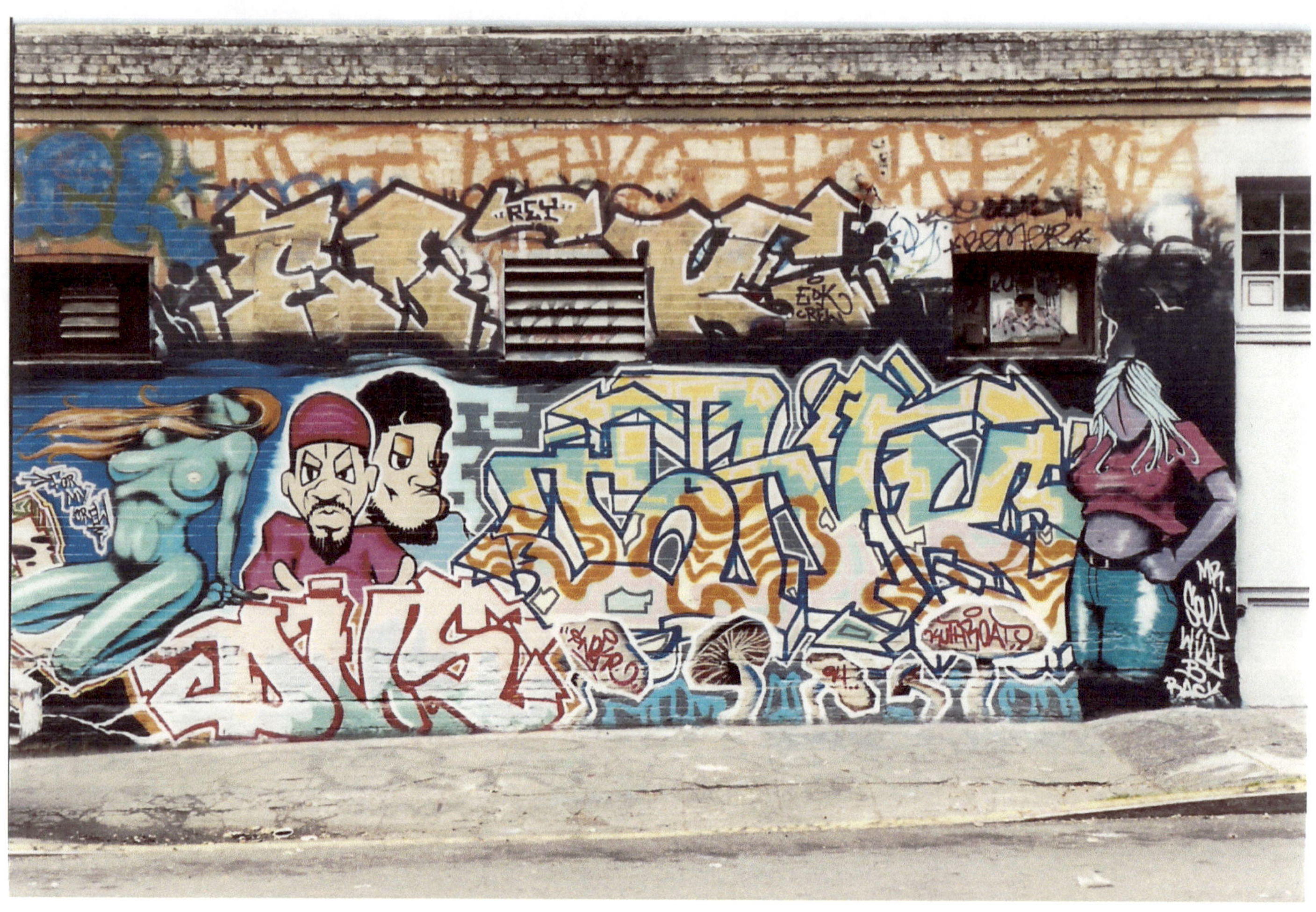

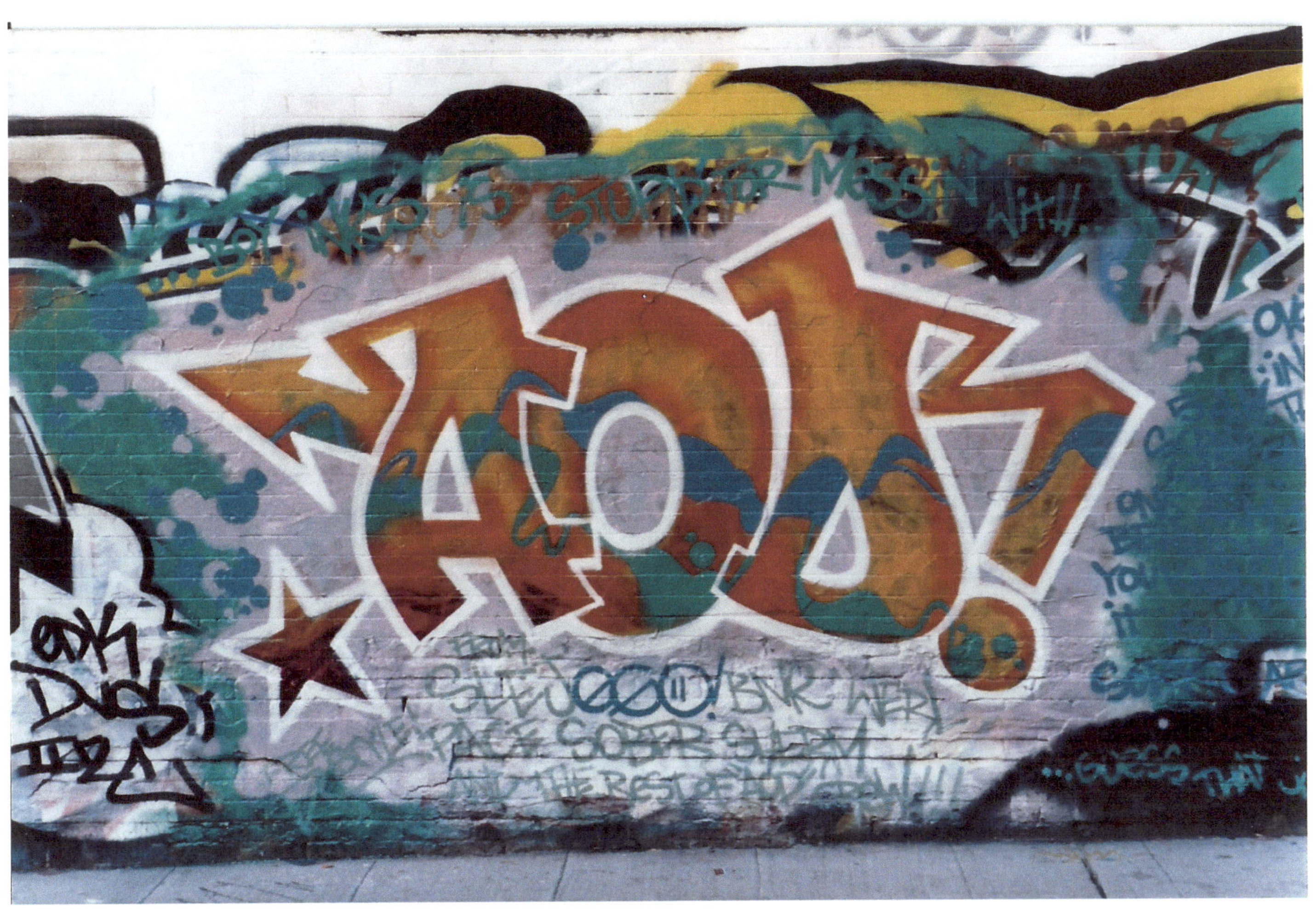

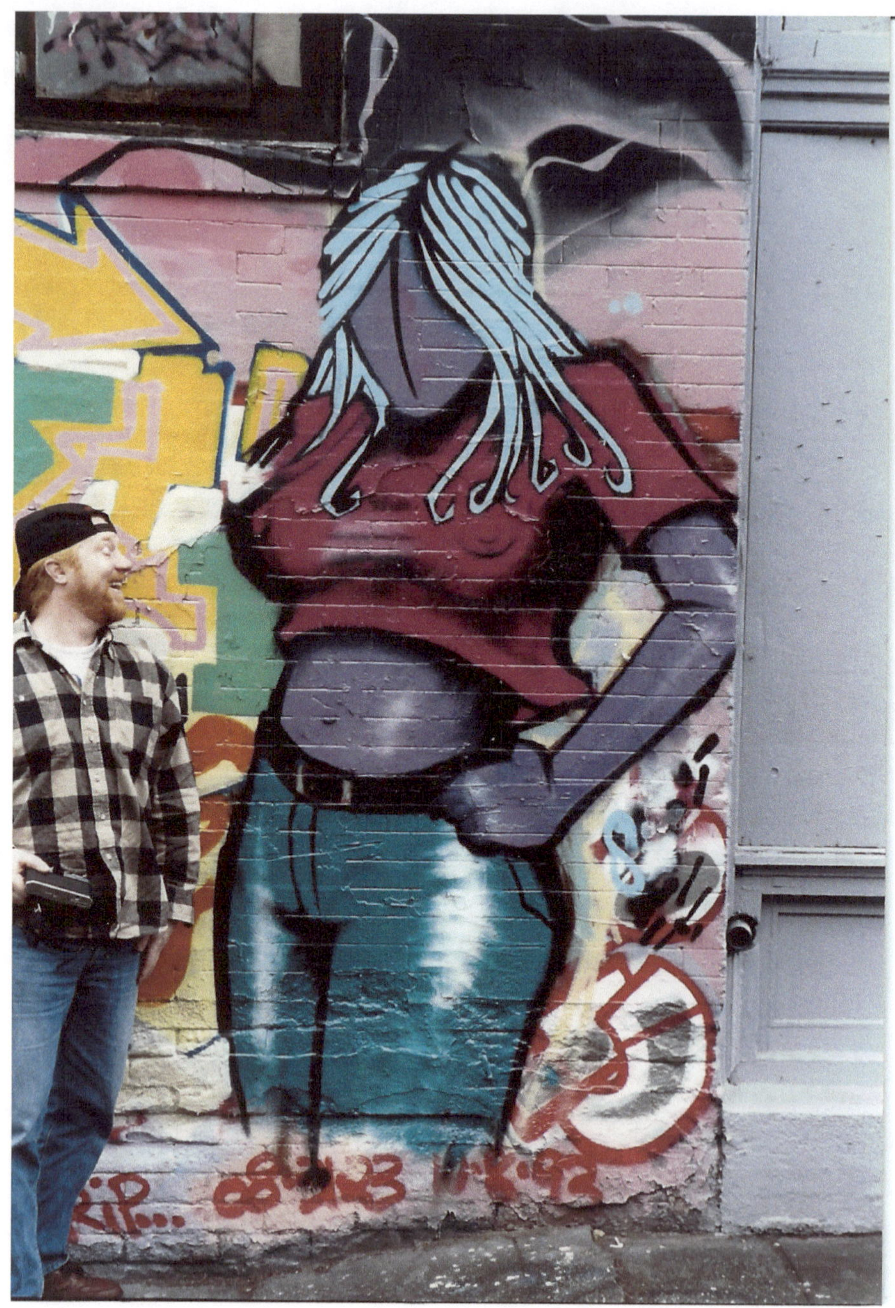

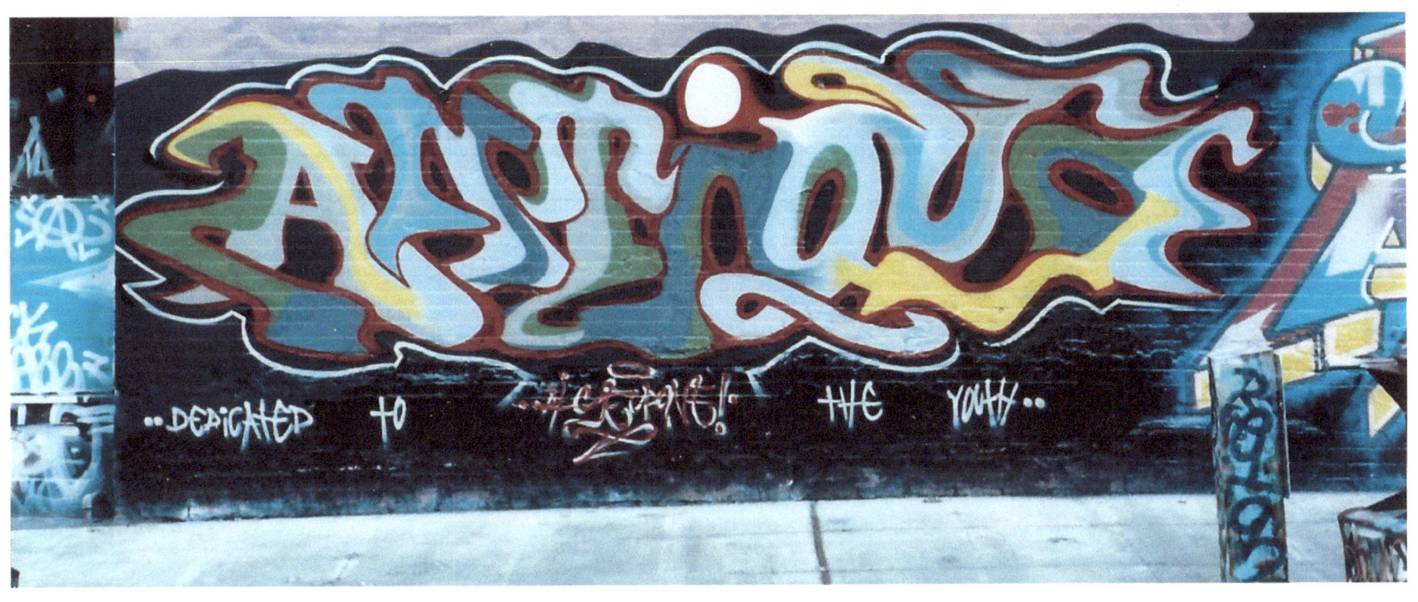
DEDICATED TO
THE YOUTH

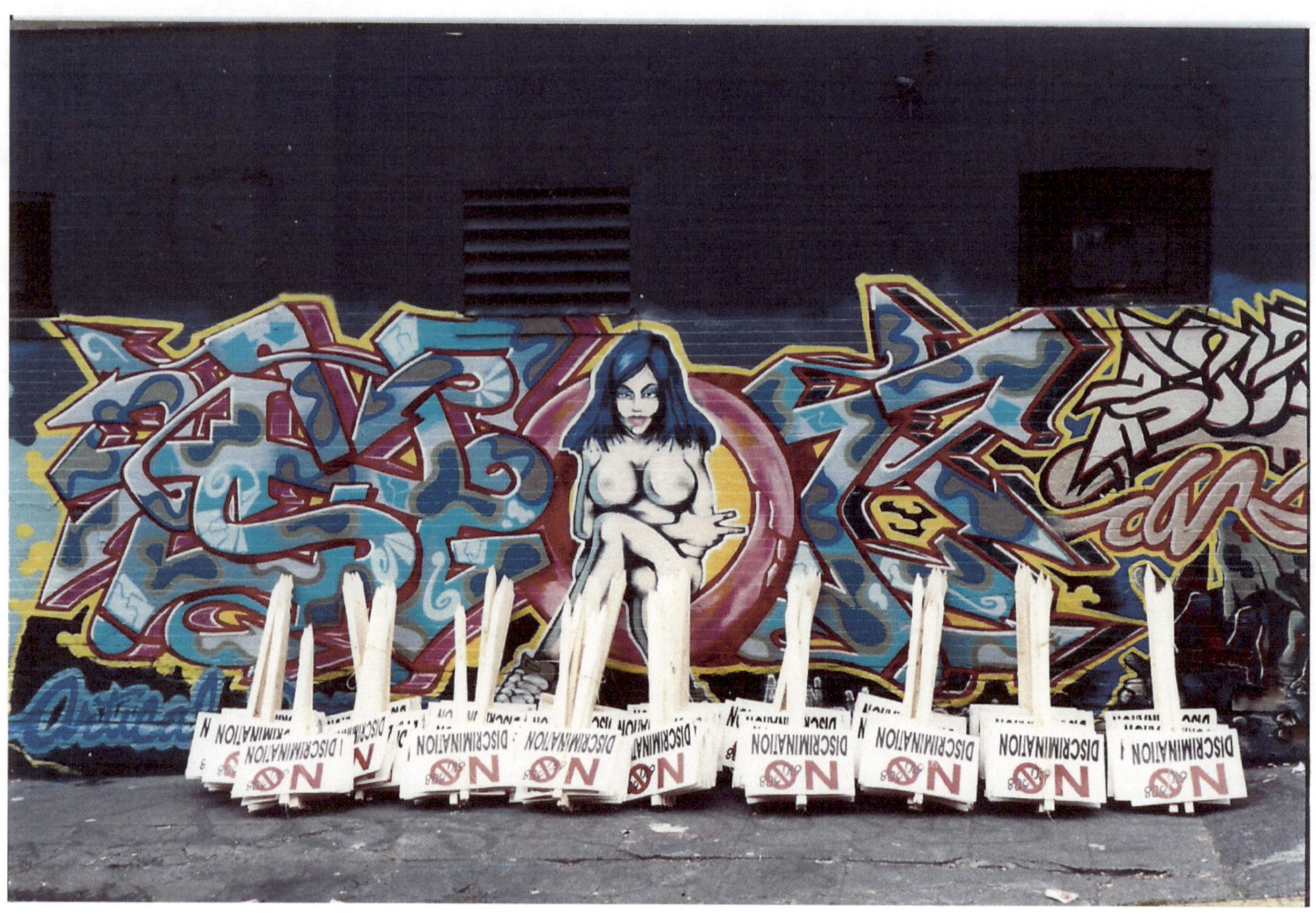
NO
DISCRIMINATION

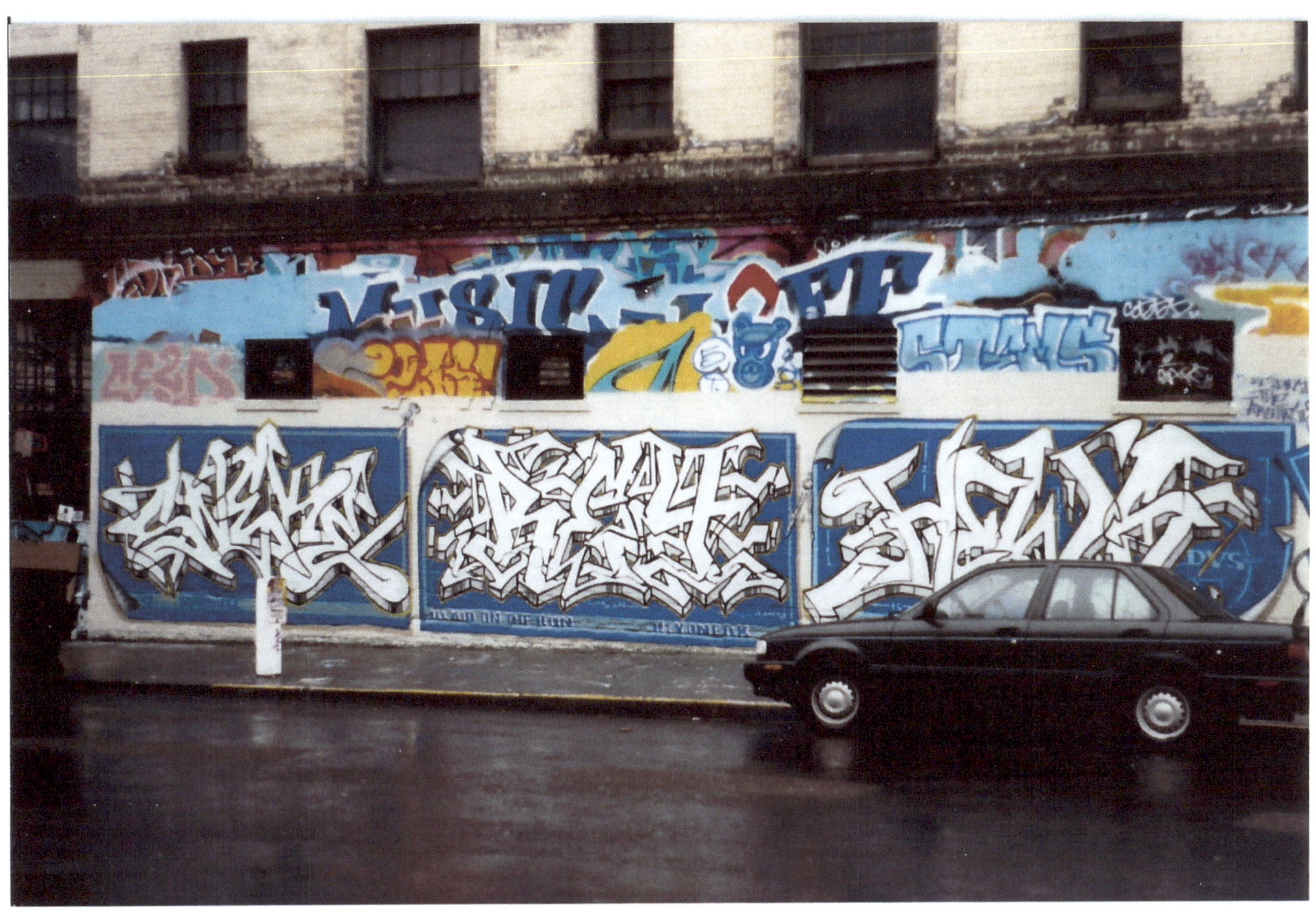

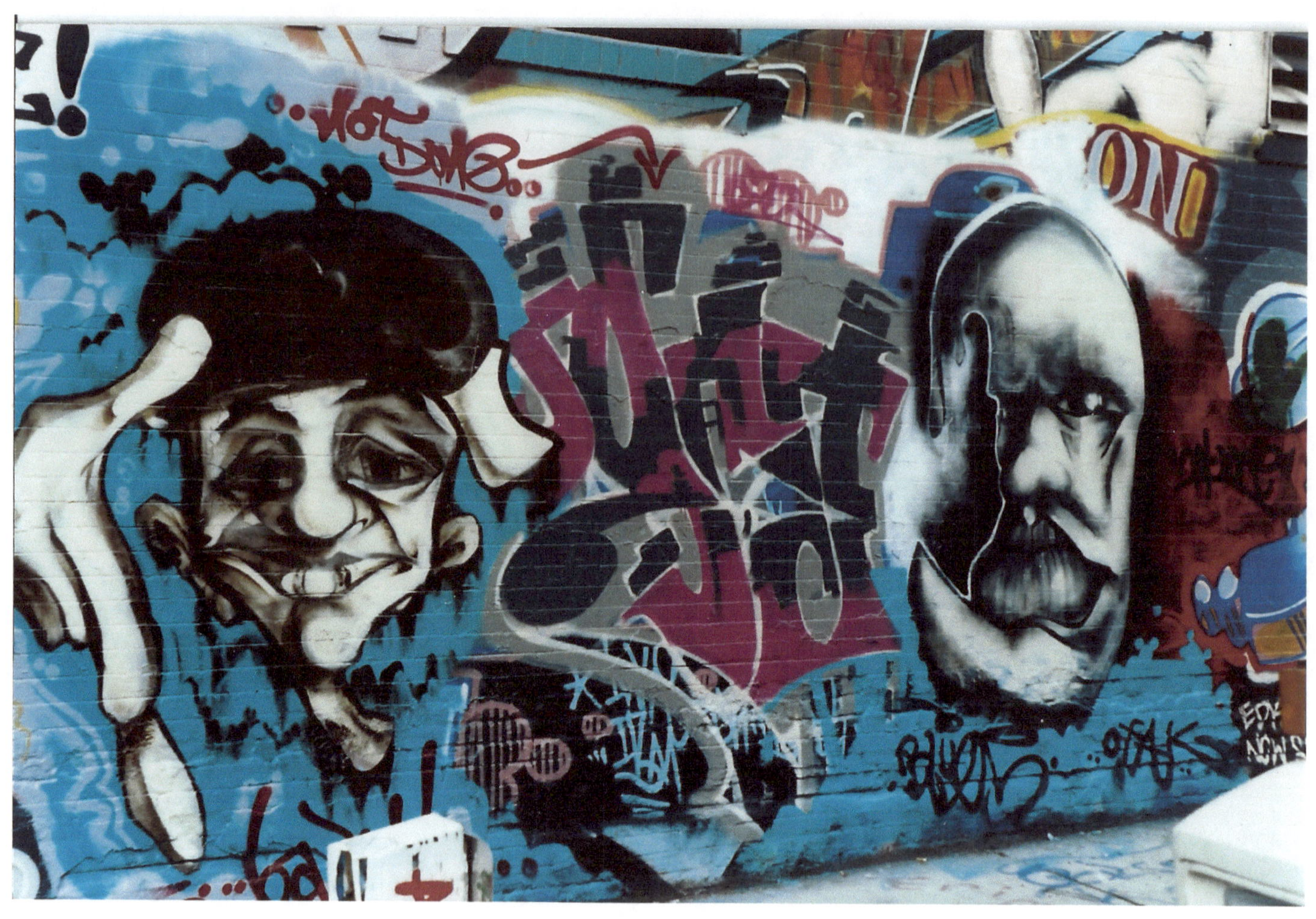
ON

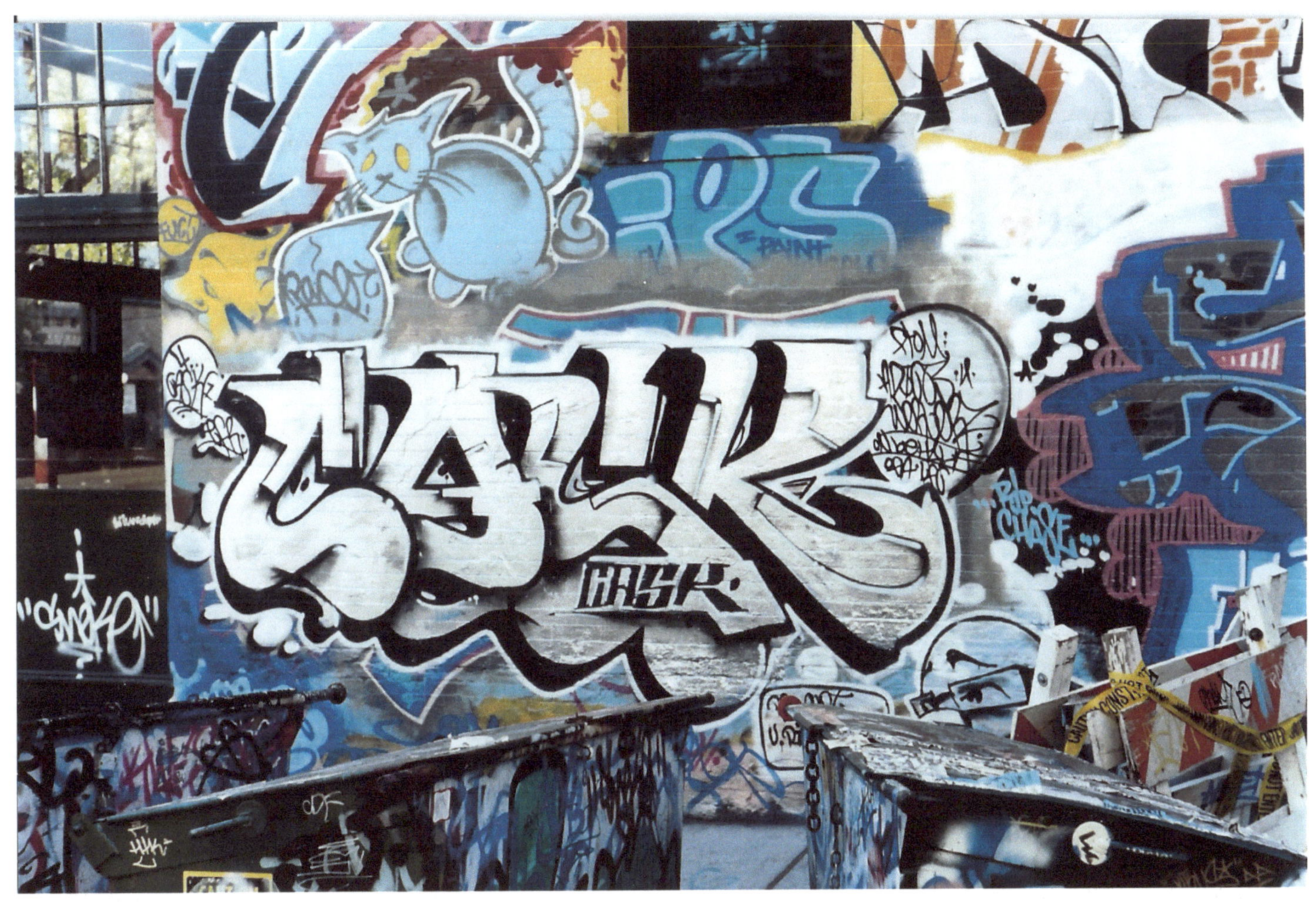

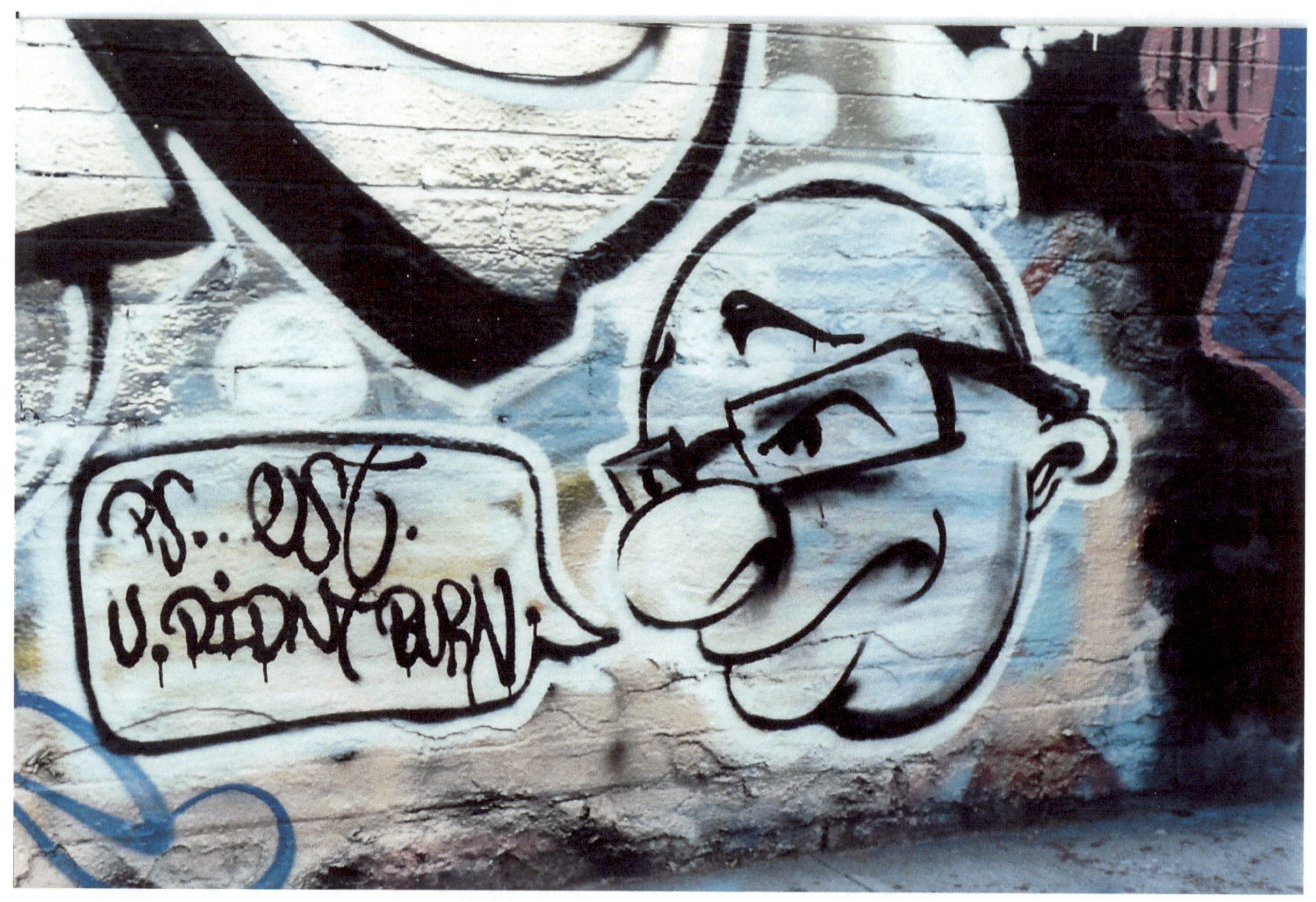
PS.. ESC.
U. DIDNT BURN.

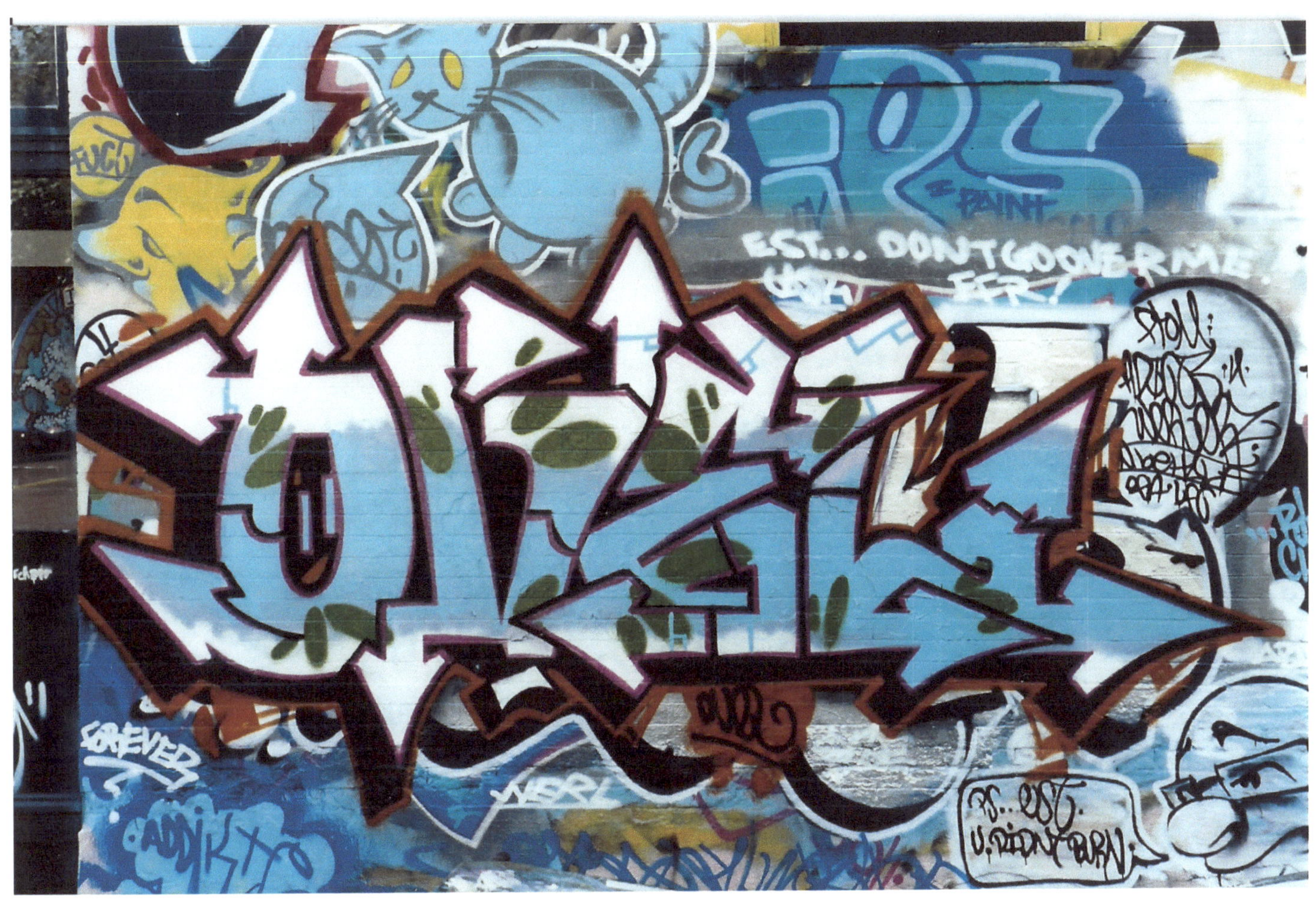
EST... DONTGOOVERME
FOREVER

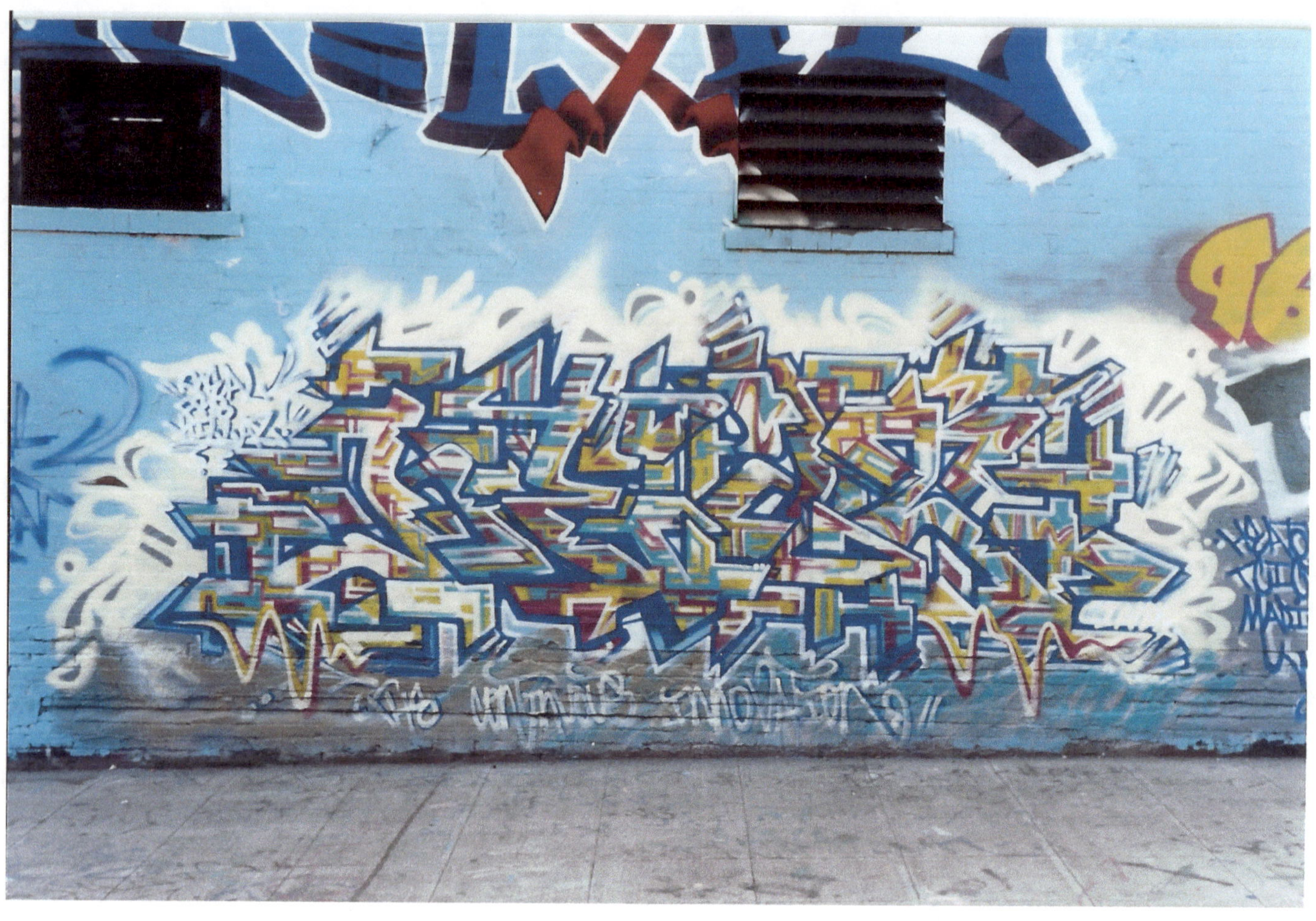

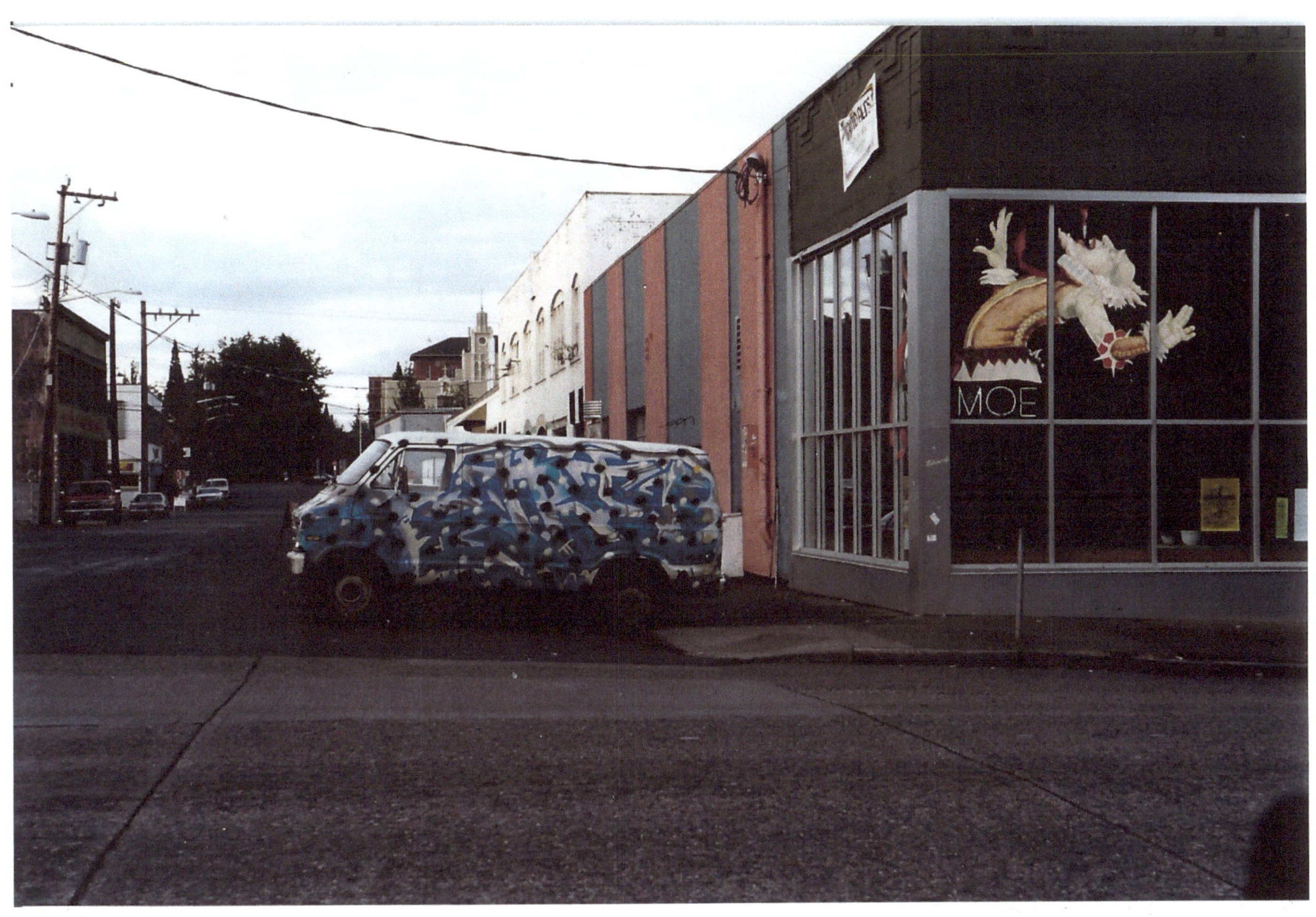
MOE

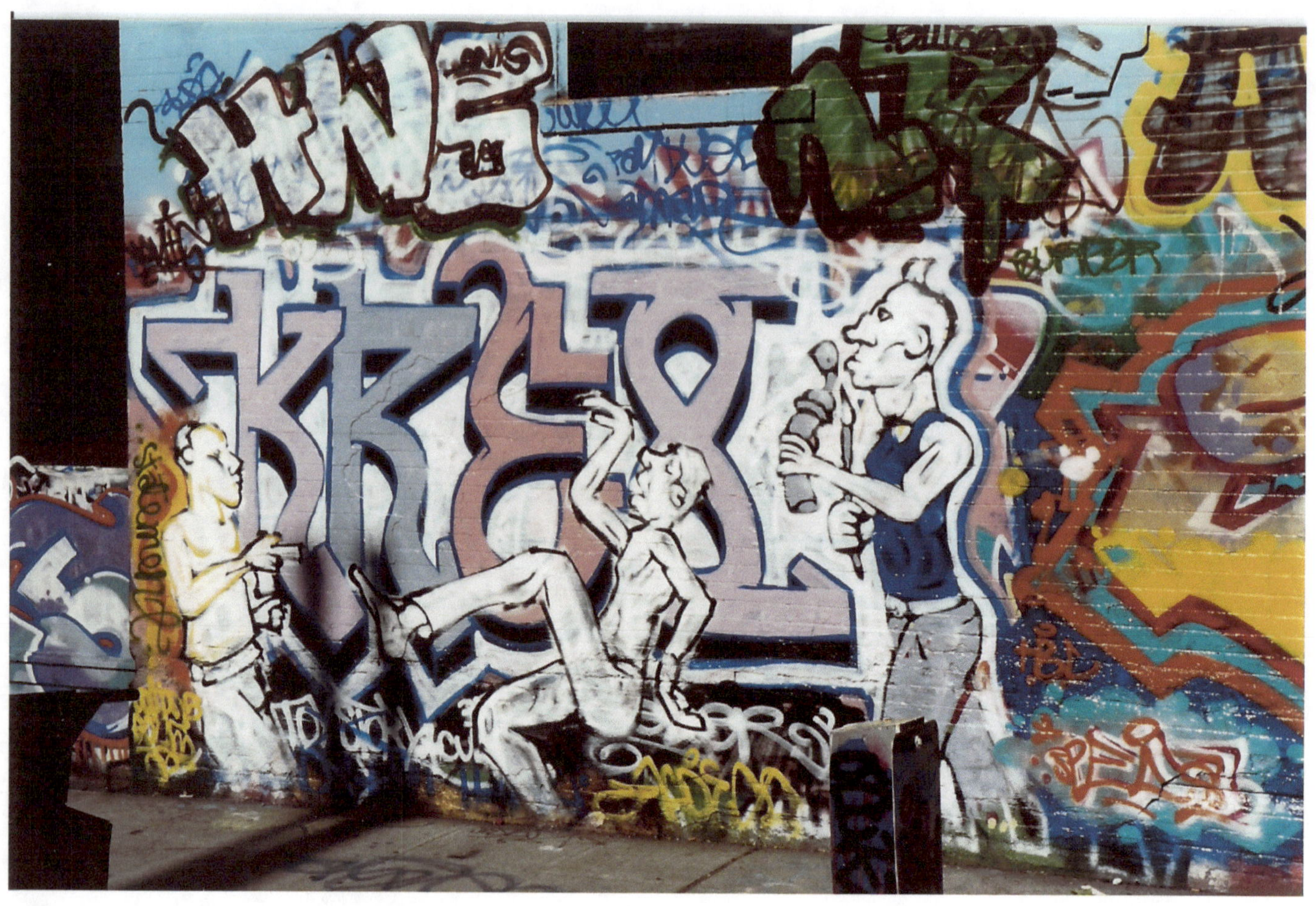

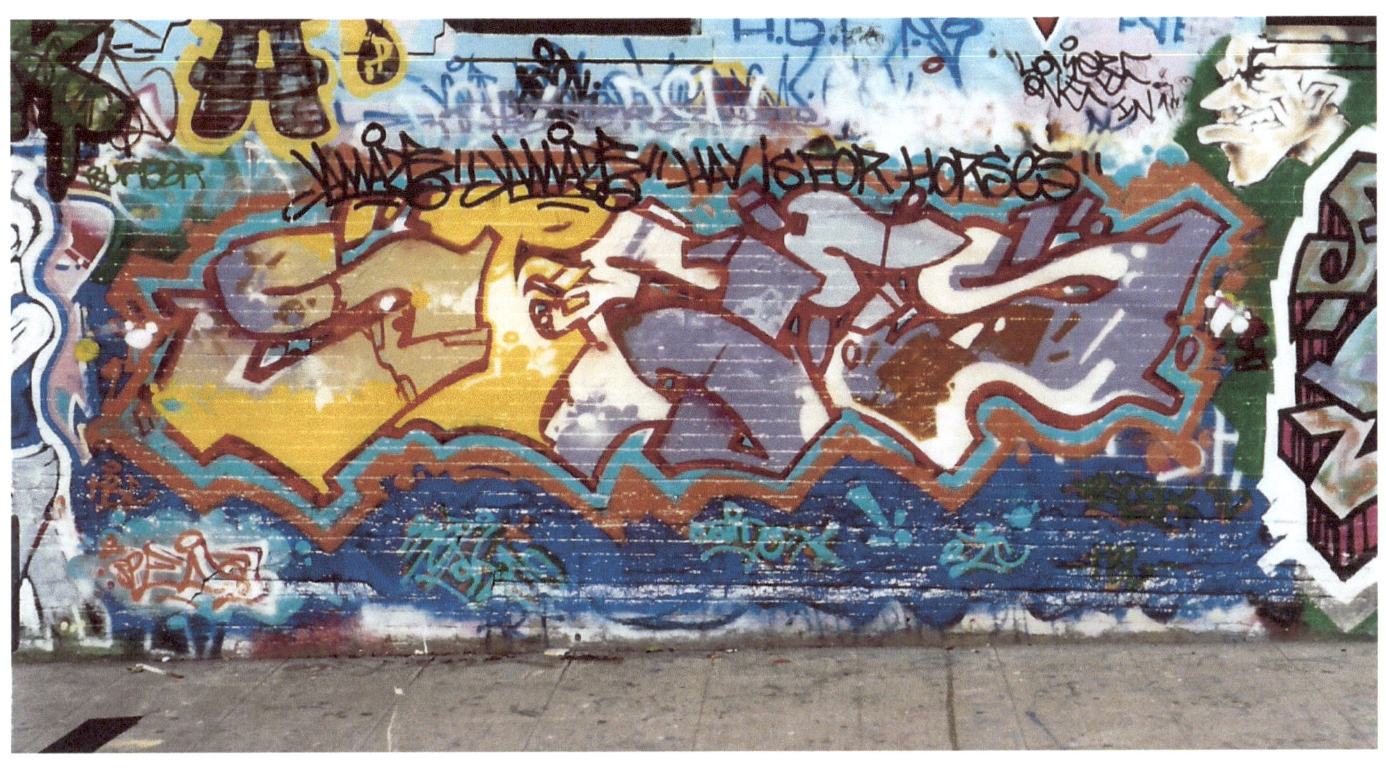
"HAY IS FOR HORSES"

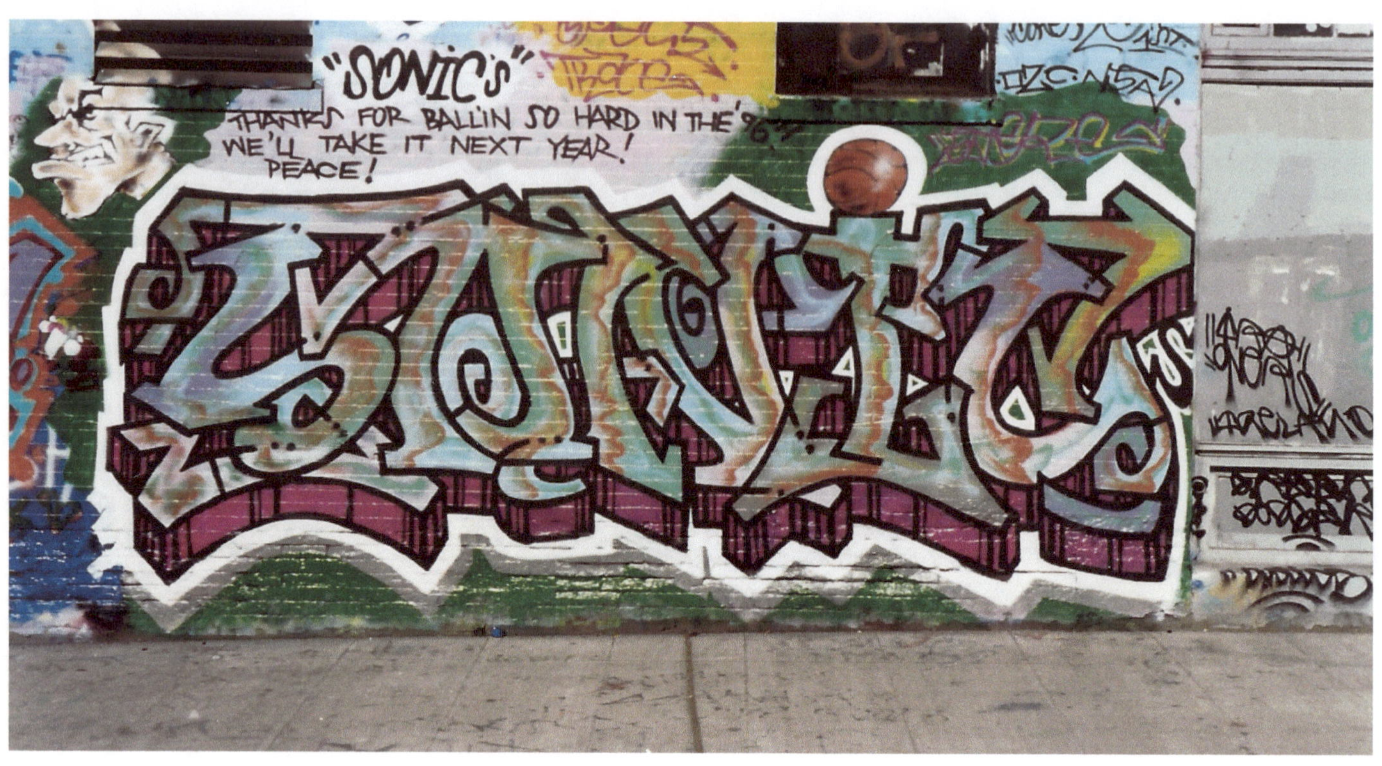
"SONIC's"
THANKS FOR BALLIN SO HARD IN THE '96
WE'LL TAKE IT NEXT YEAR!
PEACE!

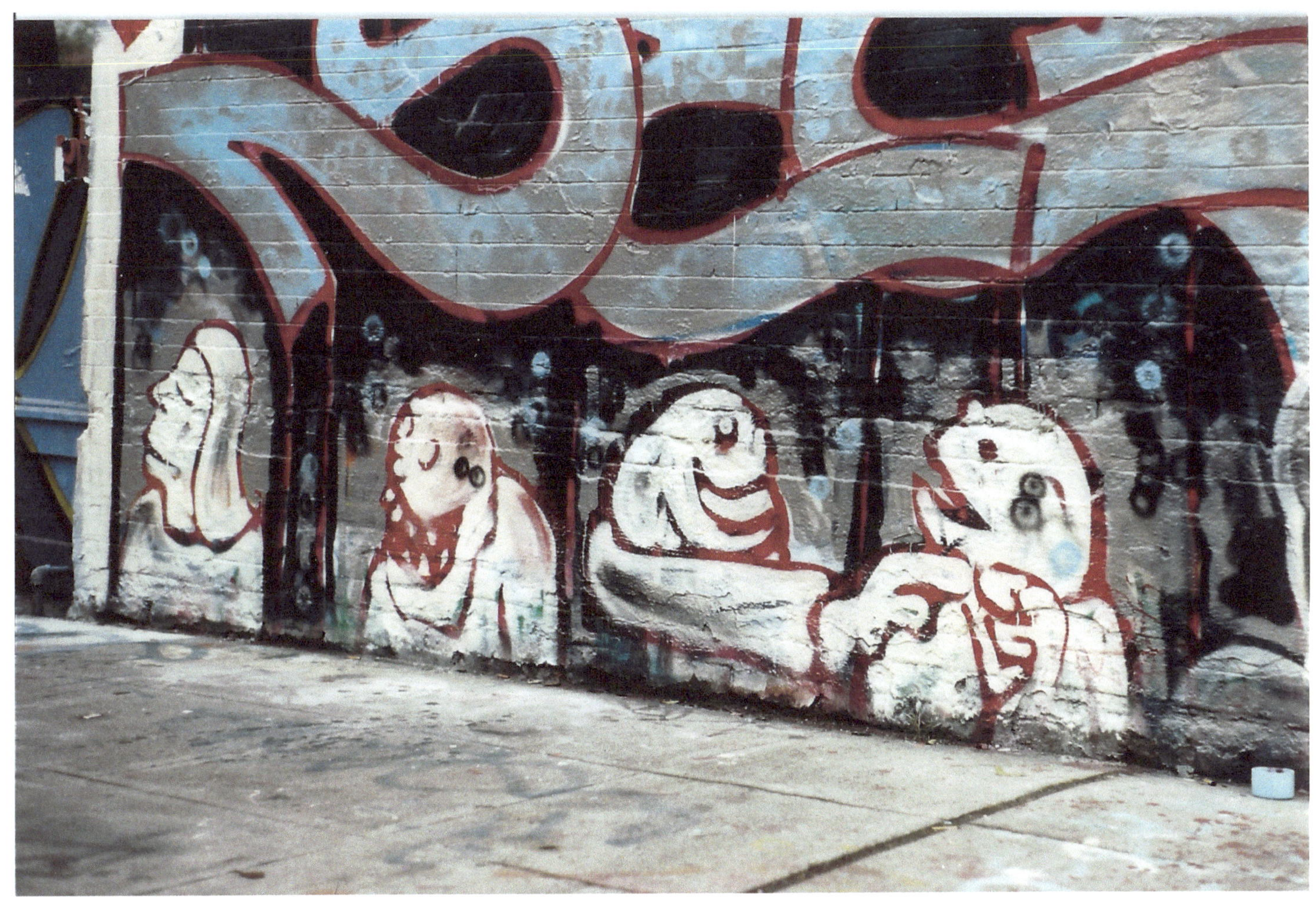

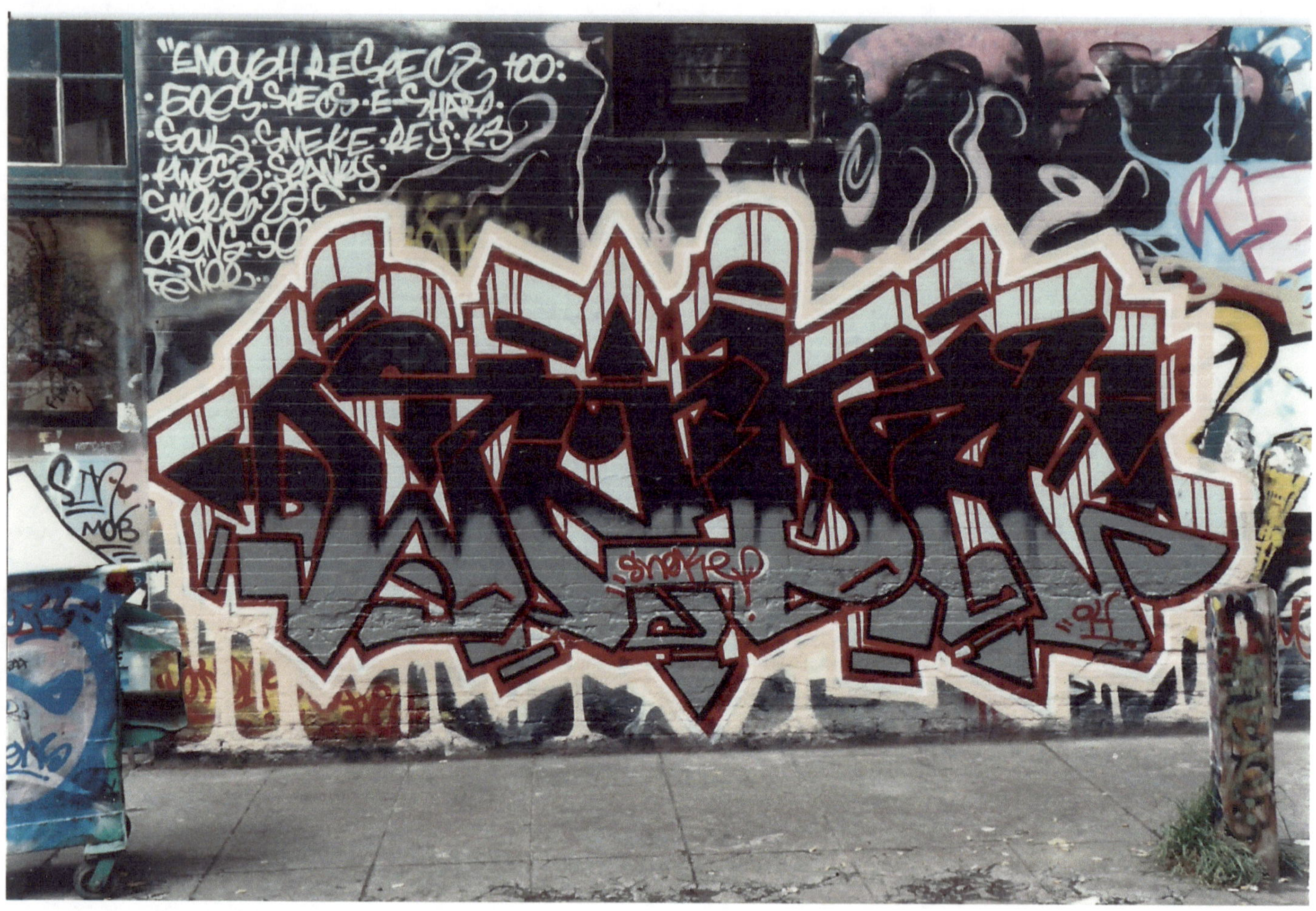

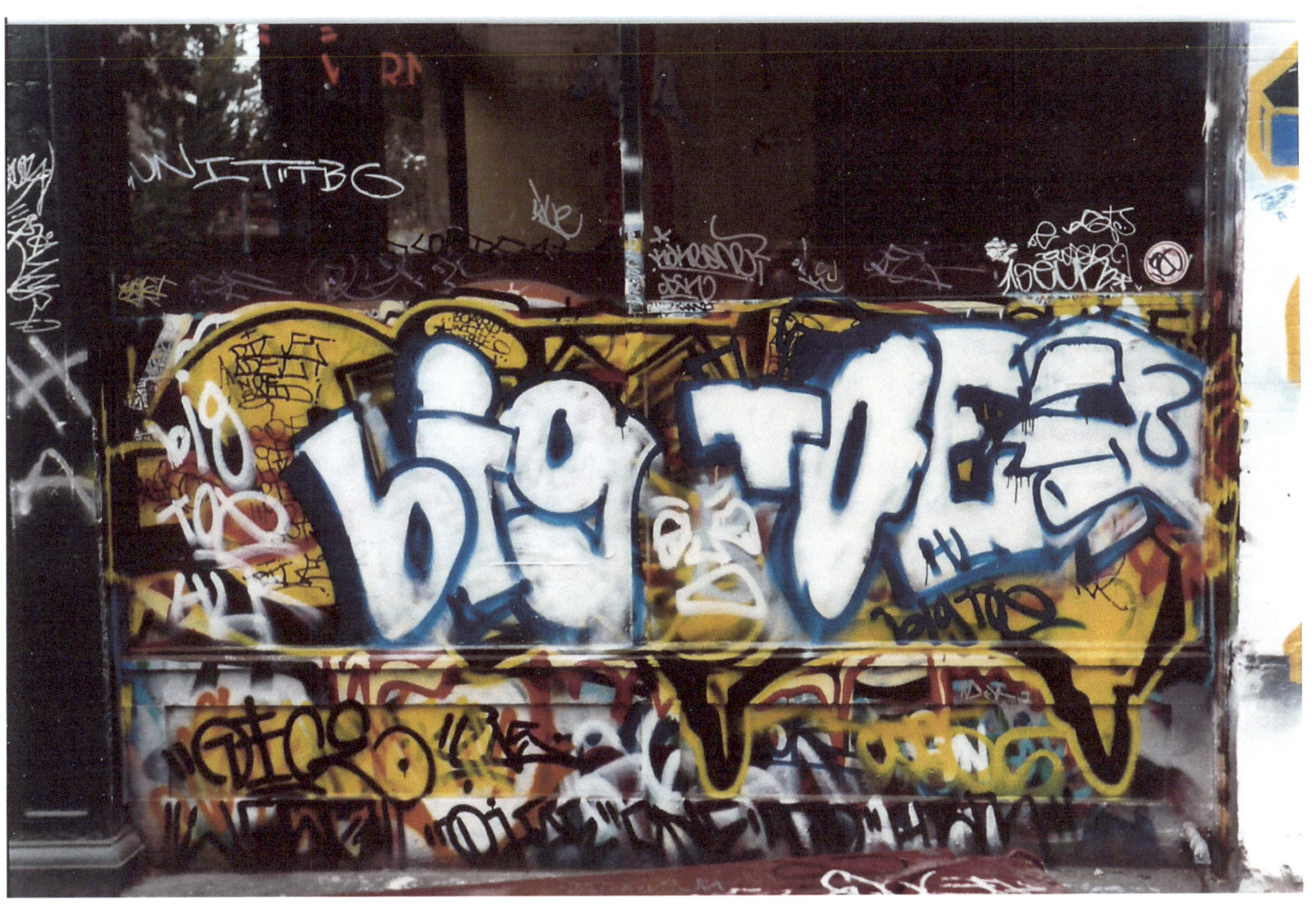

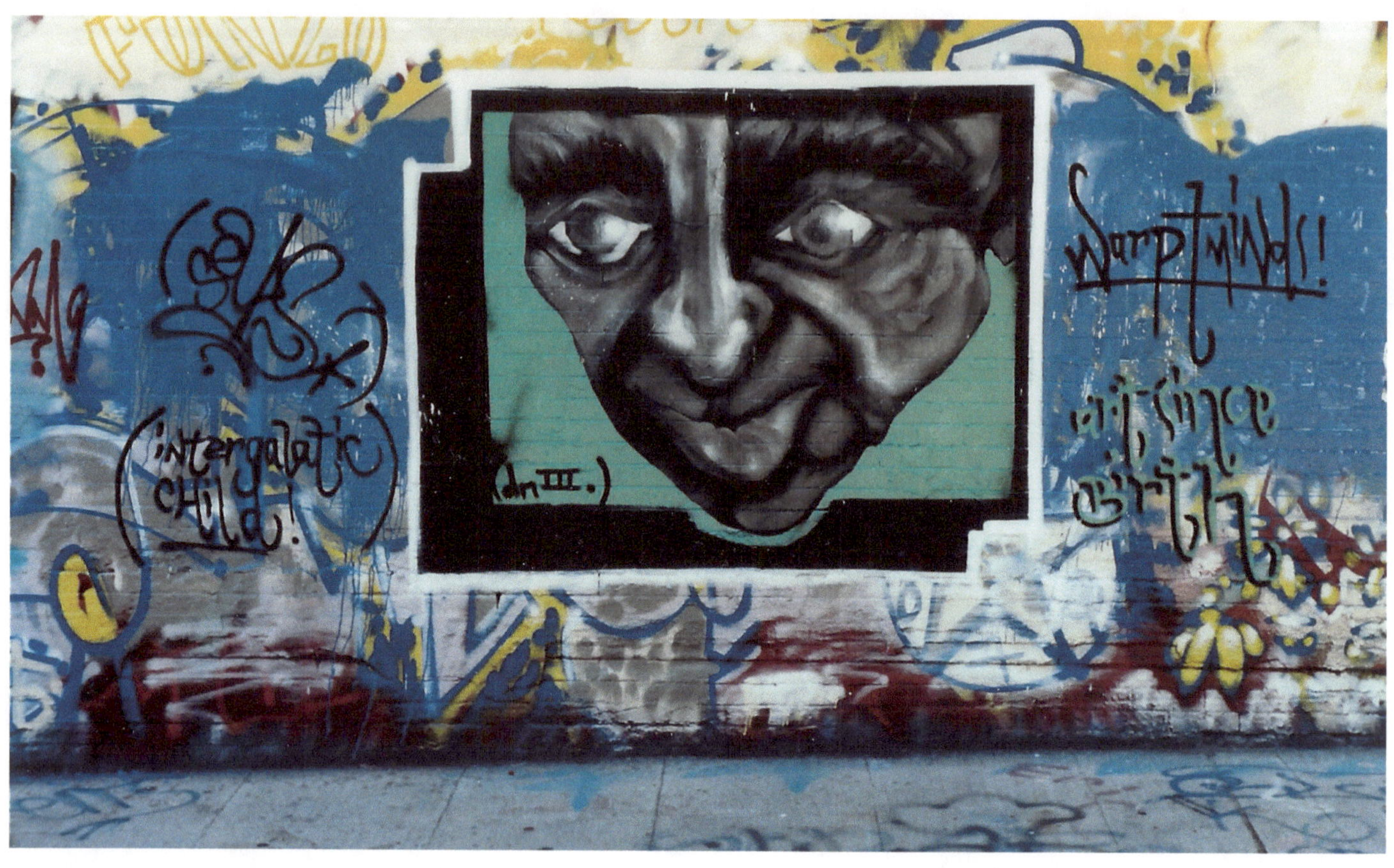
intergalatic
CHILD!
Warp7minds!

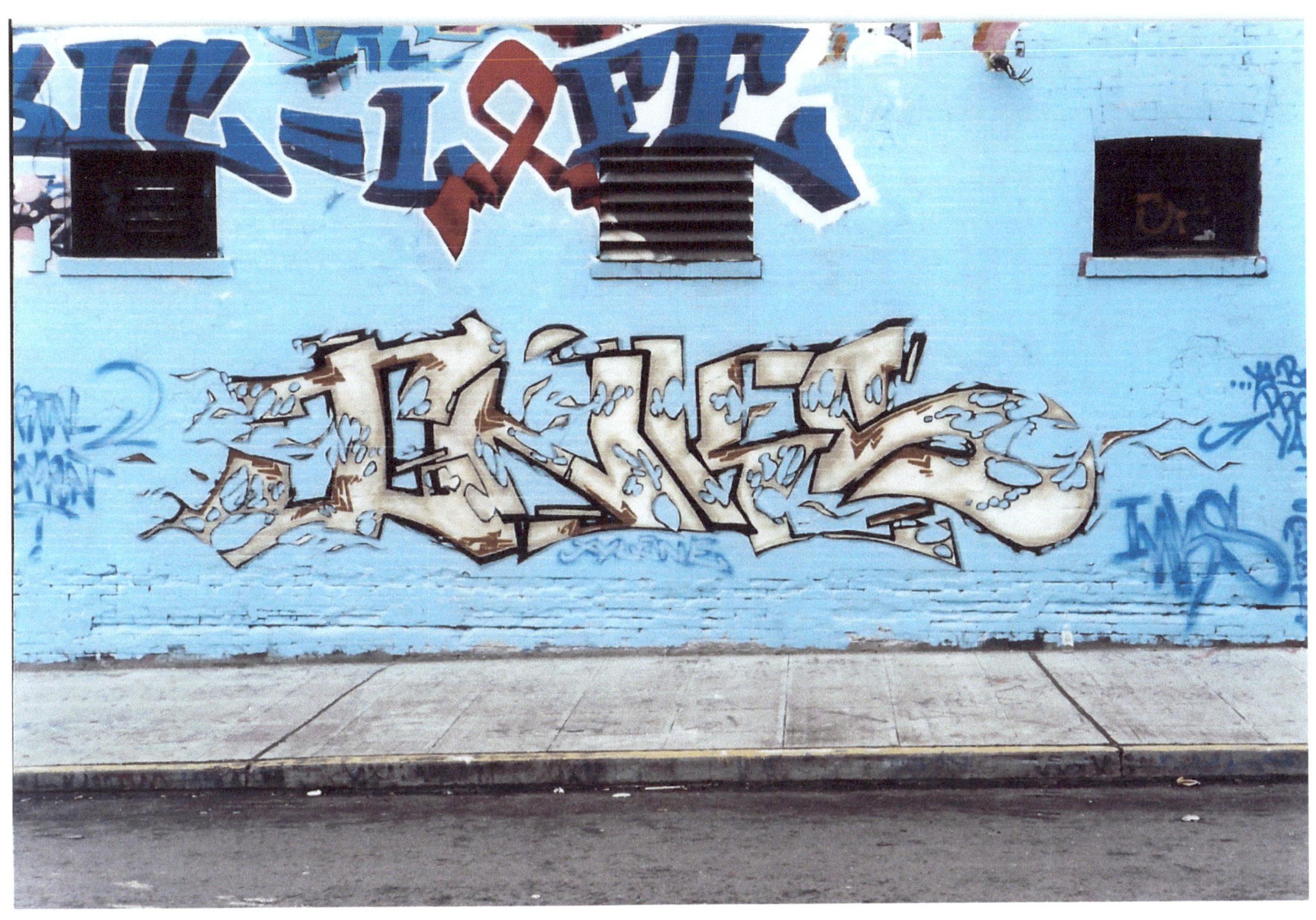

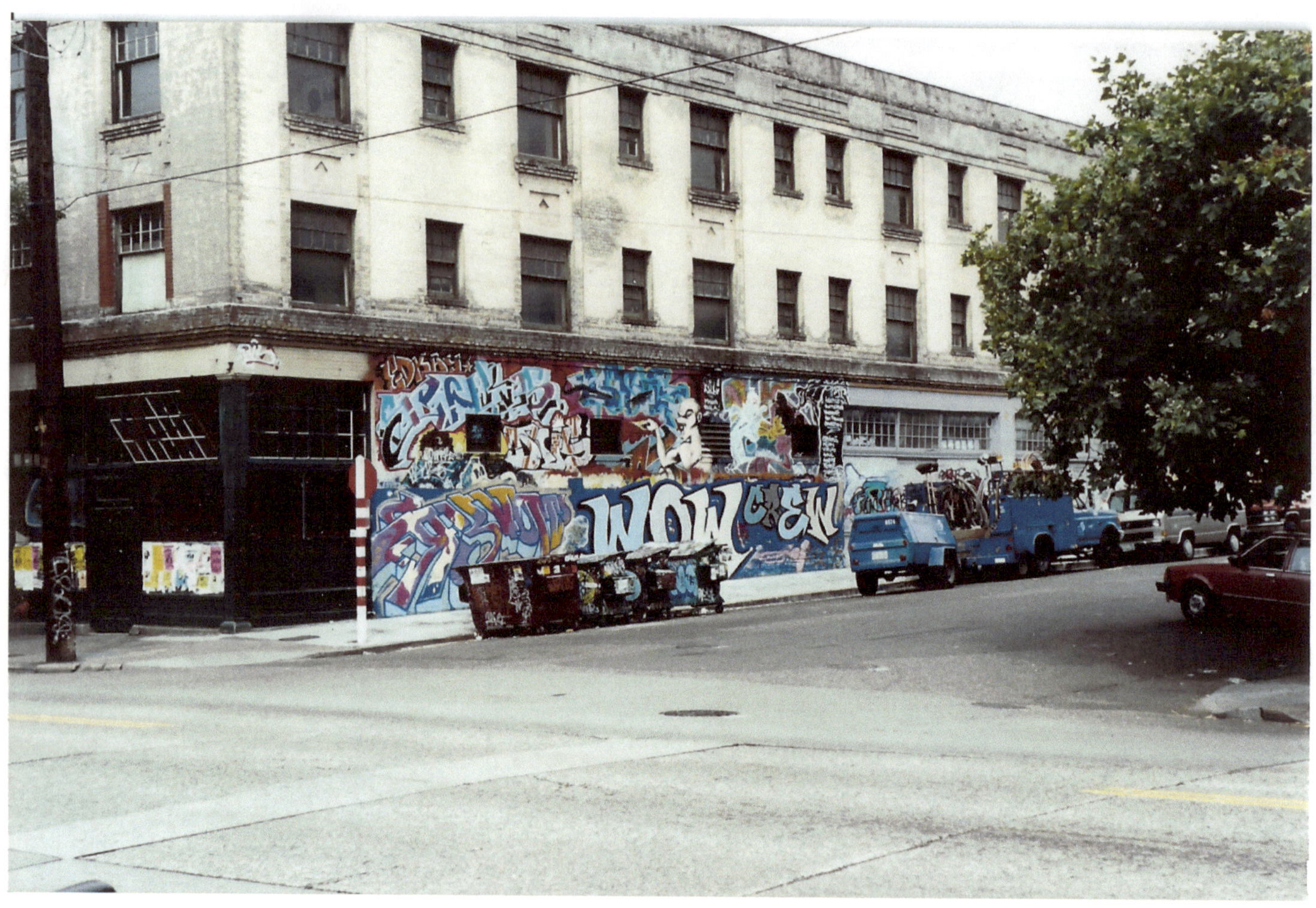
WOW

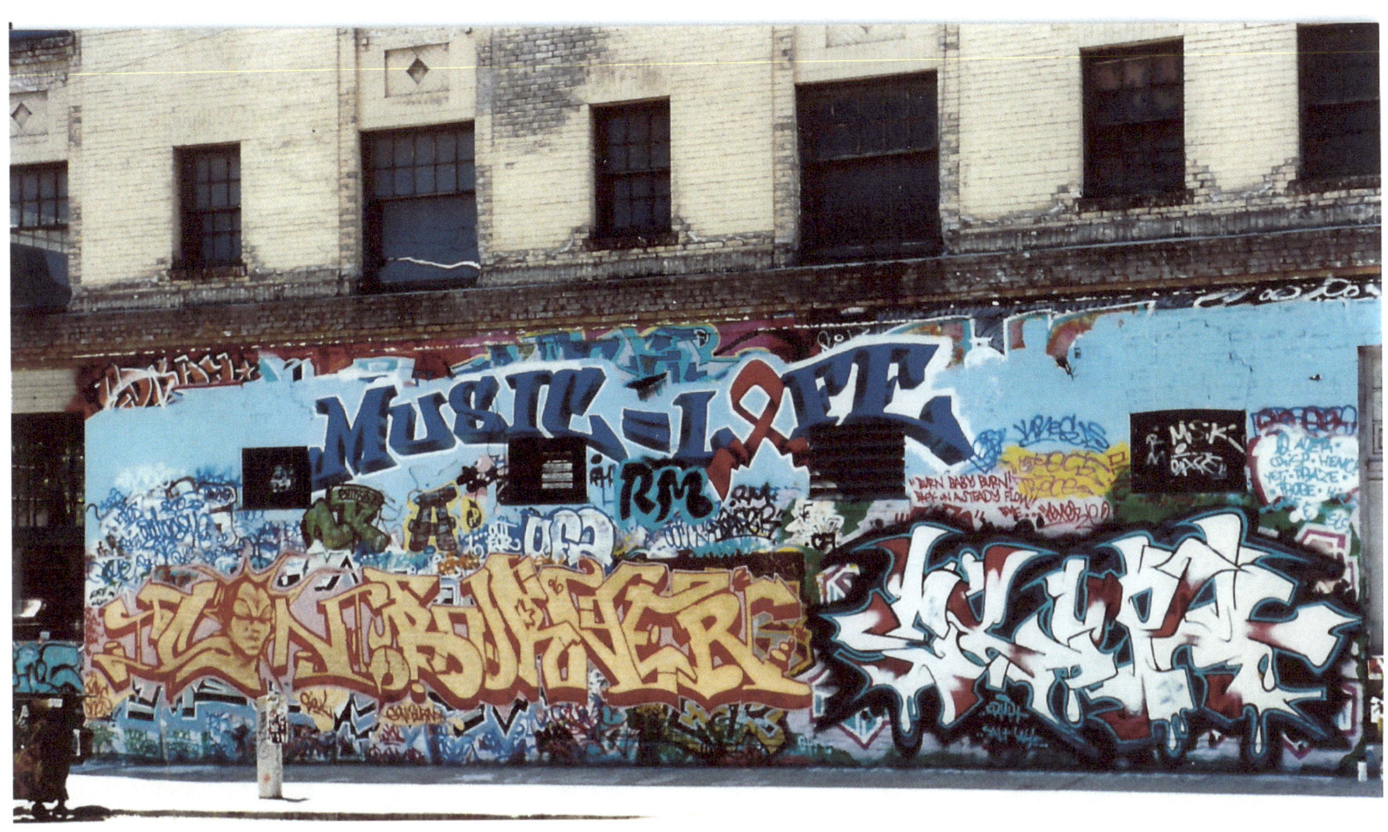
"BURN BABY BURN!
BACK ON A STEADY FLOW!"

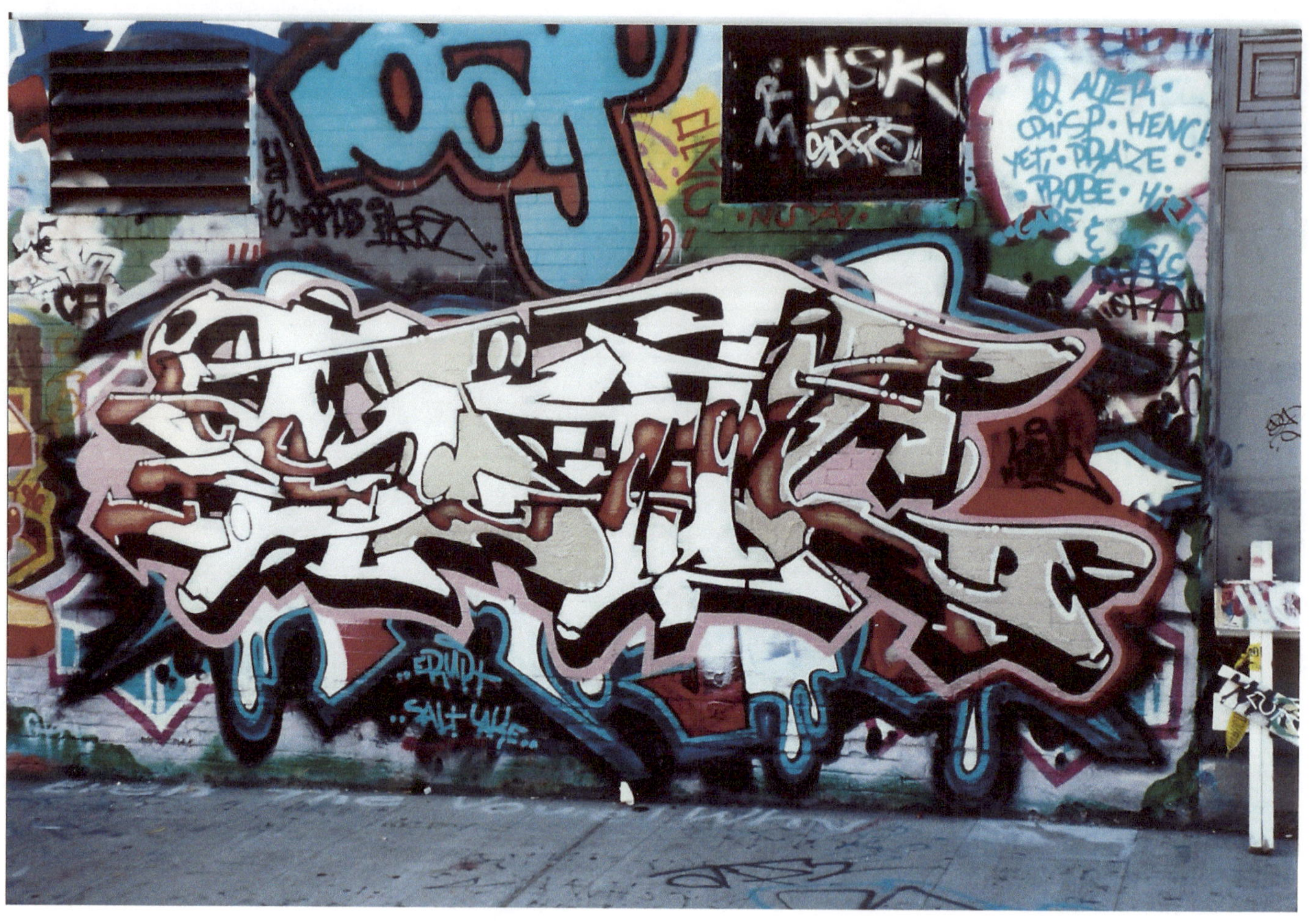
MSK
YETI • PRAZE •
• PROBE •
..SALT LAKE..

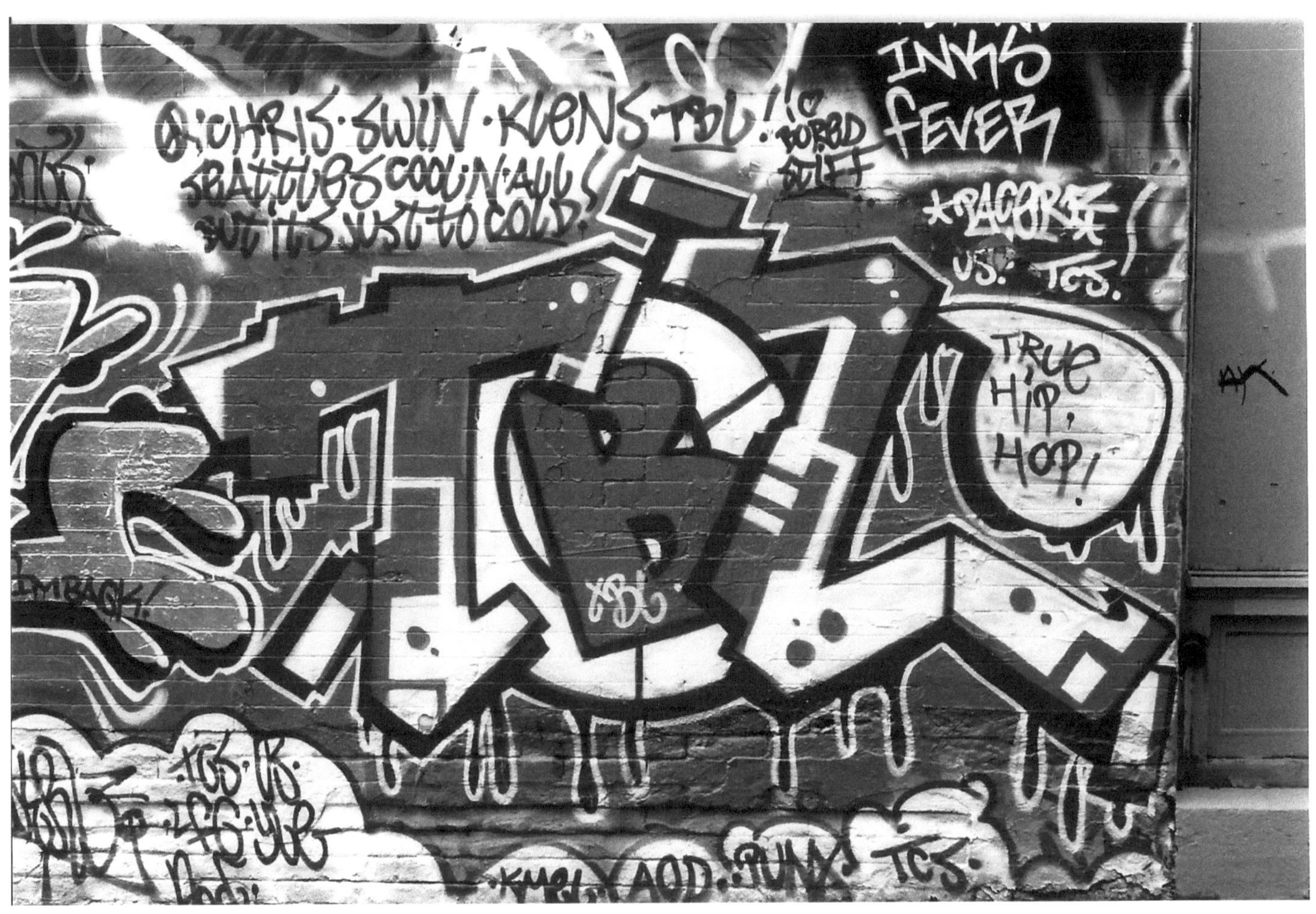
INKS
FEVER
TRUE
HIP,
HOP!

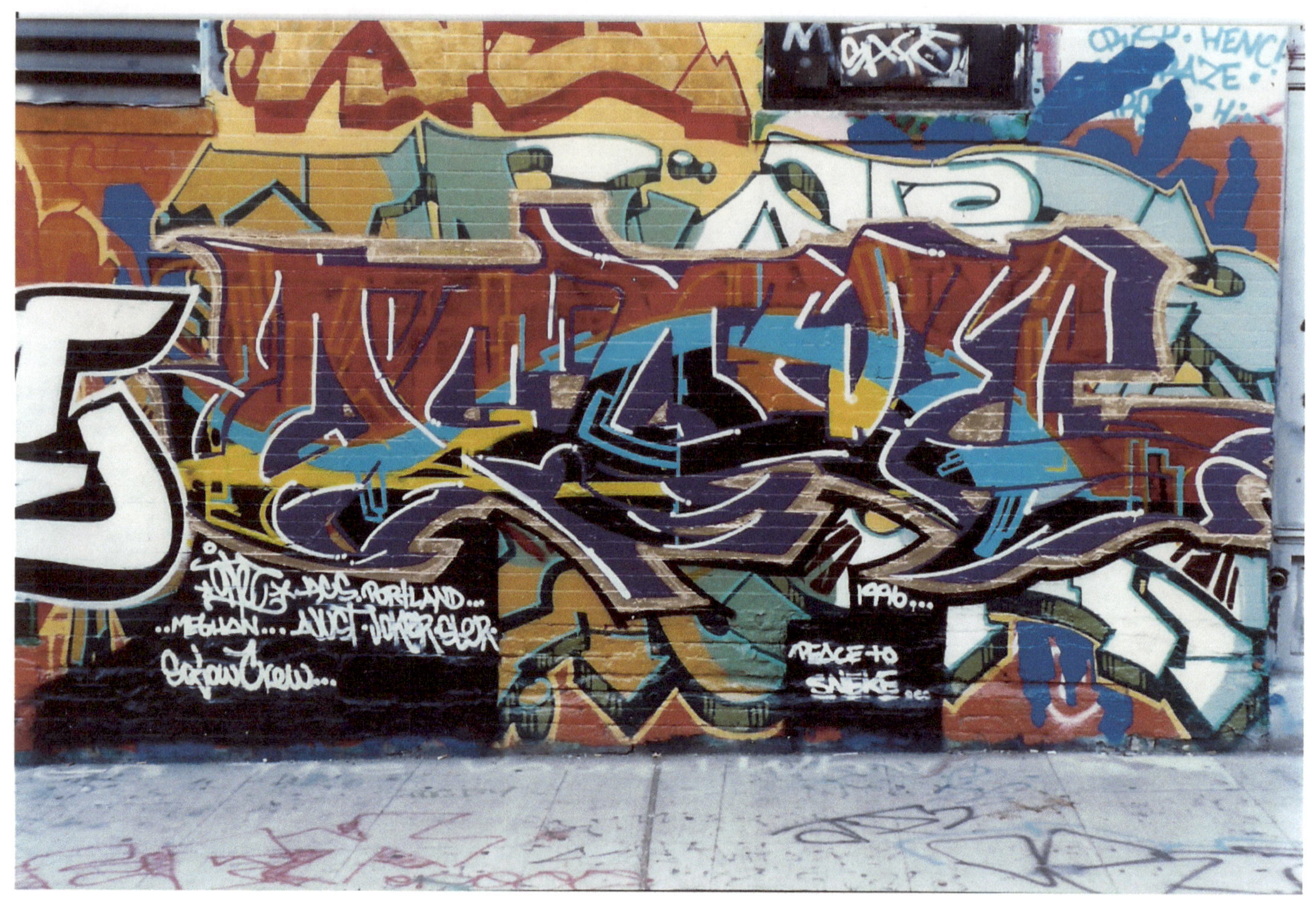

1996,...
PEACE TO

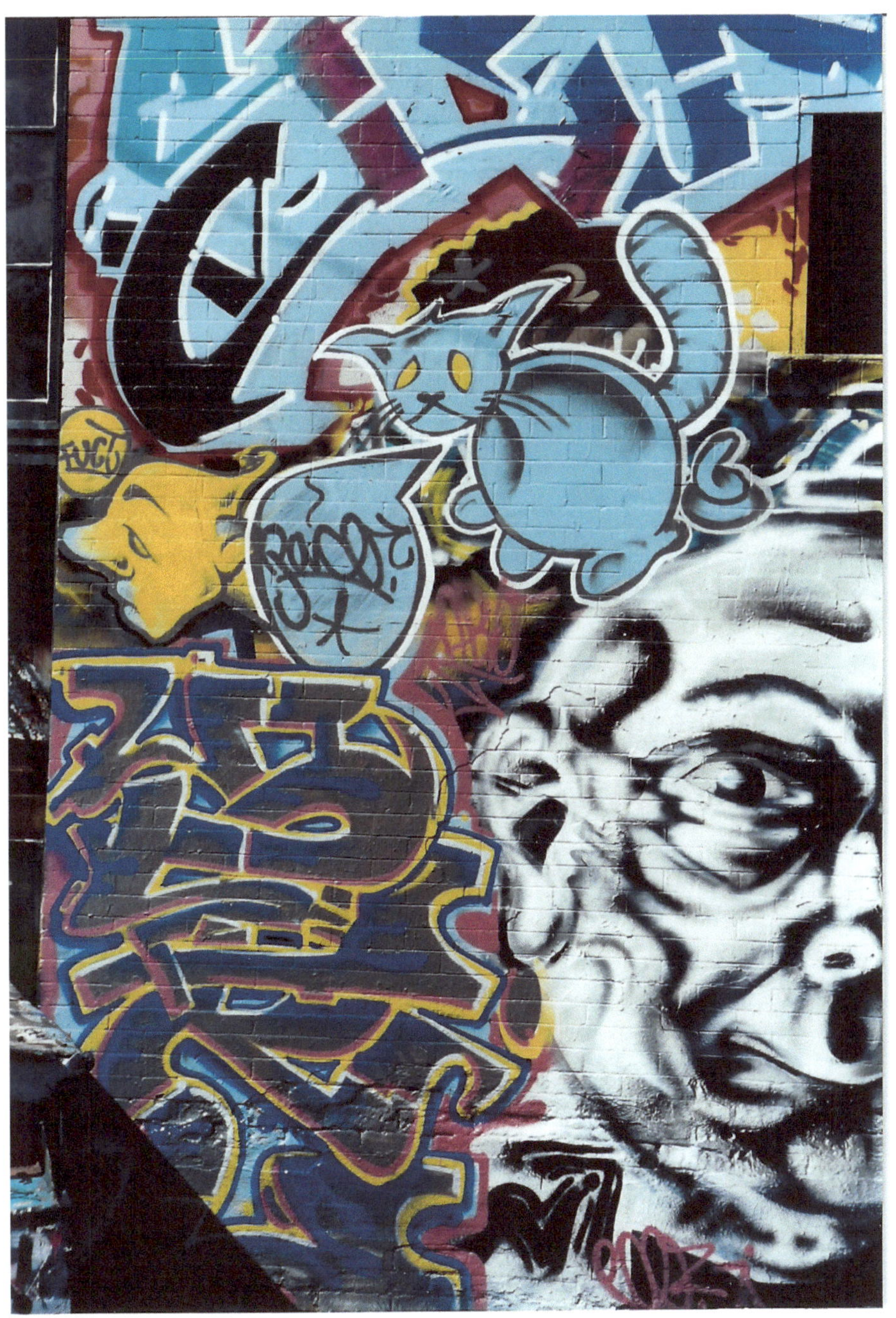

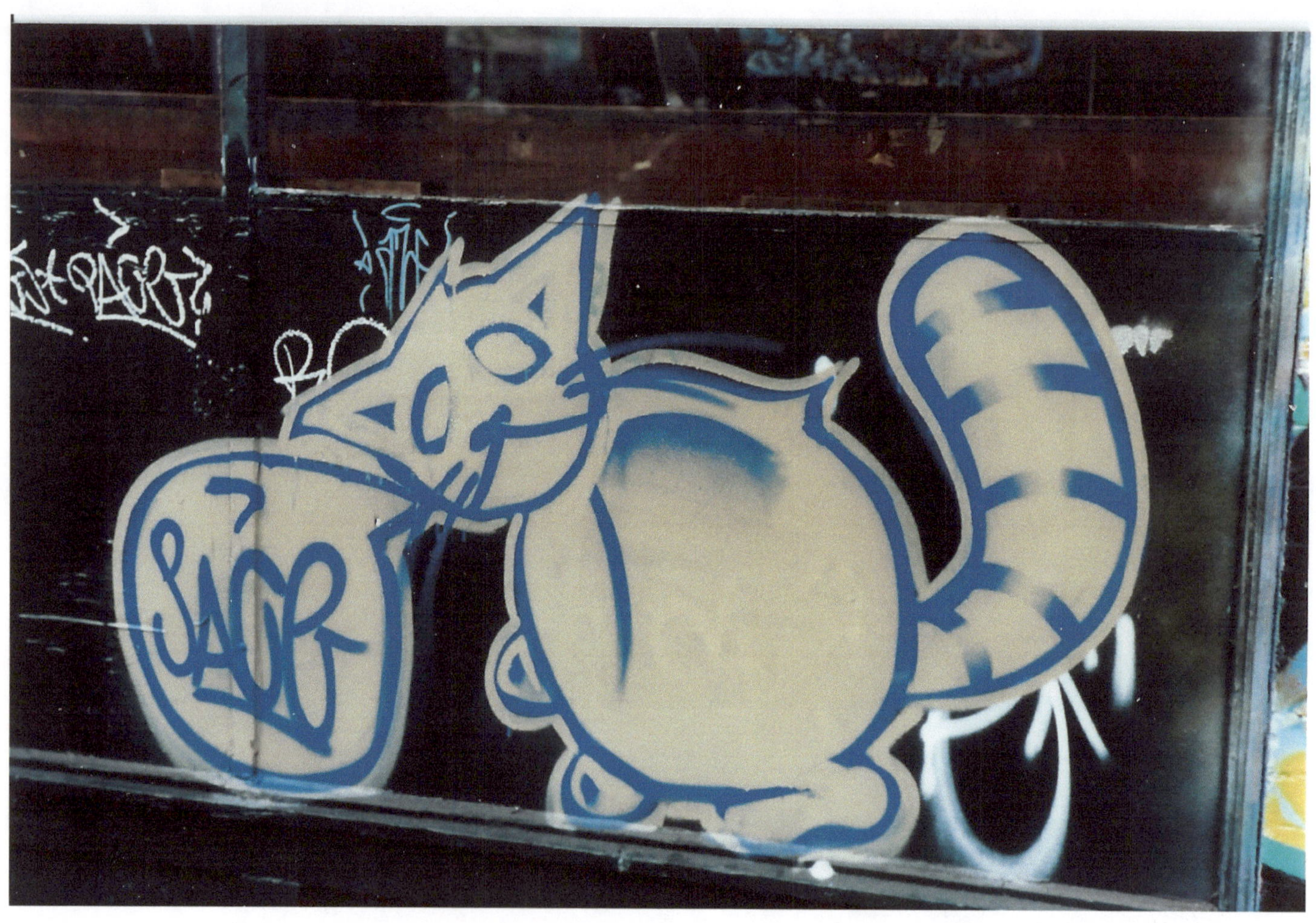

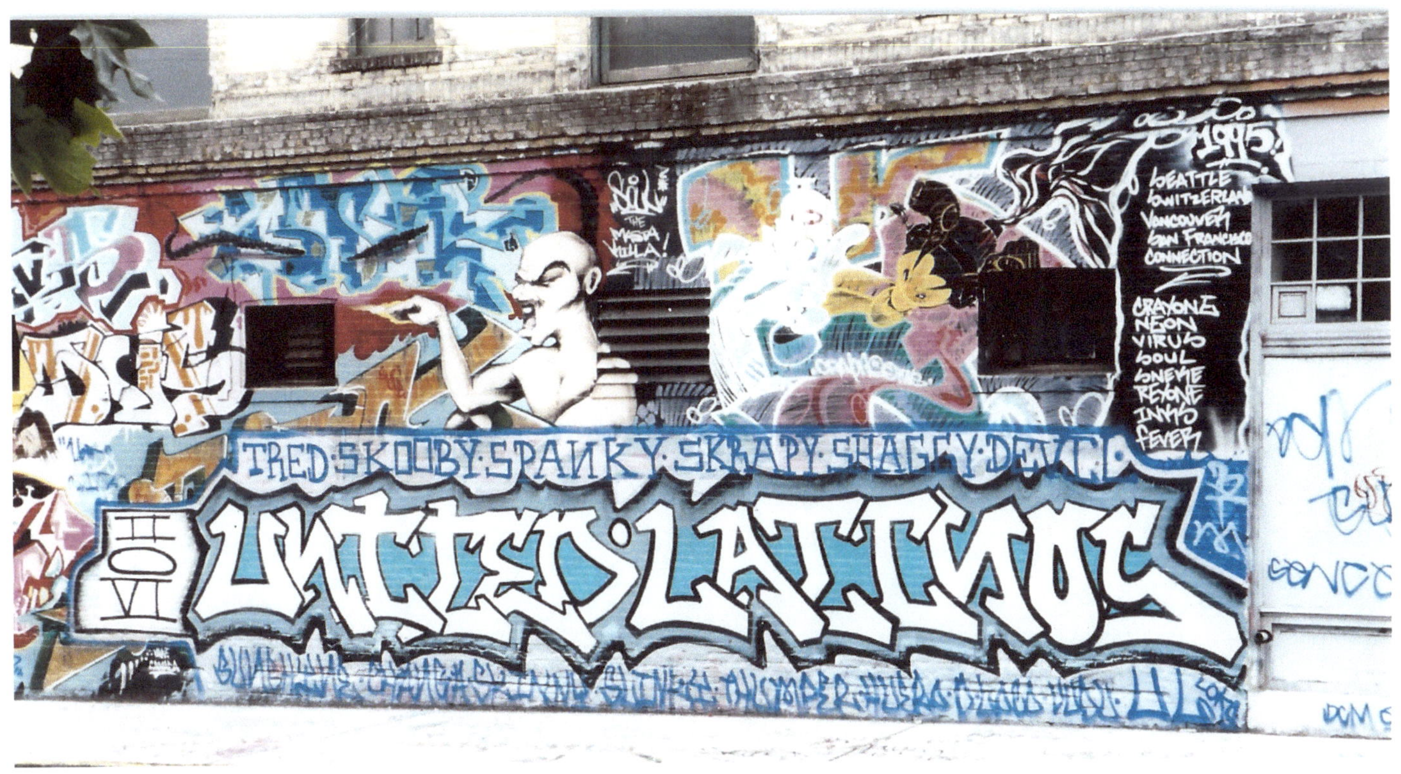
1995
SEATTLE
SWITZERLAN
VANCOUVER
SAN FRANCISCO
CONNECTION
CRAYONE
NEON
VIRUS
SOUL
SNEKE
REXONE
INKS
FEVER
TRED·SKOOBY·SPANKY·SKRAPY·SHAGGY

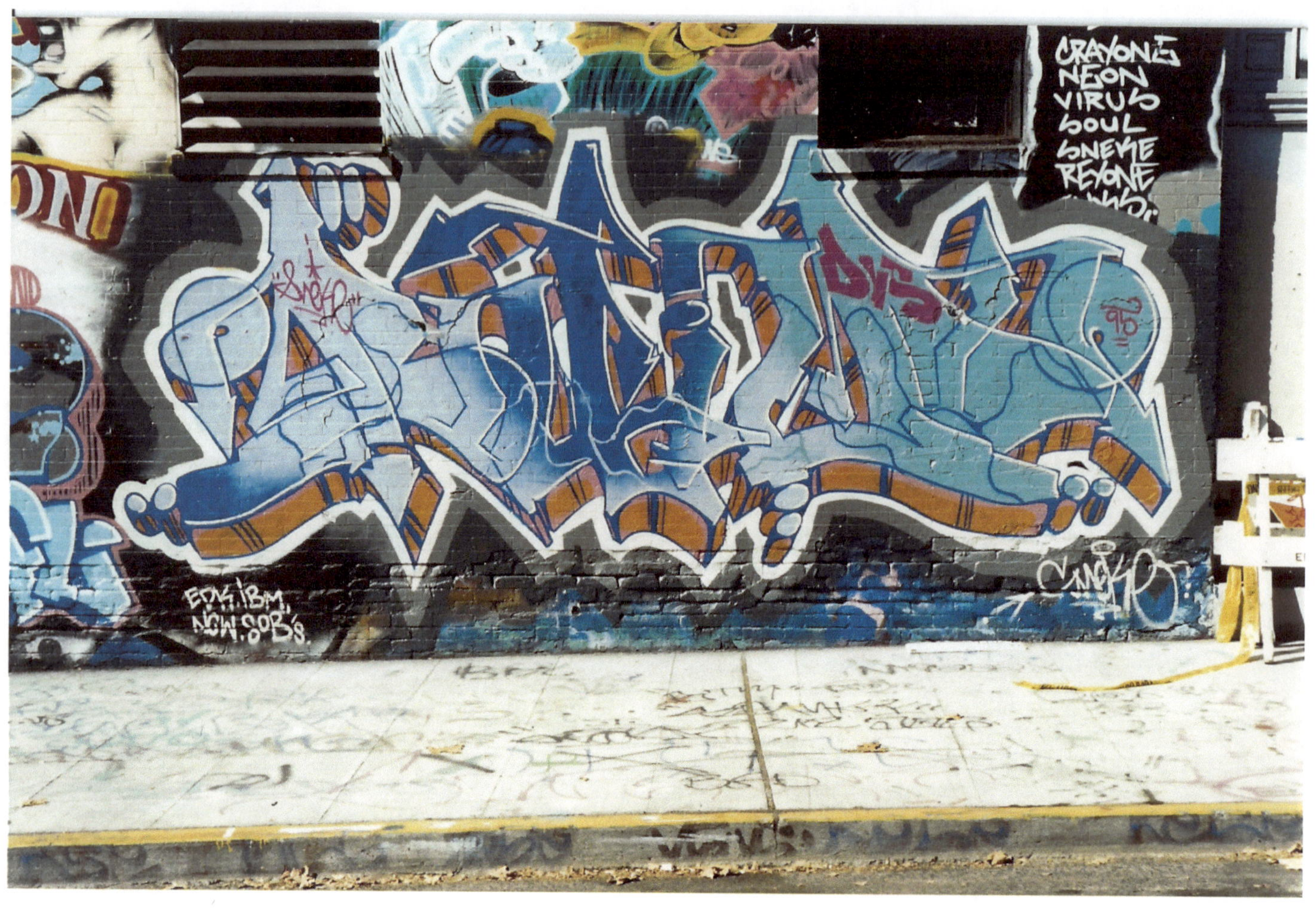
CRAYONE
NEON
VIRUS
SOUL
SNEKE
REYONE
EDS. IBM,
NEW. SOB'S

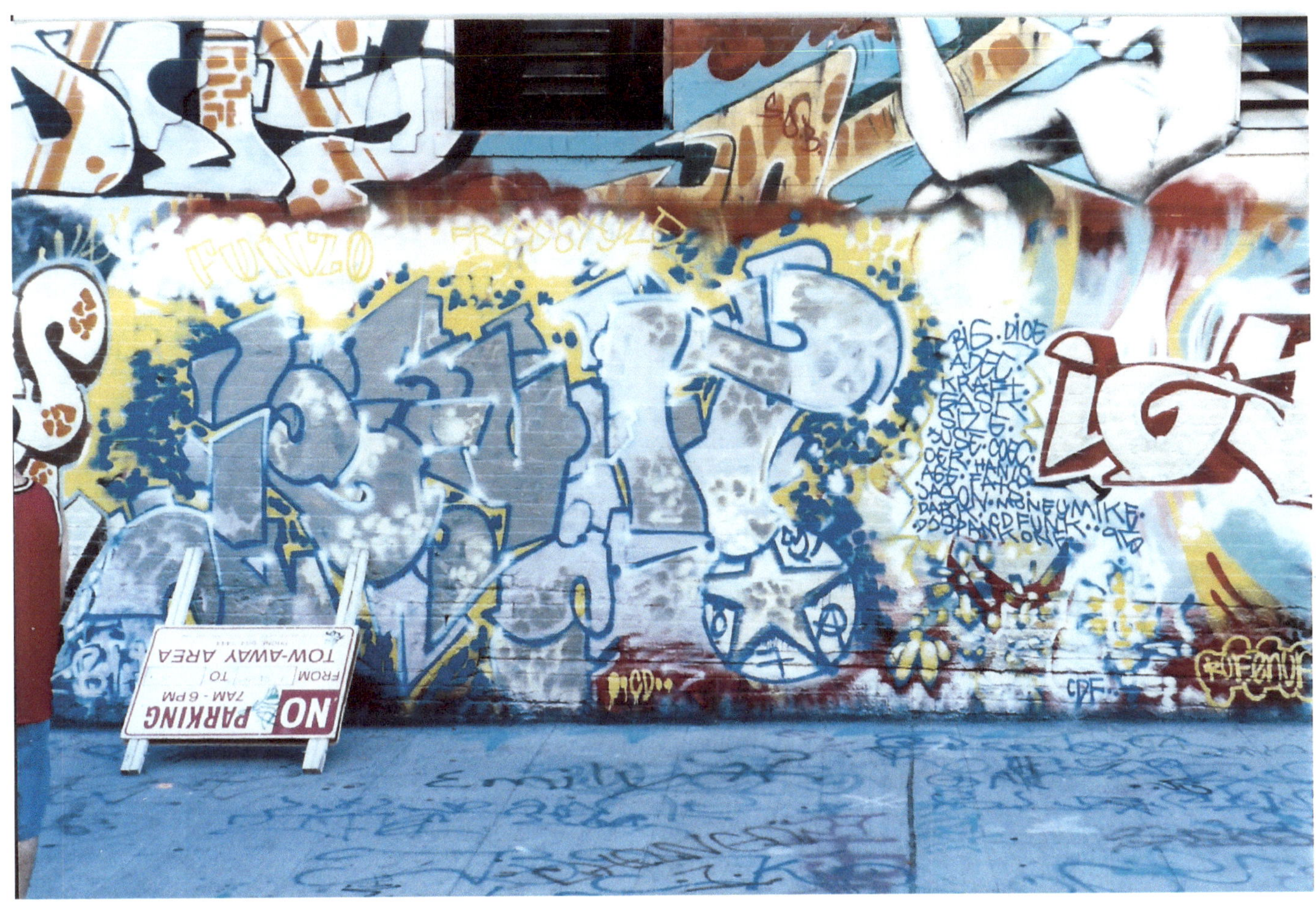
NO PARKING
7AM - 6PM
FROM TO
TOW-AWAY AREA

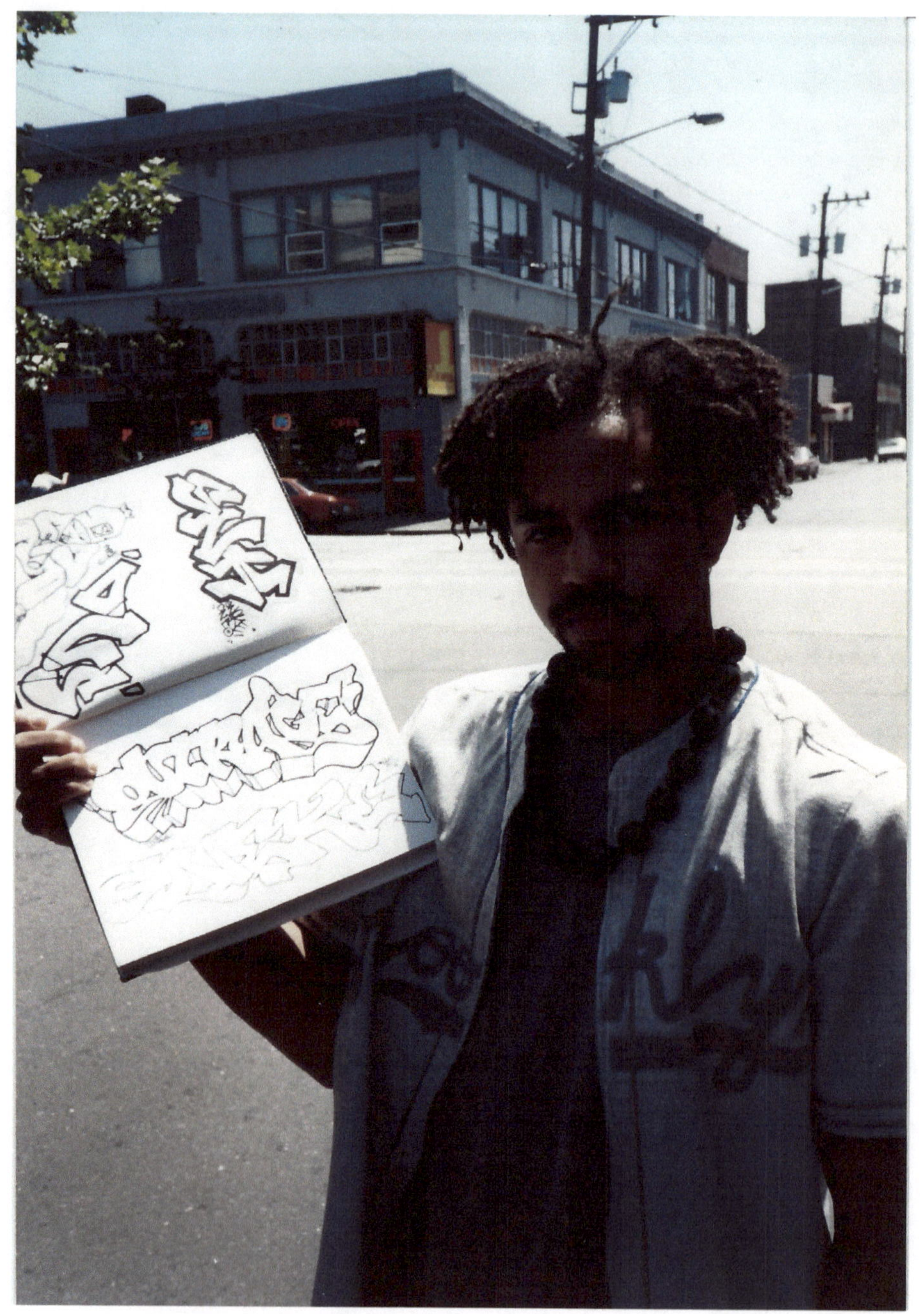

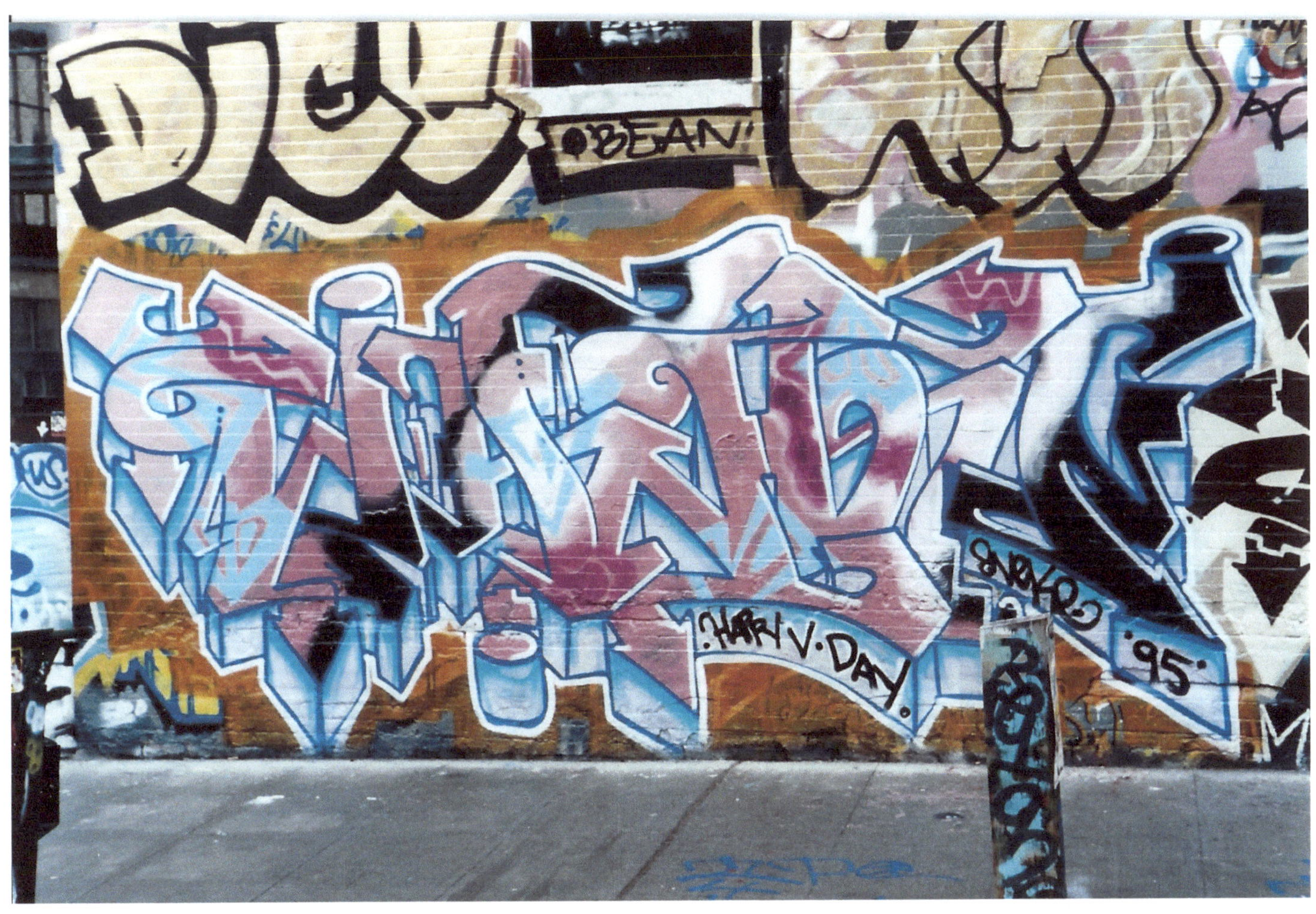
BEAN
V·DAY
95

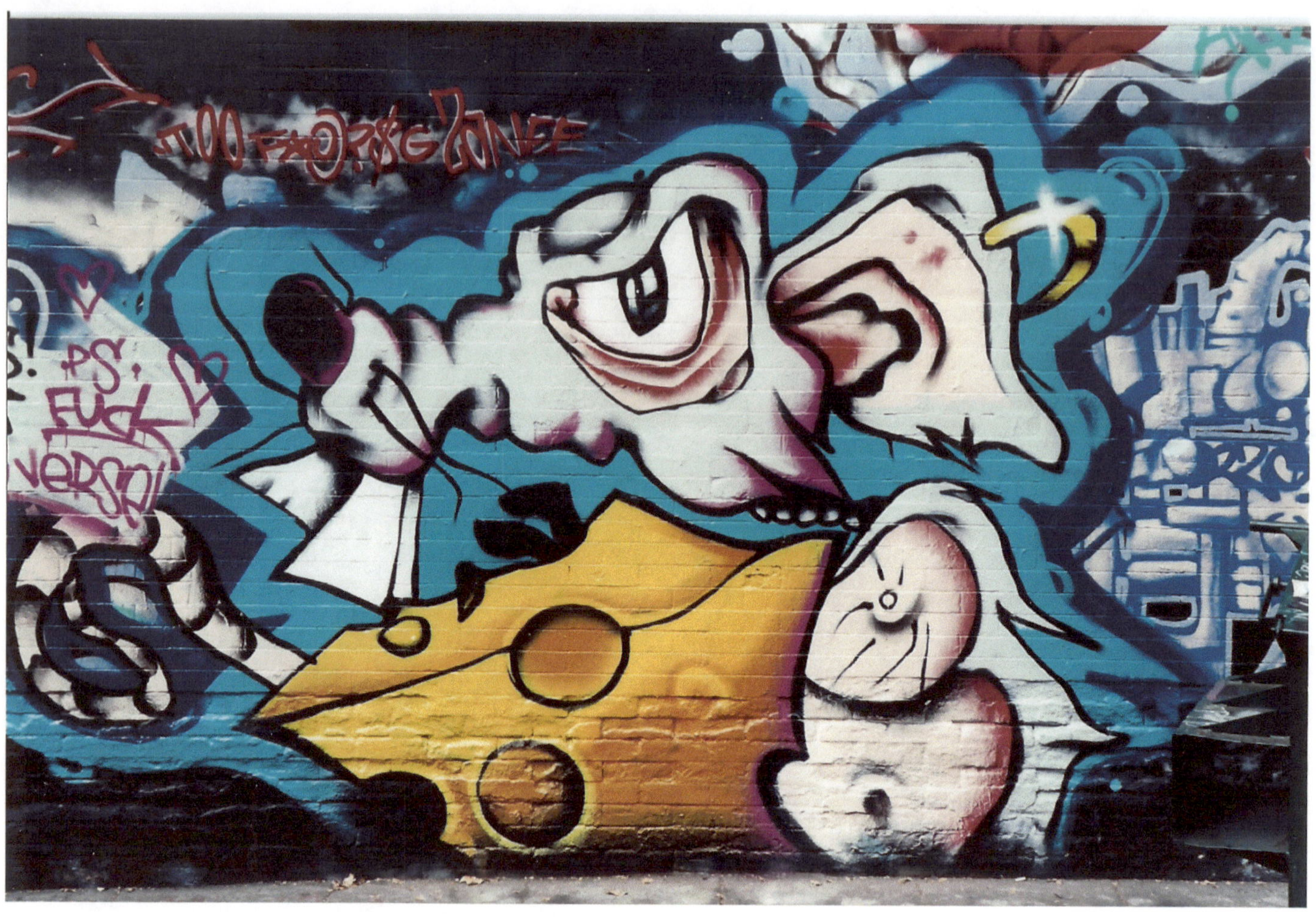
PS.
FUCK

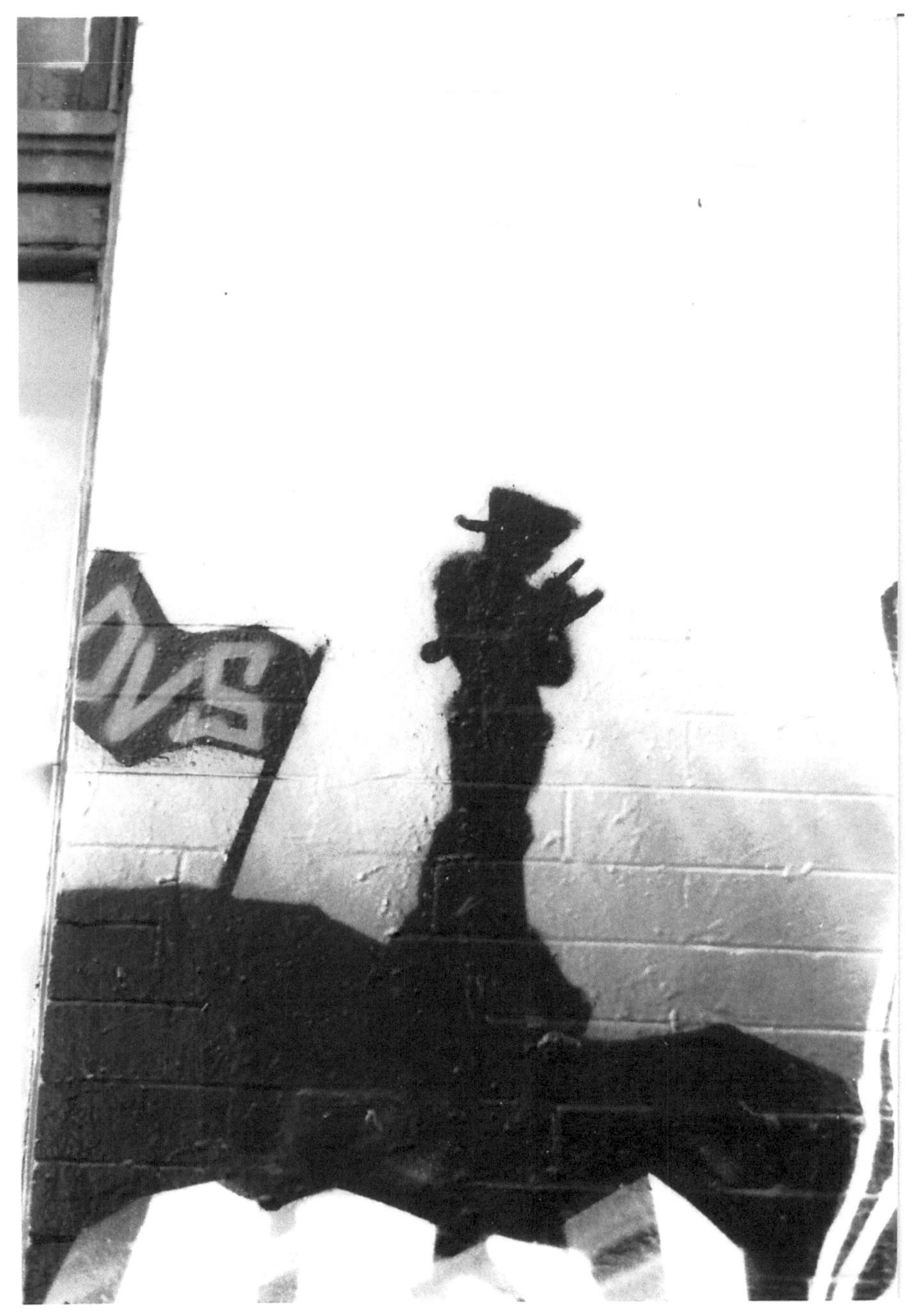

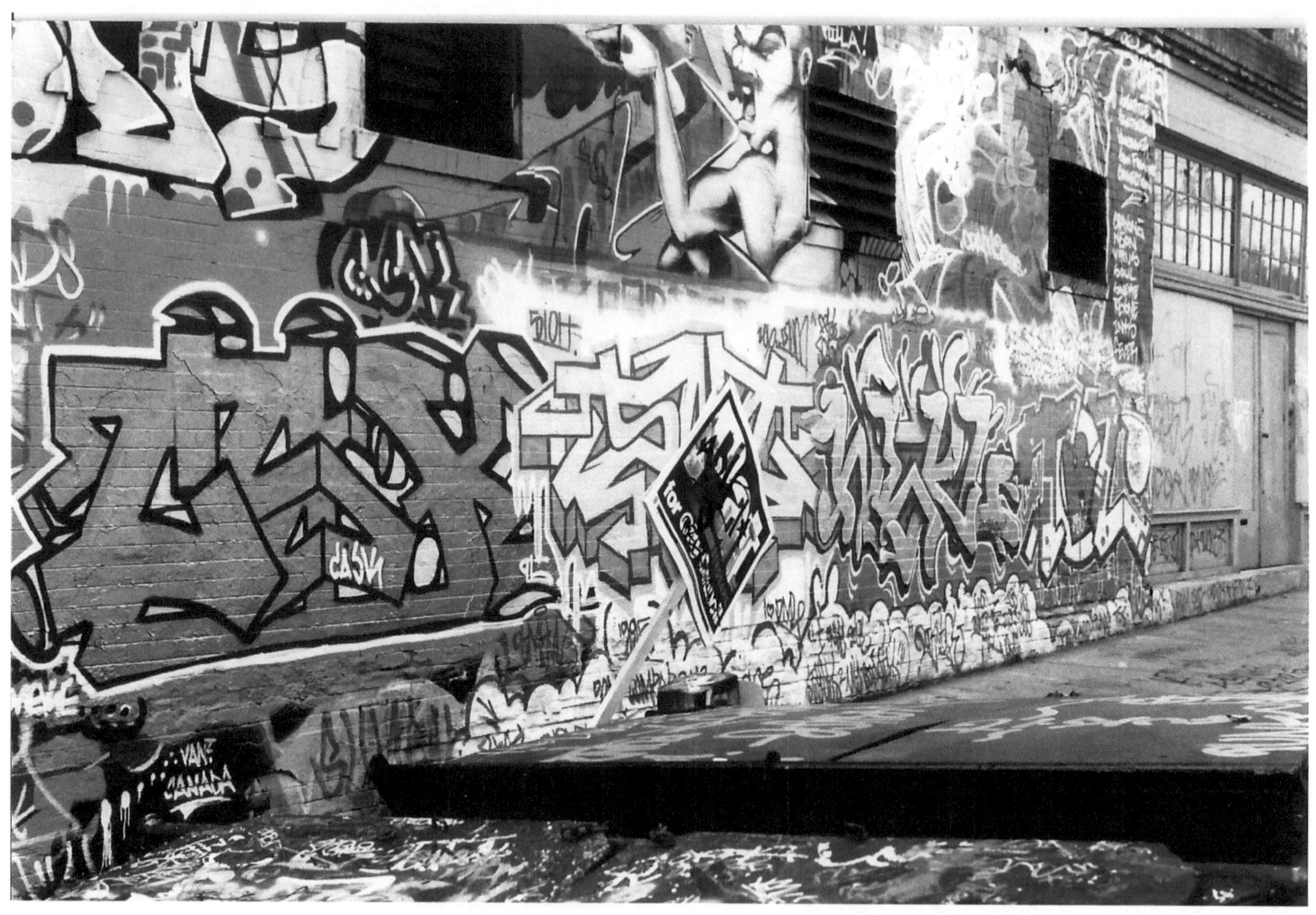

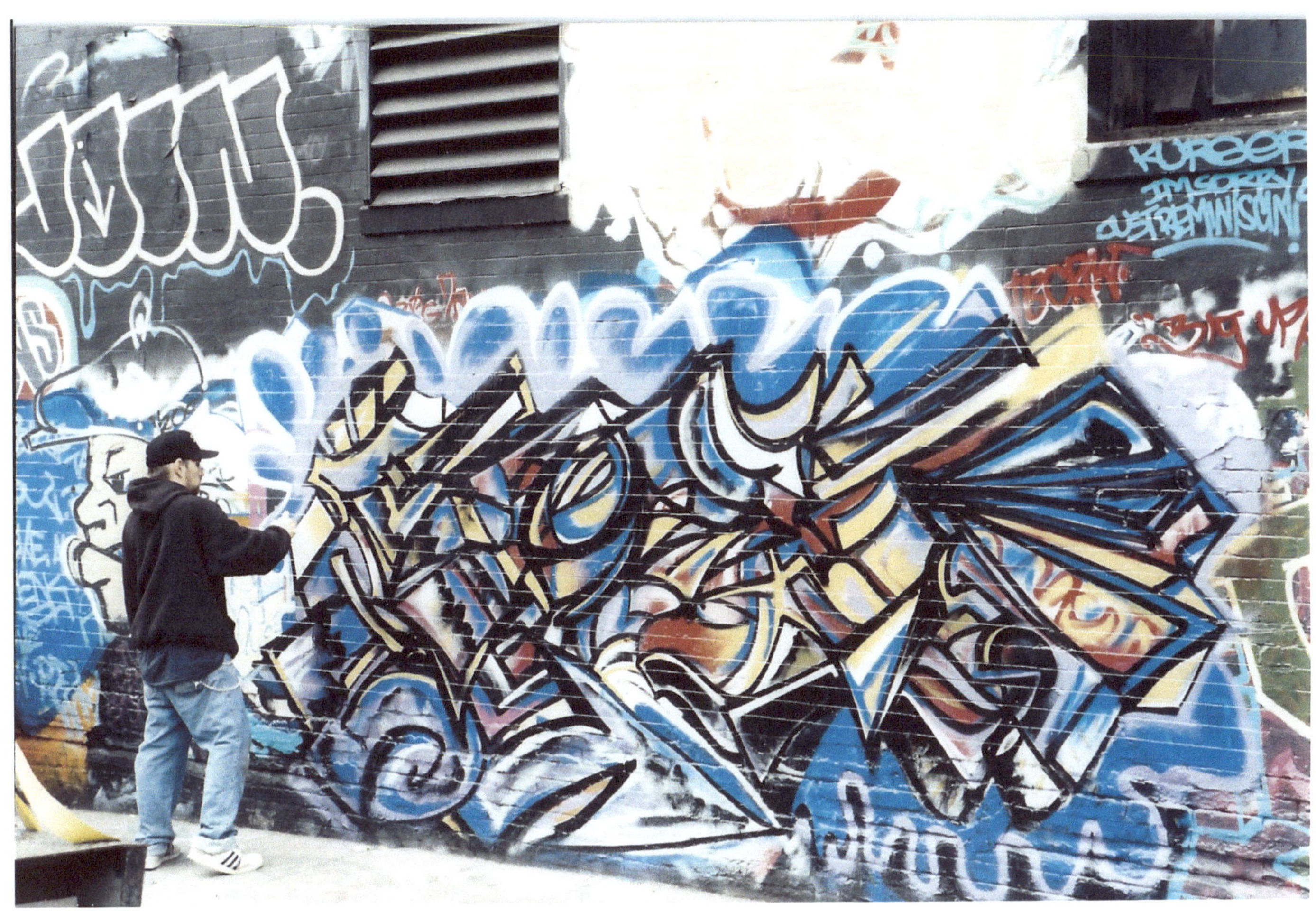

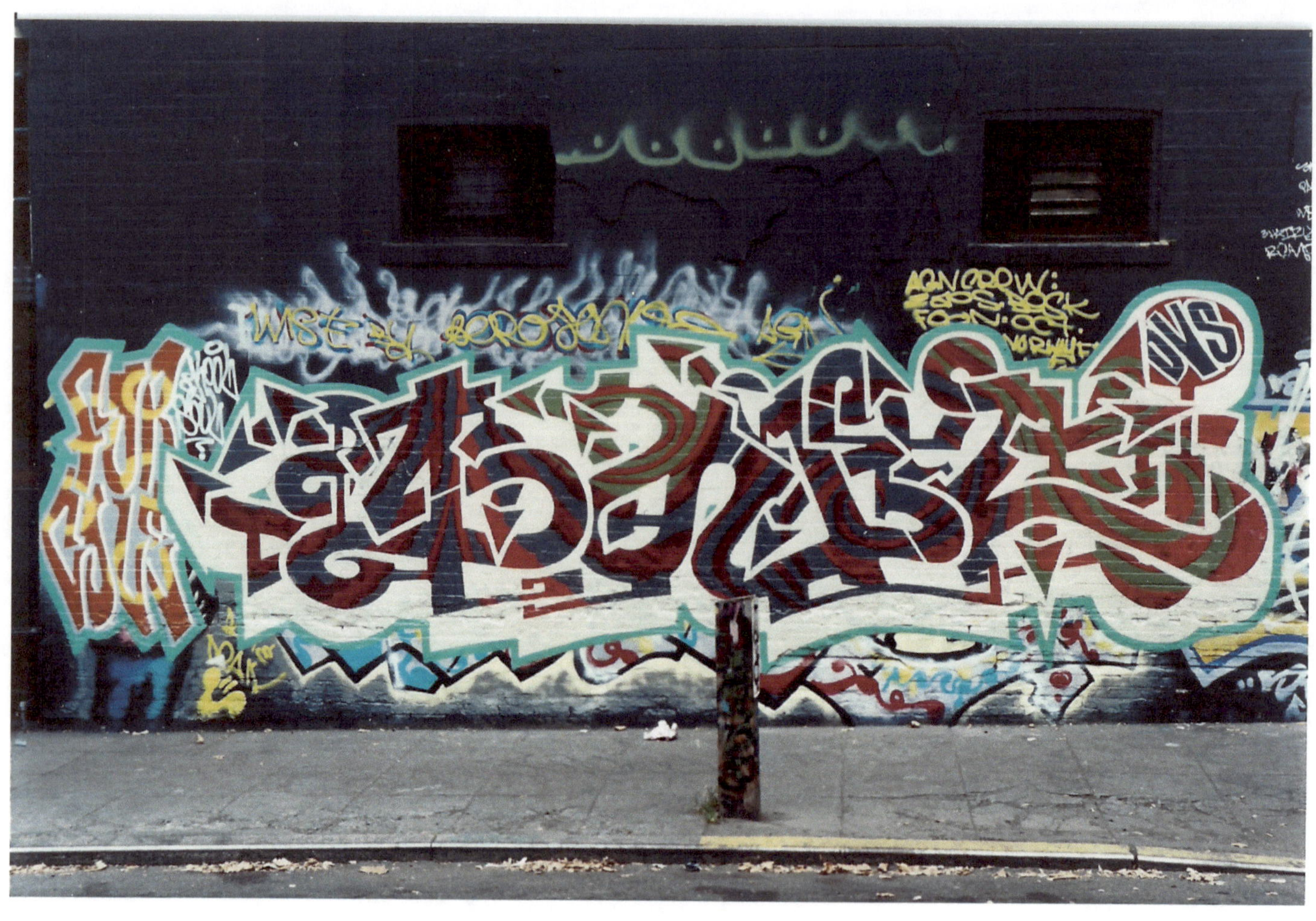

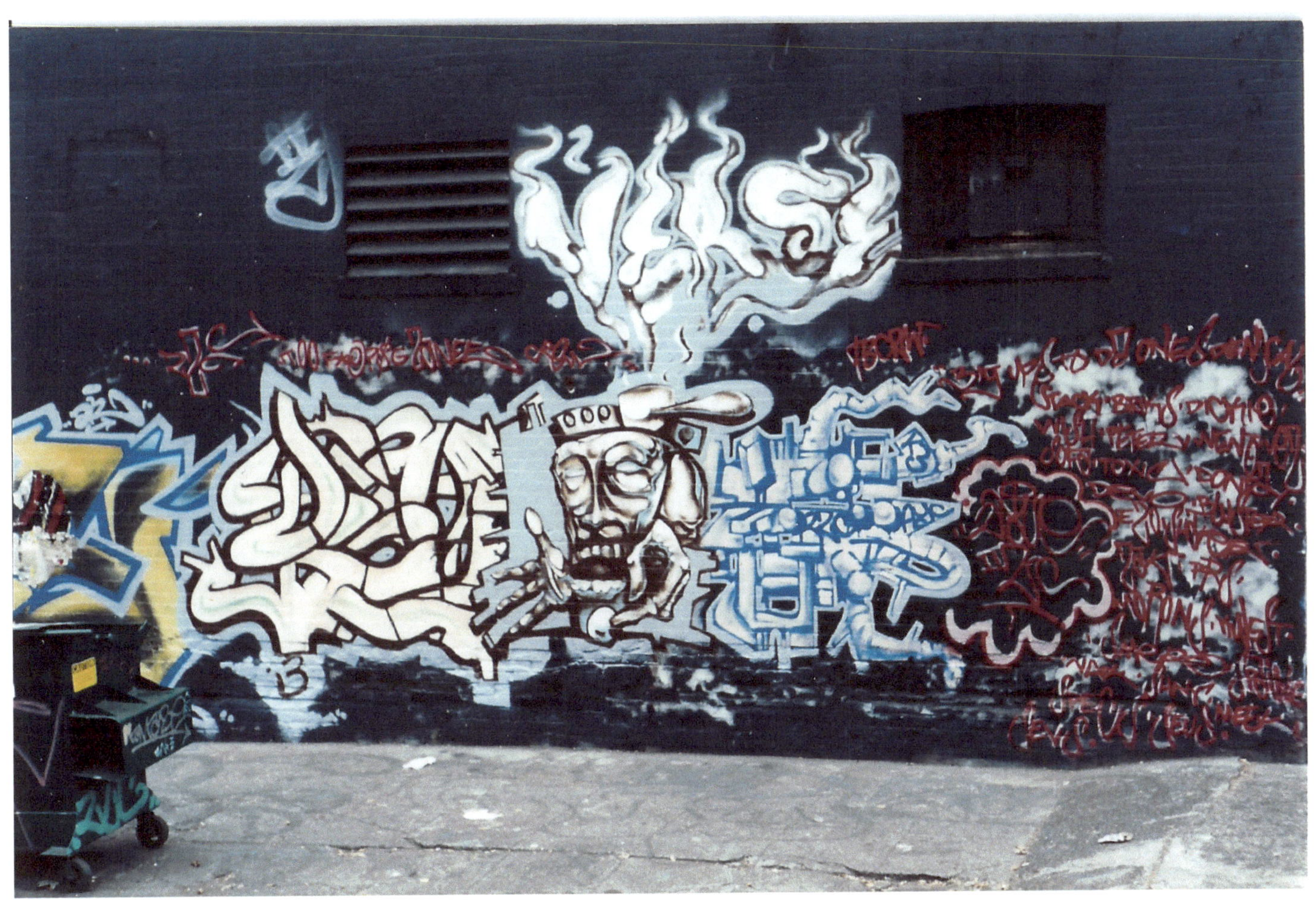

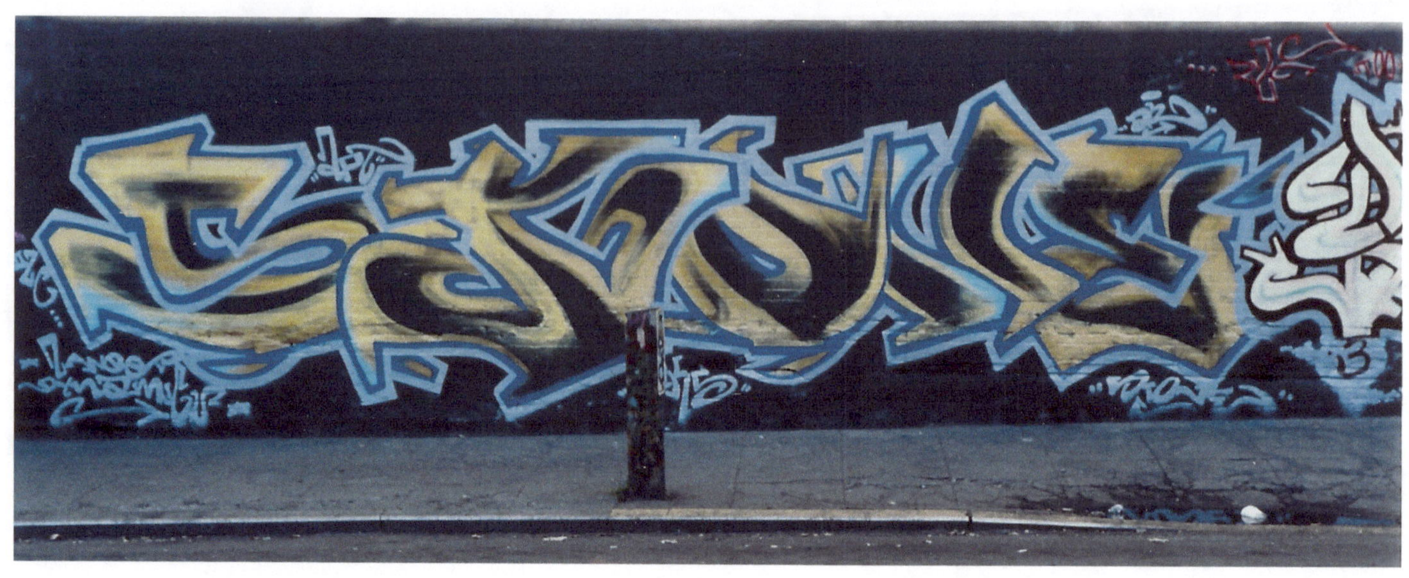

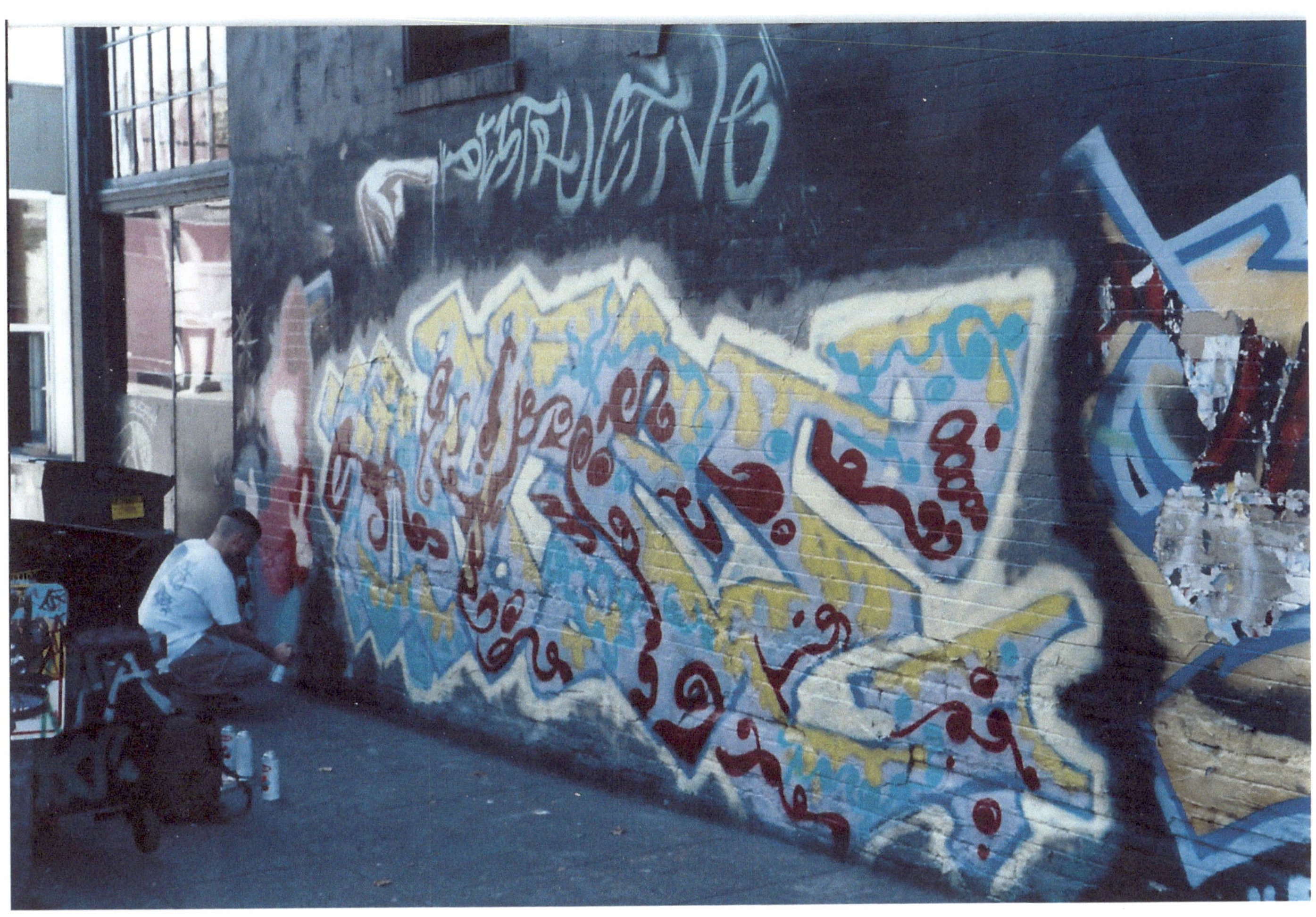

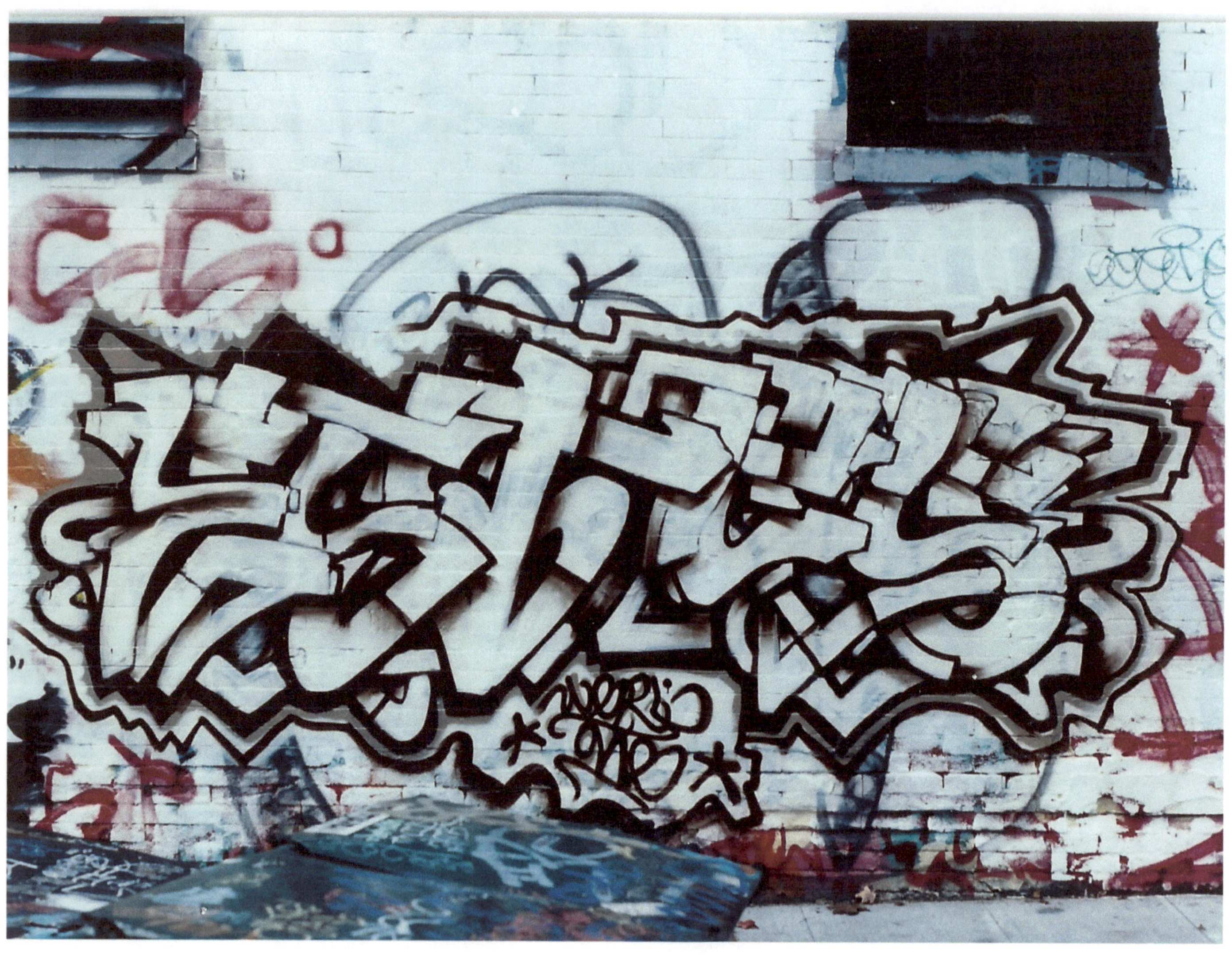

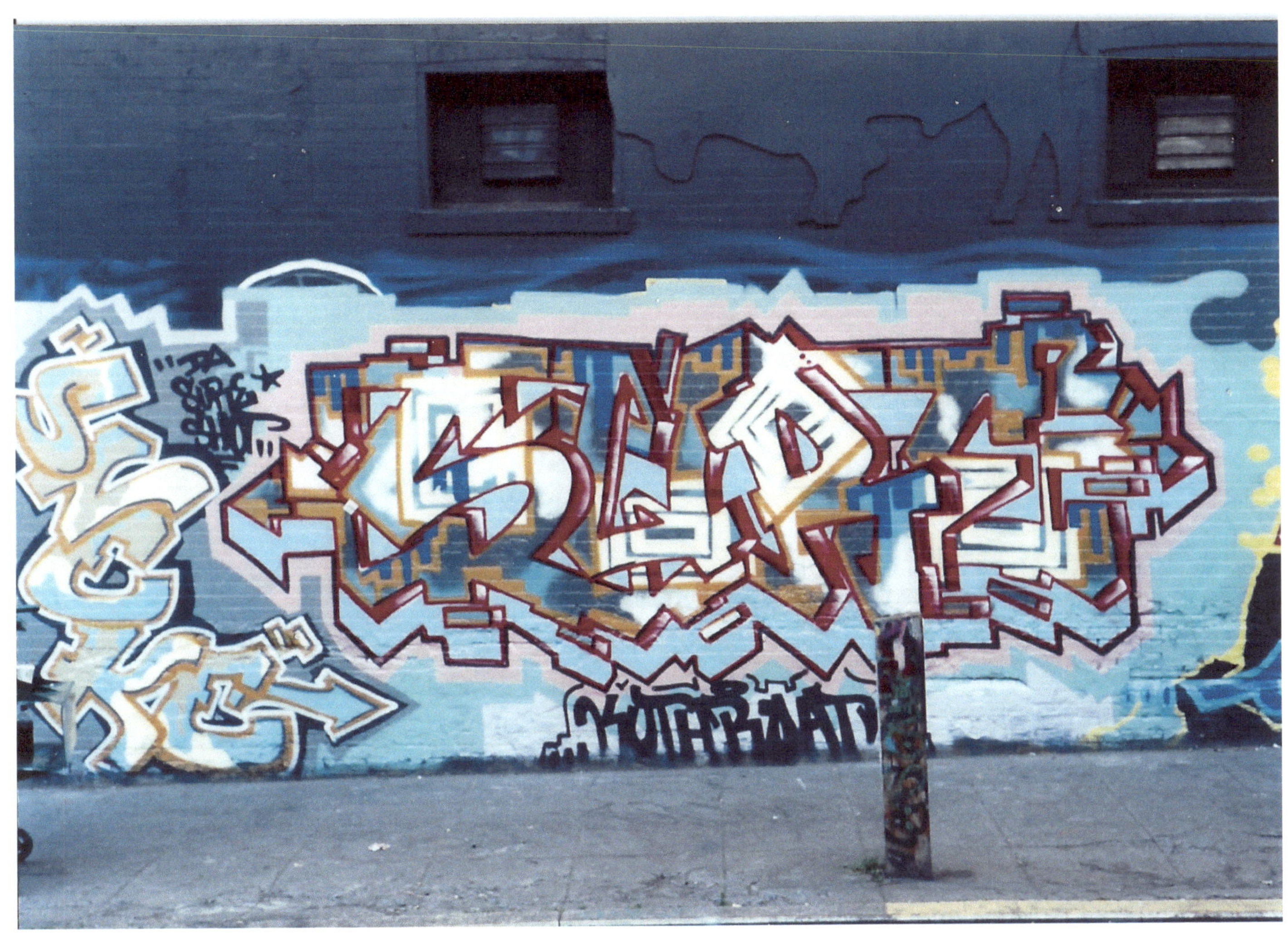

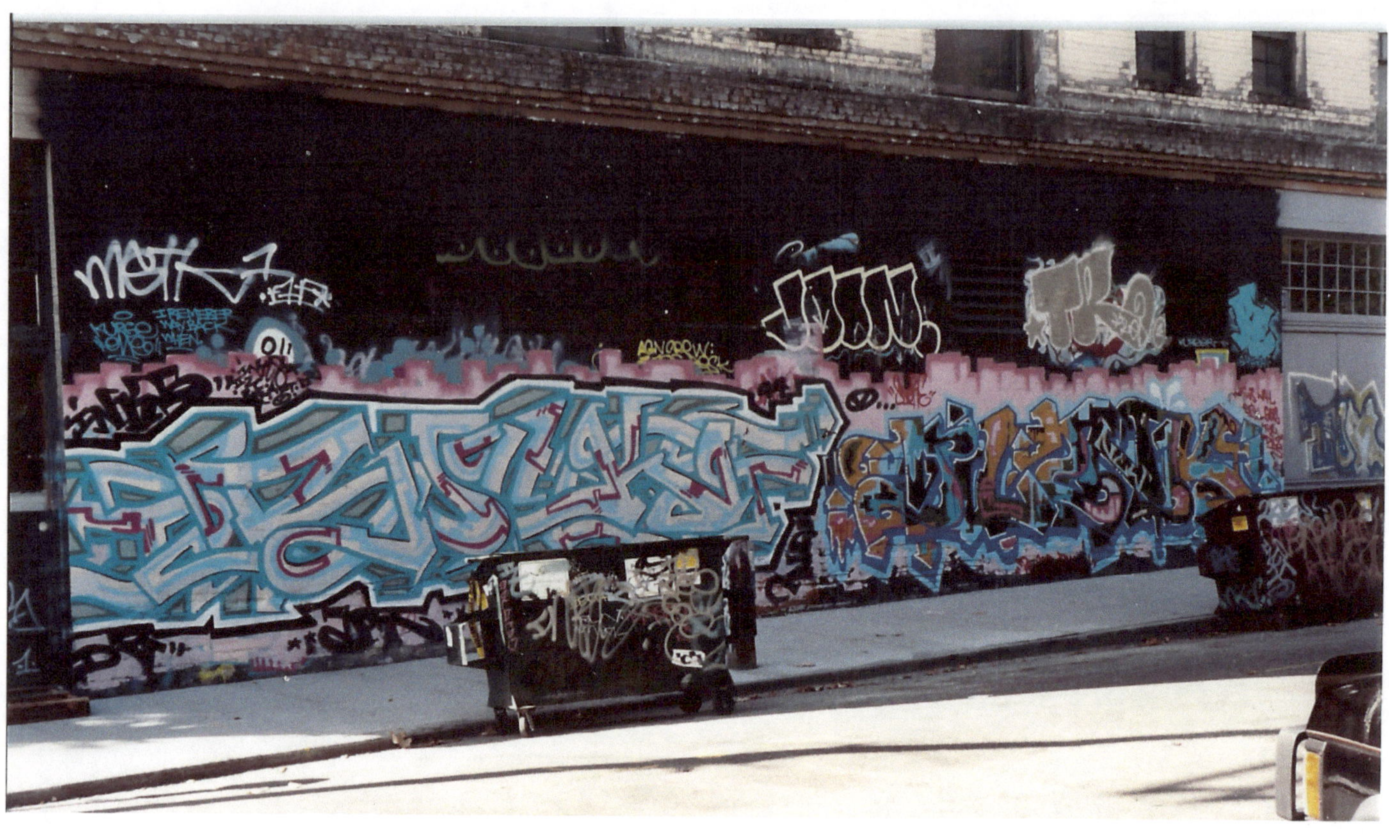

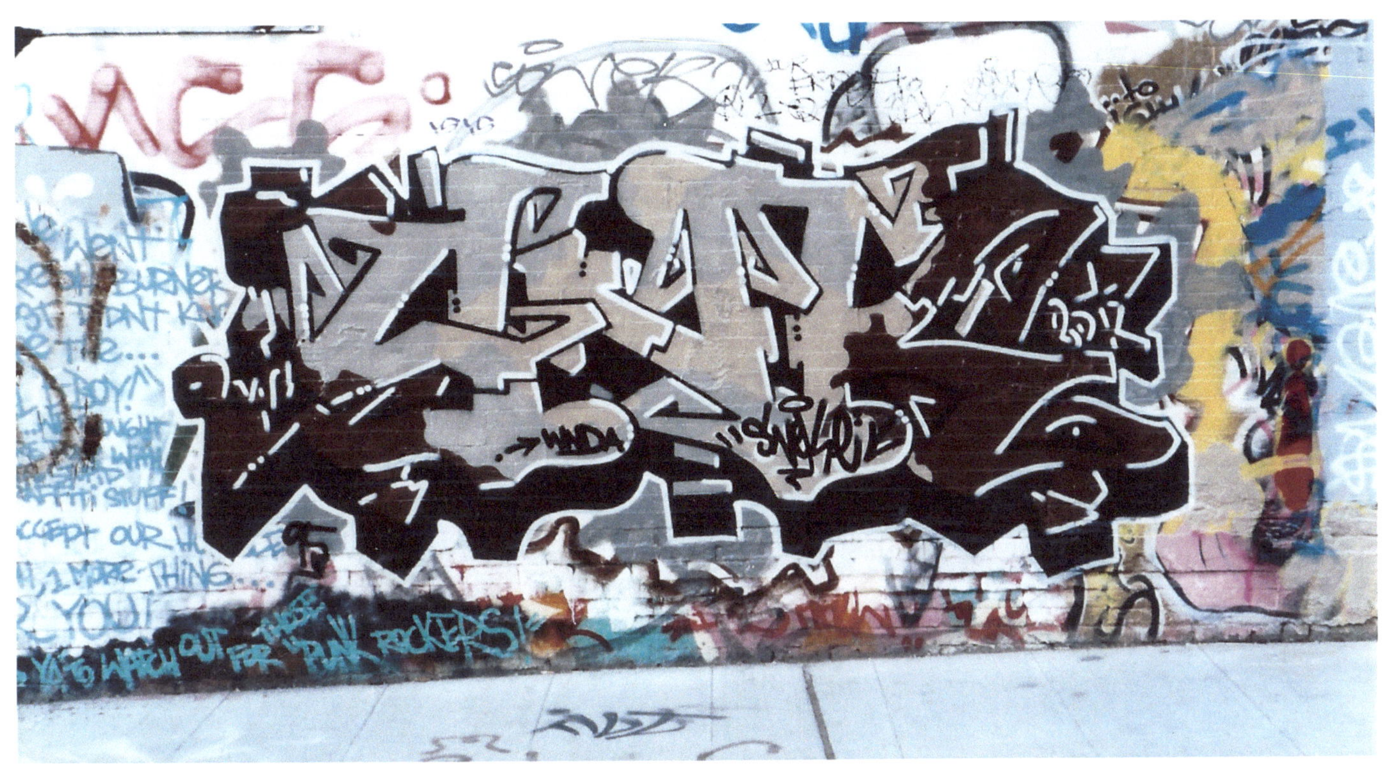
WANDA
WATCH OUT FOR THESE PUNK ROCKERS!

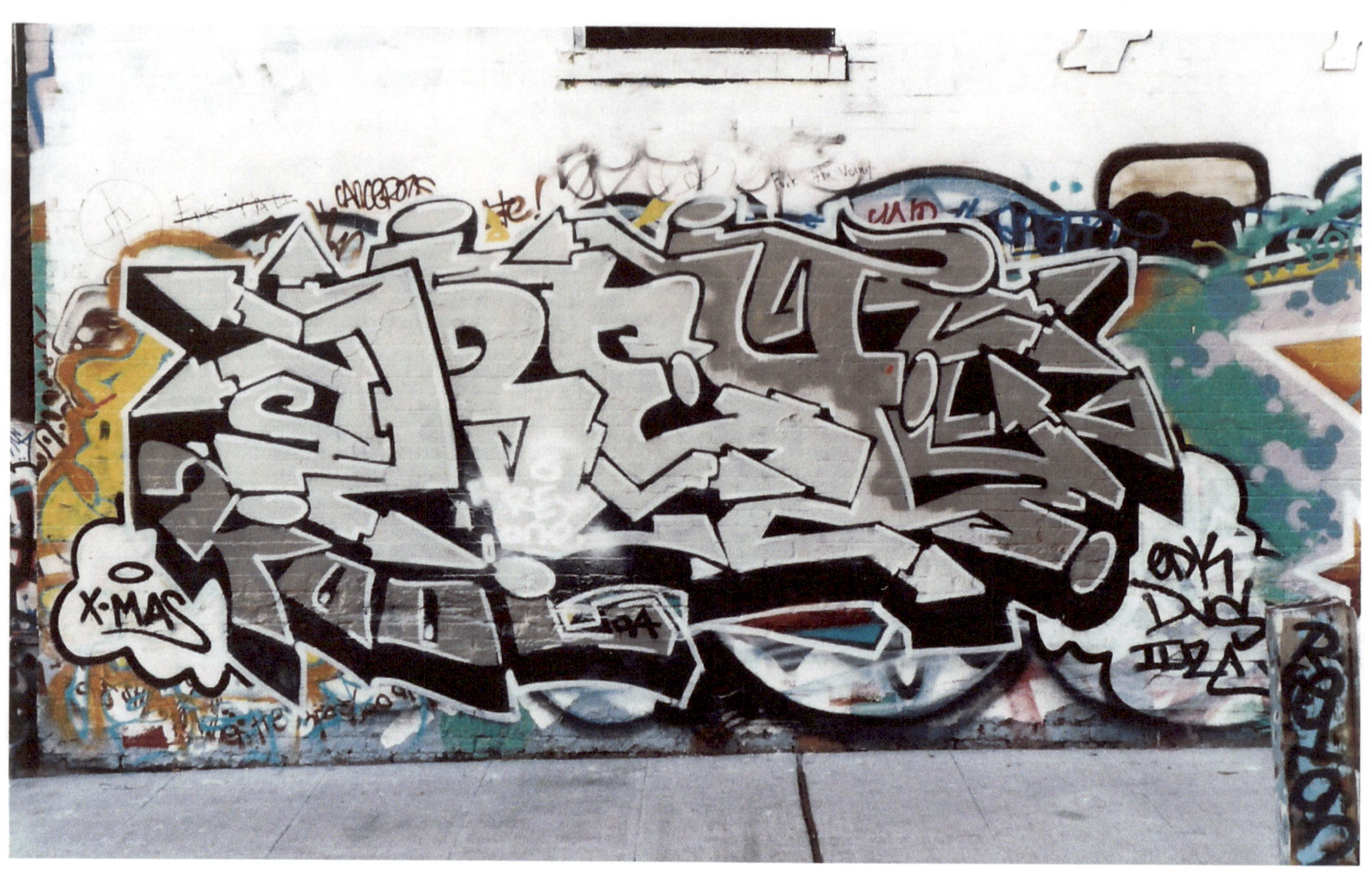
X-MAS

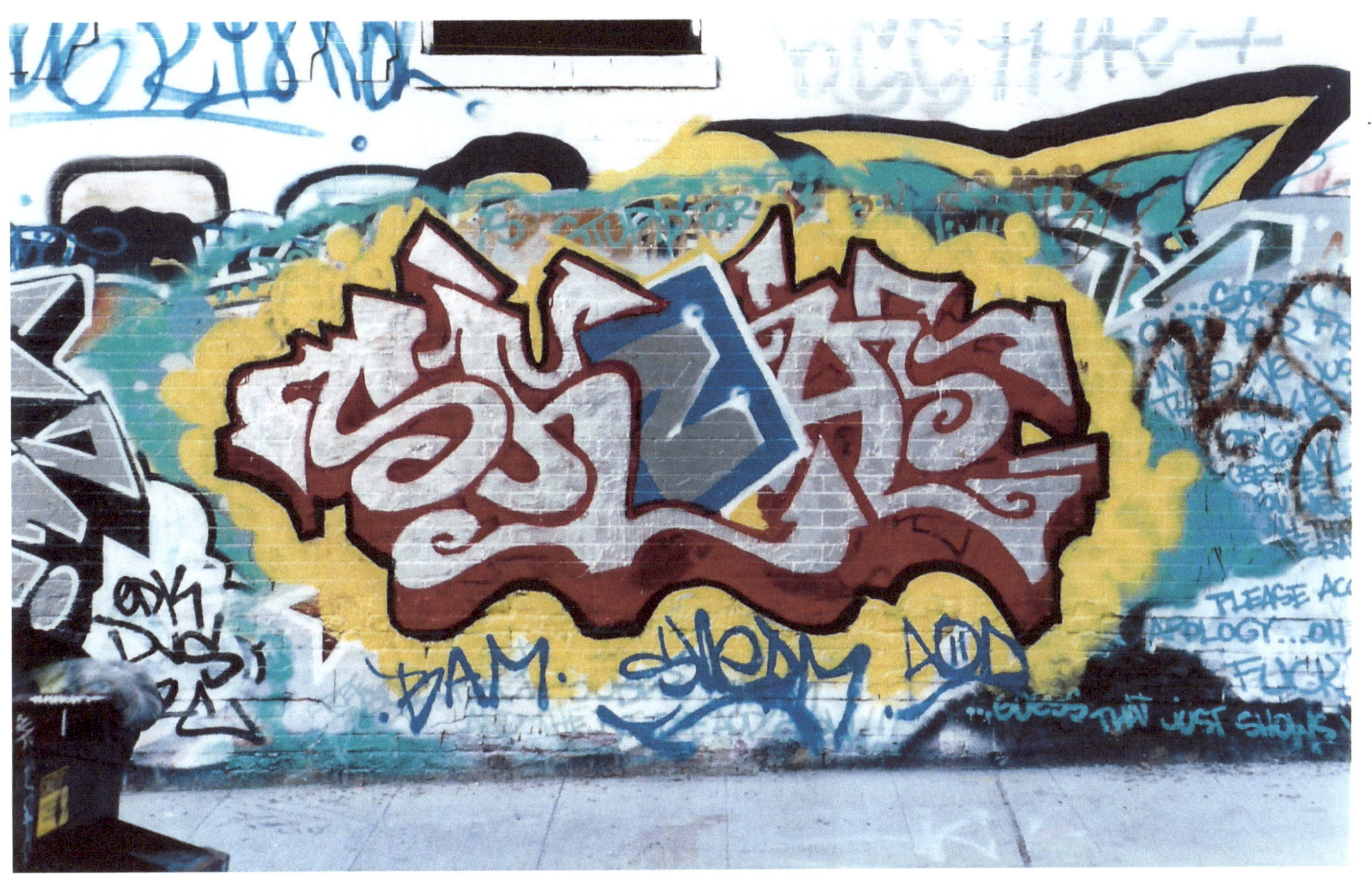

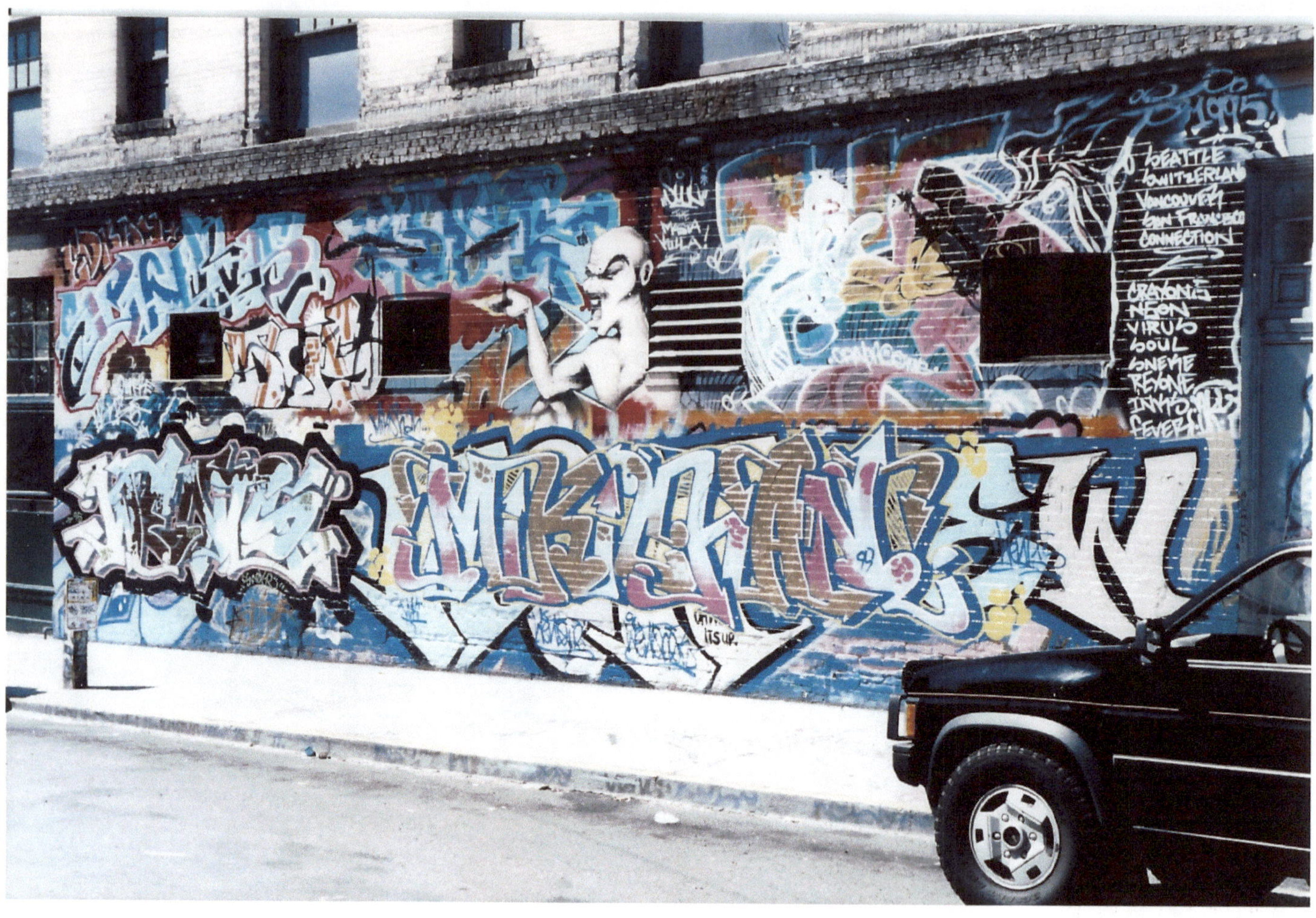
1995
SEATTLE
VANCOUVER
CONNECTION
CRAYONE
NEON
VIRUS
SOUL
SNEKE
REYONE
FEVER
its up.

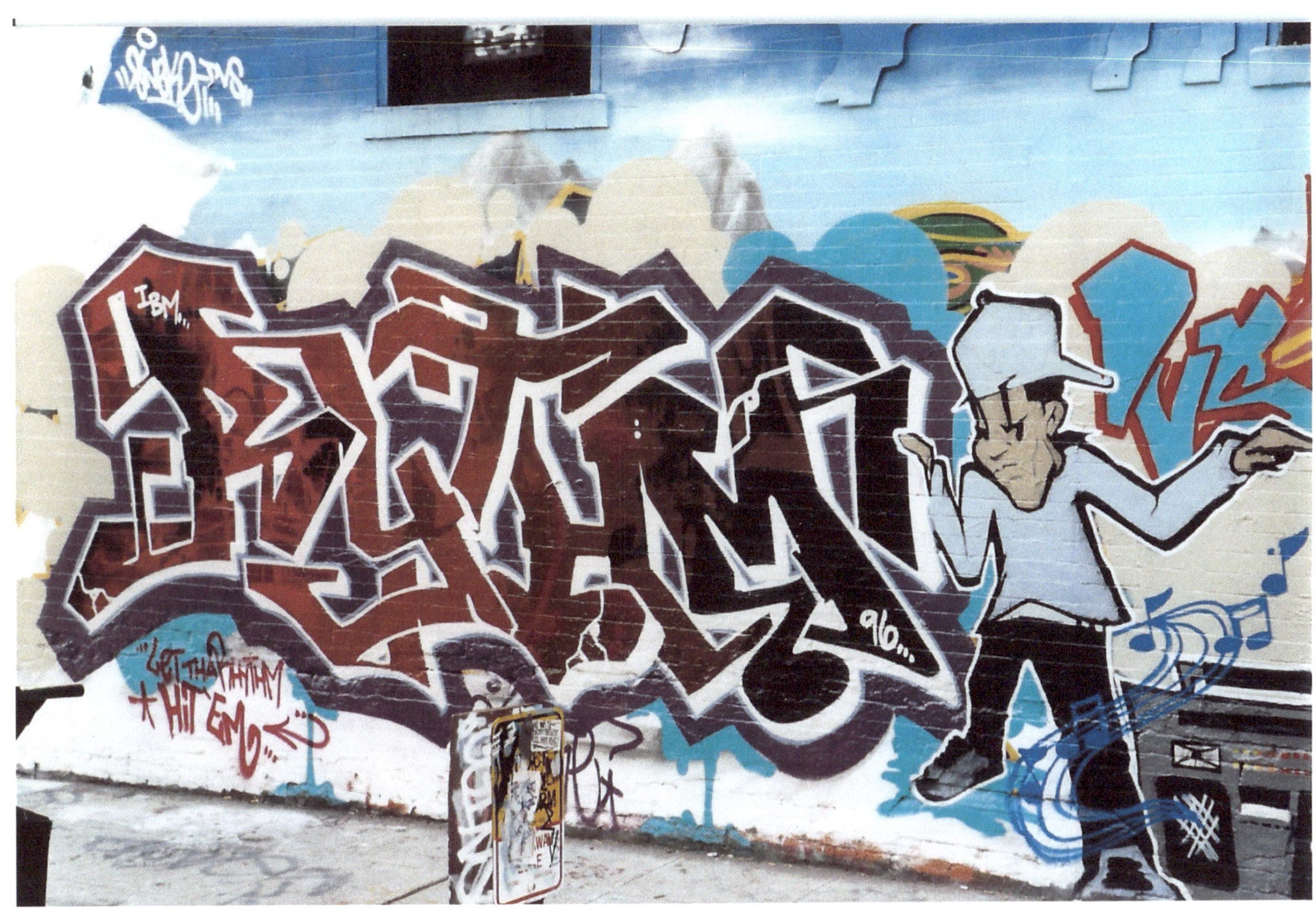
IBM
GET THA RHYTHM
HIT EM
96

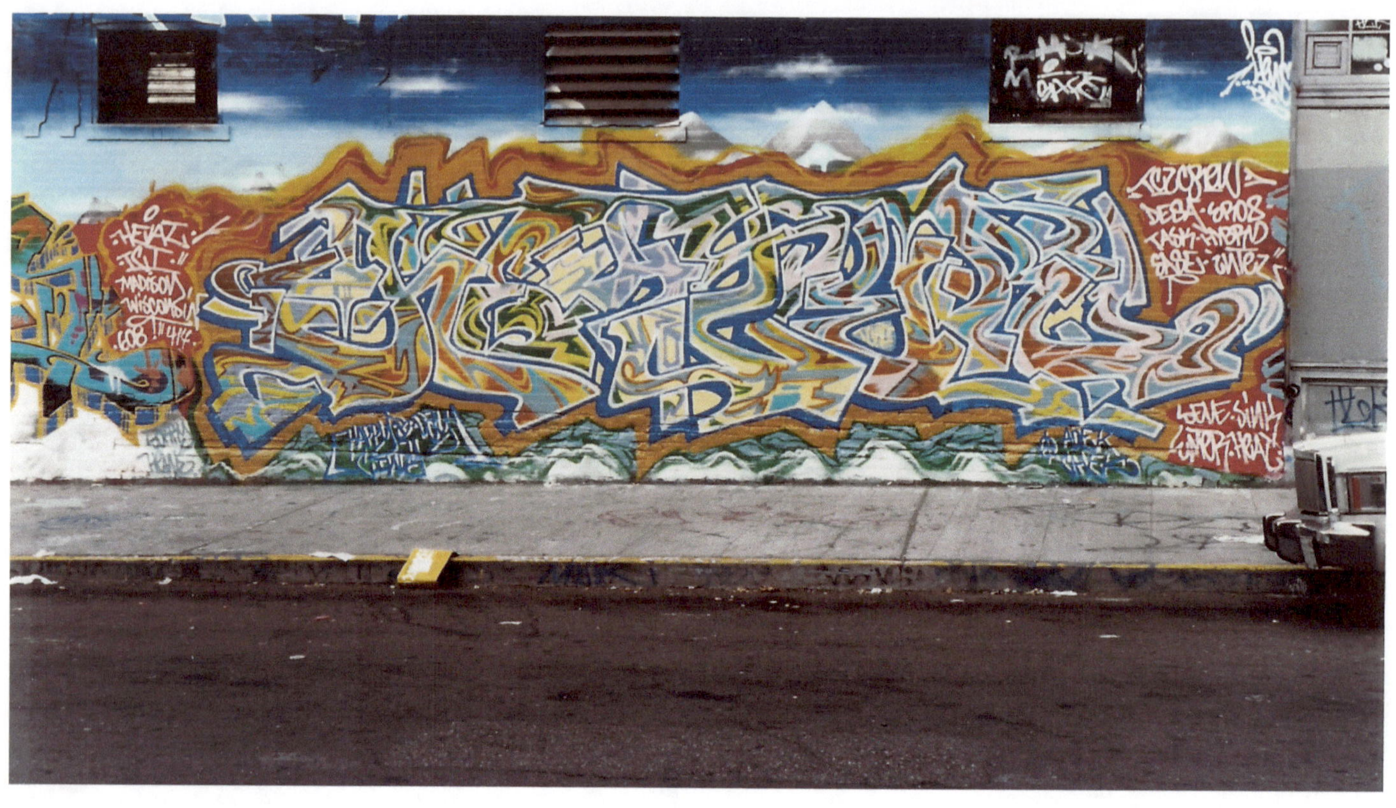
MADISON
WISCONSIN
608 414

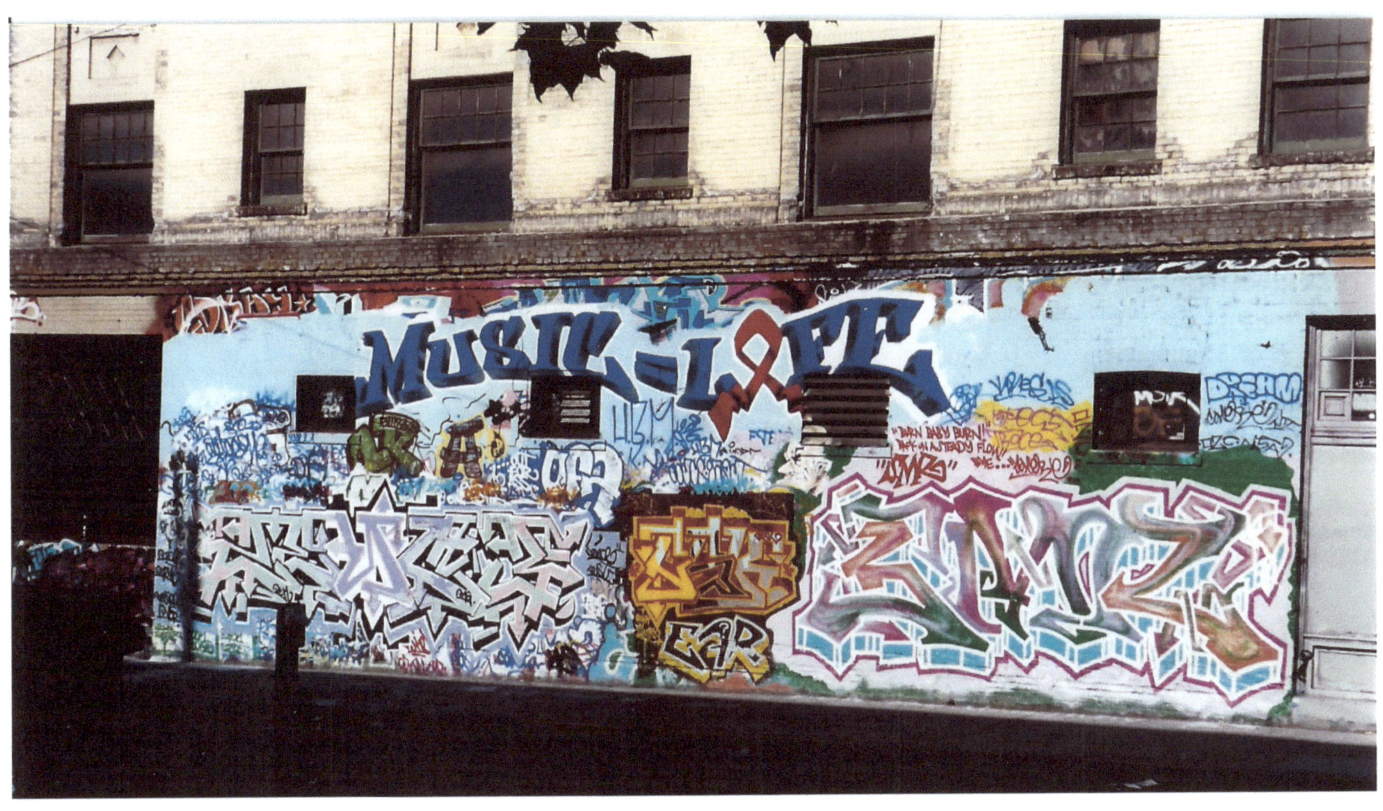

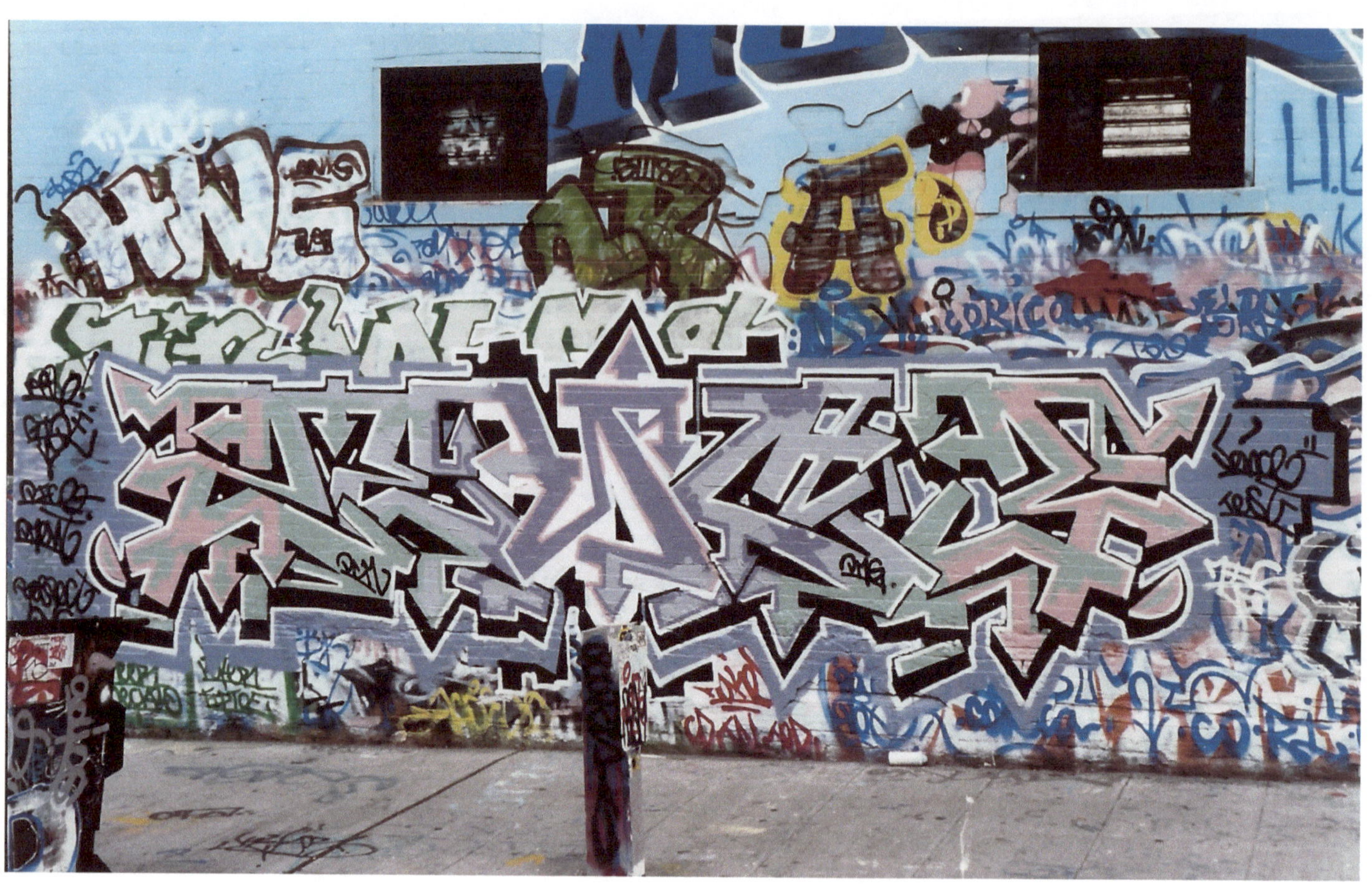

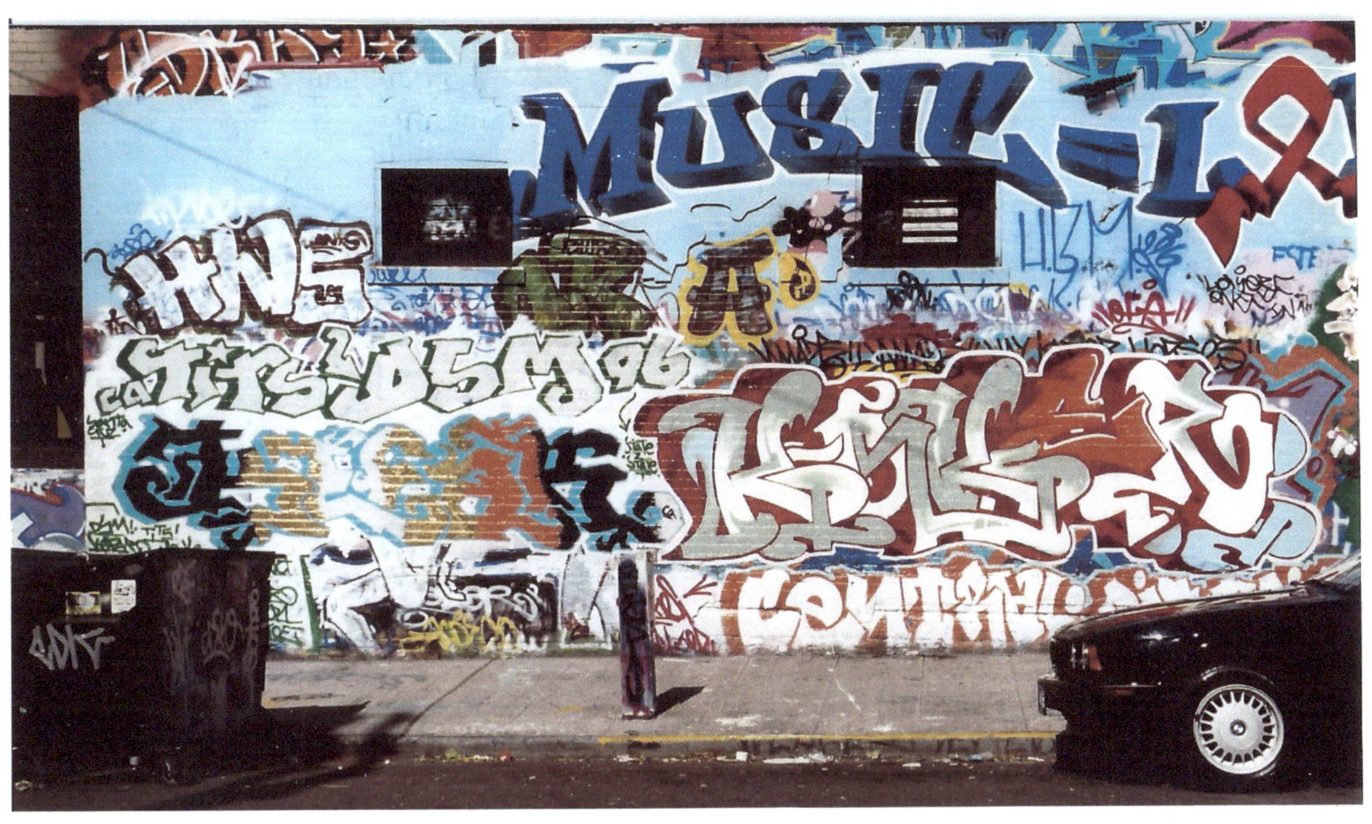
MUSIC-L

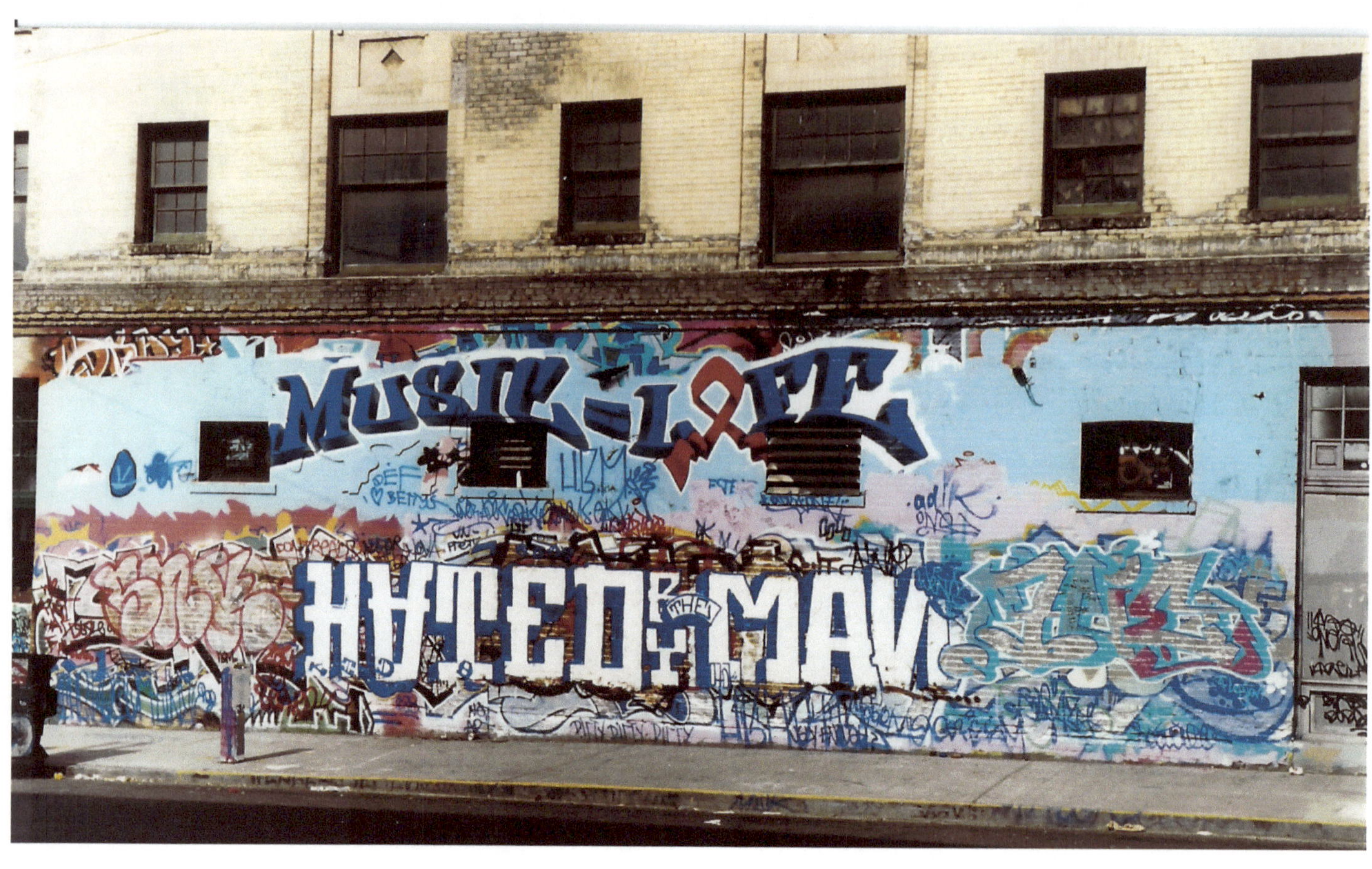

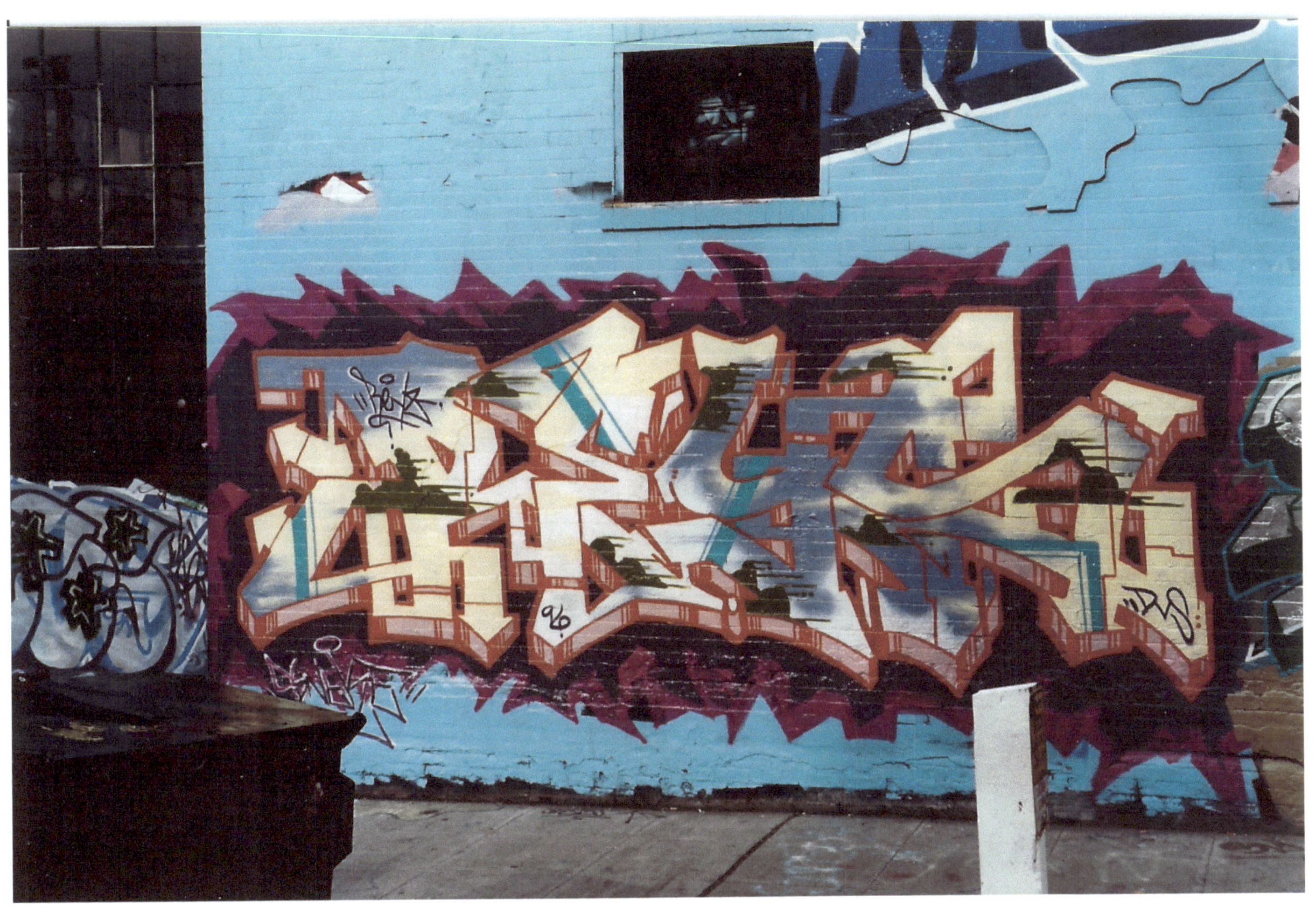

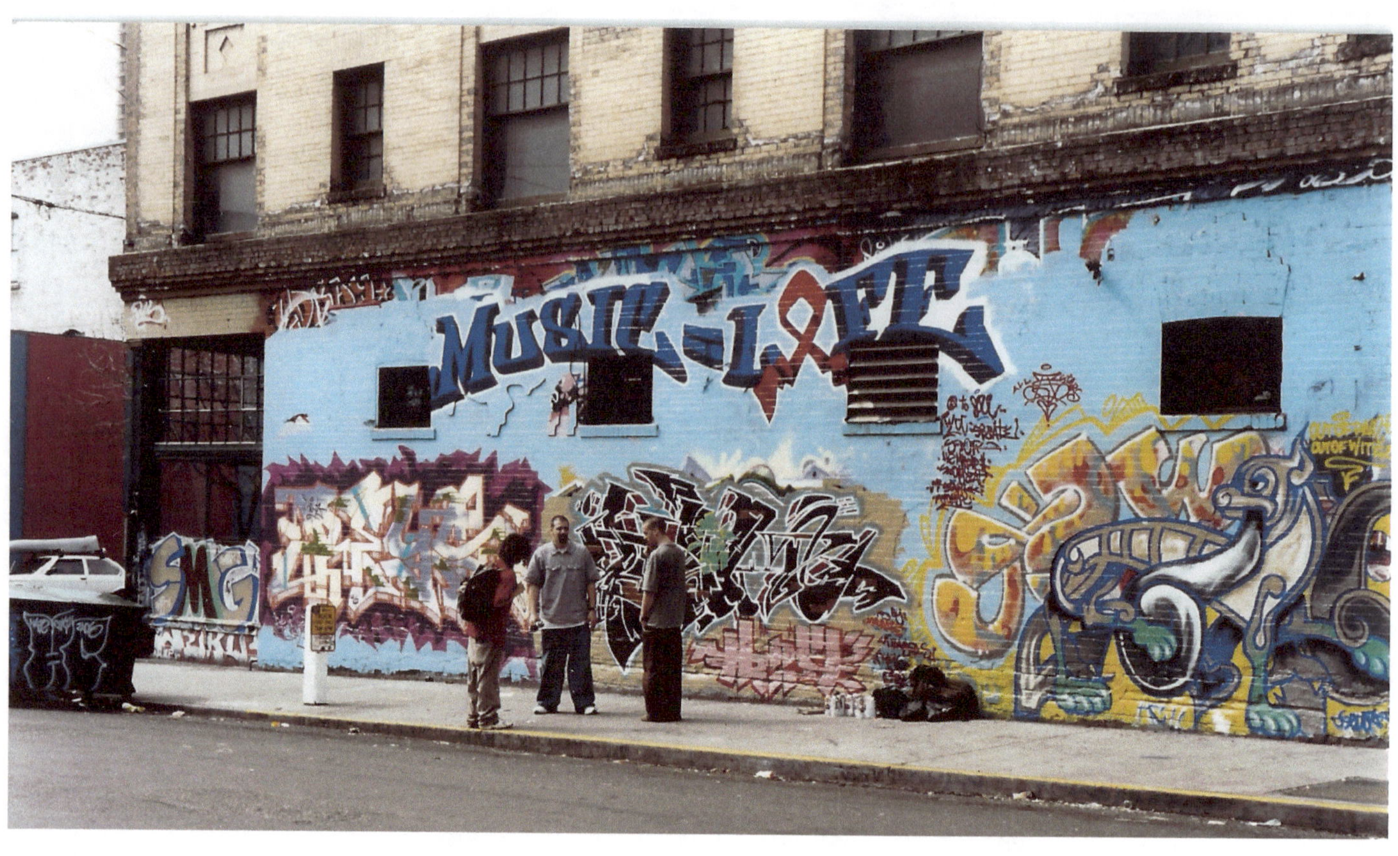
SMG

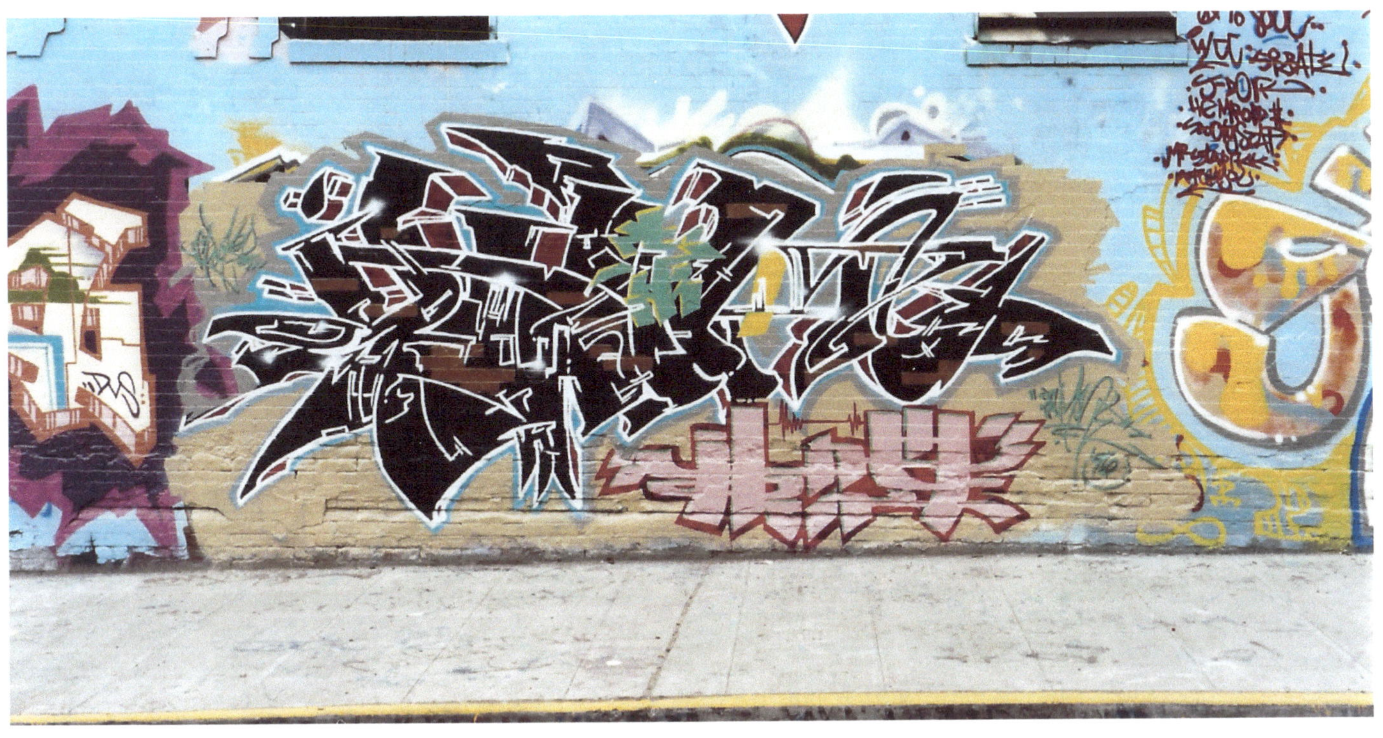

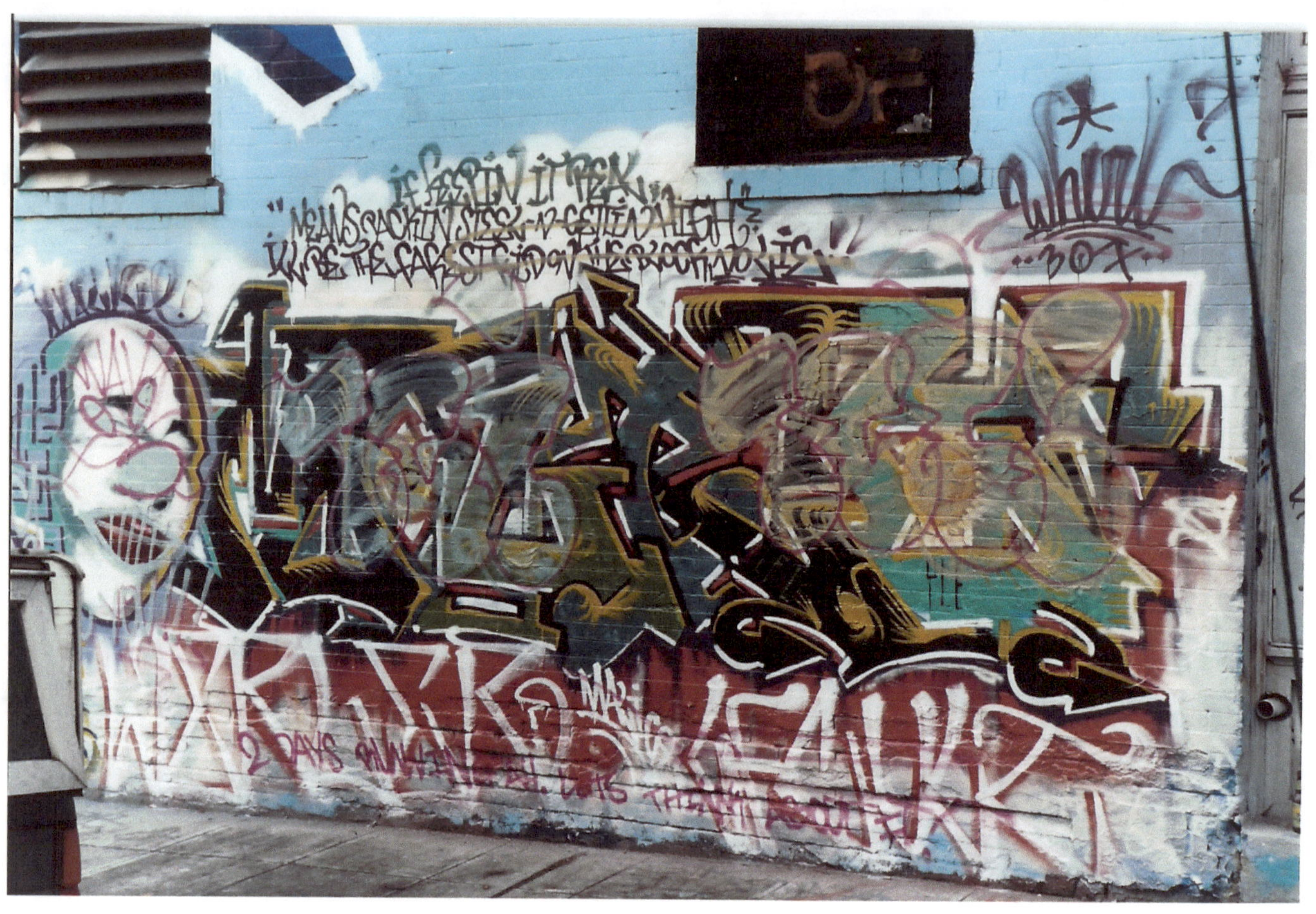

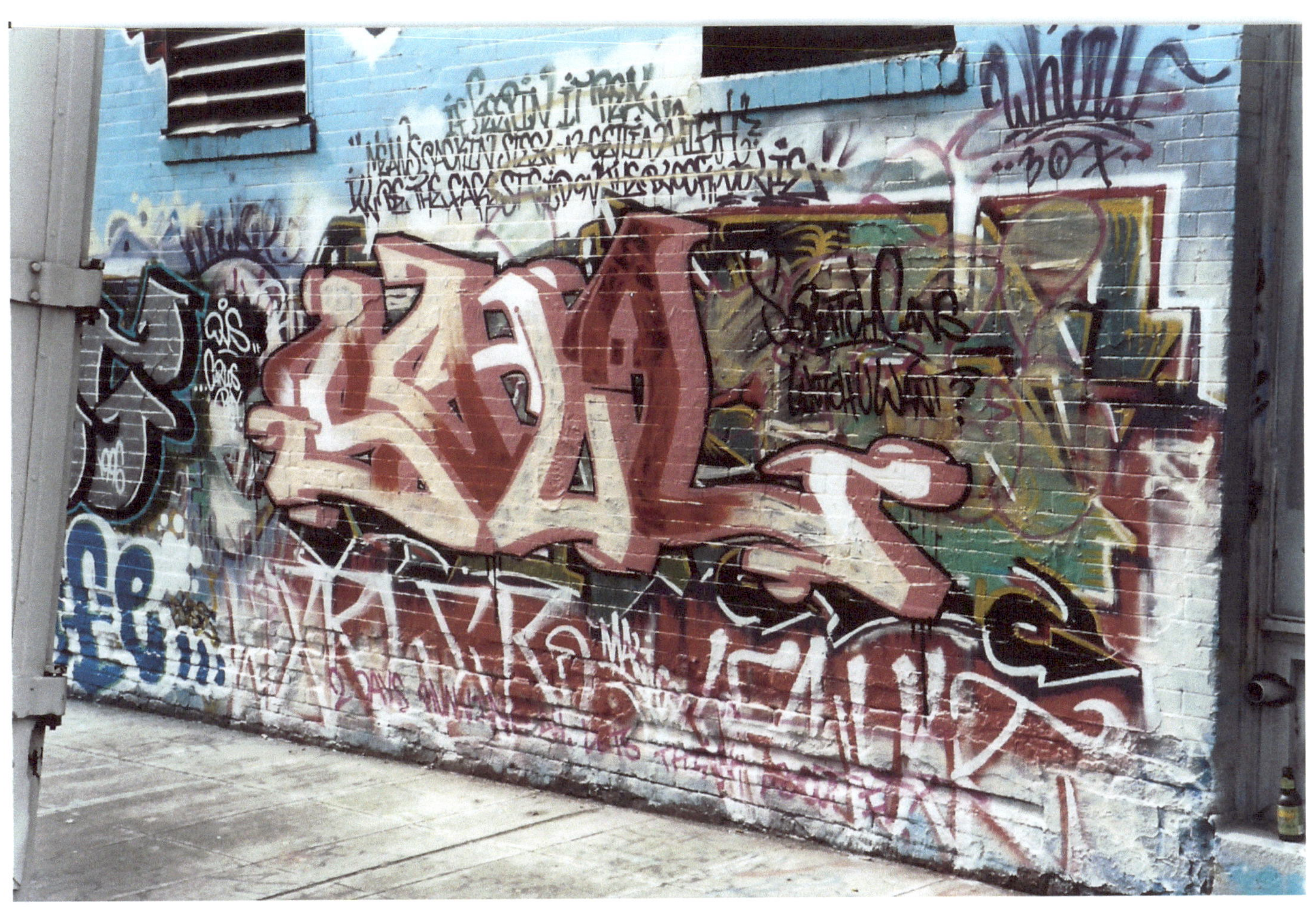

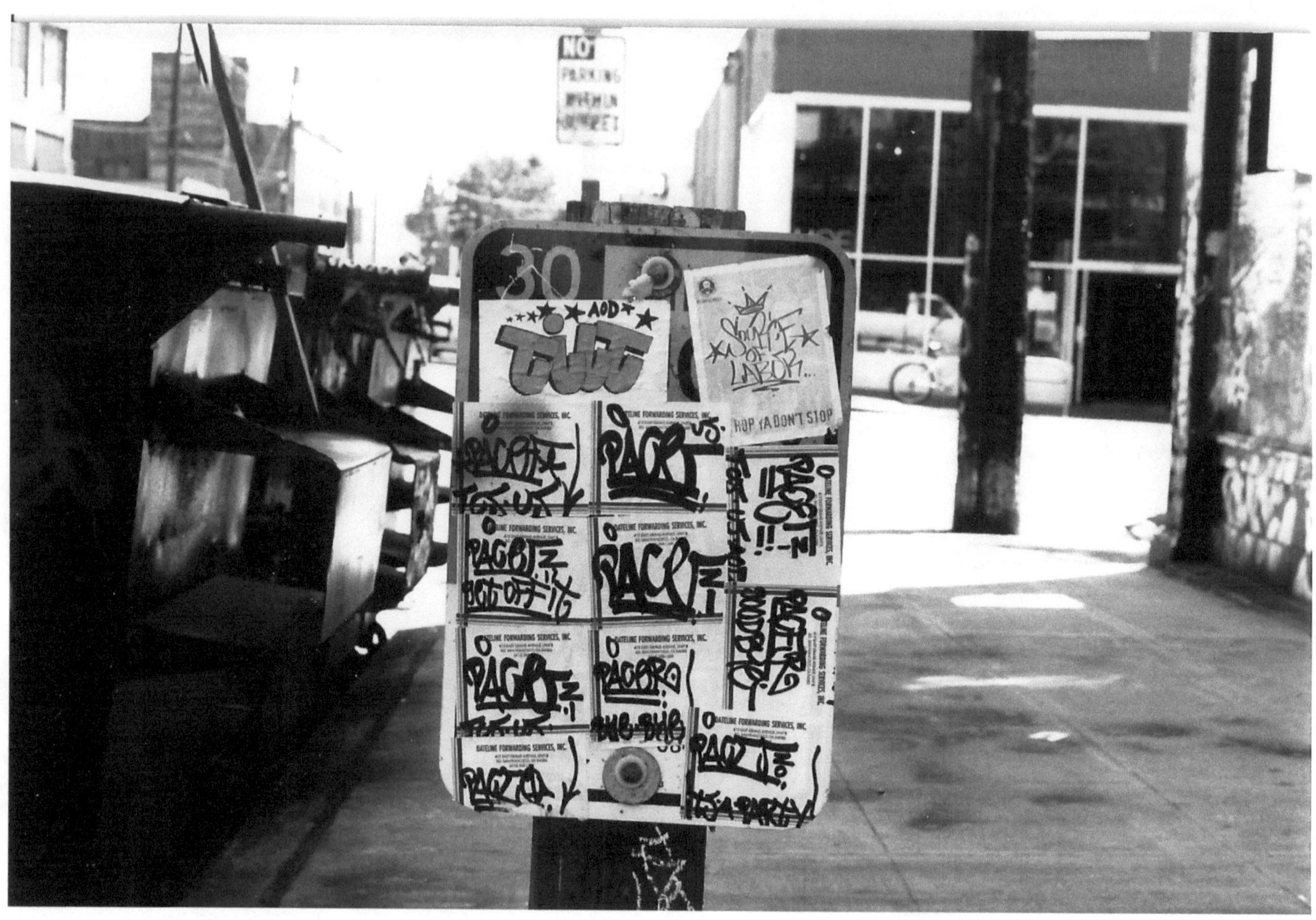
NO
30
AOD
HOP YA DON'T STOP
DATELINE FORWARDING SERVICES, INC.

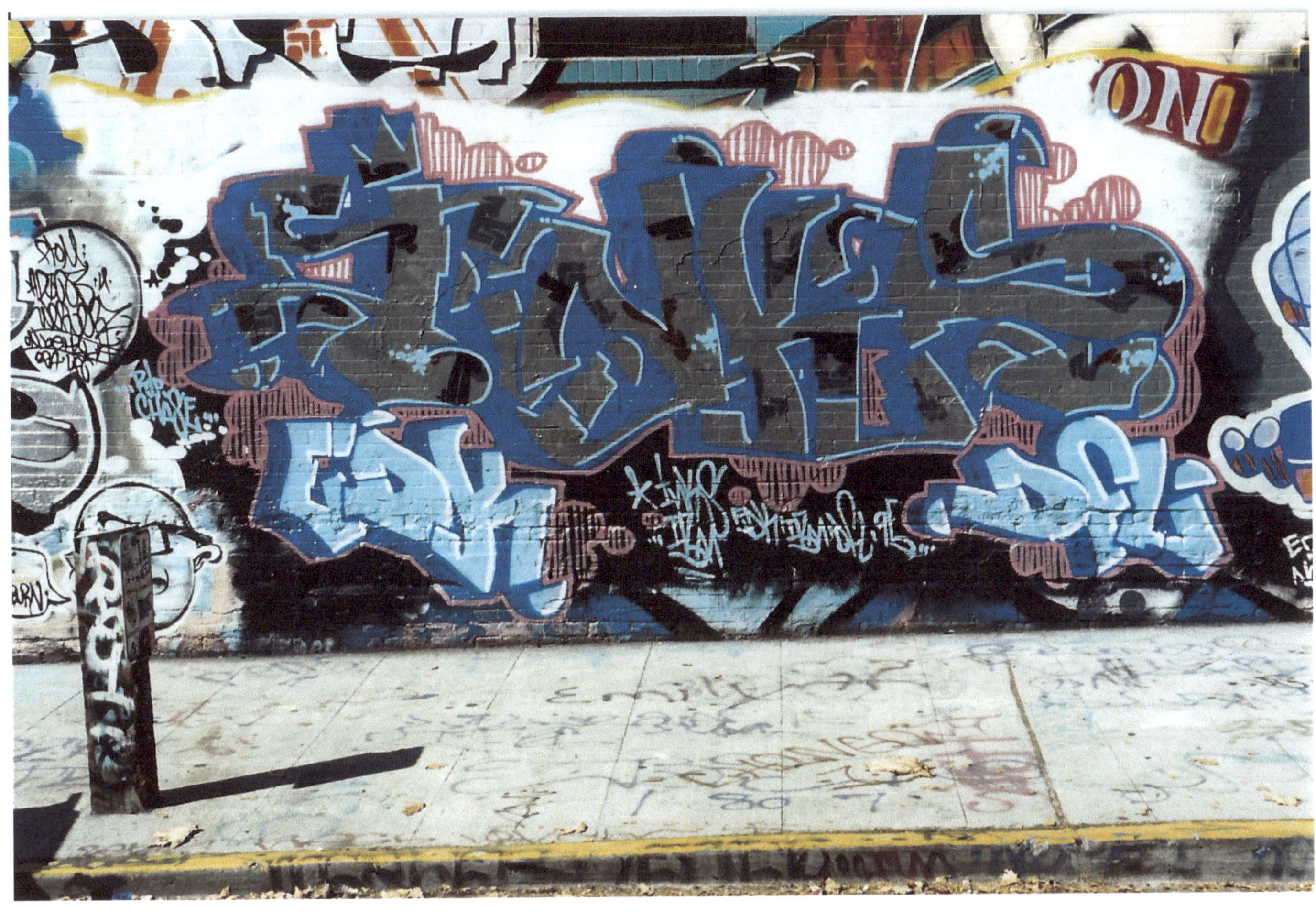

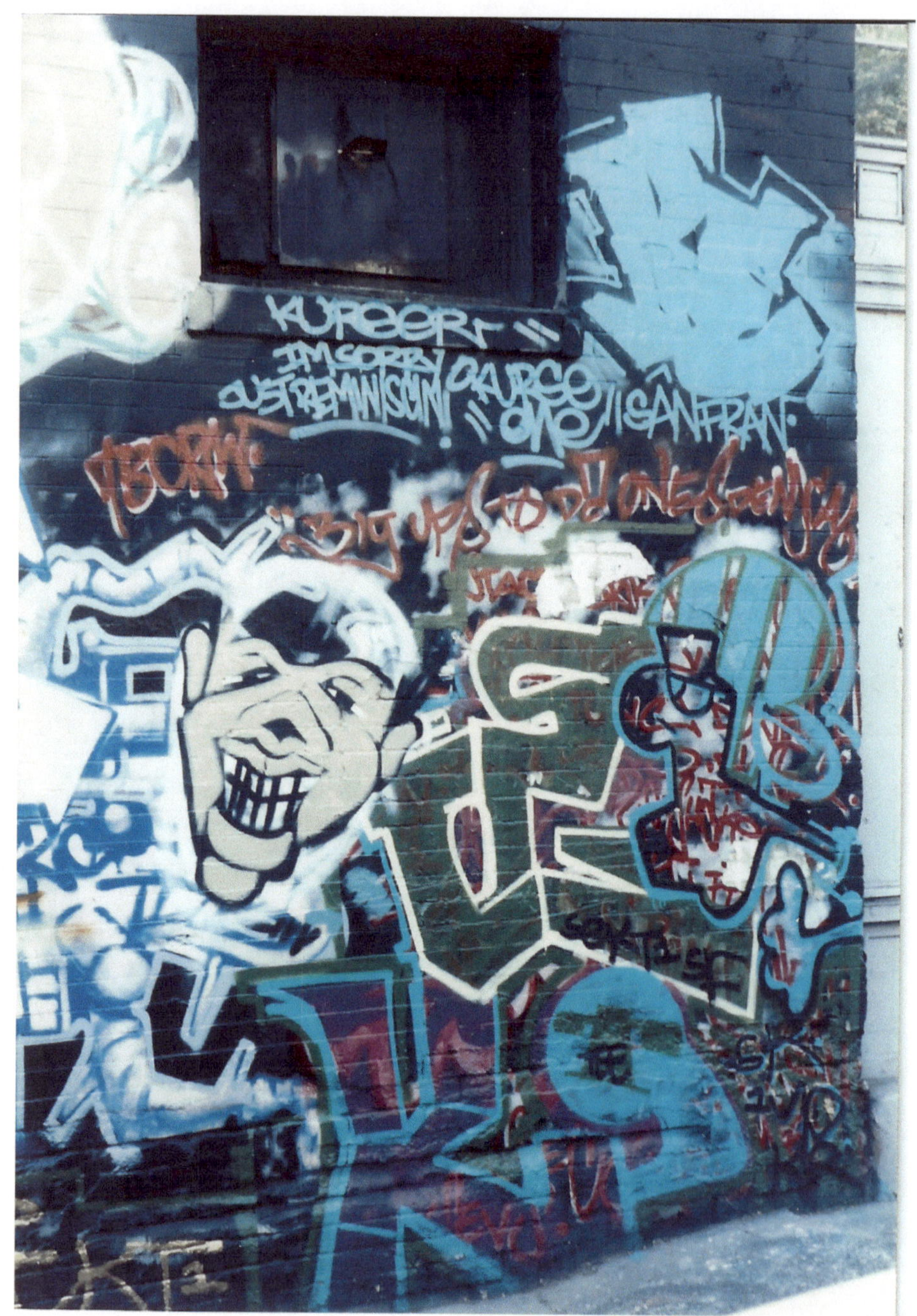

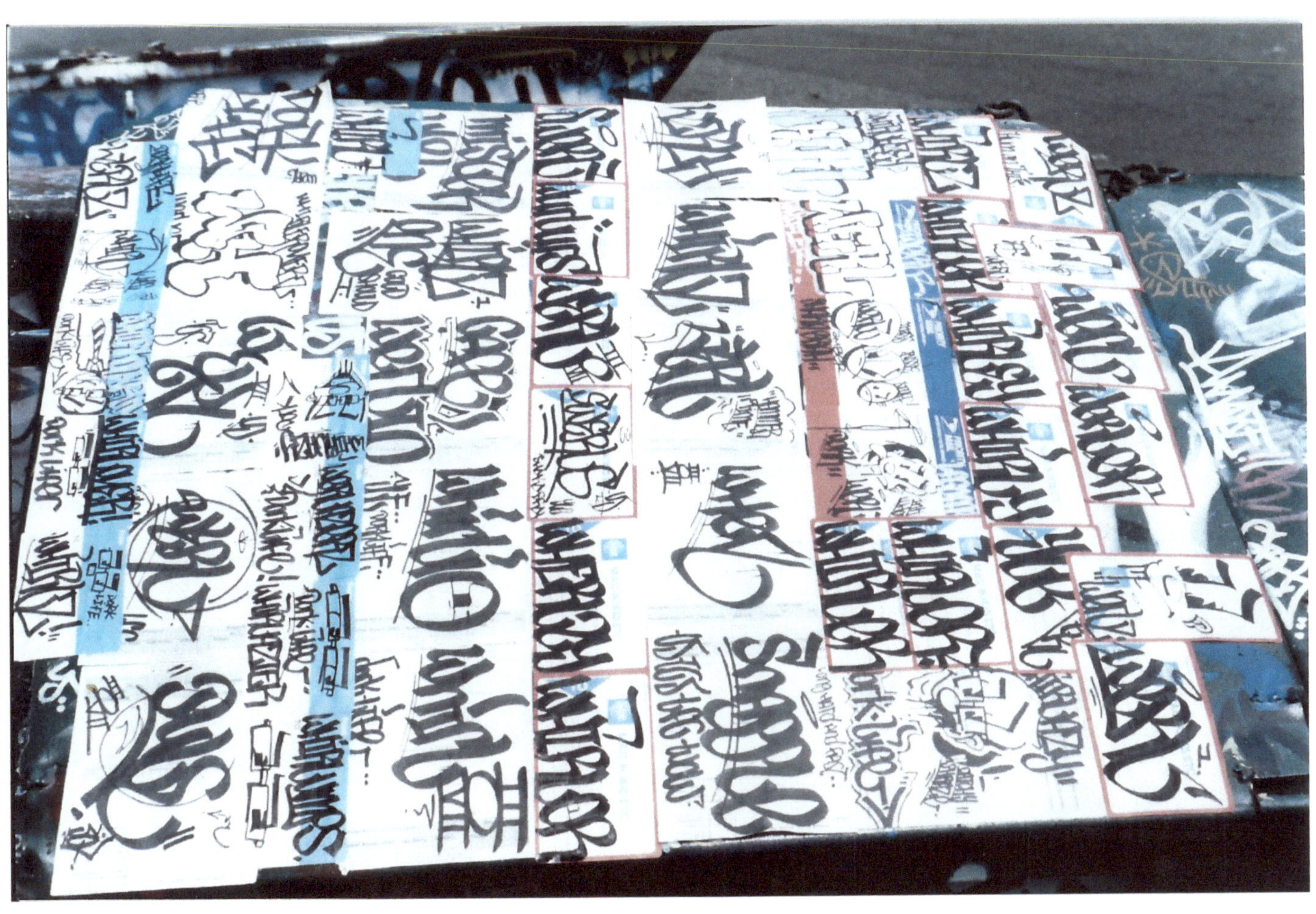

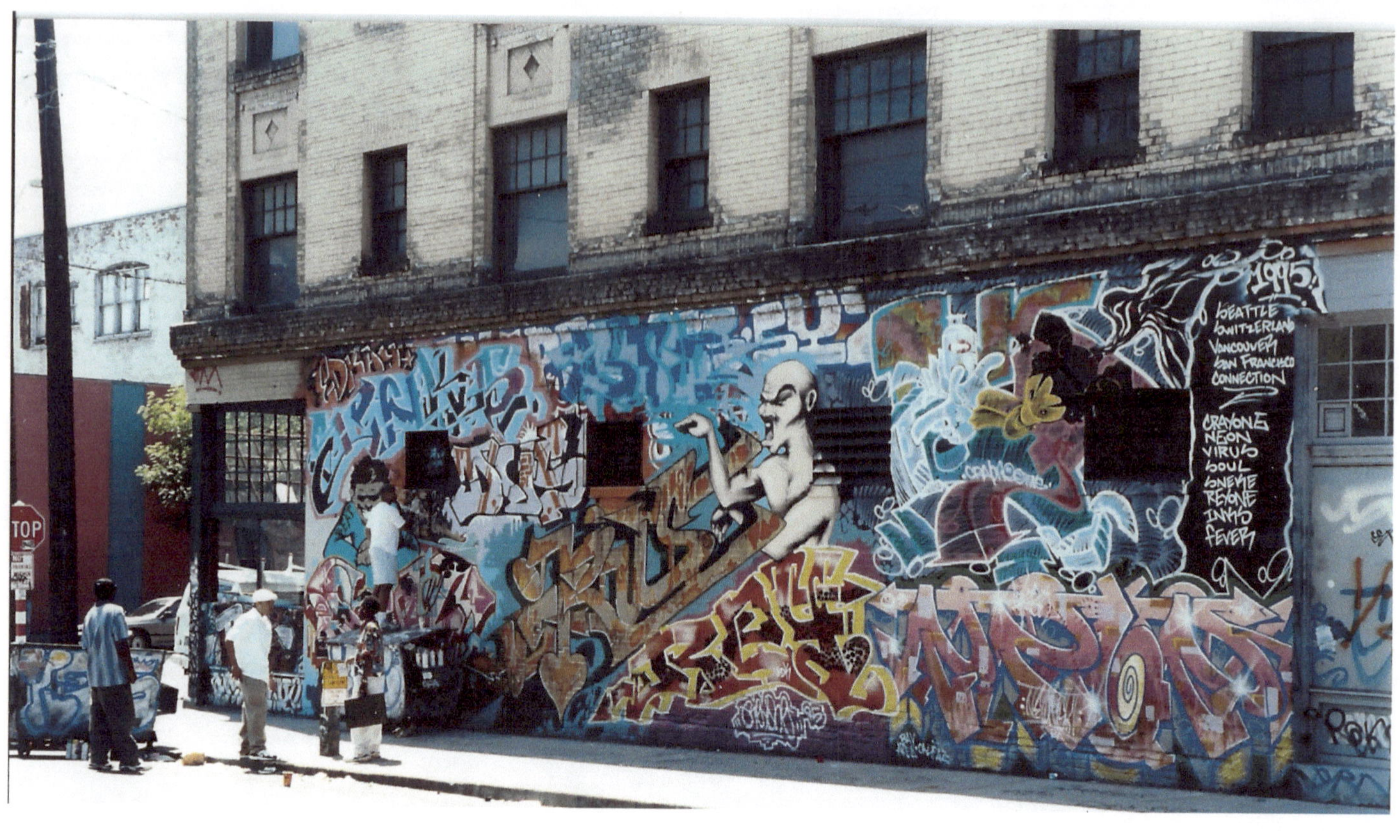
1995
SEATTLE
SWITZERLAND
VANCOUVER
SAN FRANCISCO
CONNECTION
CRAYONE
NEON
VIRUS
SOUL
ONEKIE
REYONE
INKS
FEVER
STOP

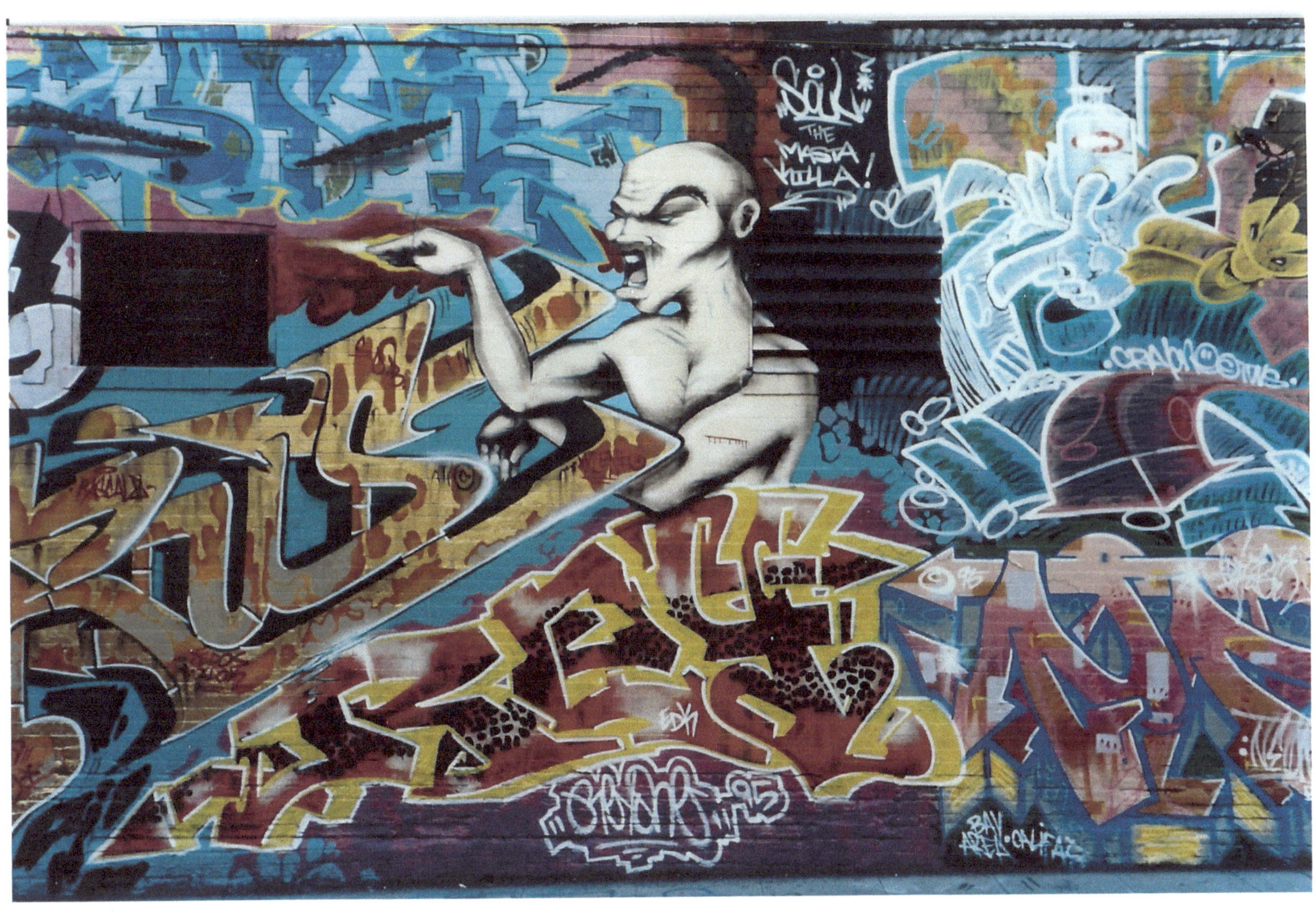
Soil
THE
MASTA
KILLA!

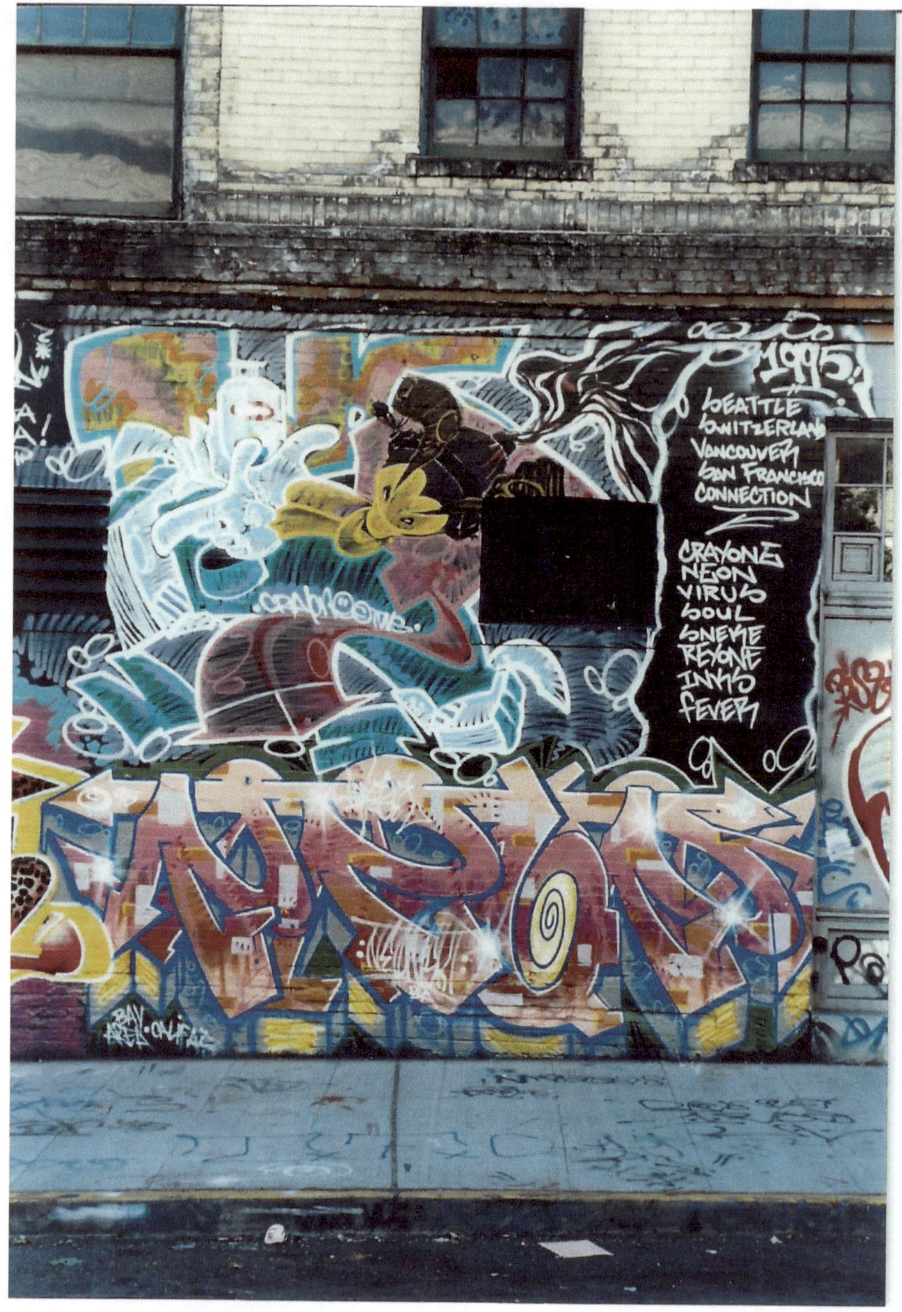
1995
SEATTLE
VANCOUVER
SAN FRANCISCO
CONNECTION
CRAYONE
NEON
VIRUS
SOUL
REYONE
FEVER

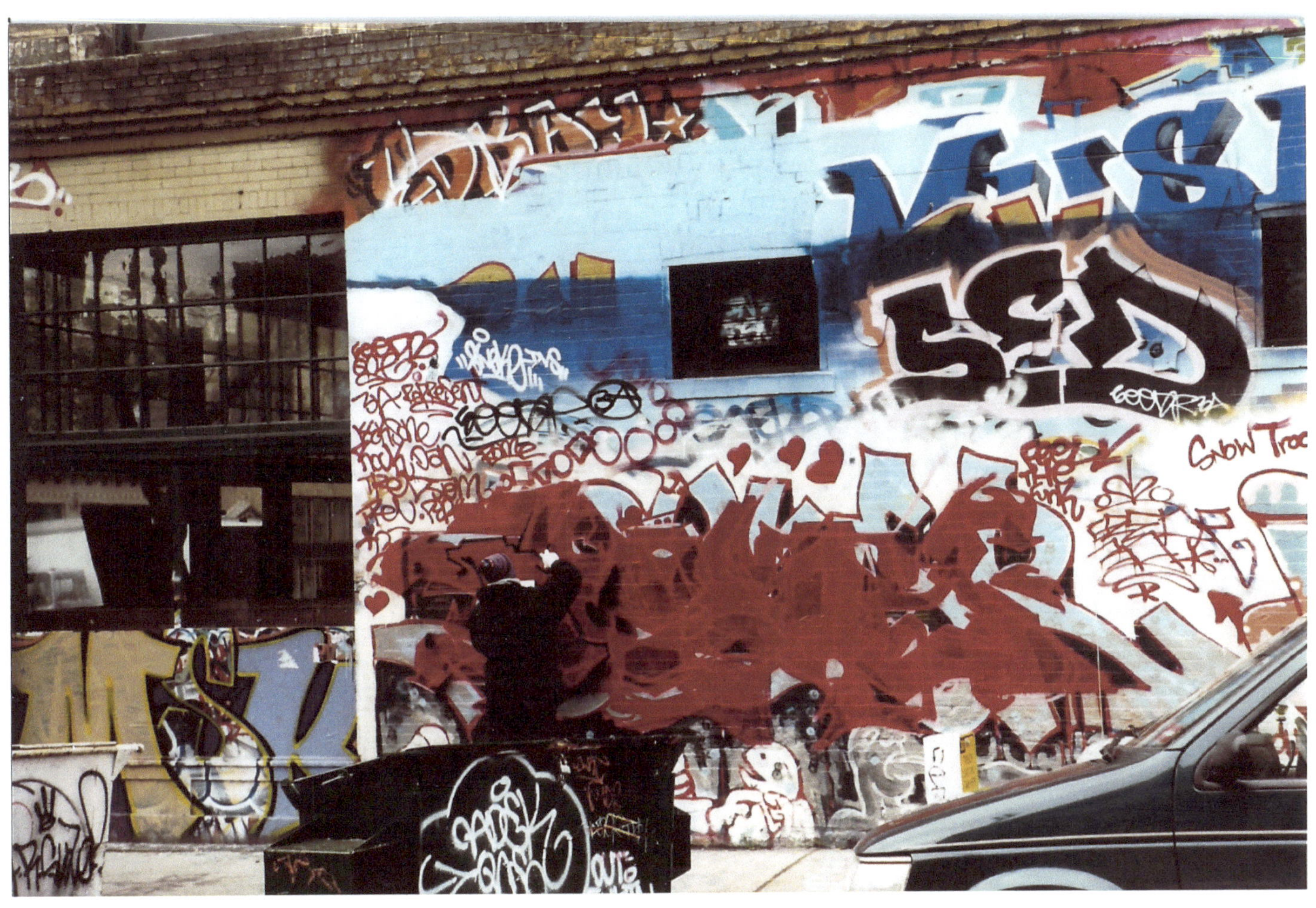

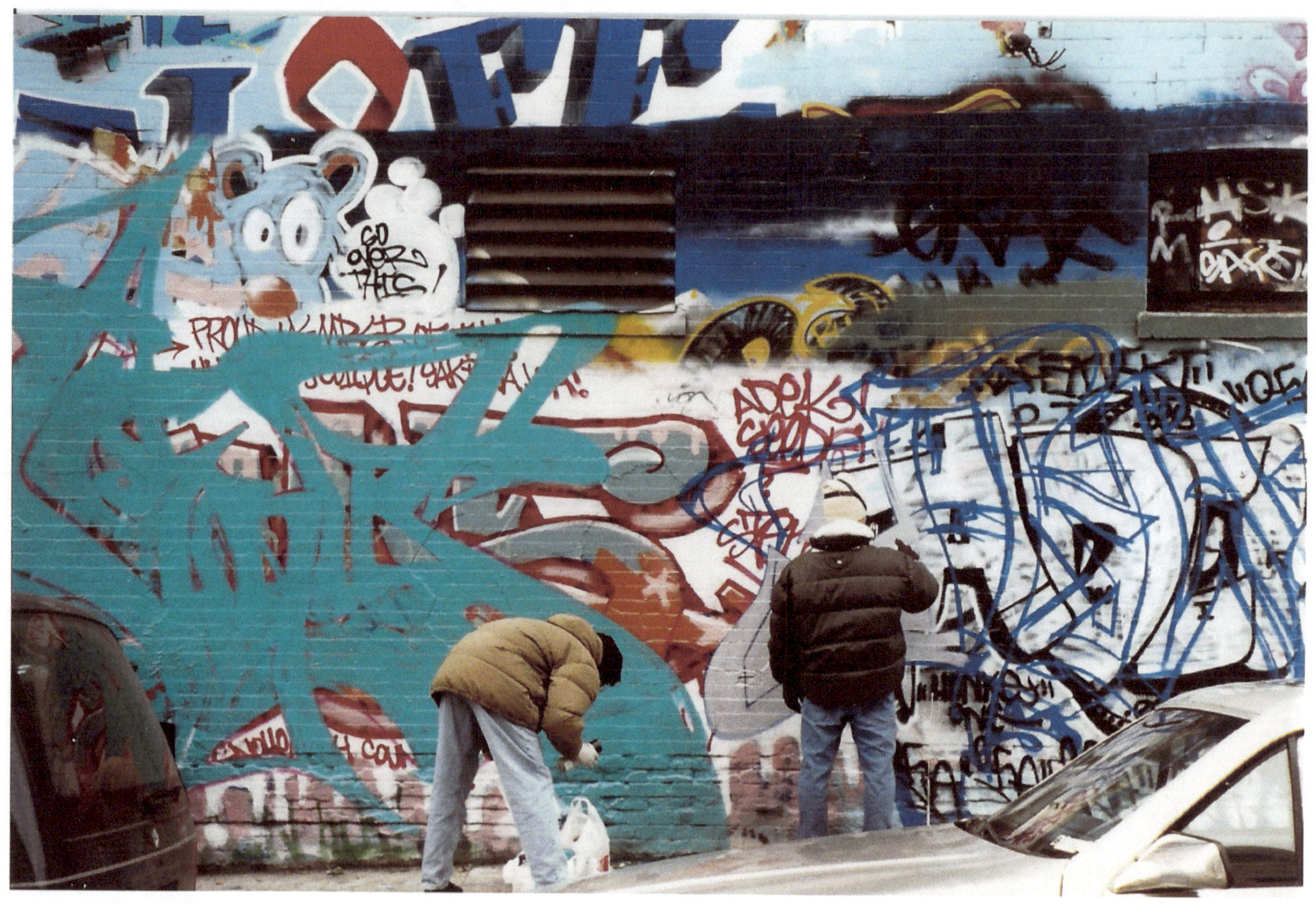
GO OVER THIS!

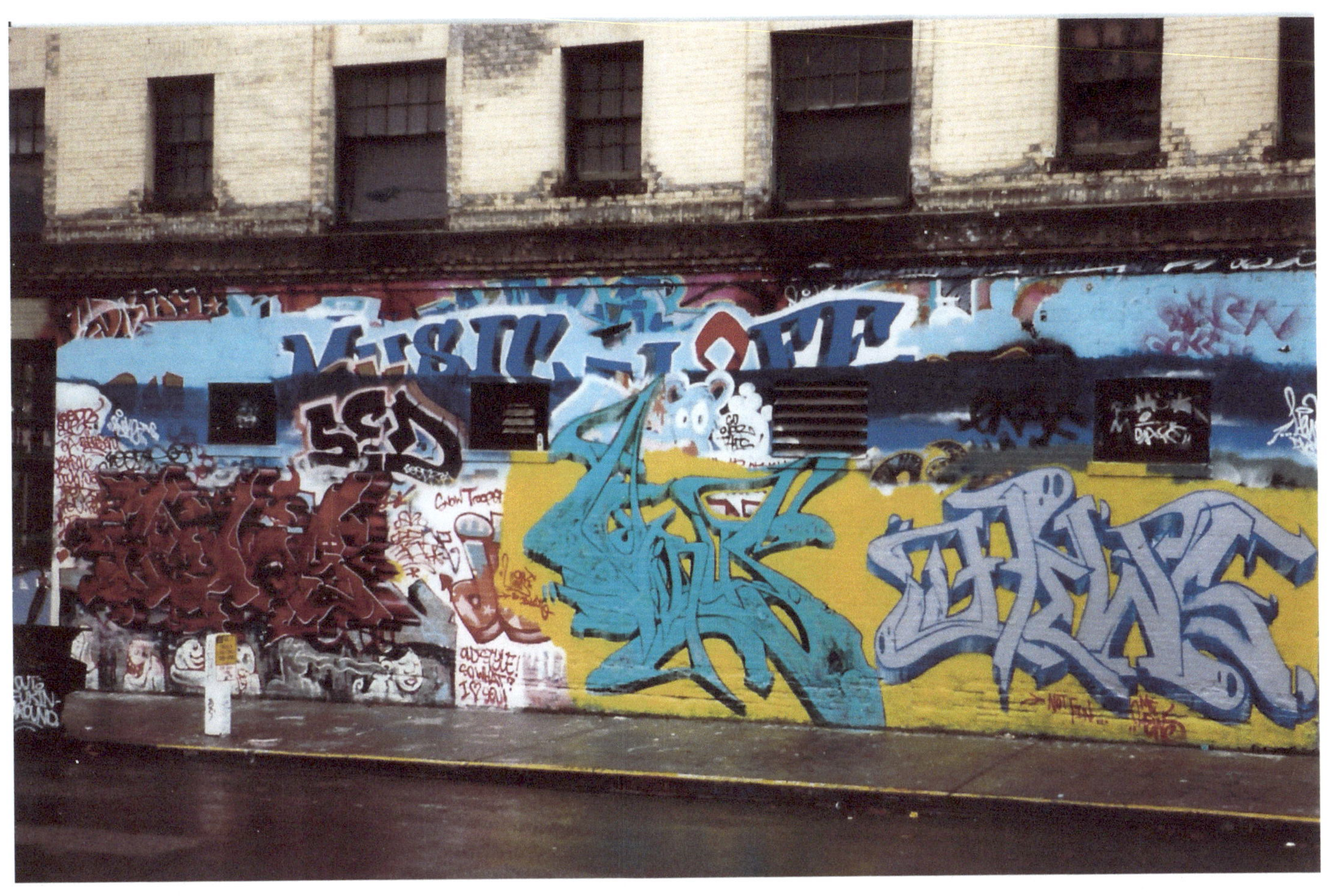

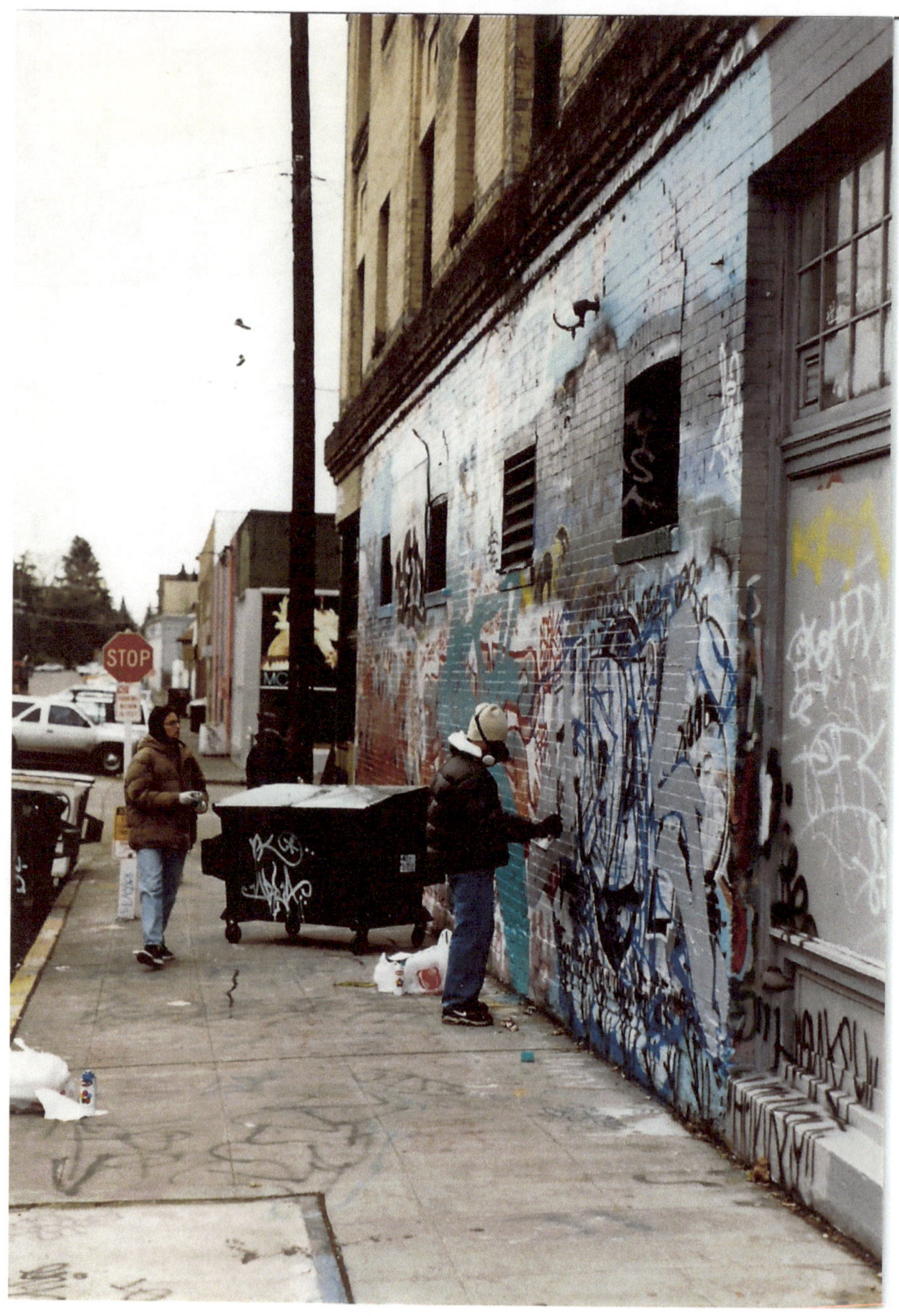
STOP

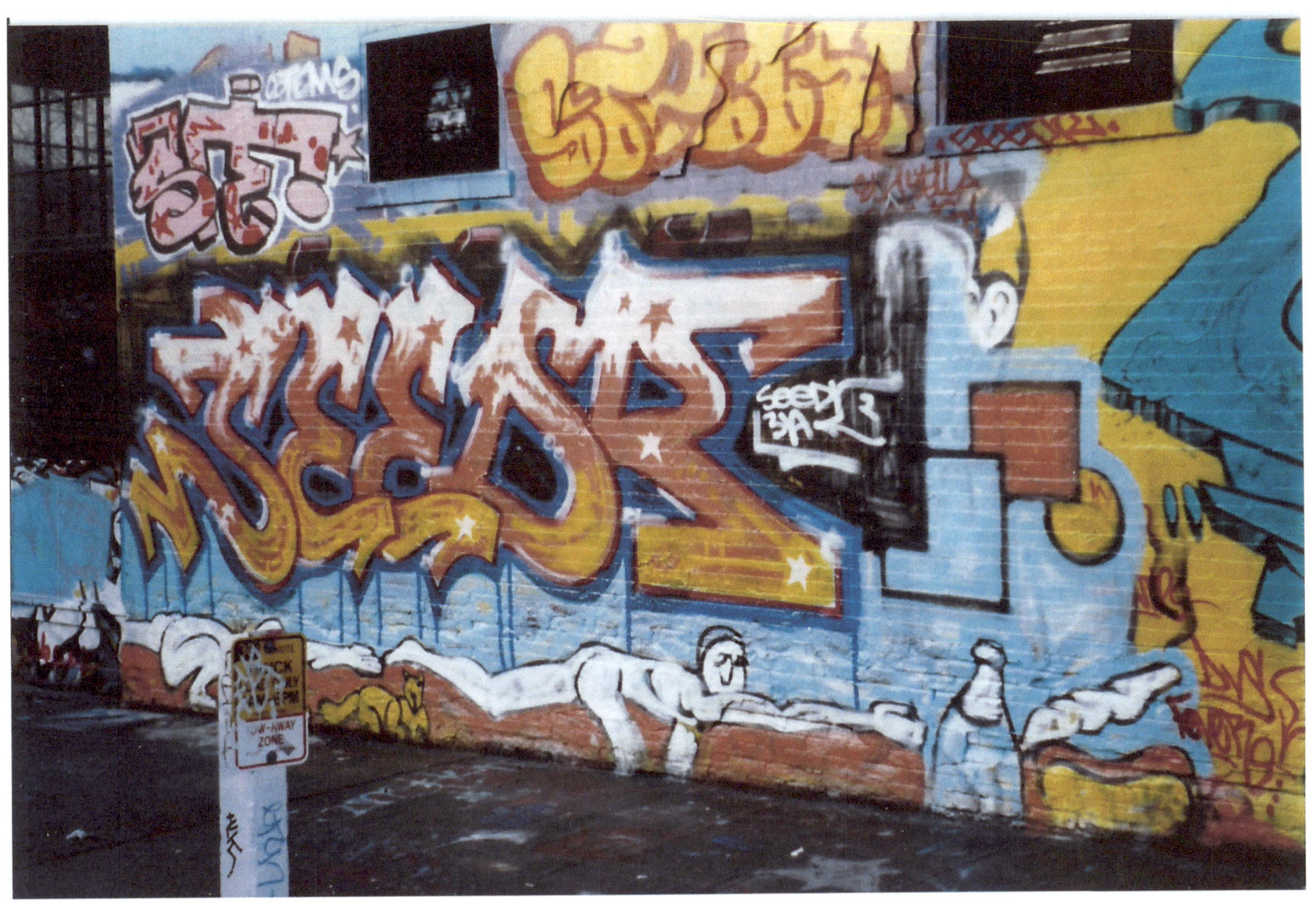
ZONE

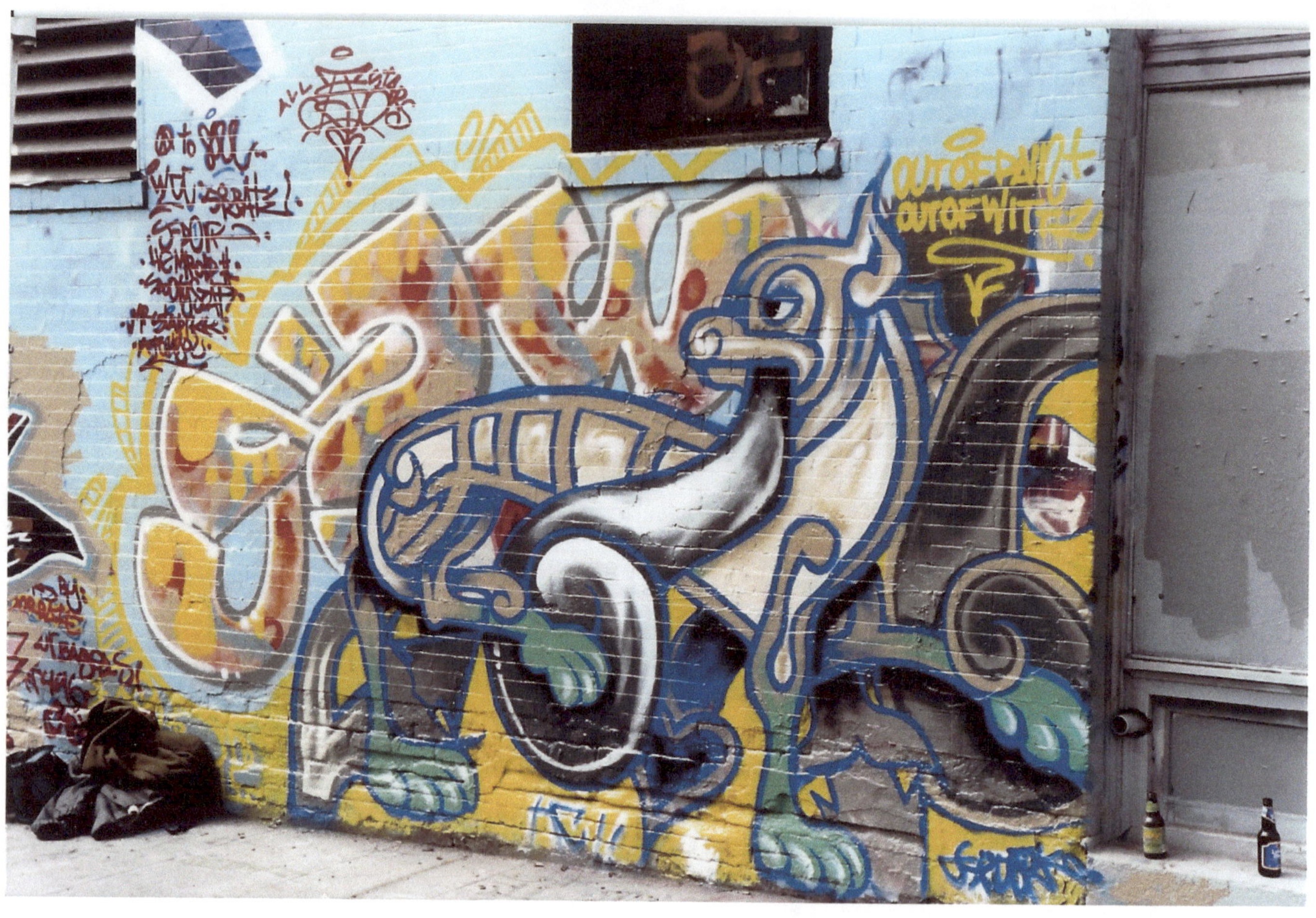

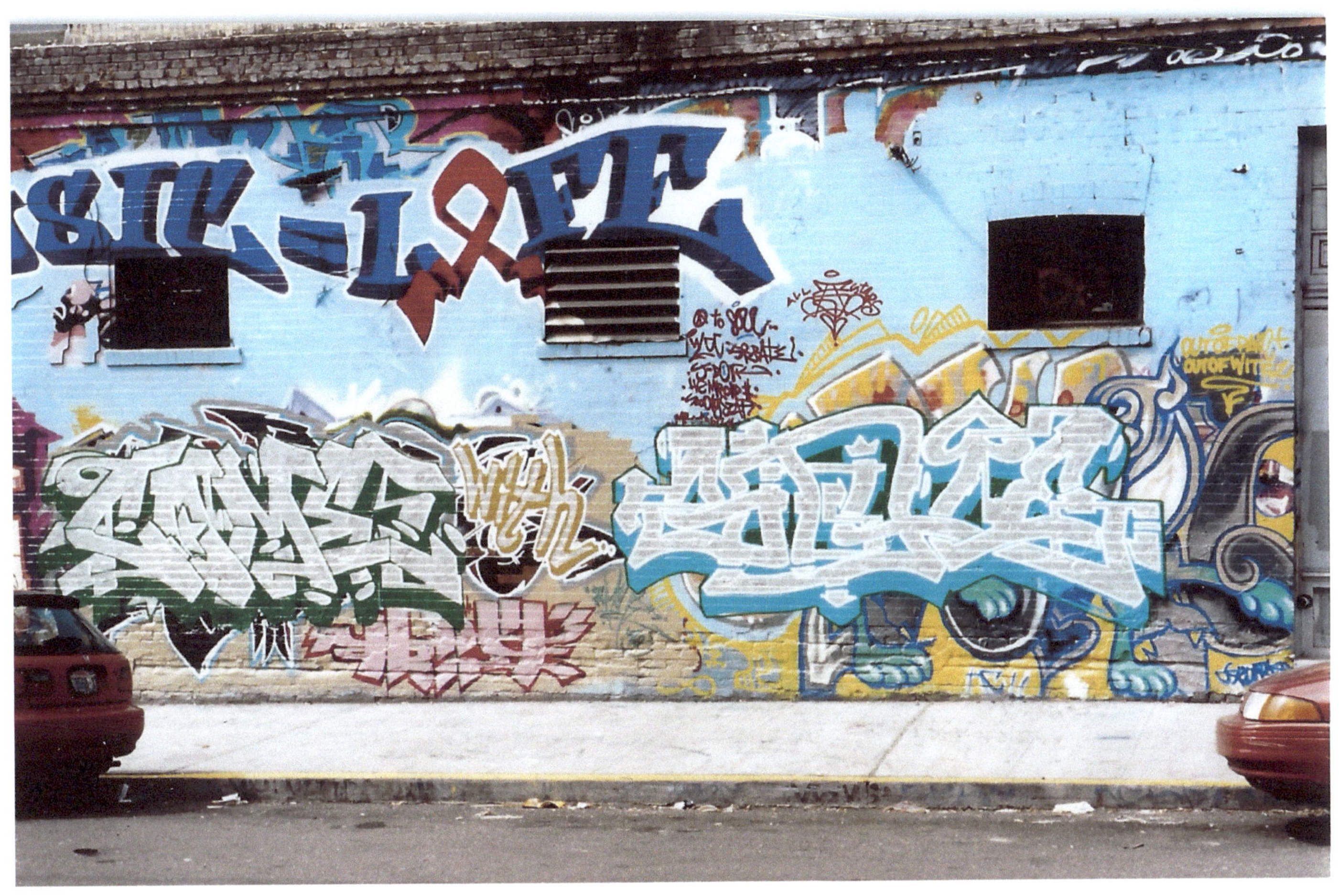

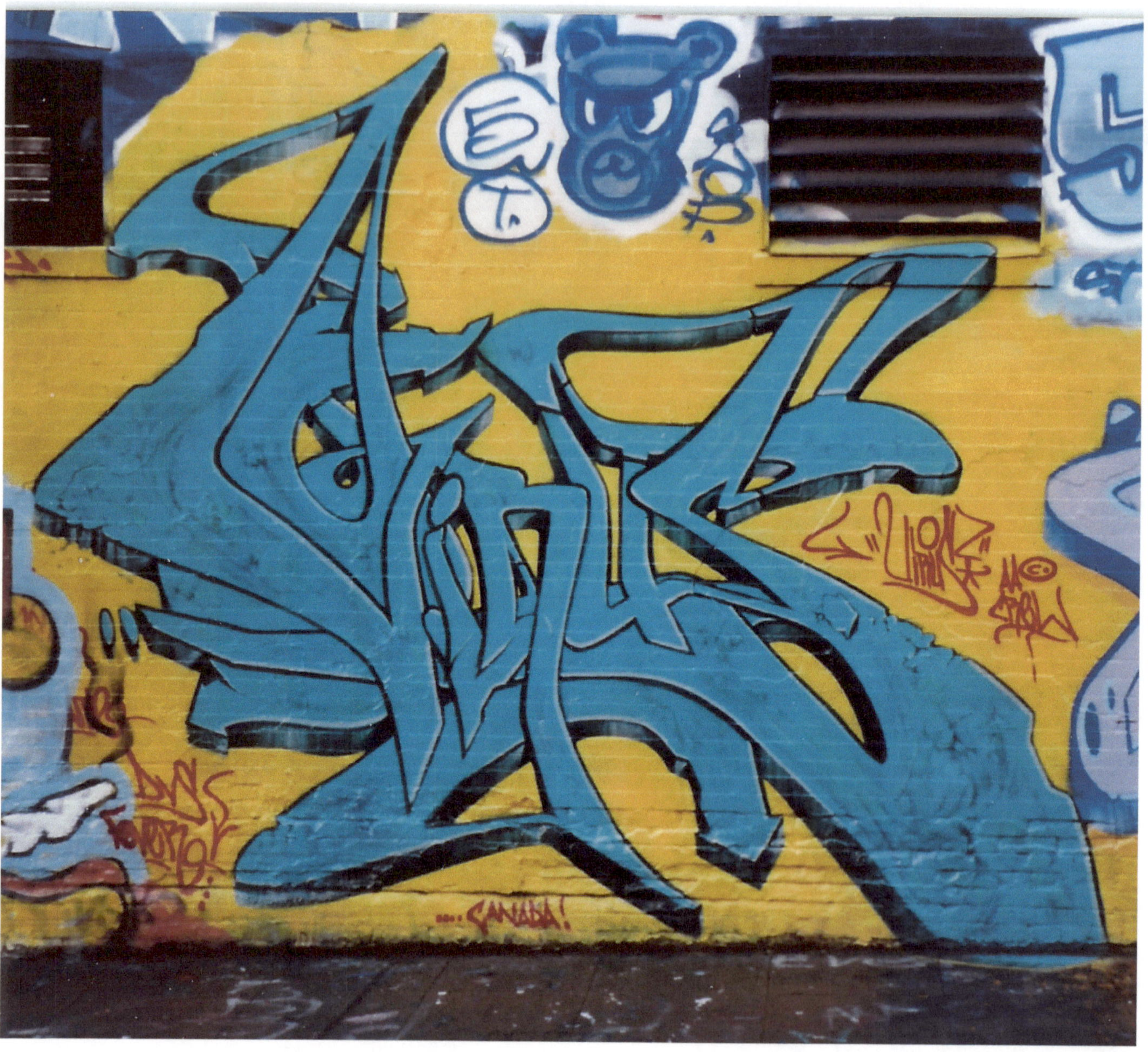
...CANADA!

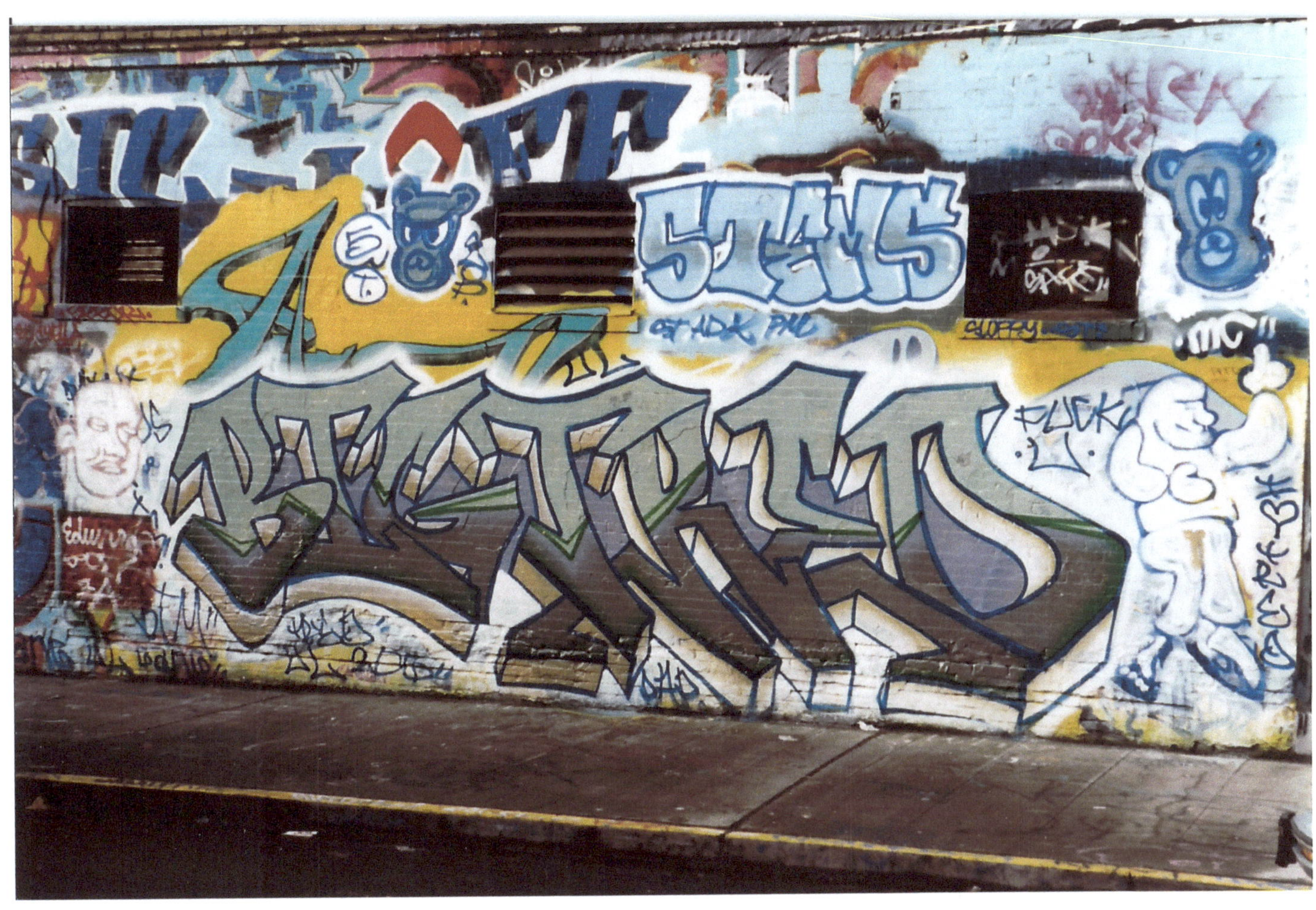

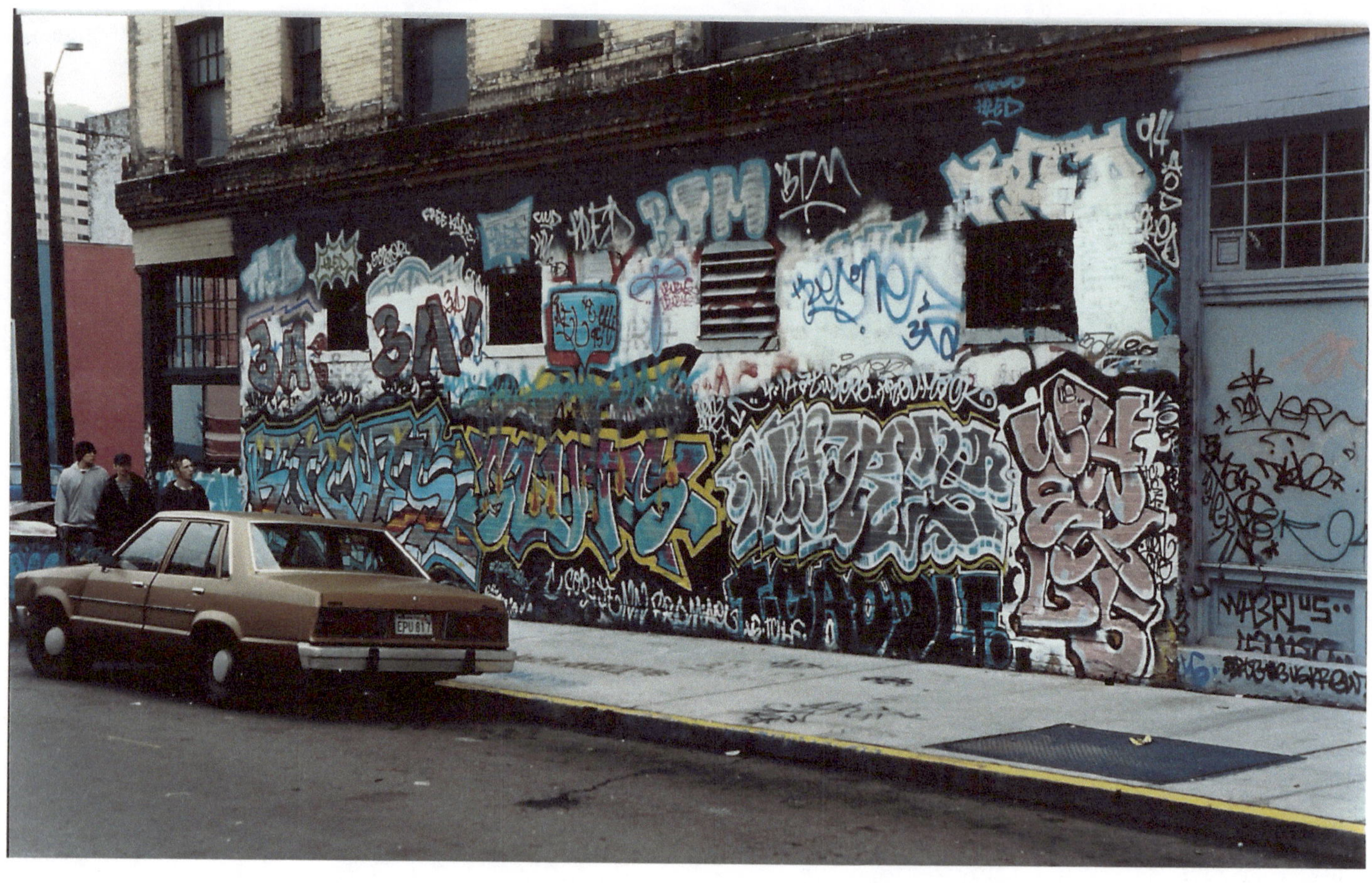
BTM
3A
3A

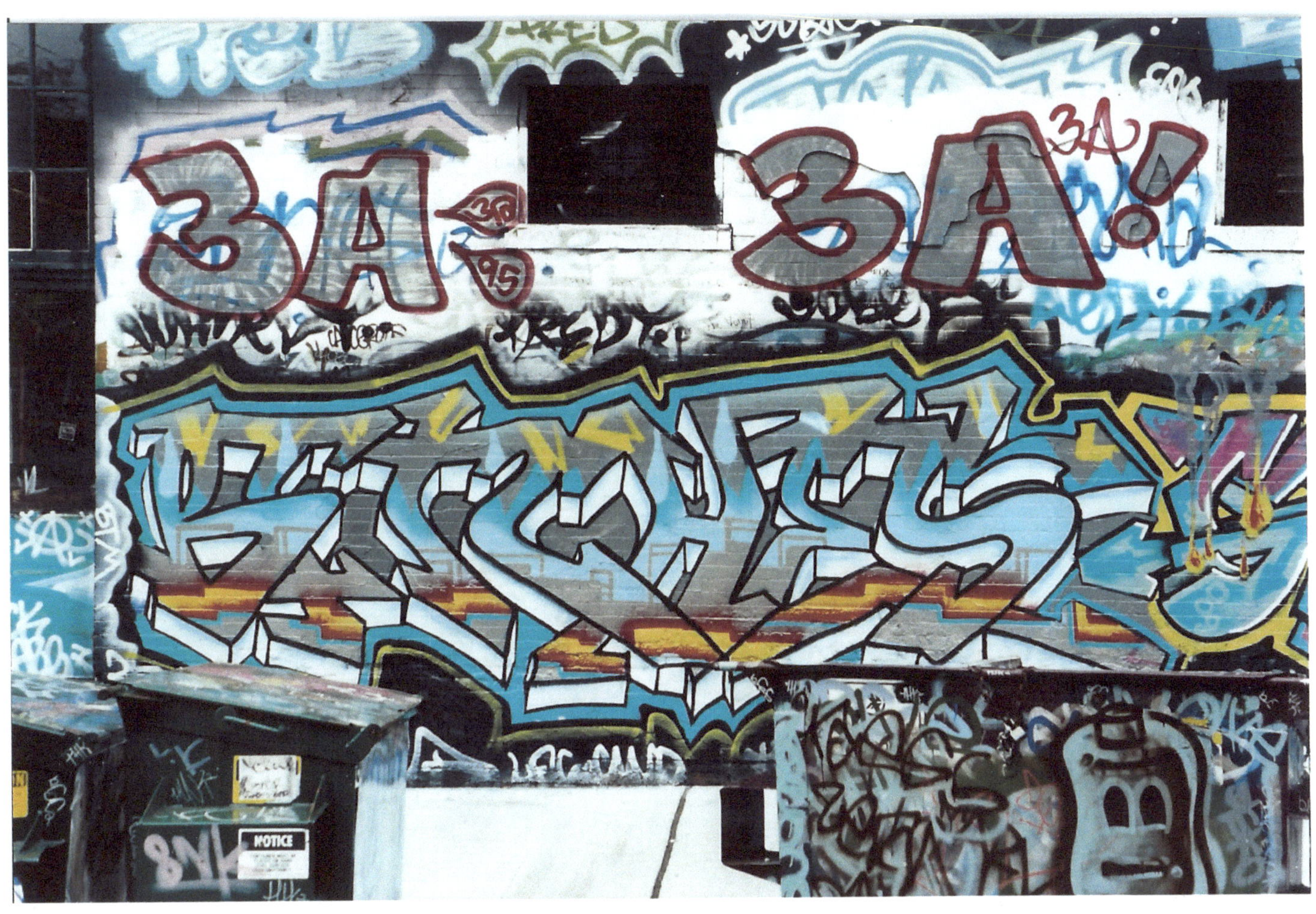
3A
3A!
NOTICE

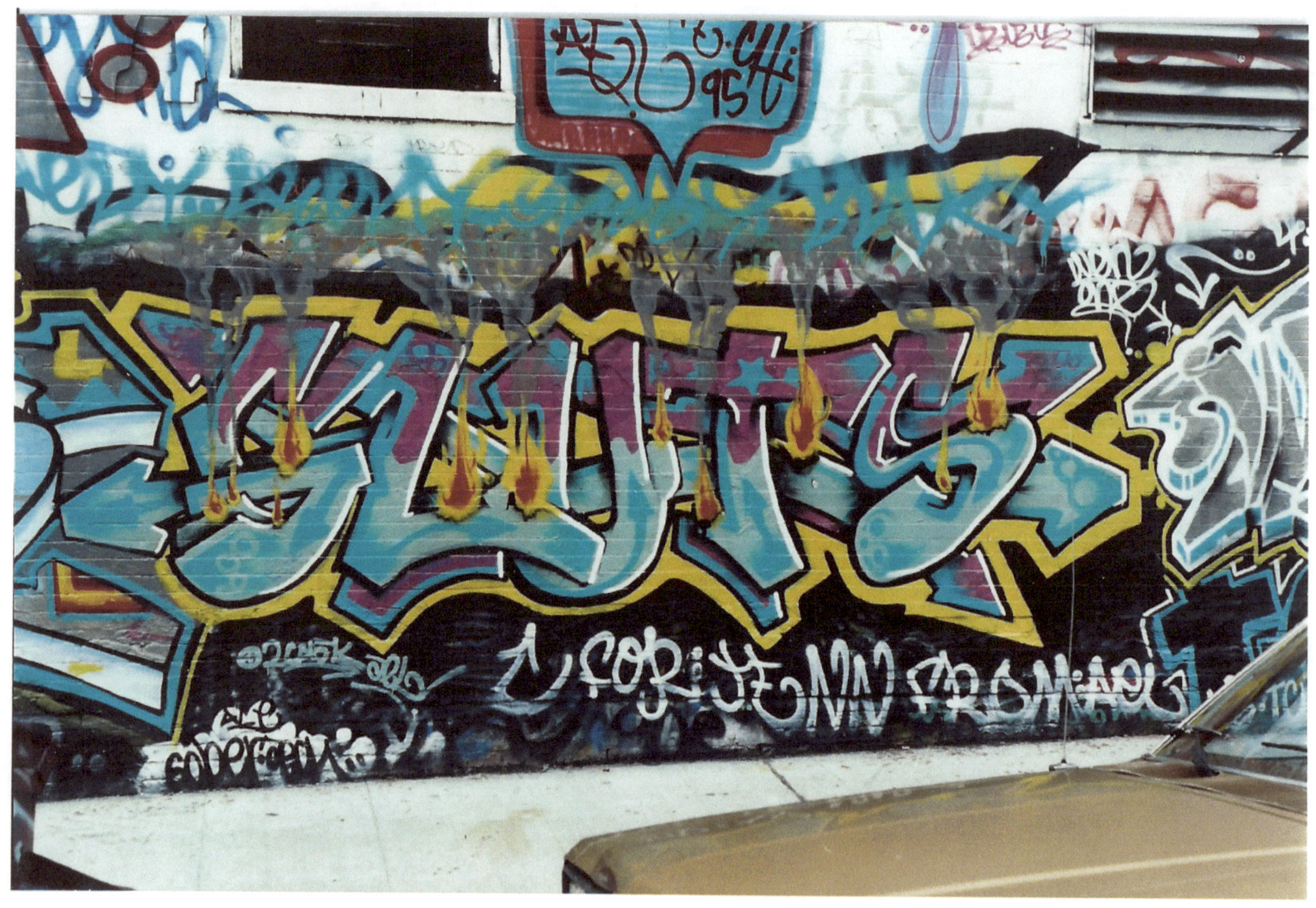

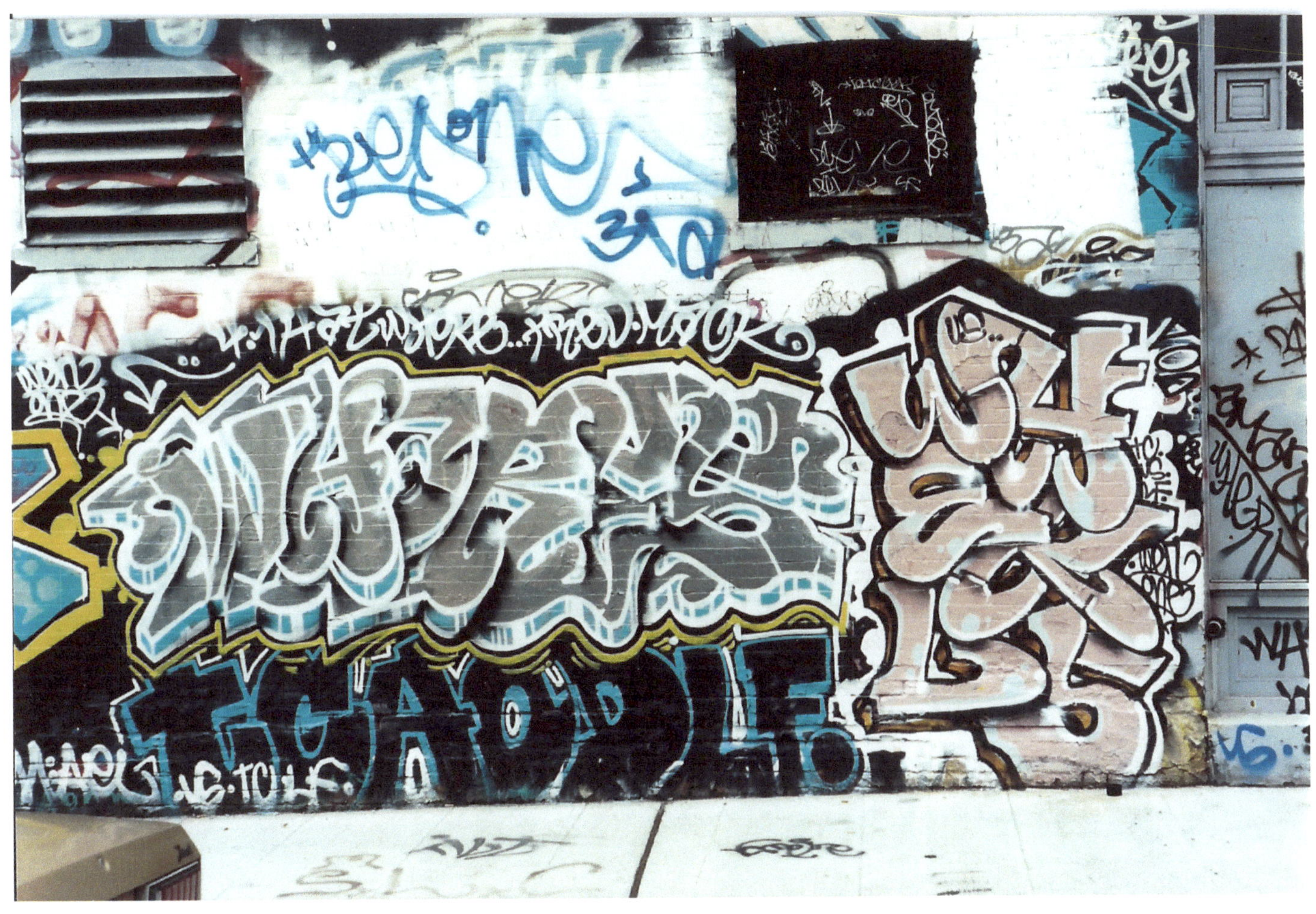

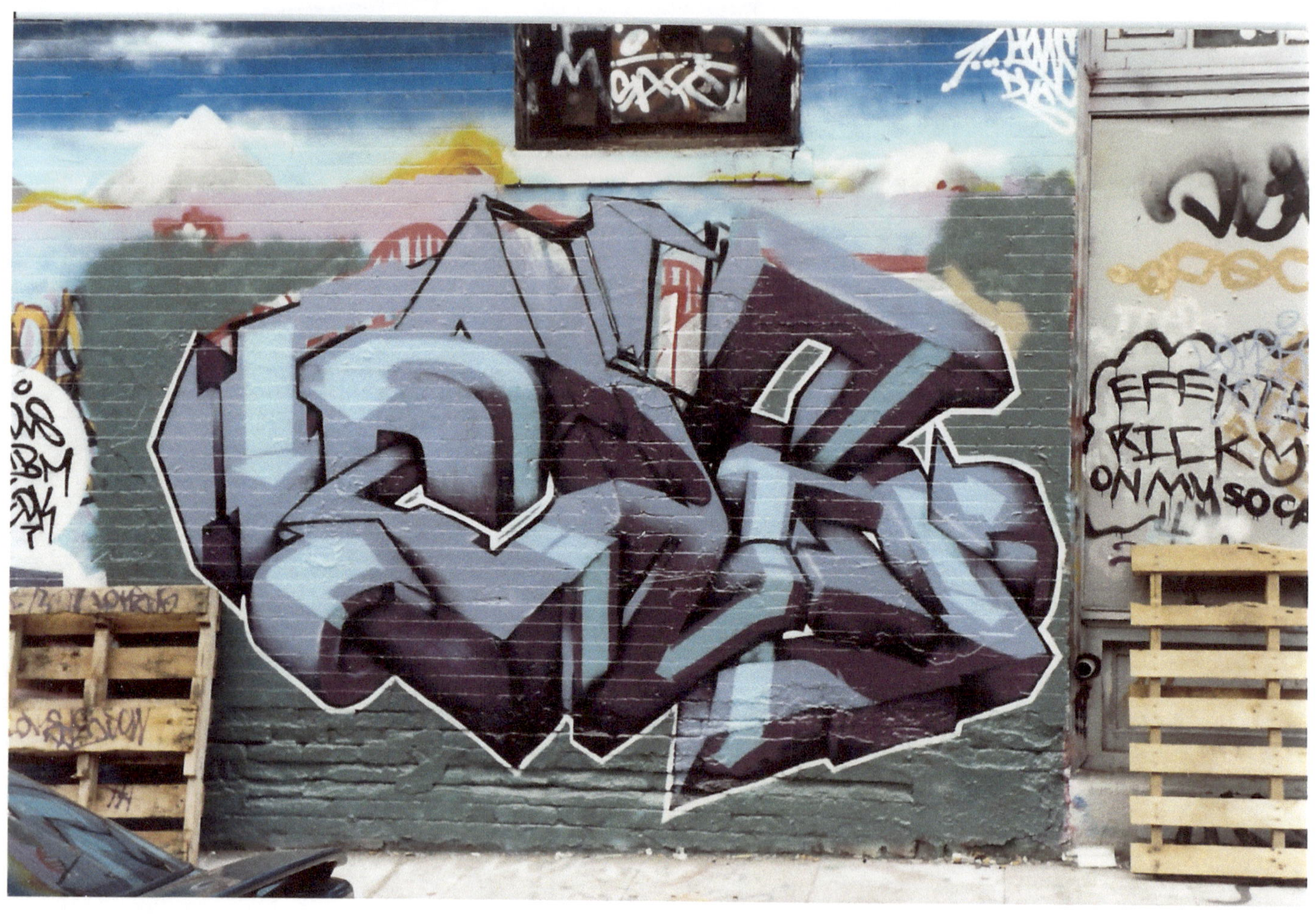

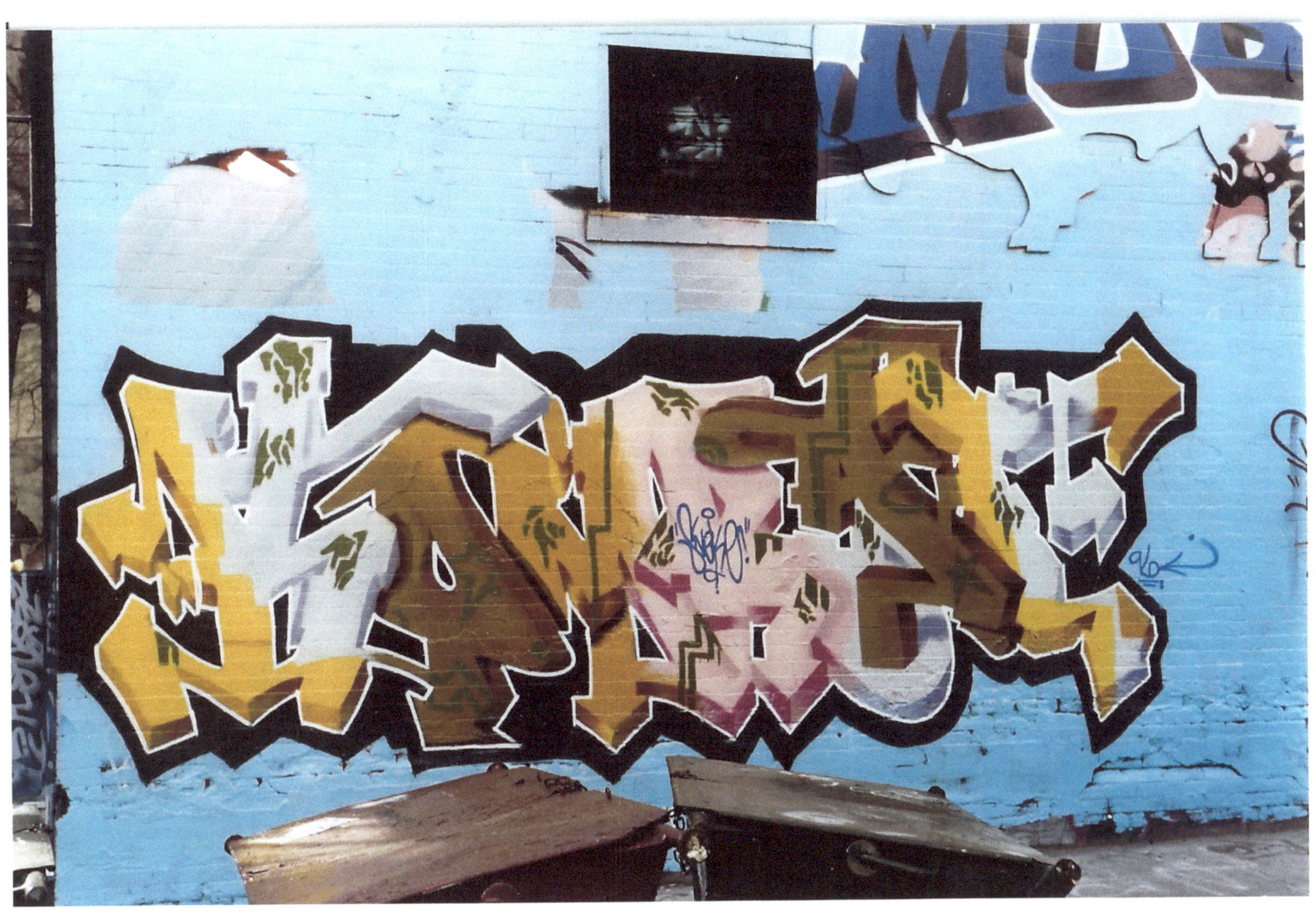

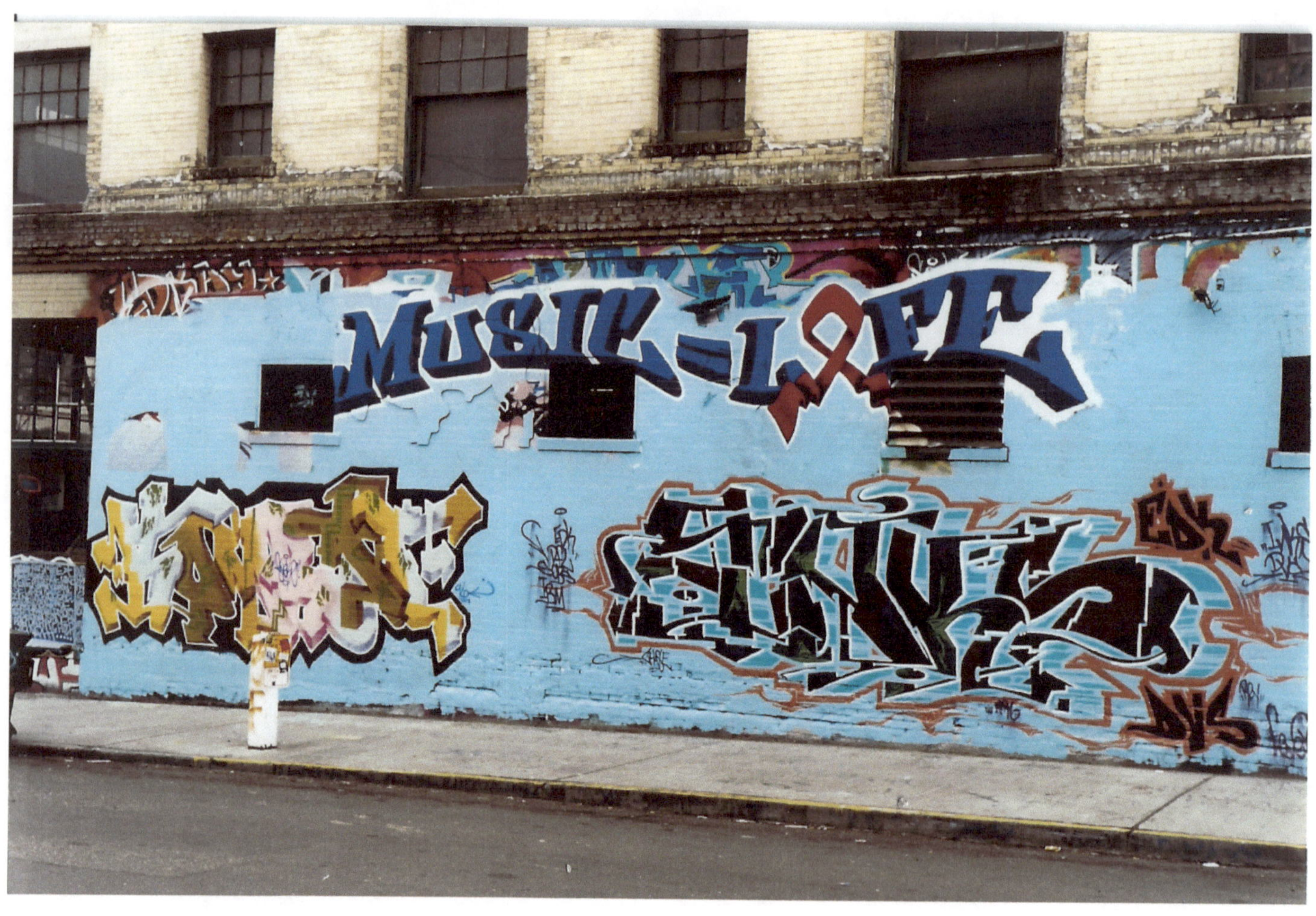

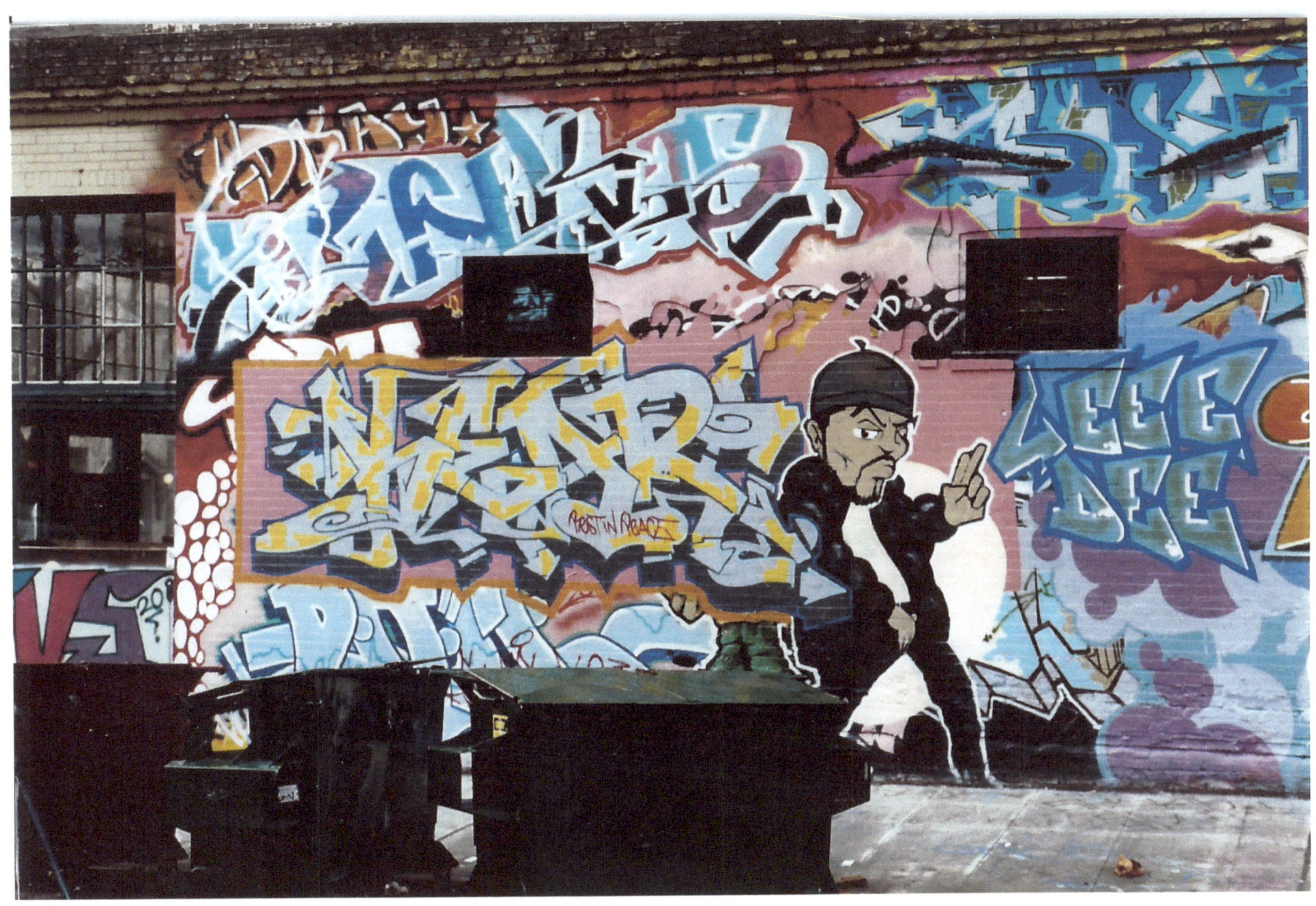

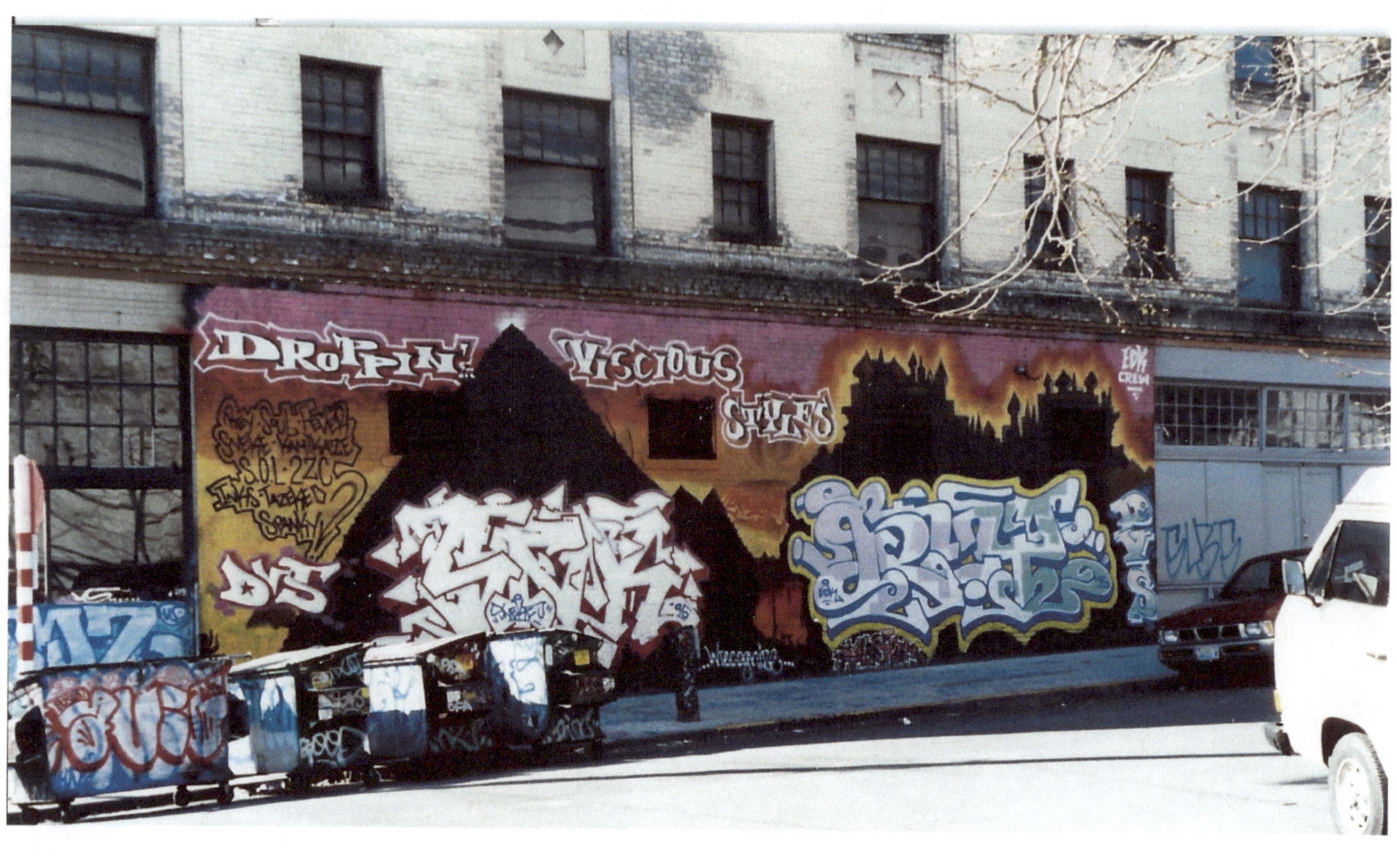
DROPPIN'
VICIOUS
STYLES

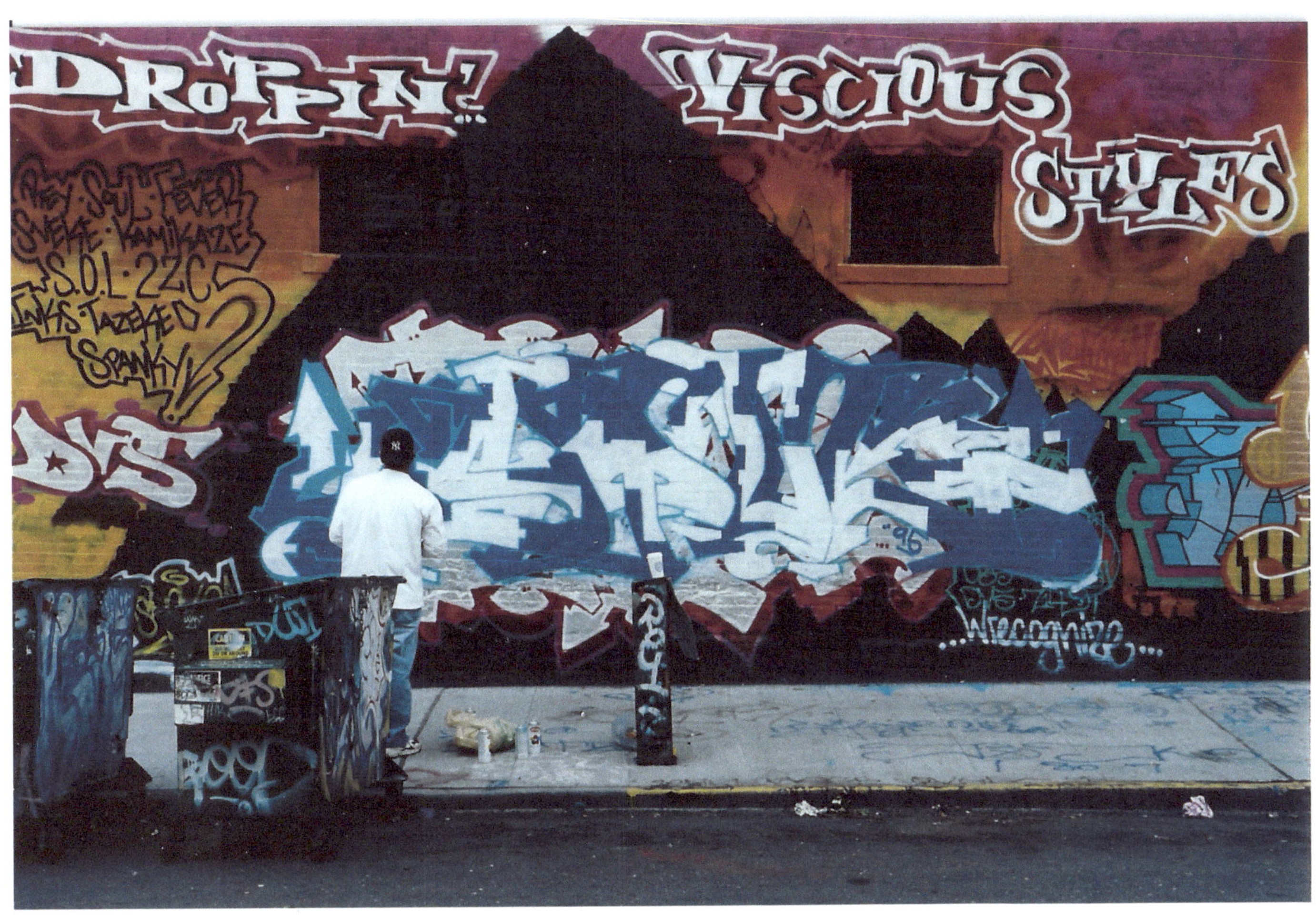
DROPPIN'
VISCIOUS
STYLES
KAMIKAZE
S.O.L·2ZC
SPANKY

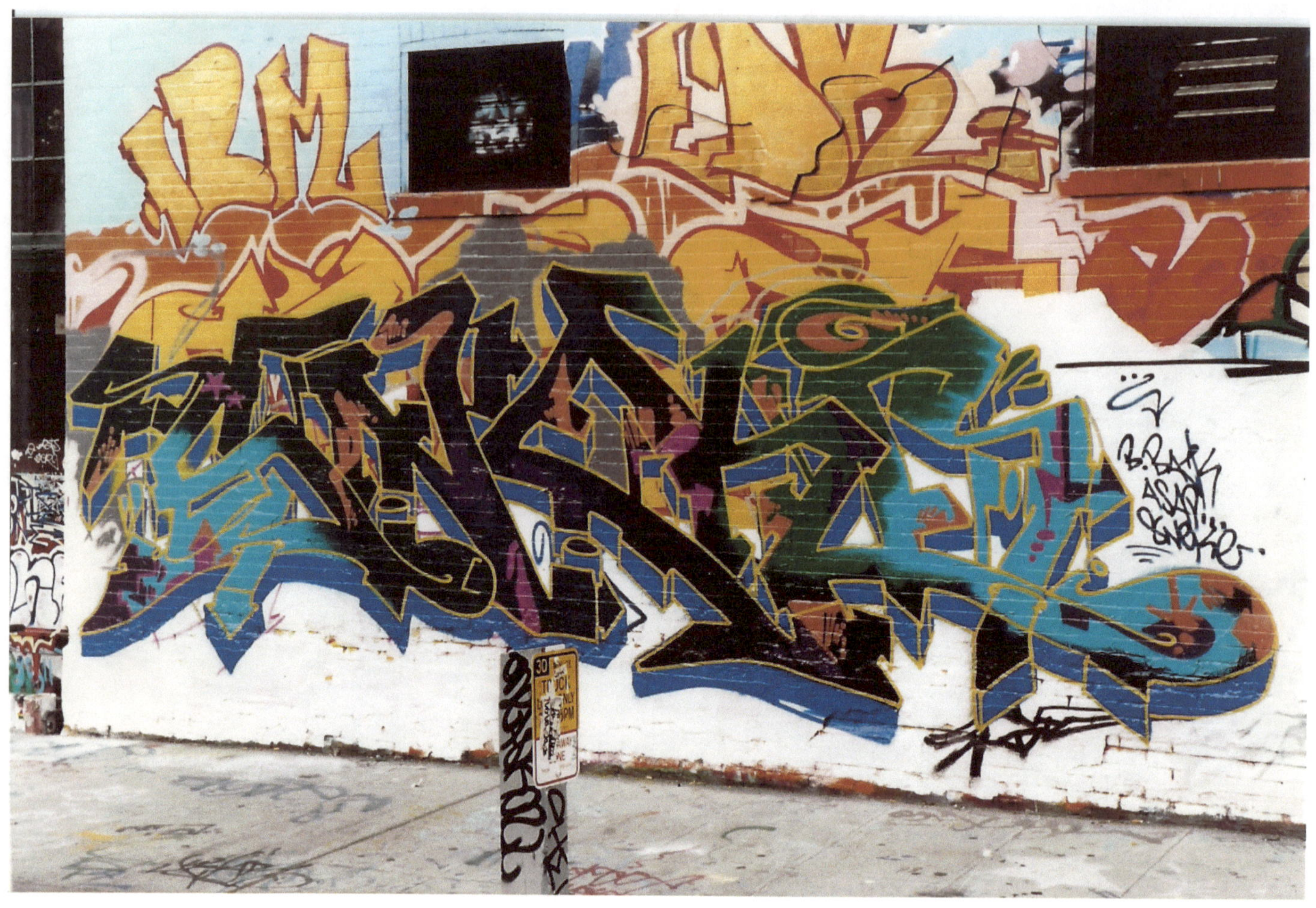

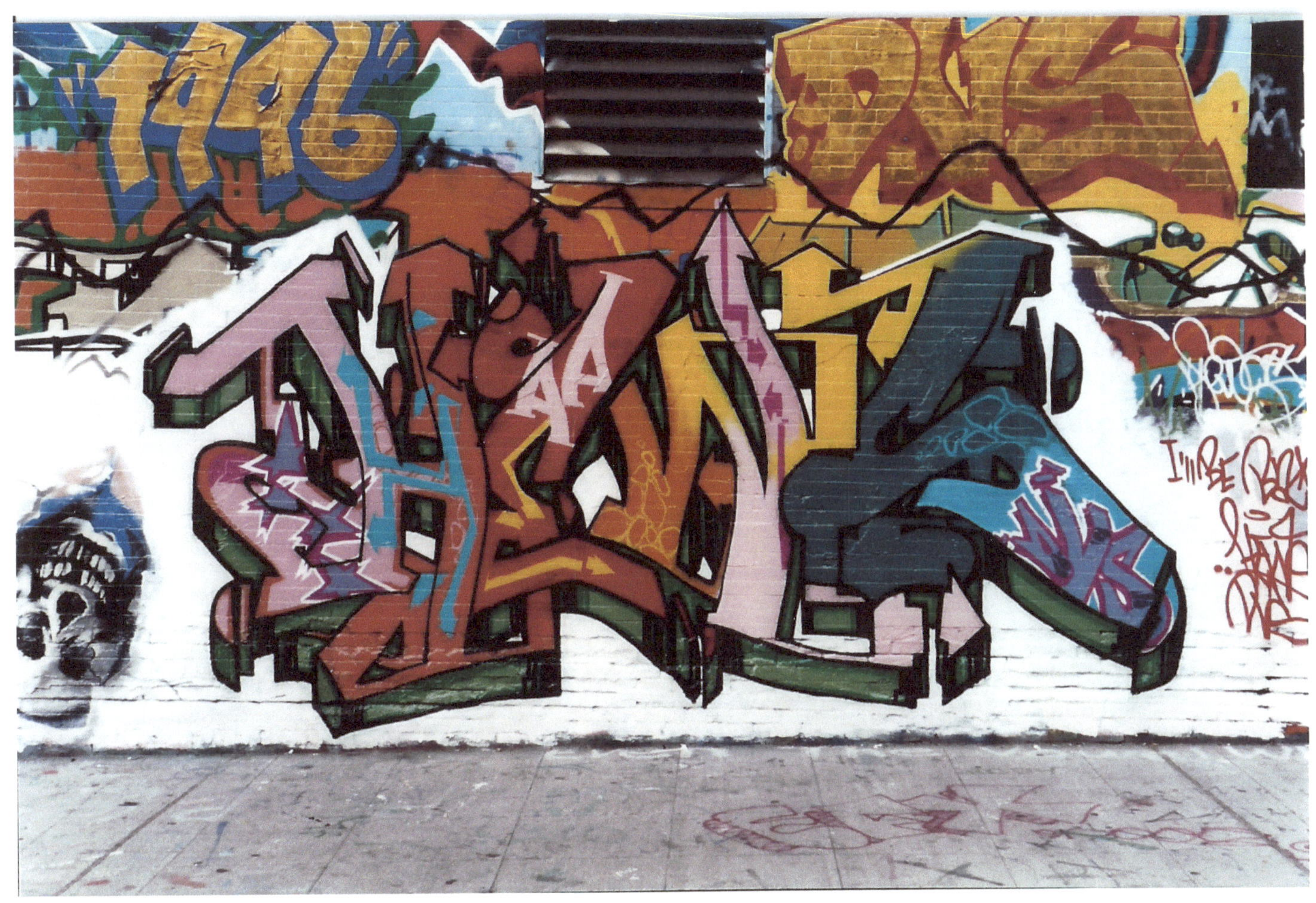

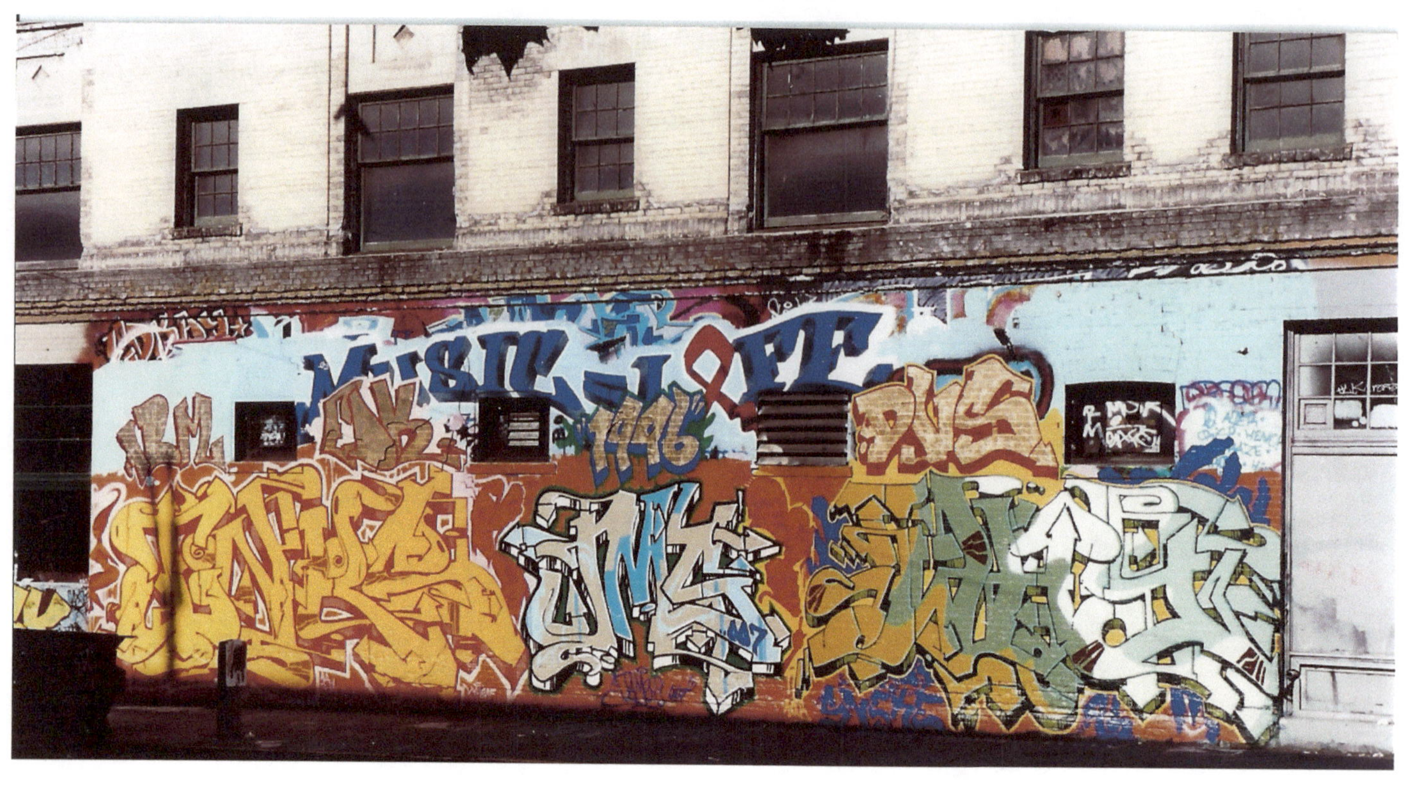

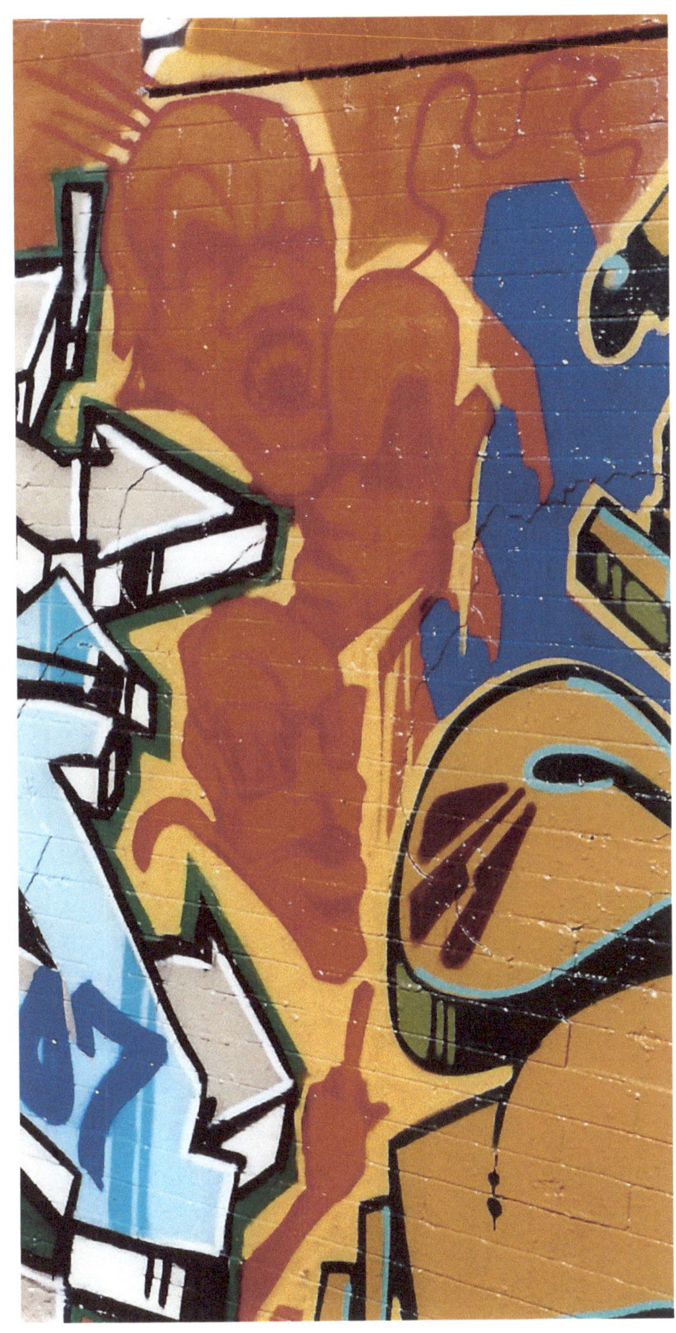

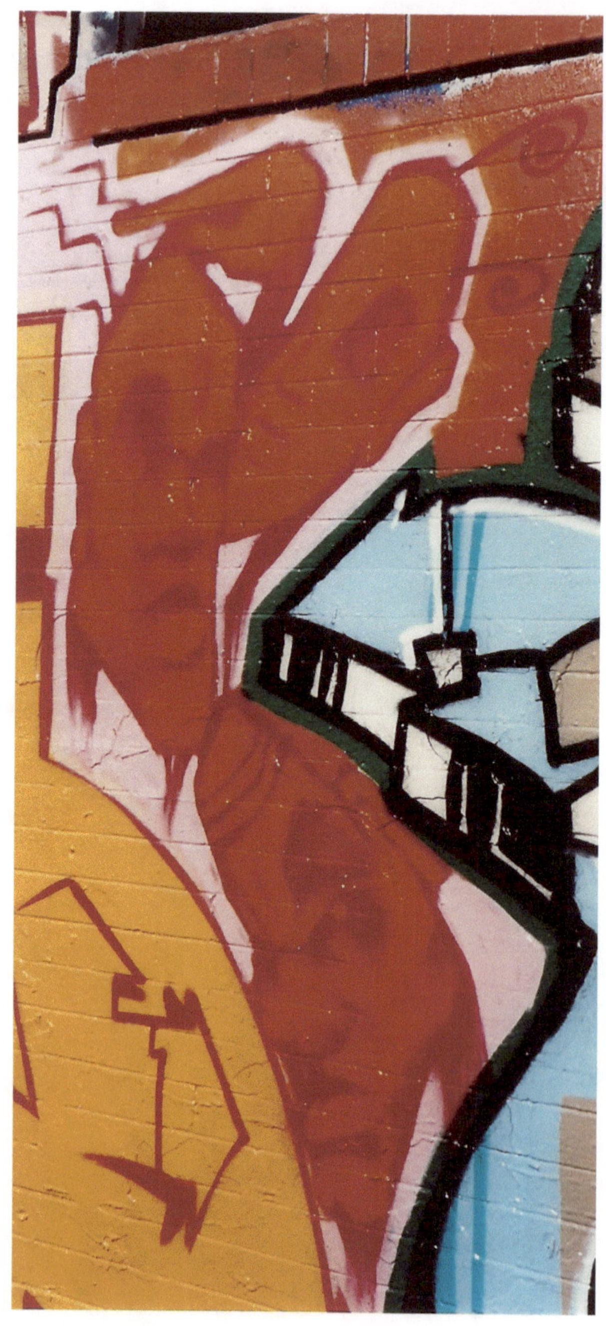

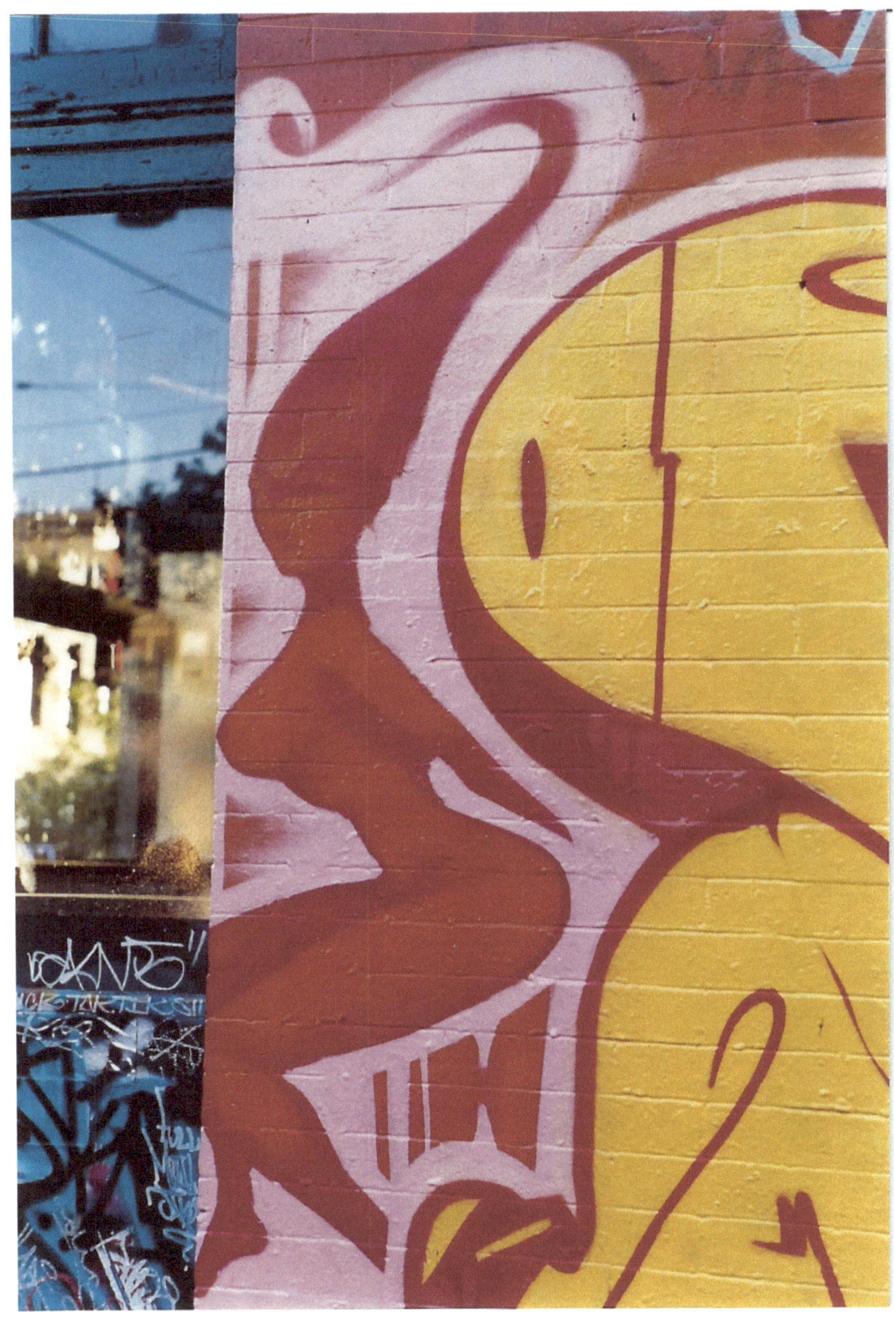

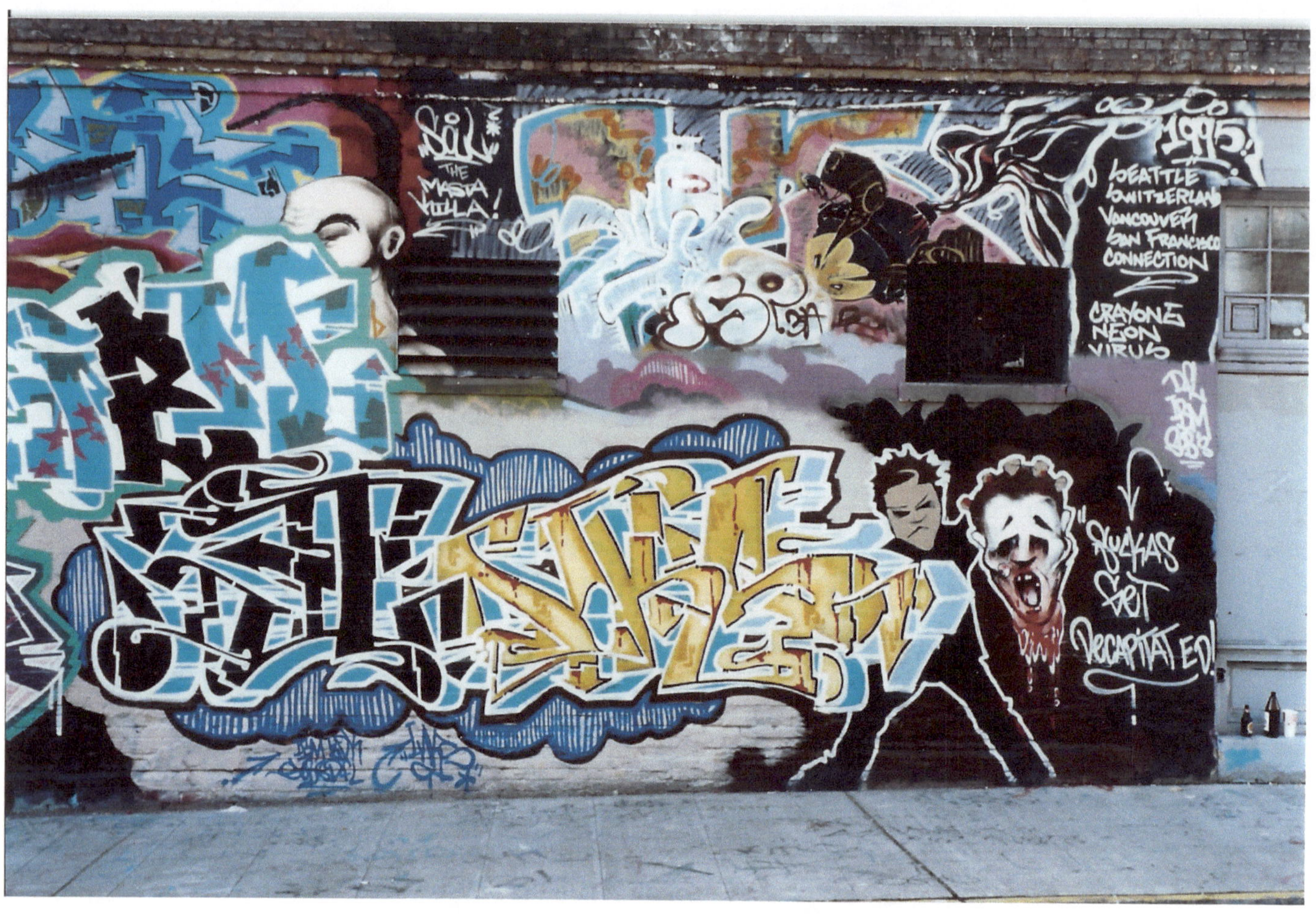
SOIL
THE MASTA KILLA!
1995
SEATTLE
SWITZERLAND
VANCOUVER
SAN FRANCISCO
CONNECTION
CRAYONE
NEON
VIRUS
"SUCKAS GET DECAPITATED!"

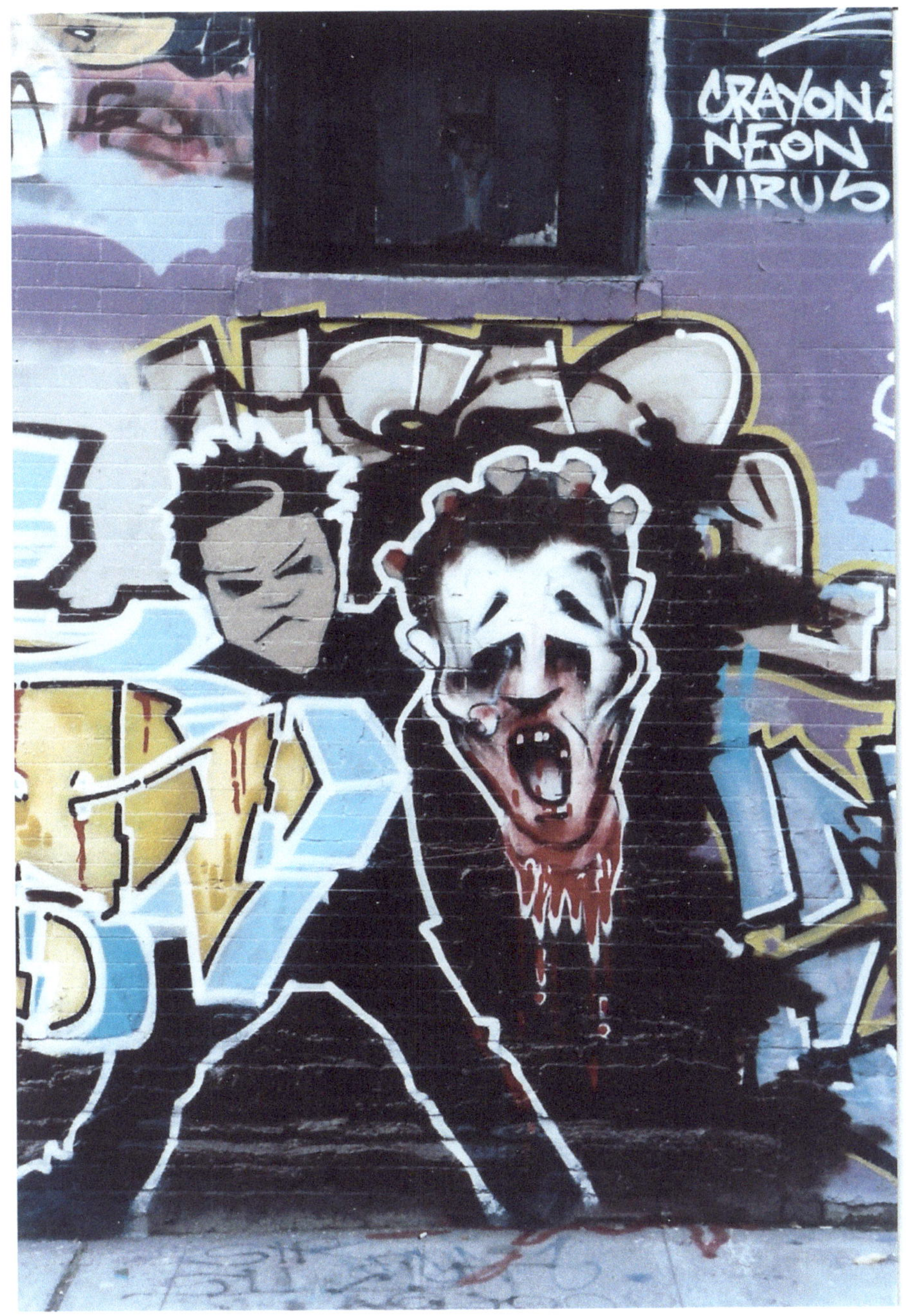
CRAYONE
NEON
VIRUS

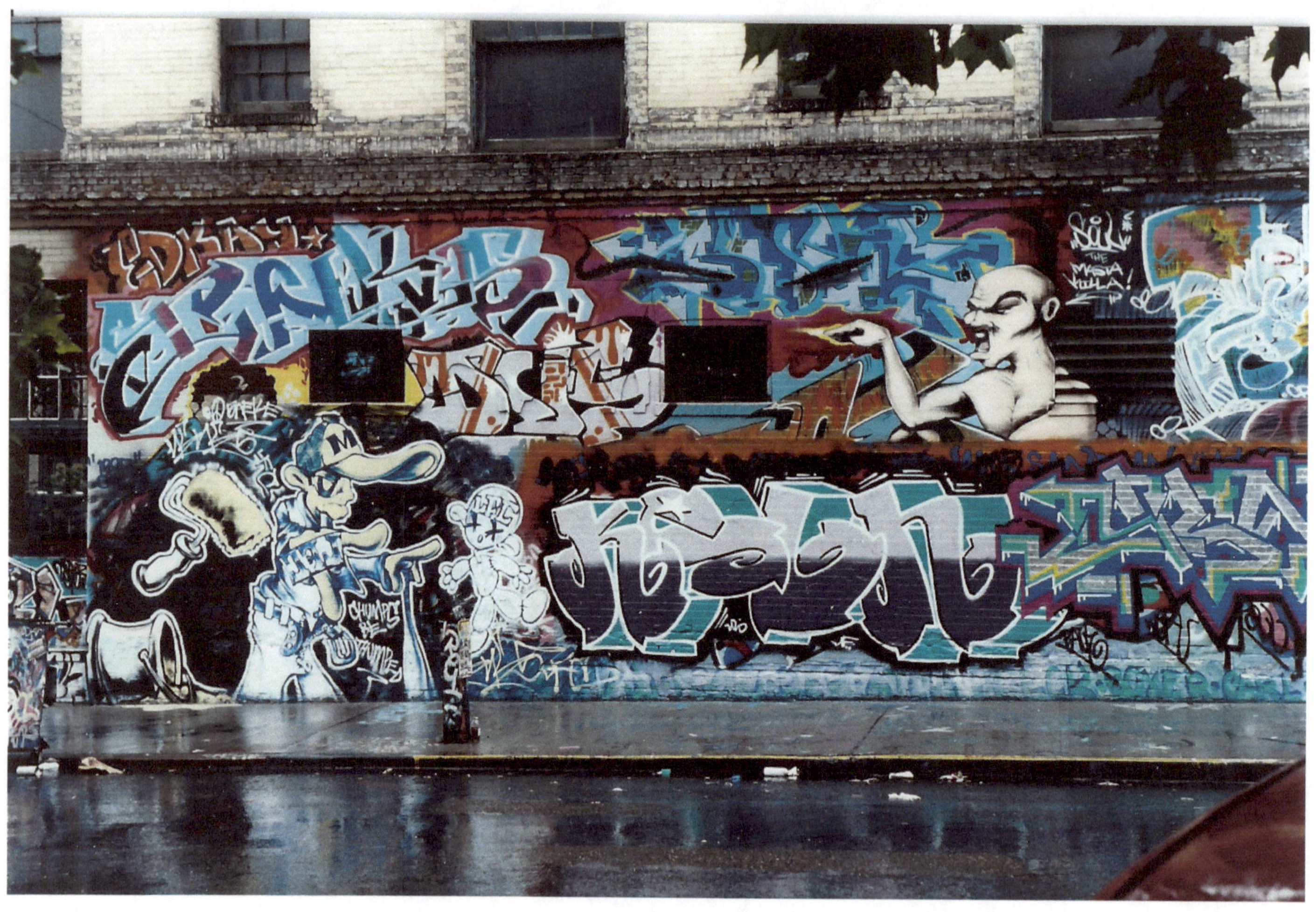

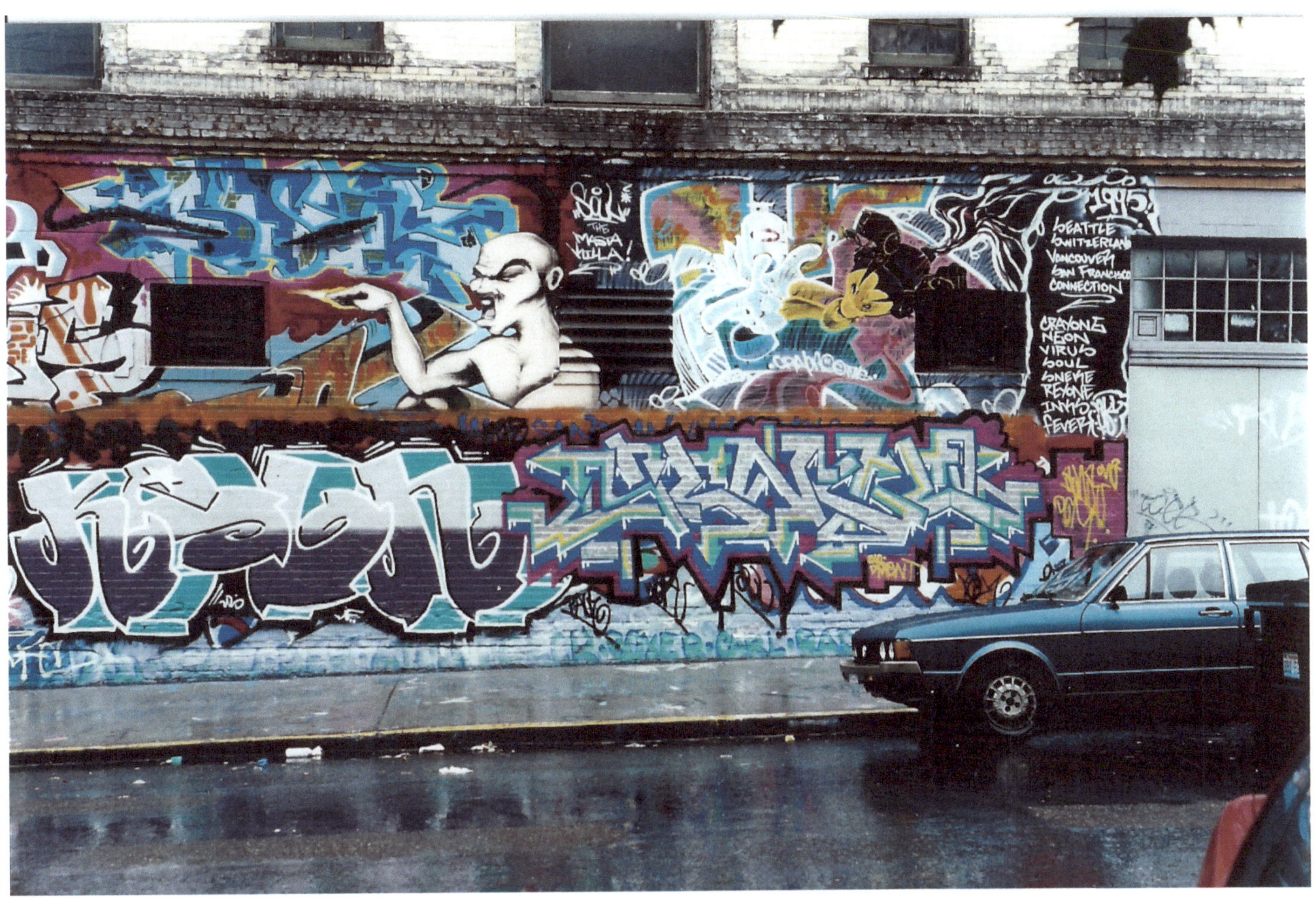
THE MASTA KILLA!
1995
SEATTLE
SWITZERLAND
VONCOUVER
SAN FRANCISCO
CONNECTION
CRAYONE
NEON
VIRUS
SOUL
ONEYE
REYONE
INKS
FEVER

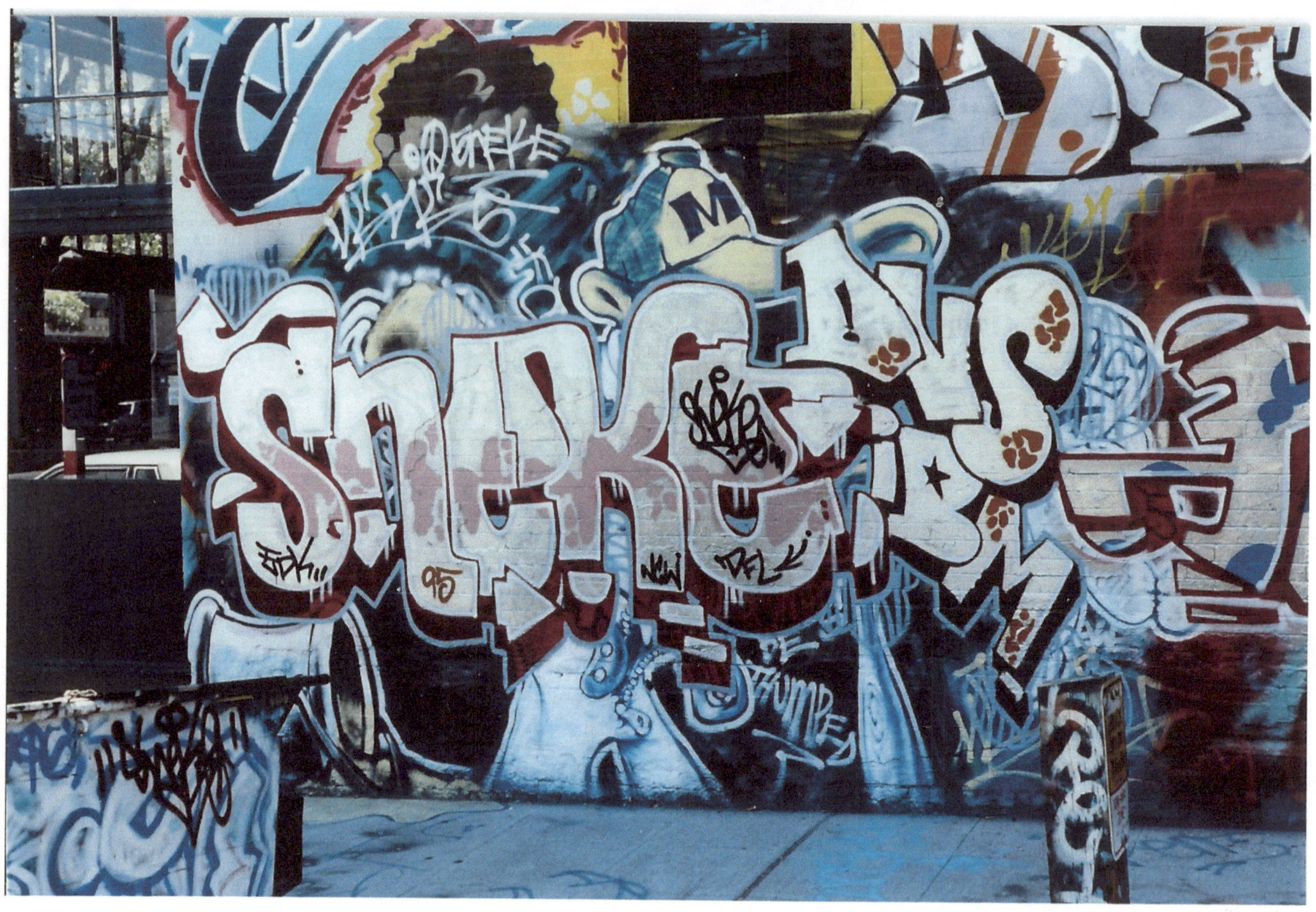

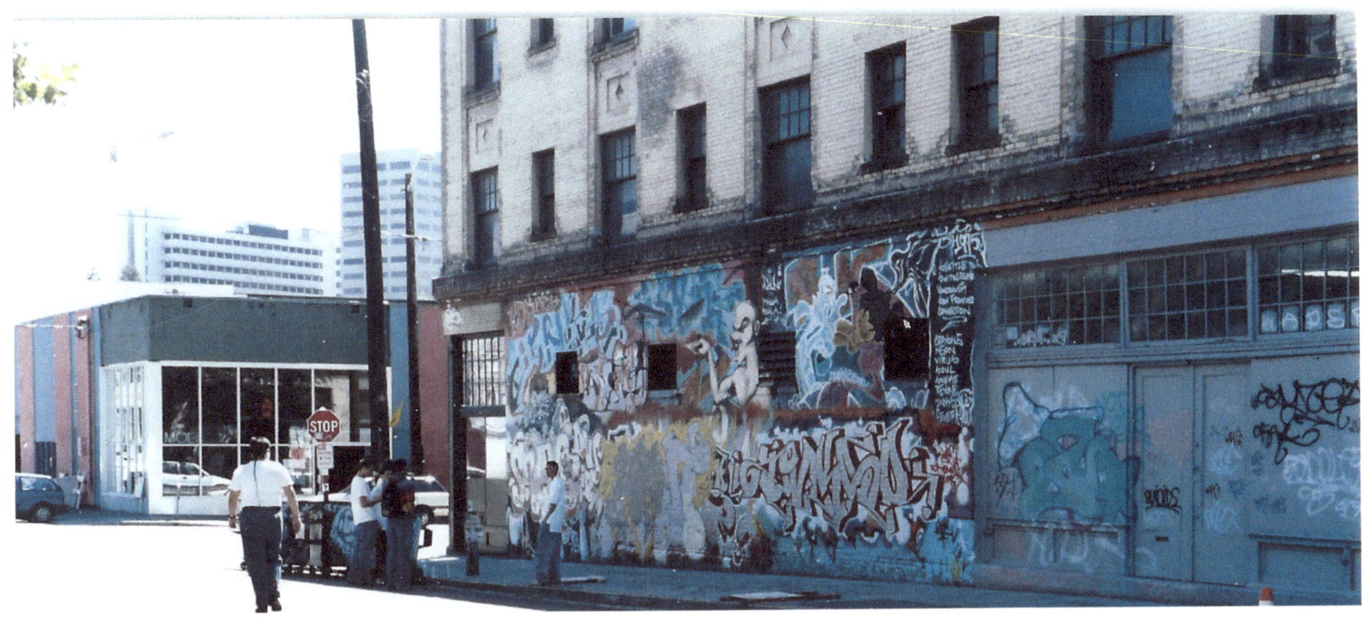
STOP

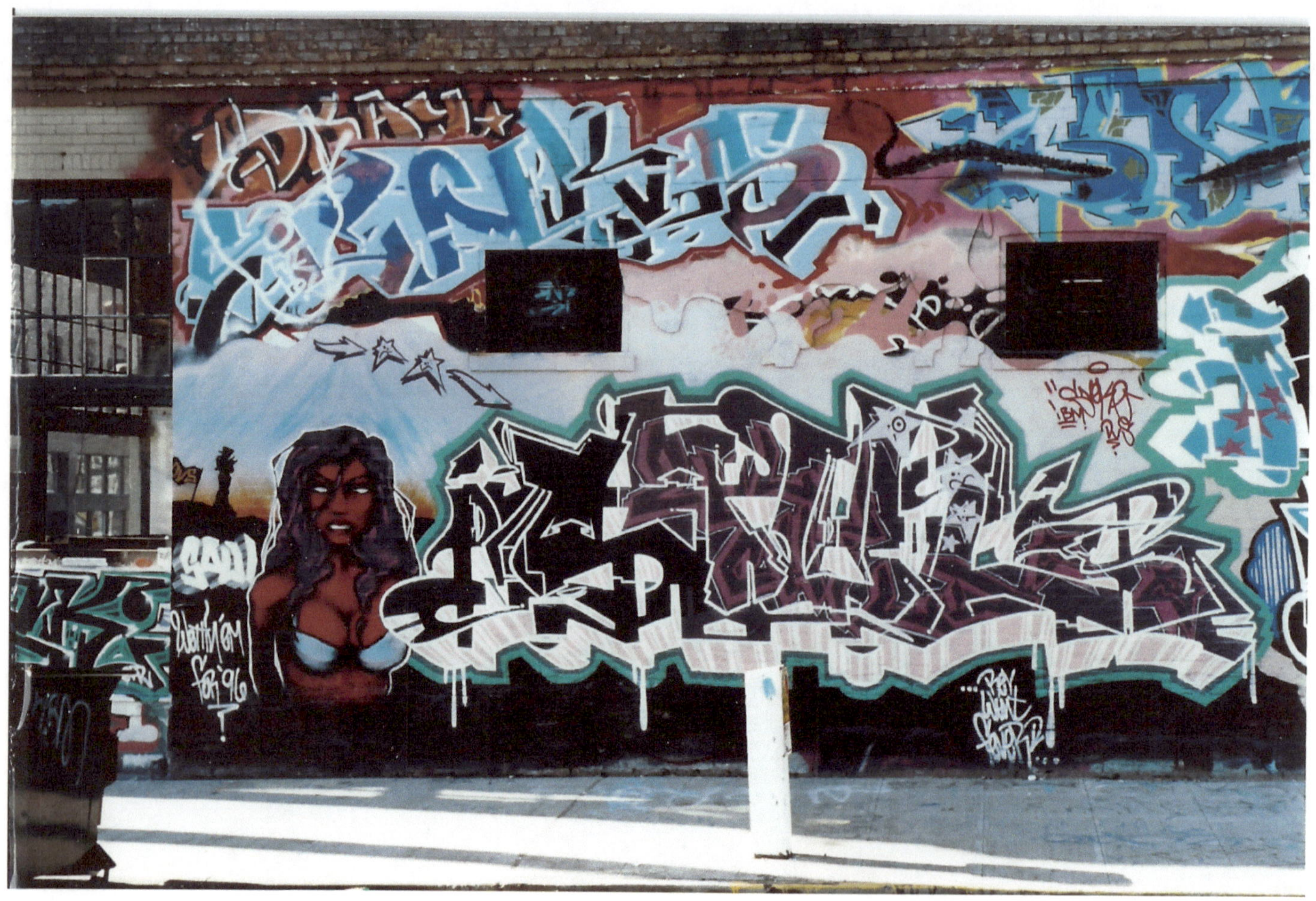

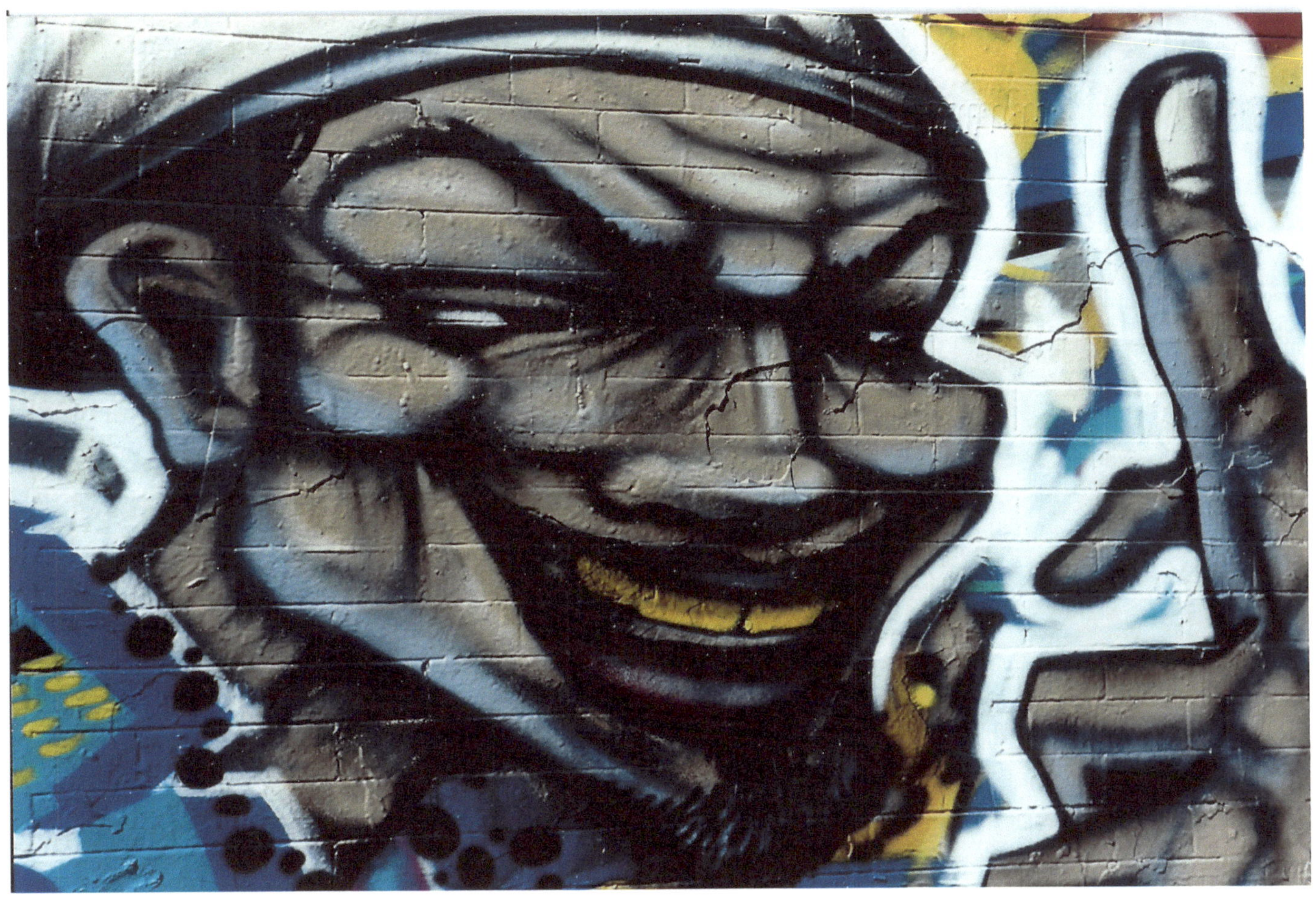

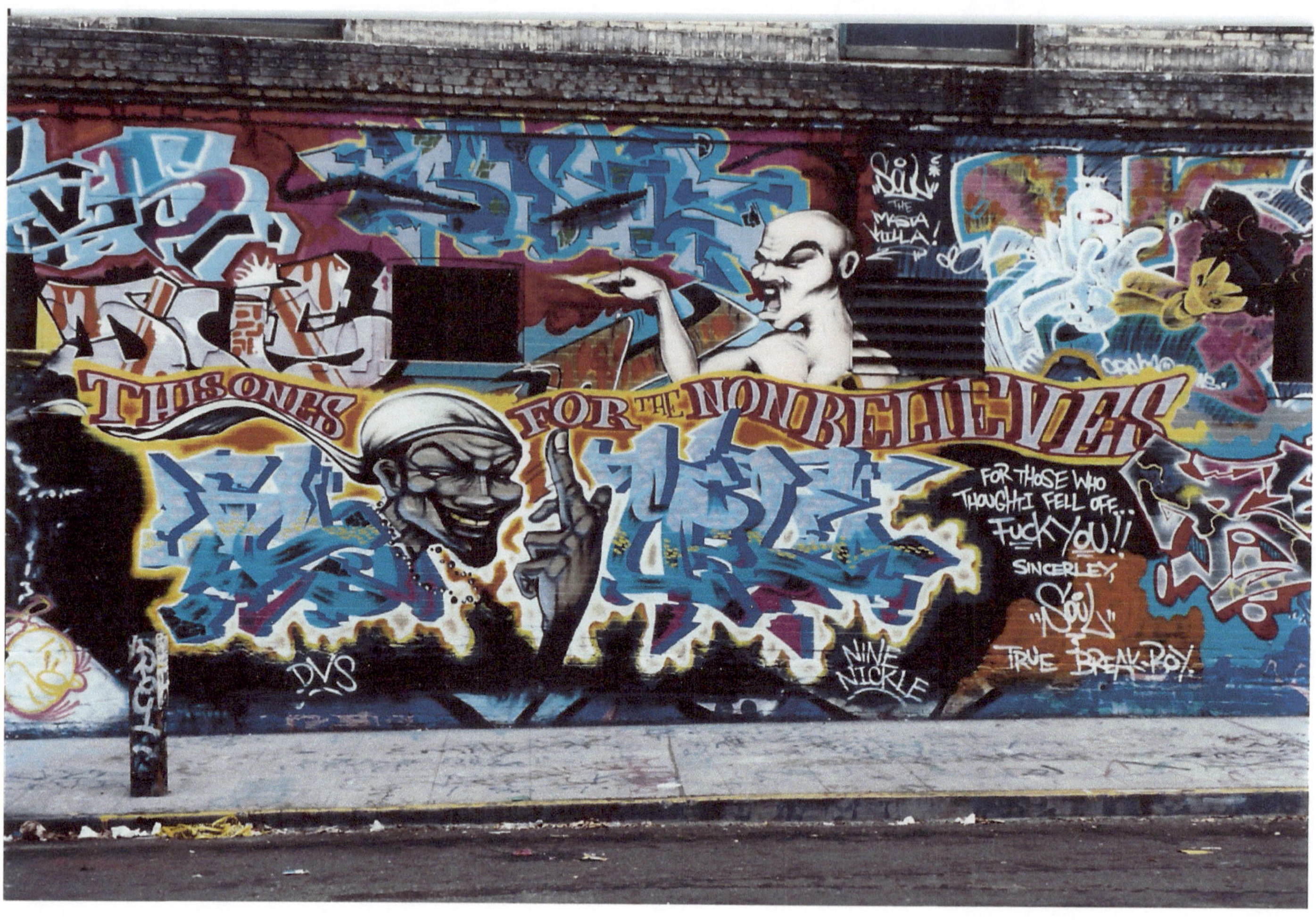
THIS ONES FOR THE NONBELIEVERS
FOR THOSE WHO THOUGHT I FELL OFF... FUCK YOU!! SINCERLEY, "SOUL" TRUE BREAK-BOY.
DVS
NINE NICKLE

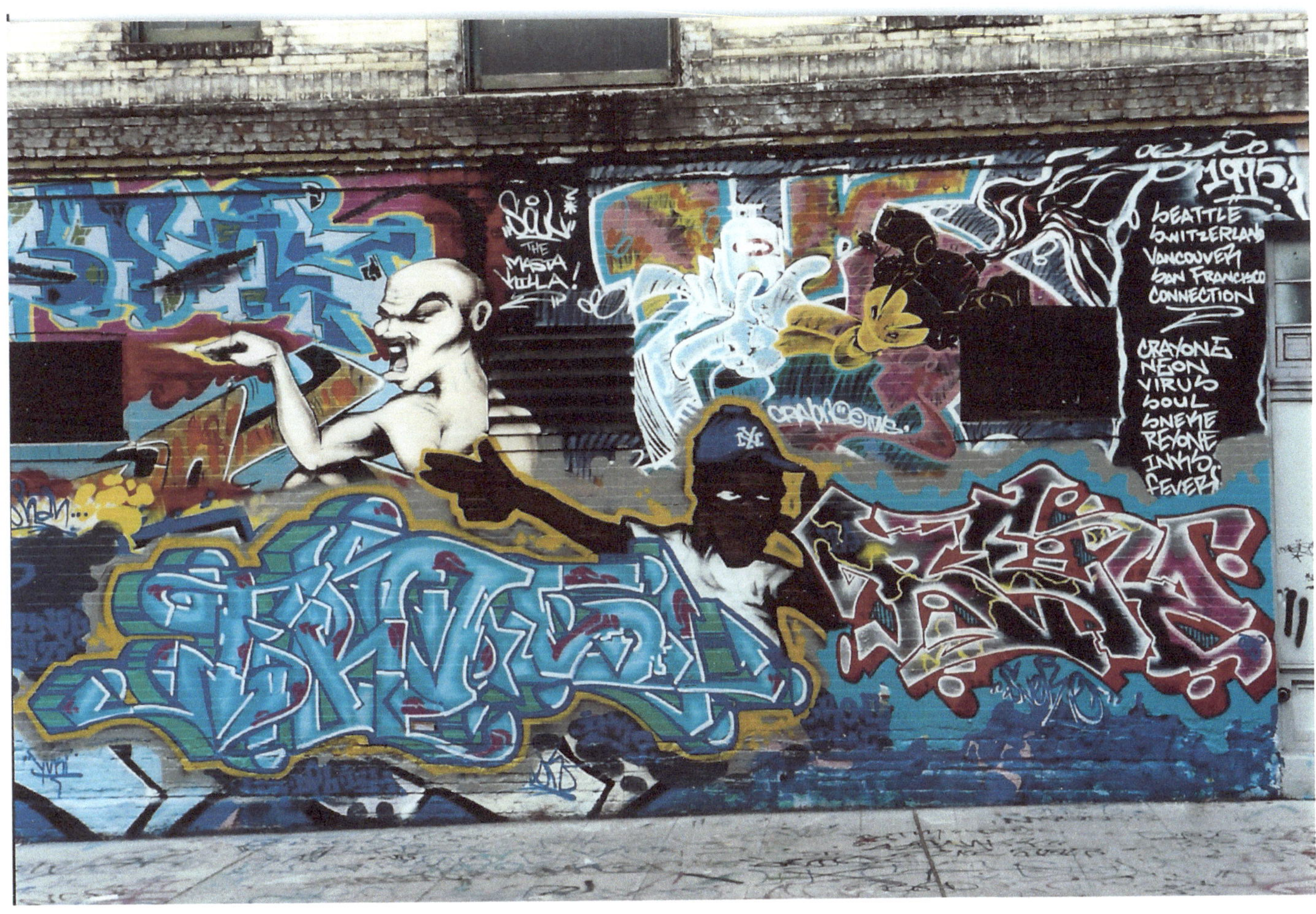
THE MASTA KILLA!
1995!
SEATTLE
SWITZERLAND
VANCOUVER
SAN FRANCISCO
CONNECTION
CRAYONE
NEON
VIRUS
SOUL
SNEKE
REYONE
INKS.
FEVER

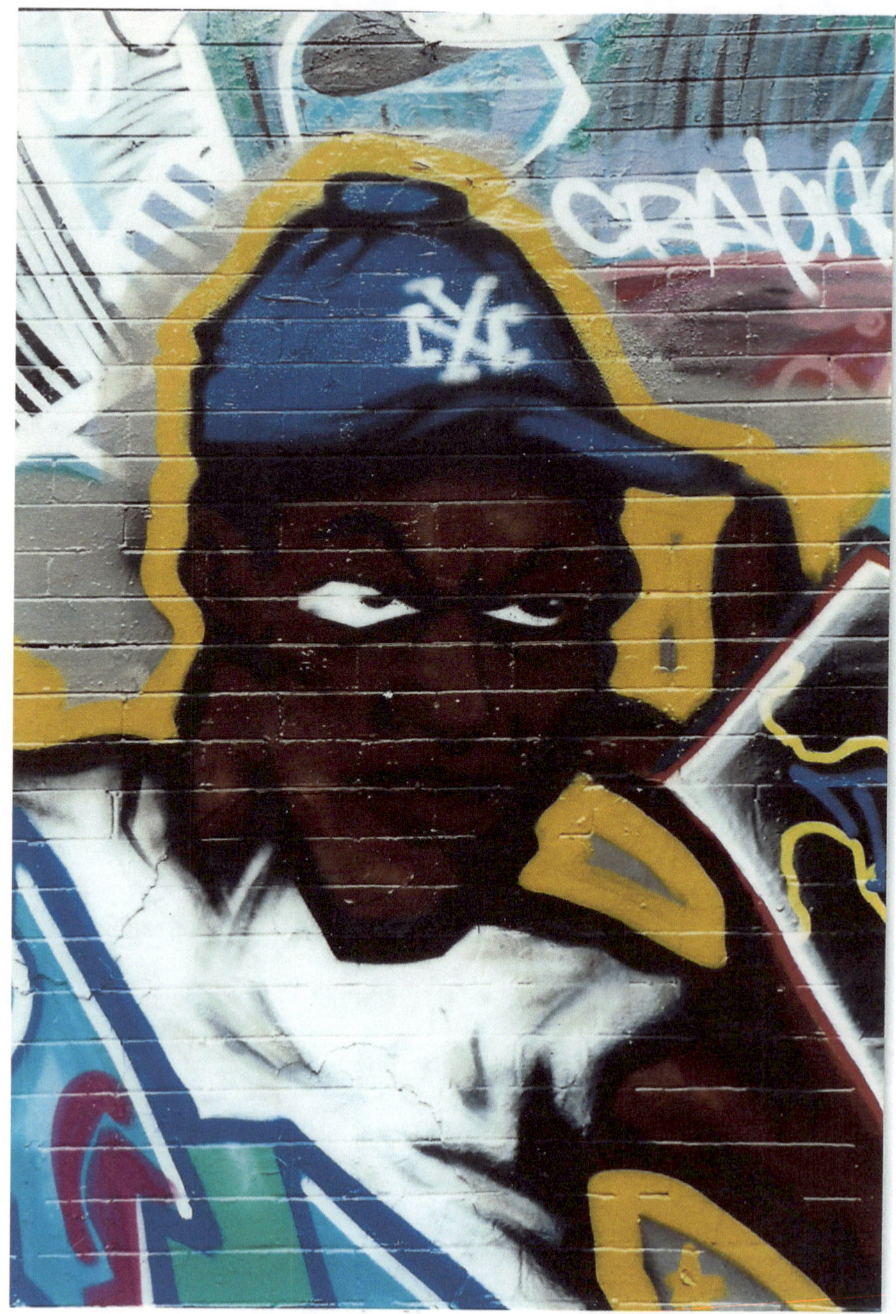
NY

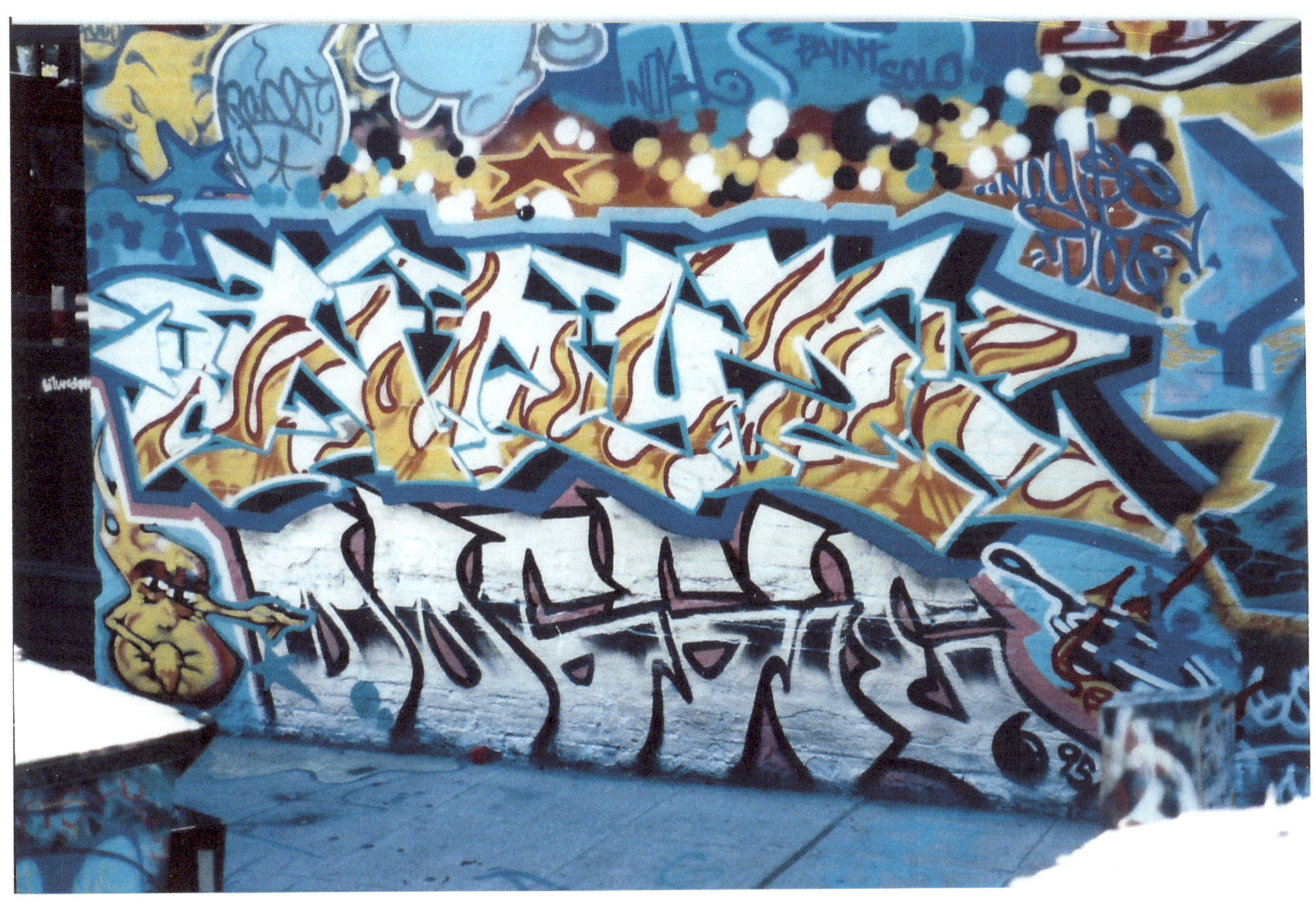
PAINT SOLO

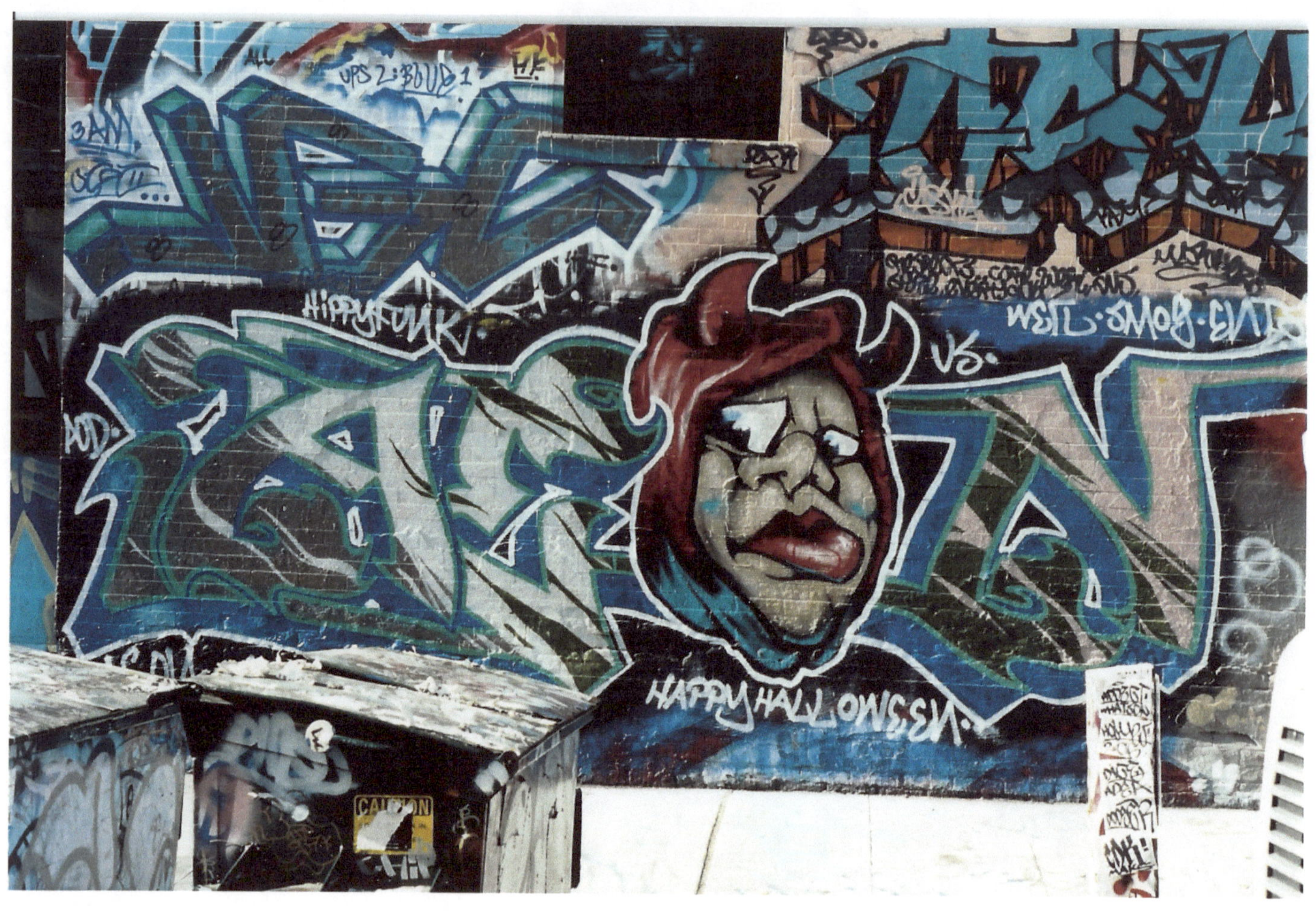
HIPPYFUNK
VS.

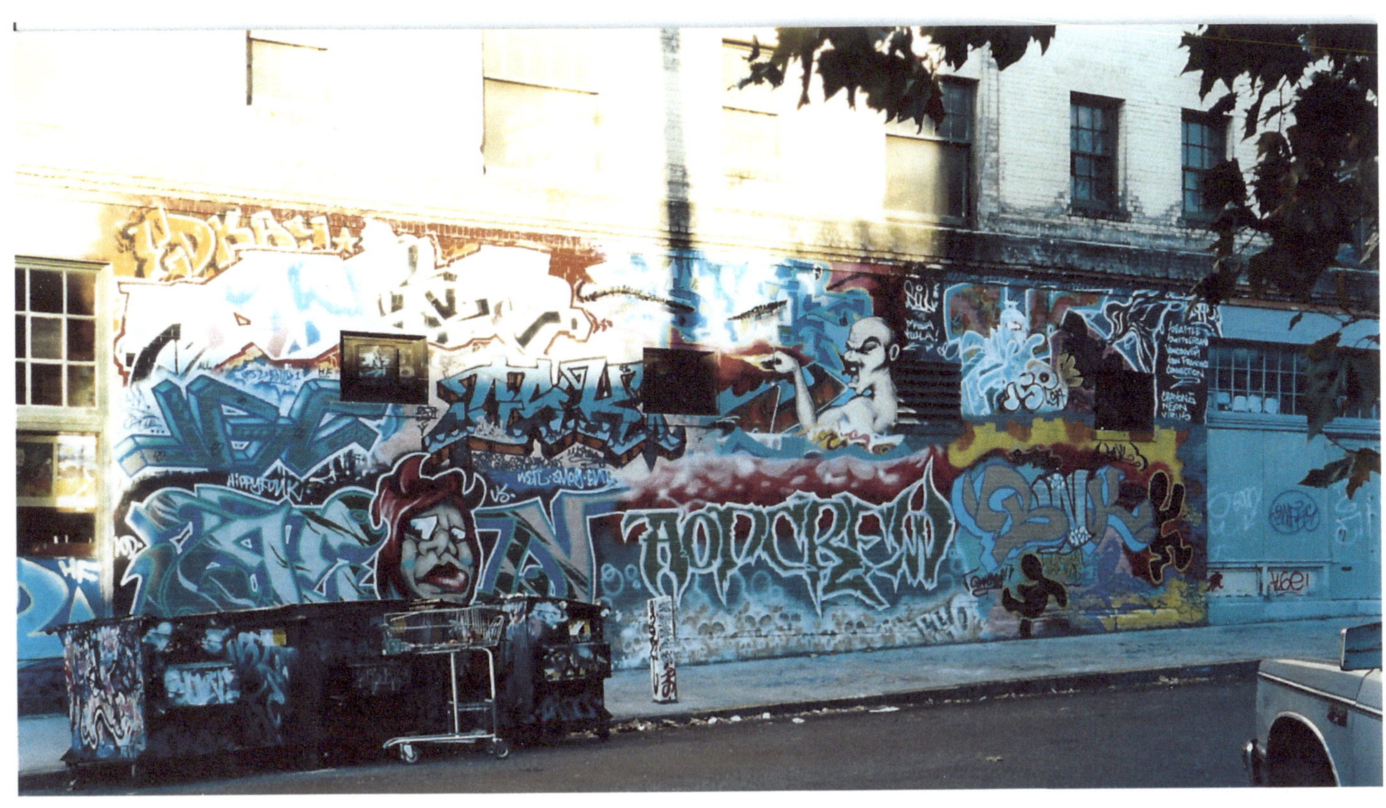

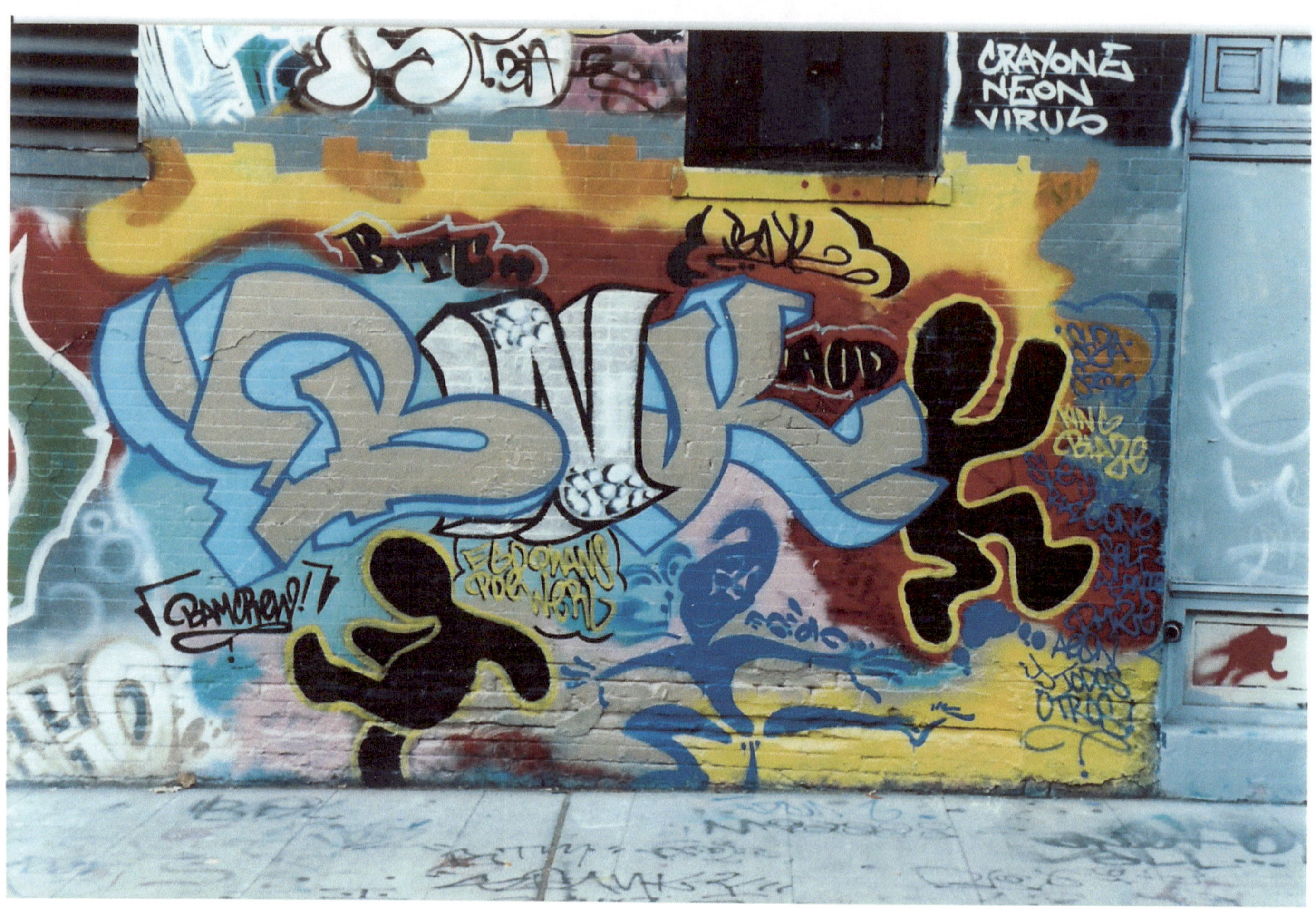
CRAYONE
NEON
VIRUS

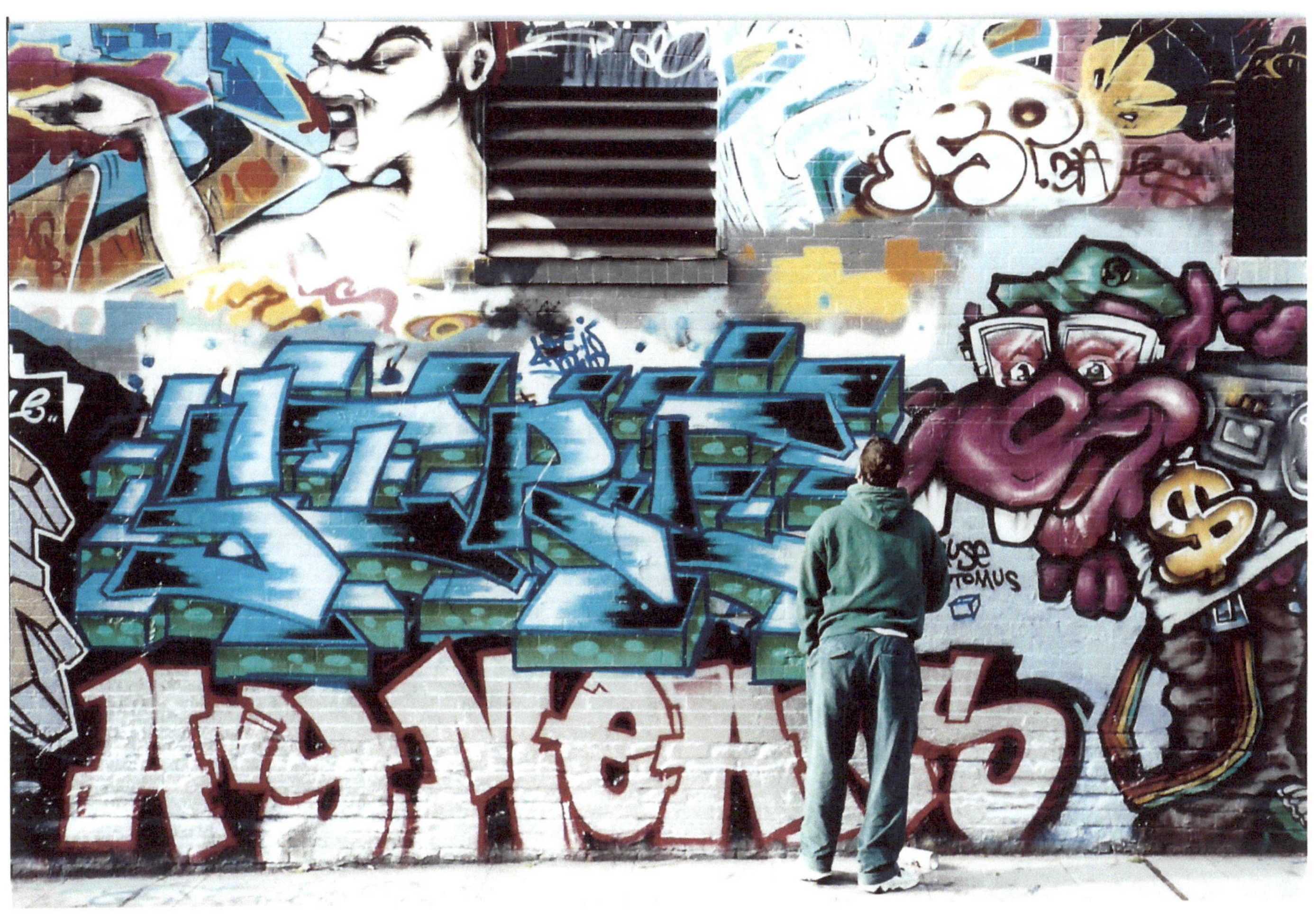

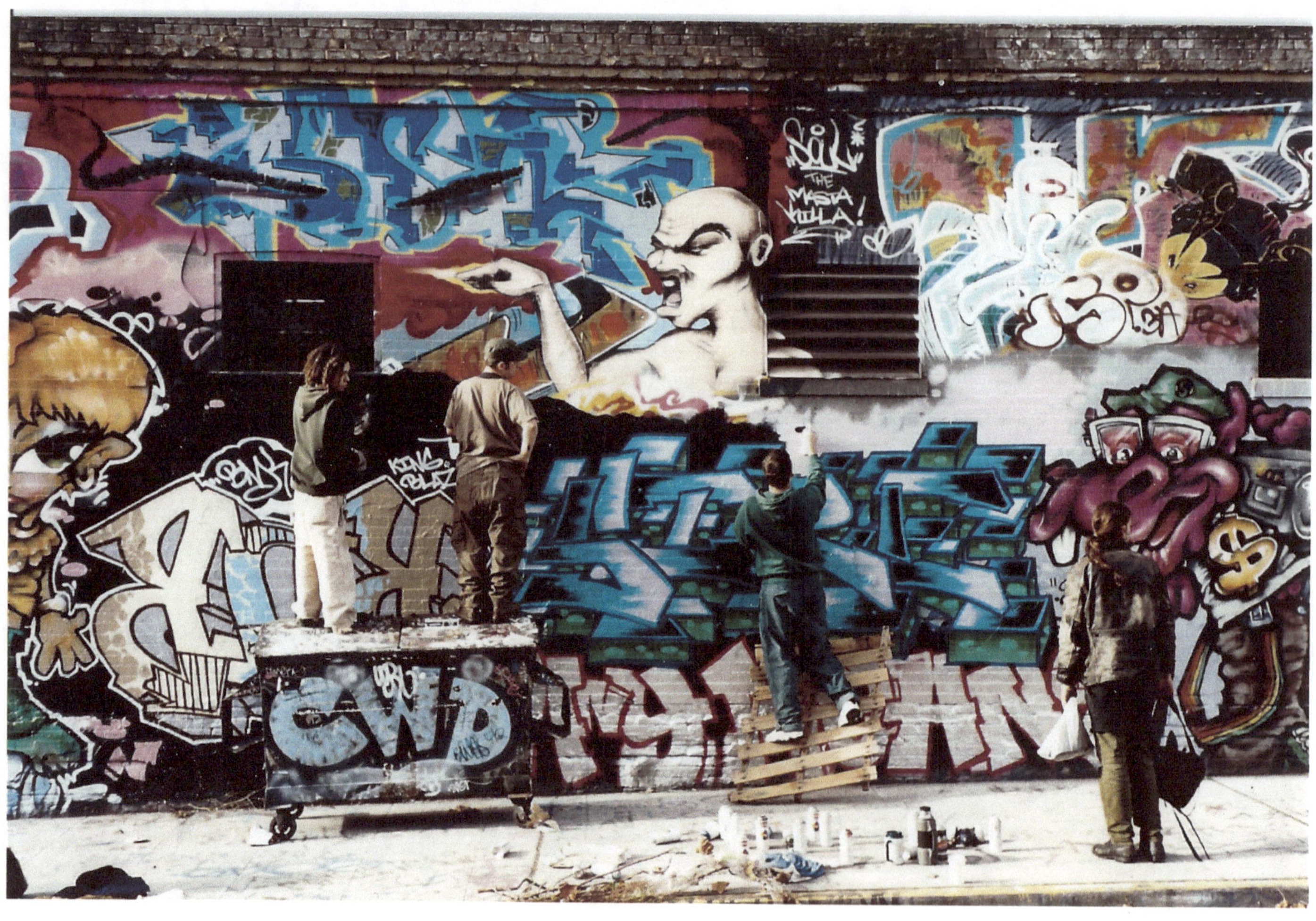
THE MASTA KILLA!
CWD

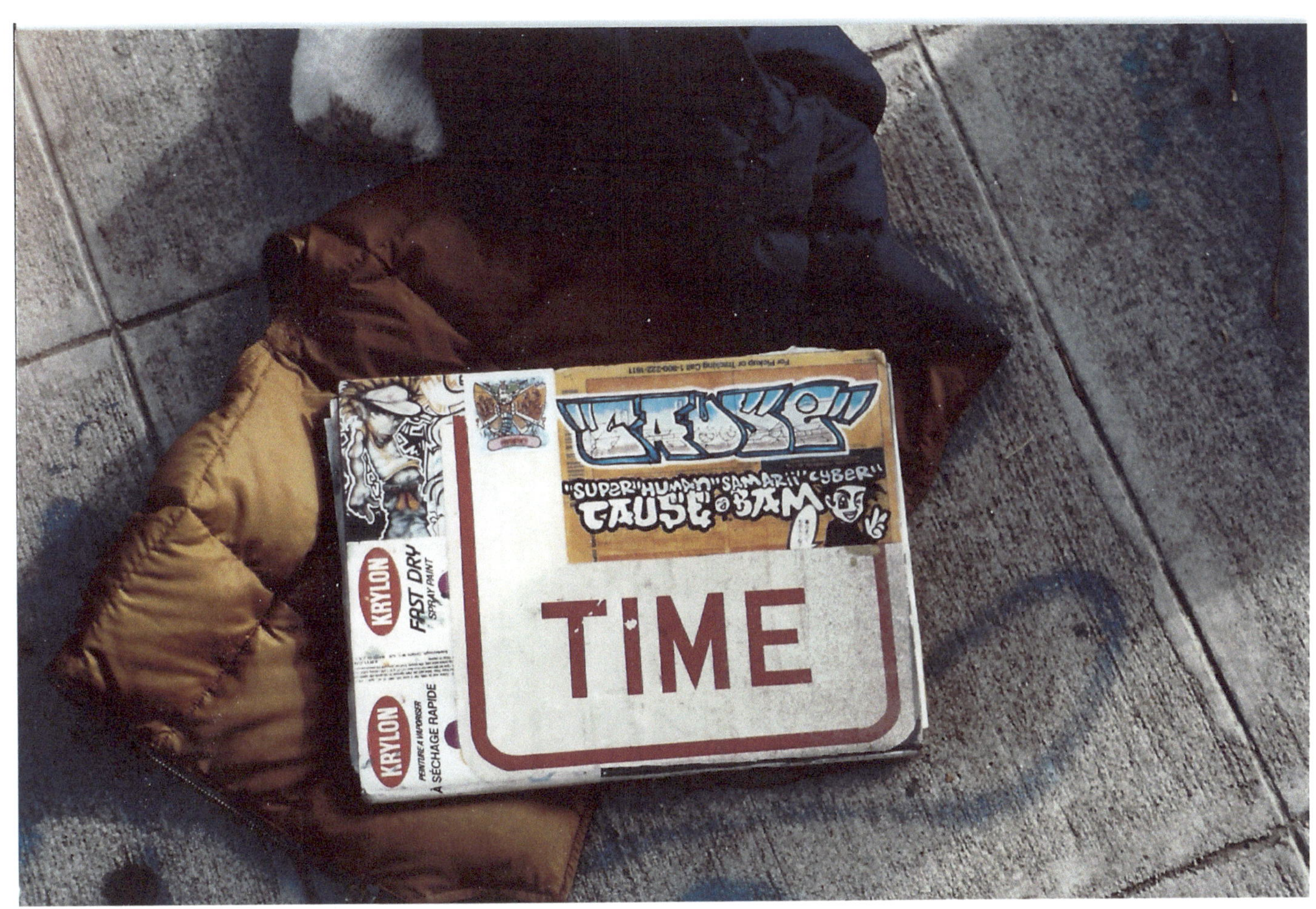
KRYLON
FAST DRY
SPRAY PAINT
KRYLON
À SÉCHAGE RAPIDE
TIME

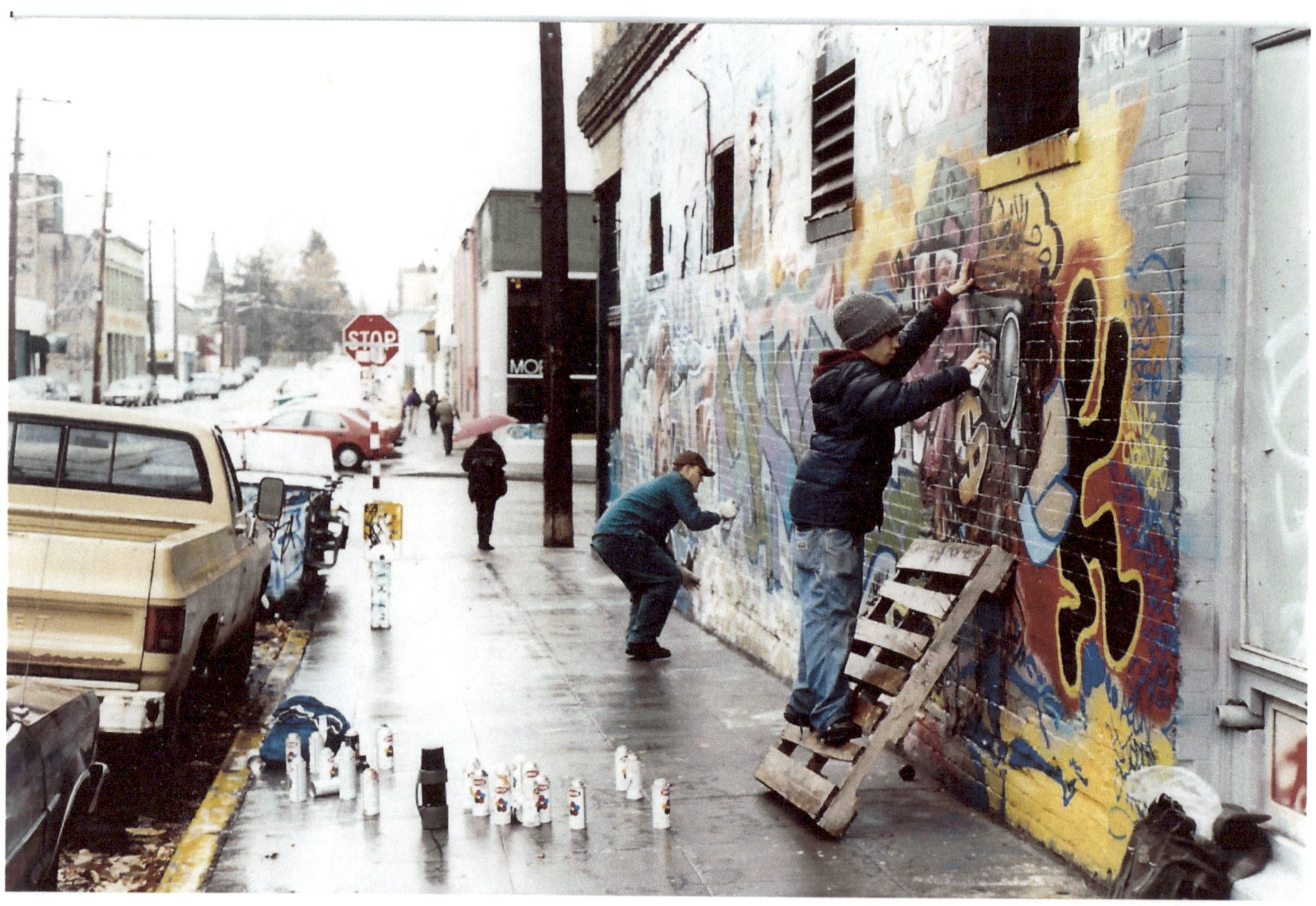
STOP

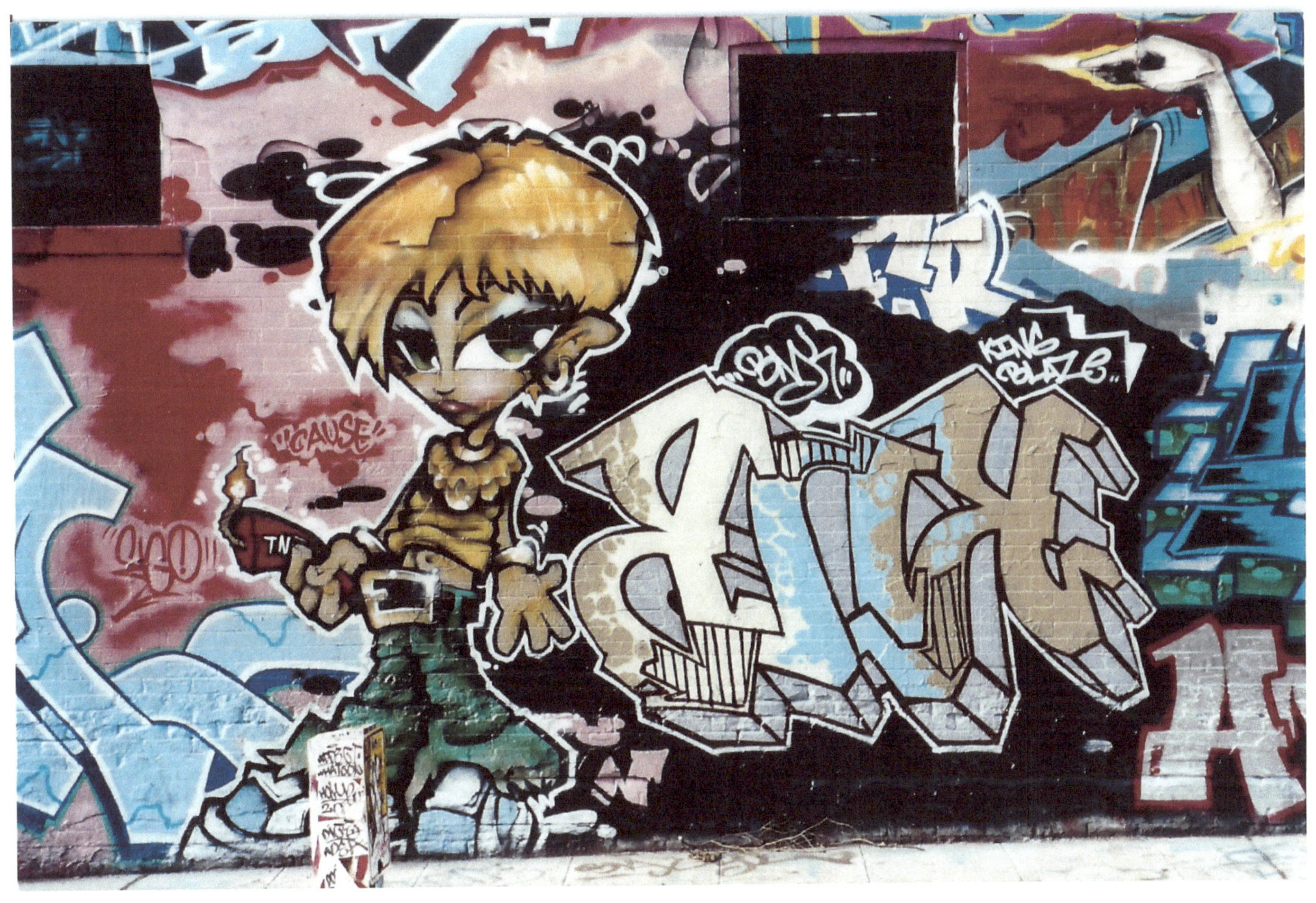
CAUSE

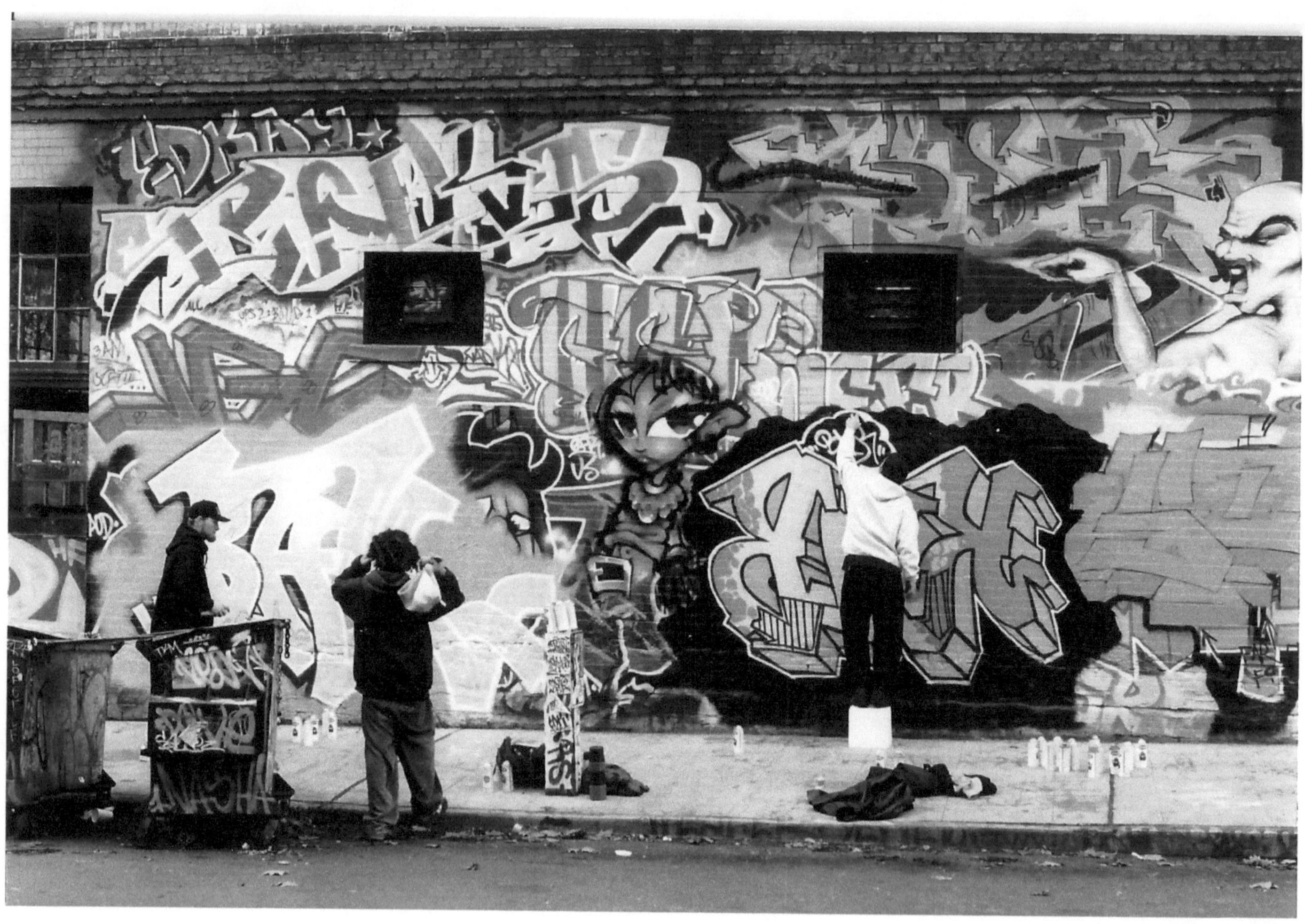

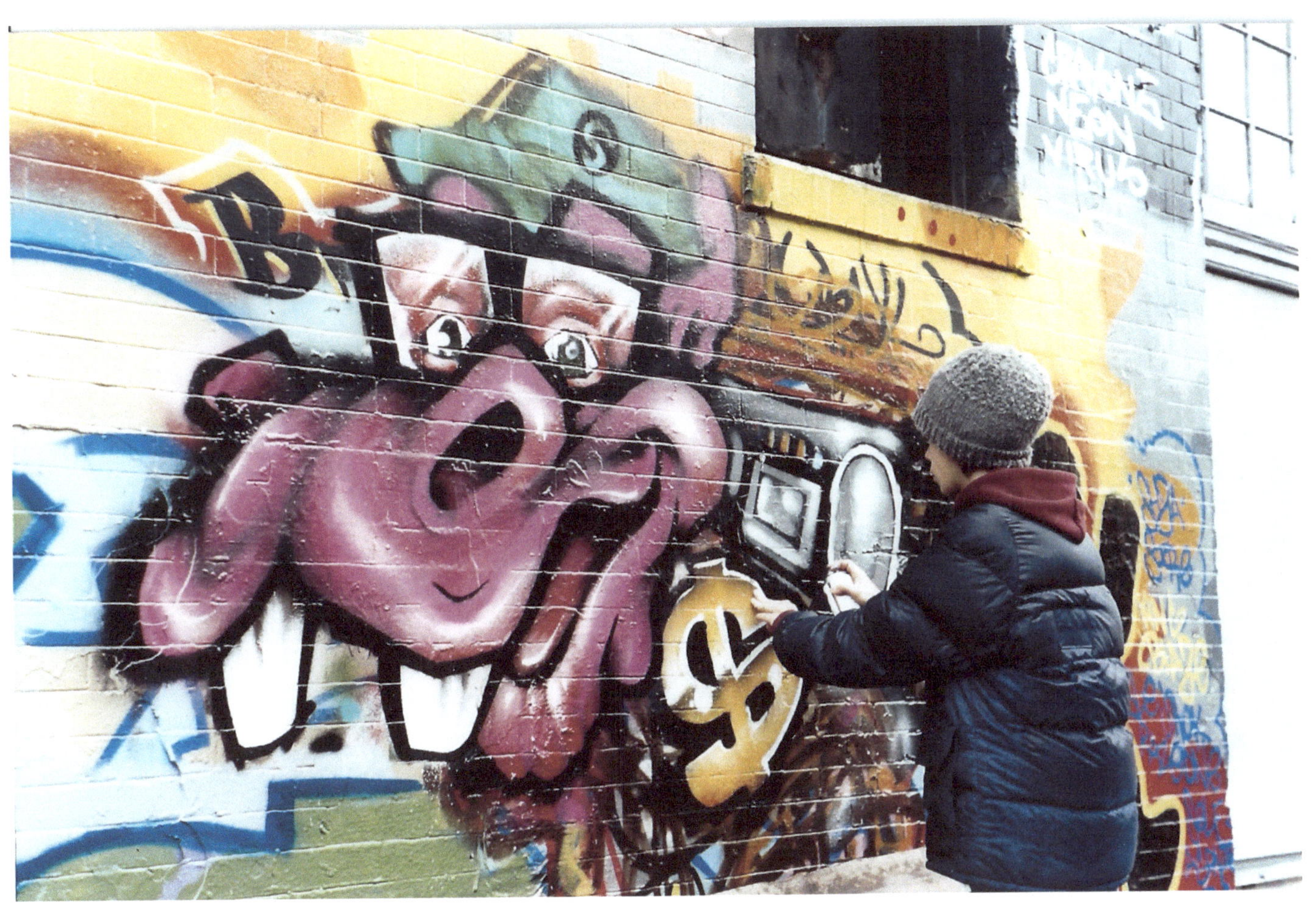

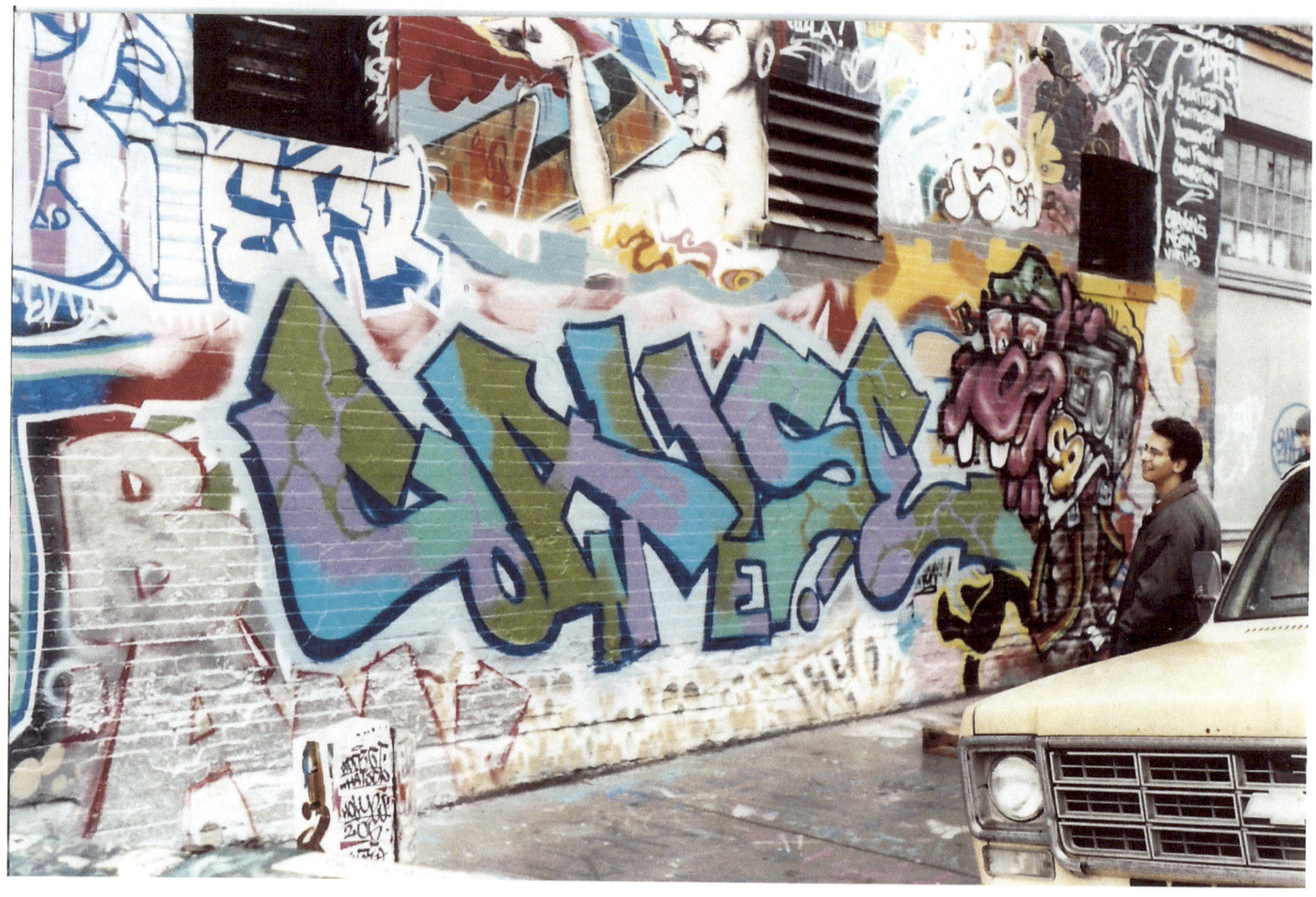

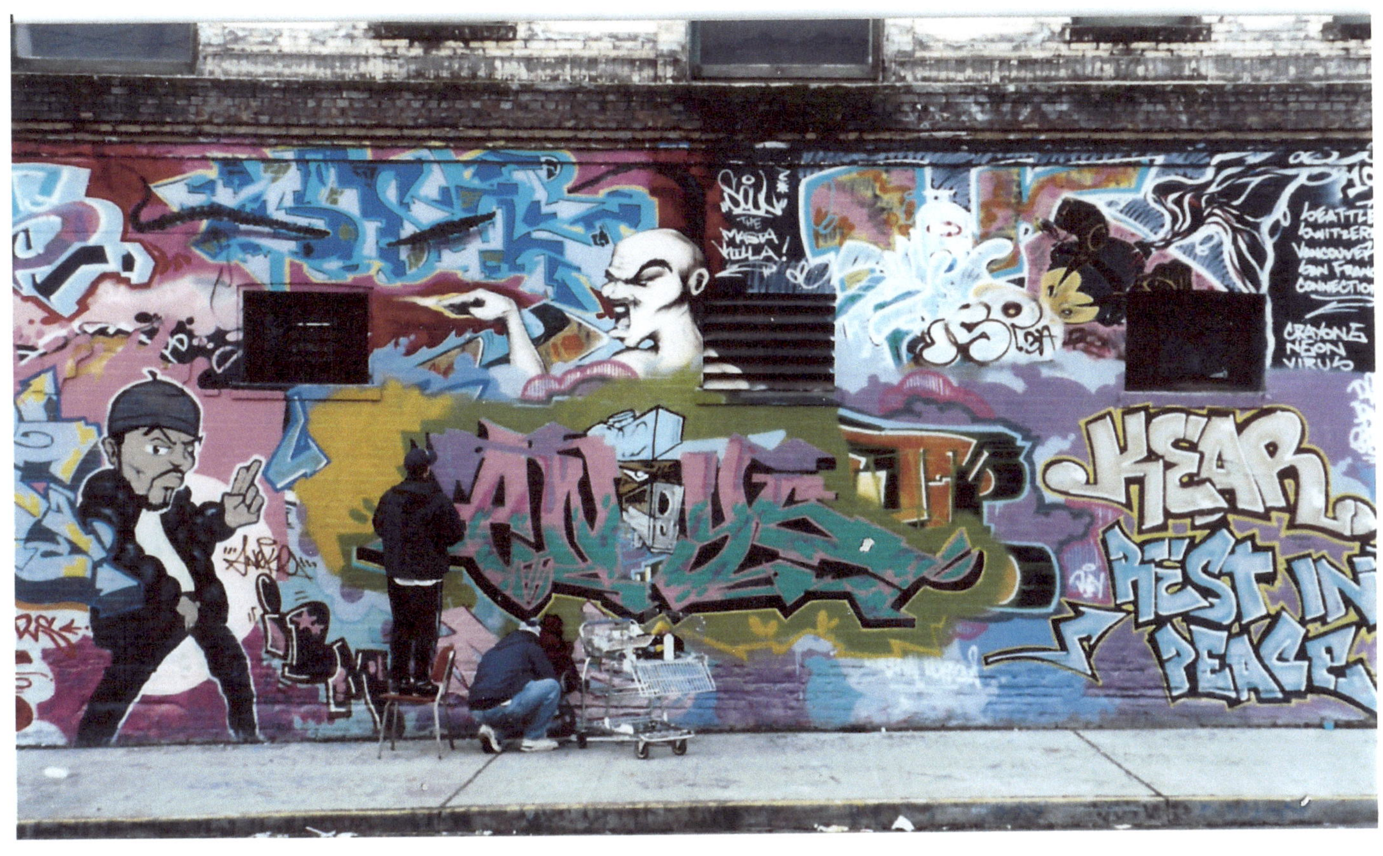
KEAR
REST IN
PEACE

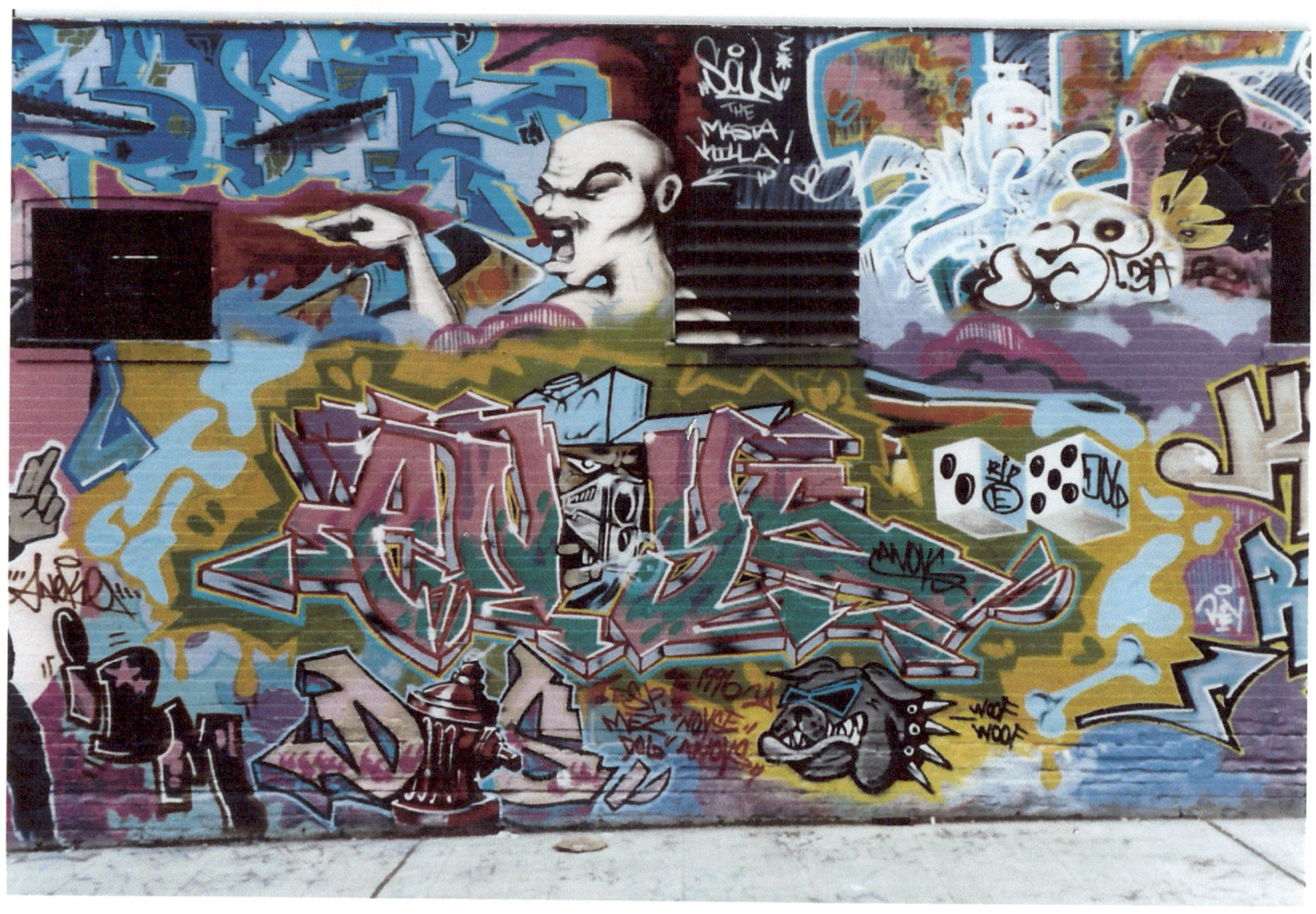
THE
MASTA
KILLA!
WOOF
WOOF

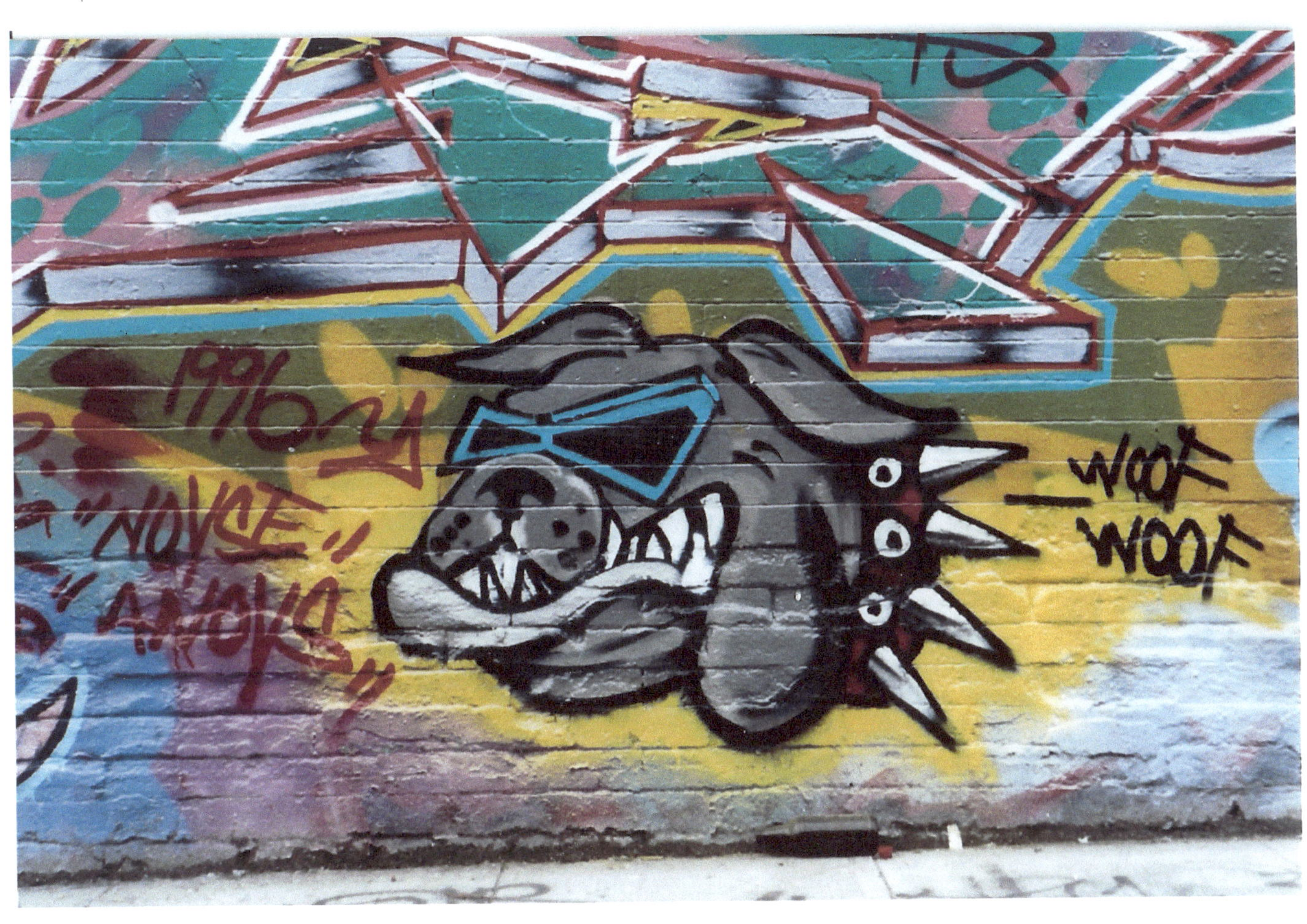
1996
WOOF
WOOF

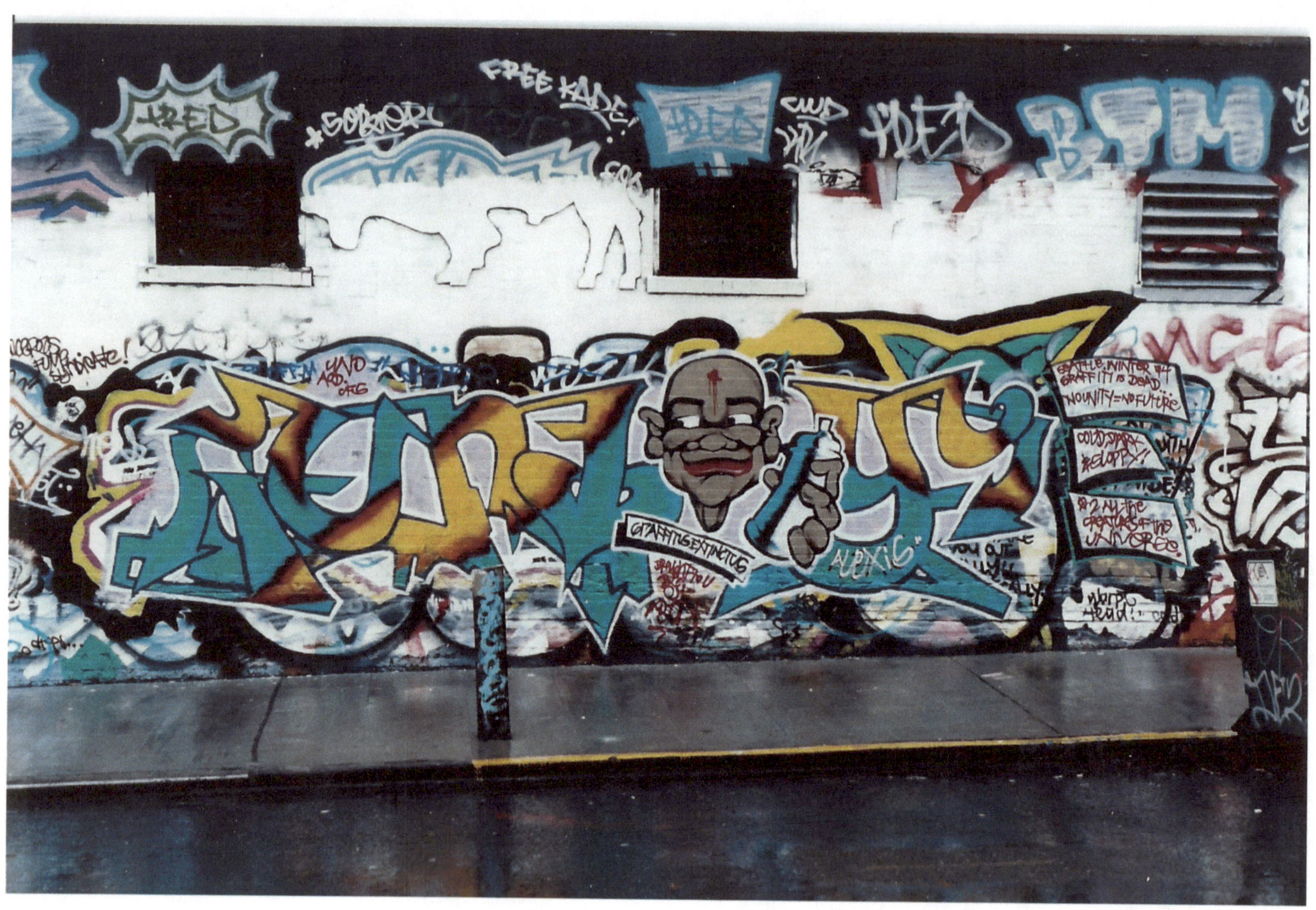
FREE KADE!
SEATTLE WINTER 94
GRAFFITI IS DEAD...
NO UNITY = NO FUTURE
2 ALL the CREATURES OF THE UNIVERSE.
GRAFFITUS EXTINCTUS

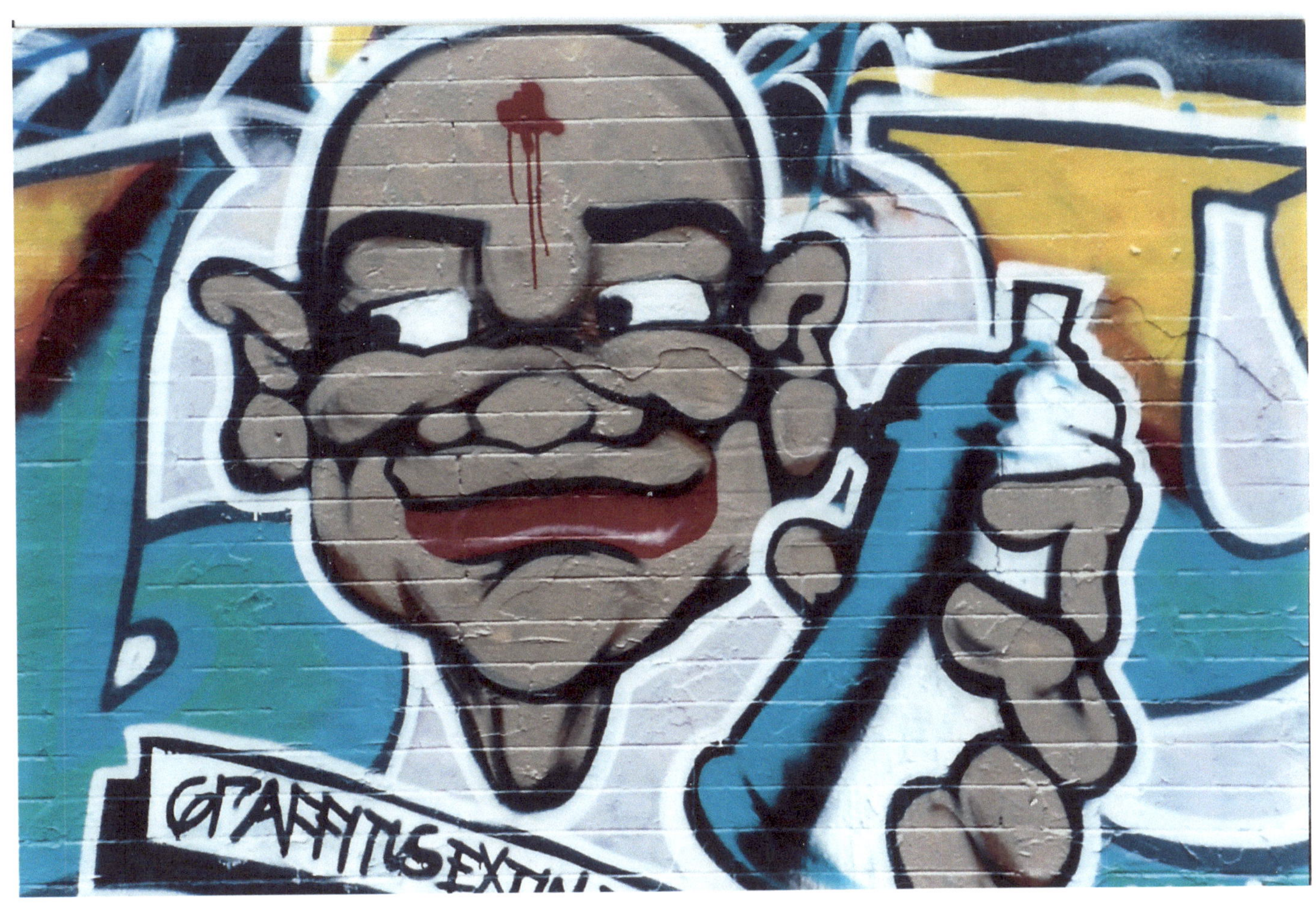
GRAFFITIS

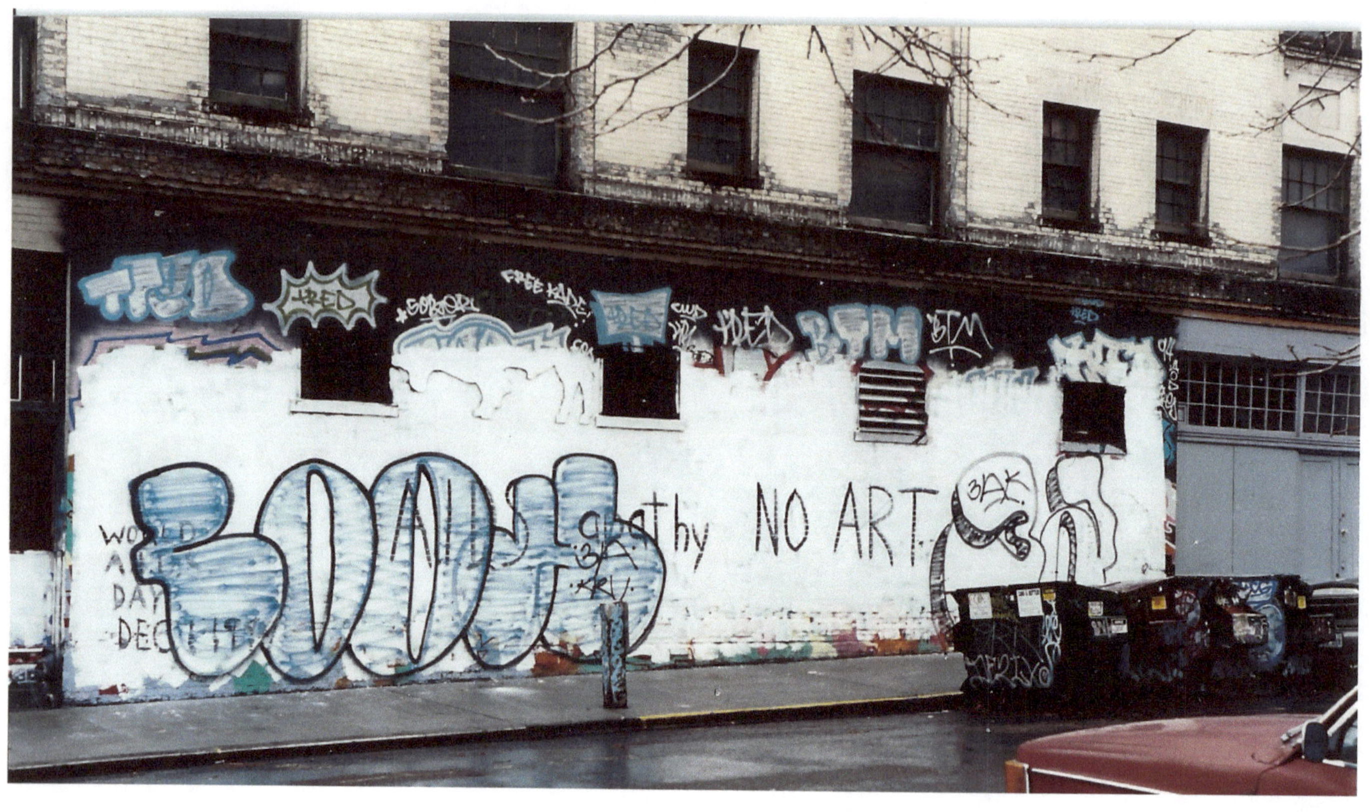
NO ART.

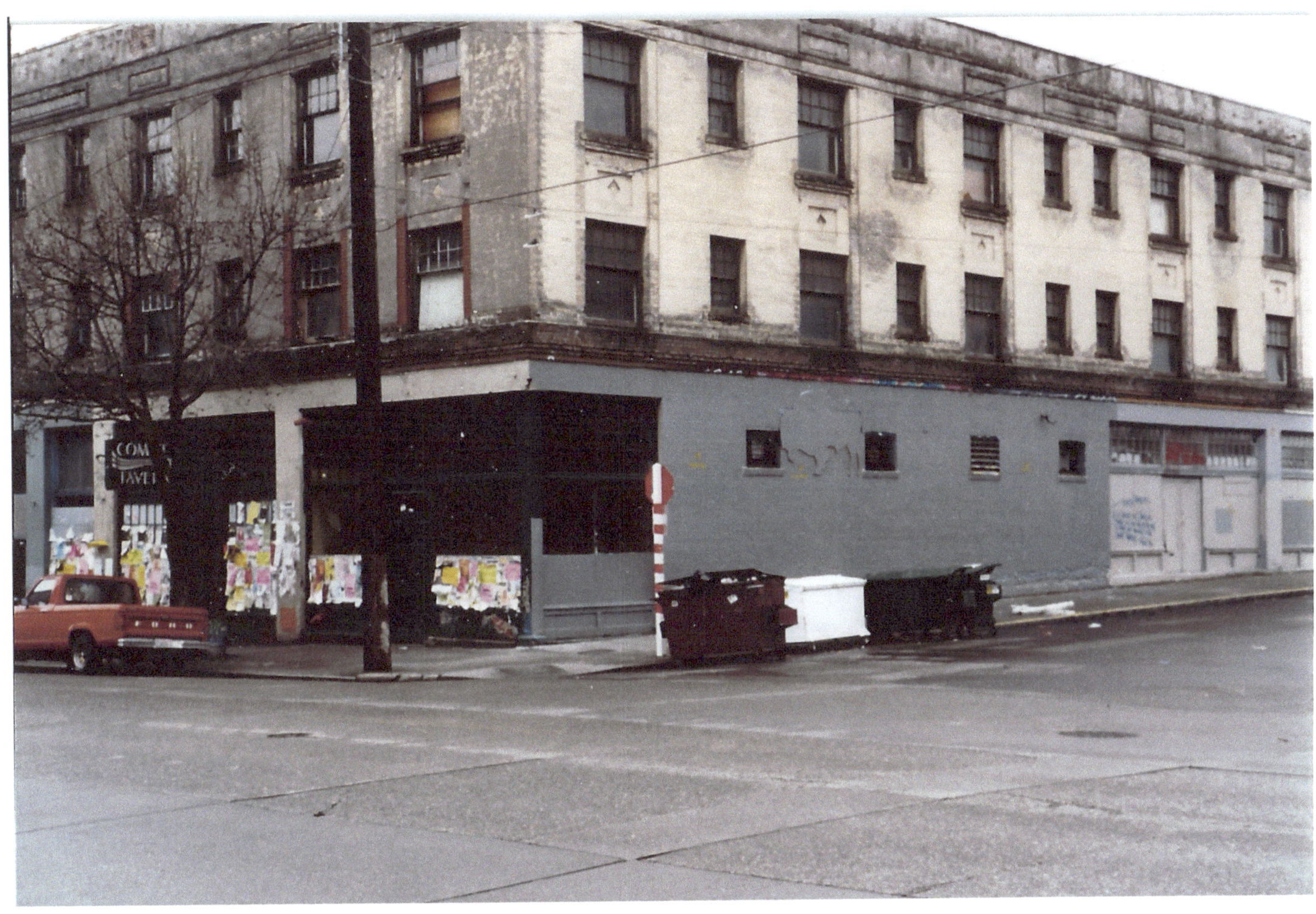

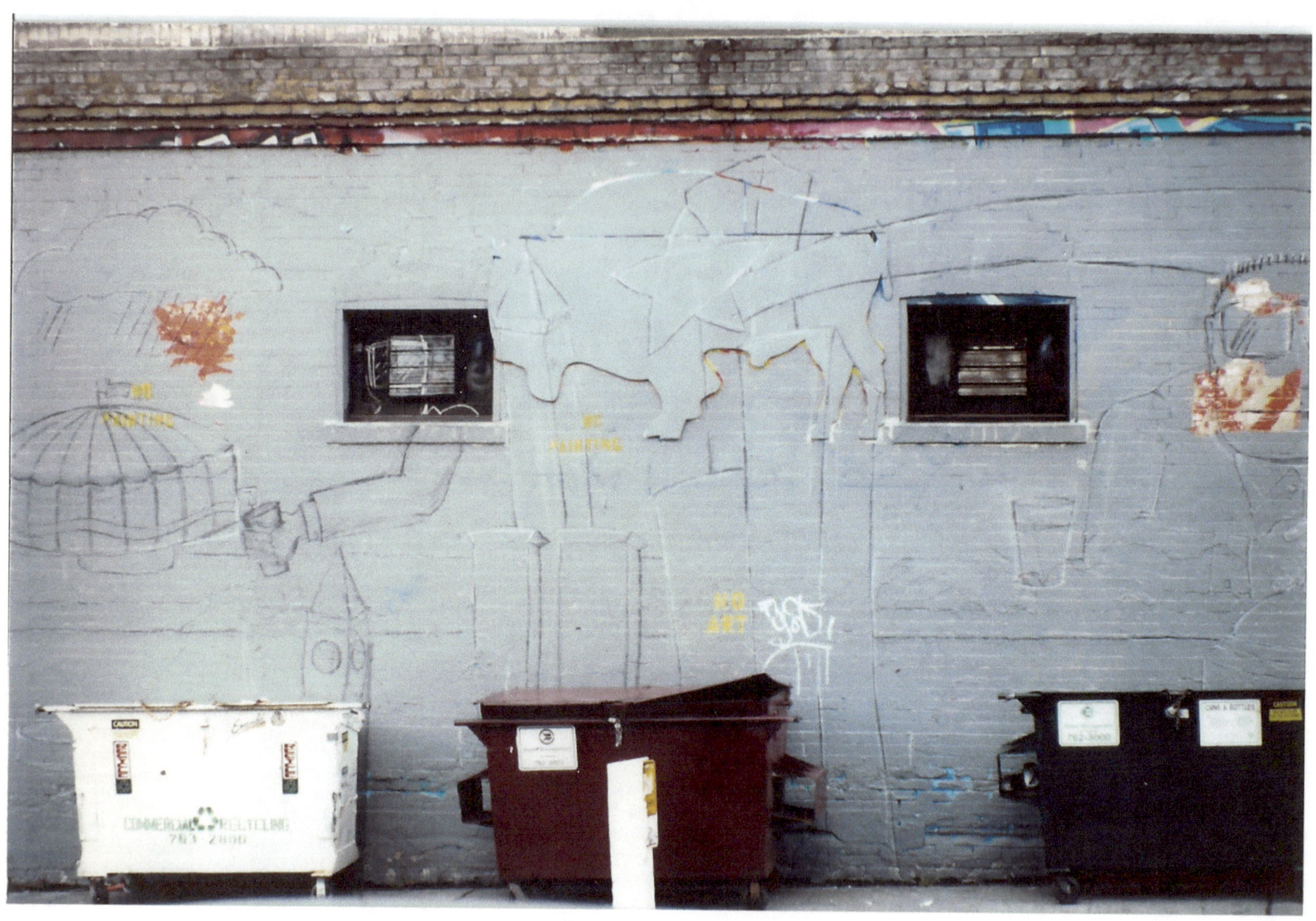
NO
PAINTING
NO
PAINTING
NO
ART
CAUTION
COMMERCIAL RECYCLING

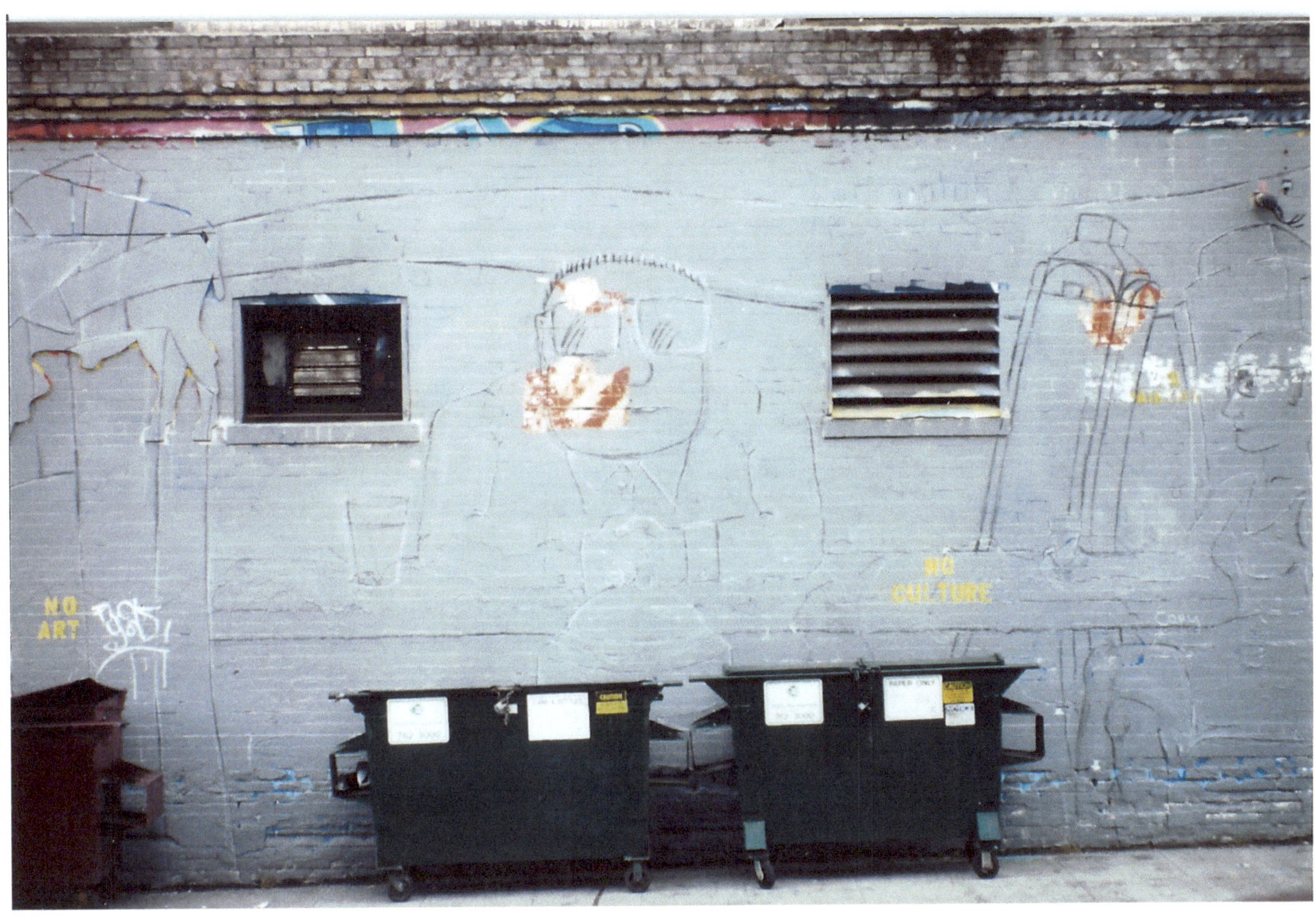
NO
ART
NO
CULTURE

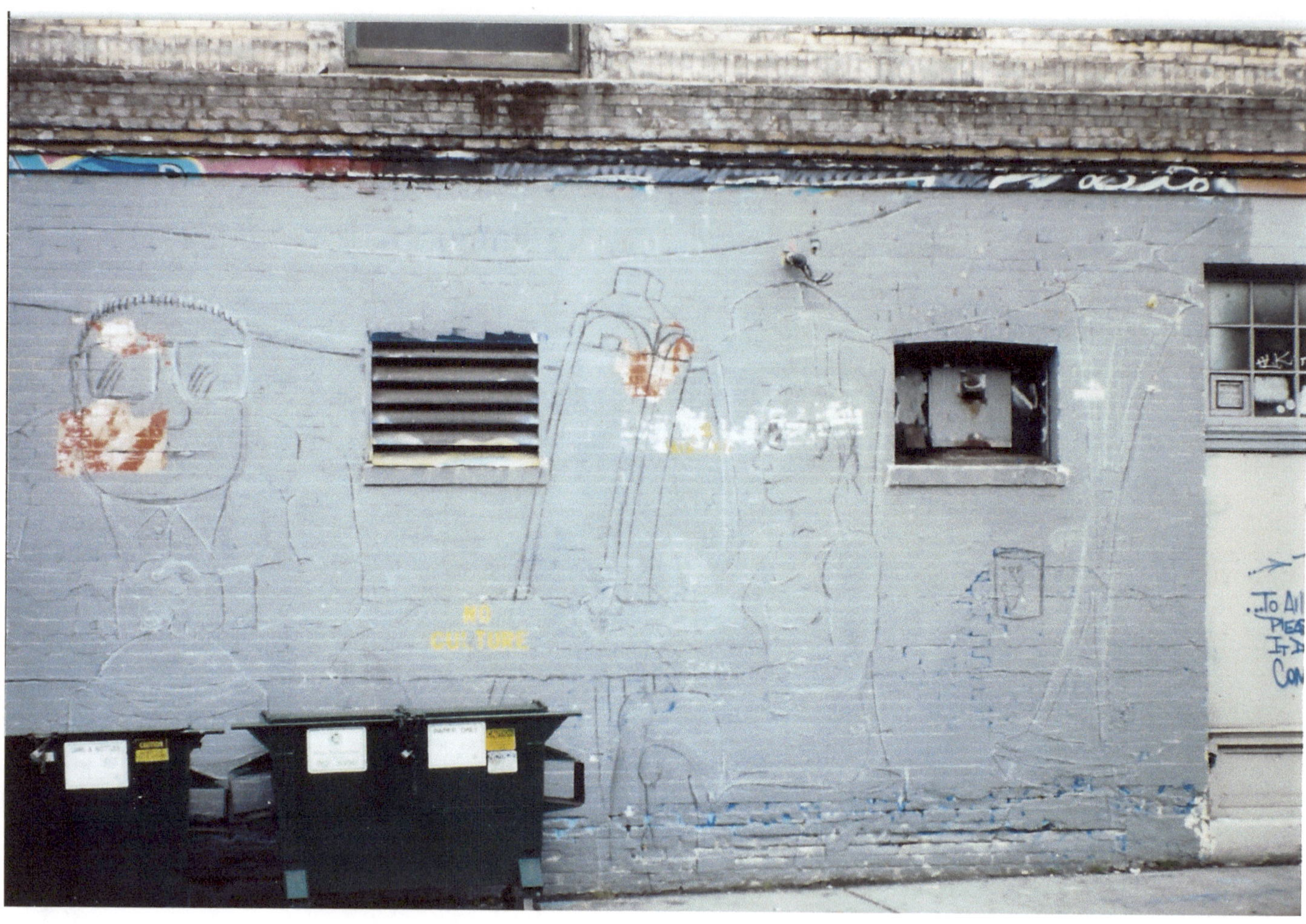
NO
CULTURE

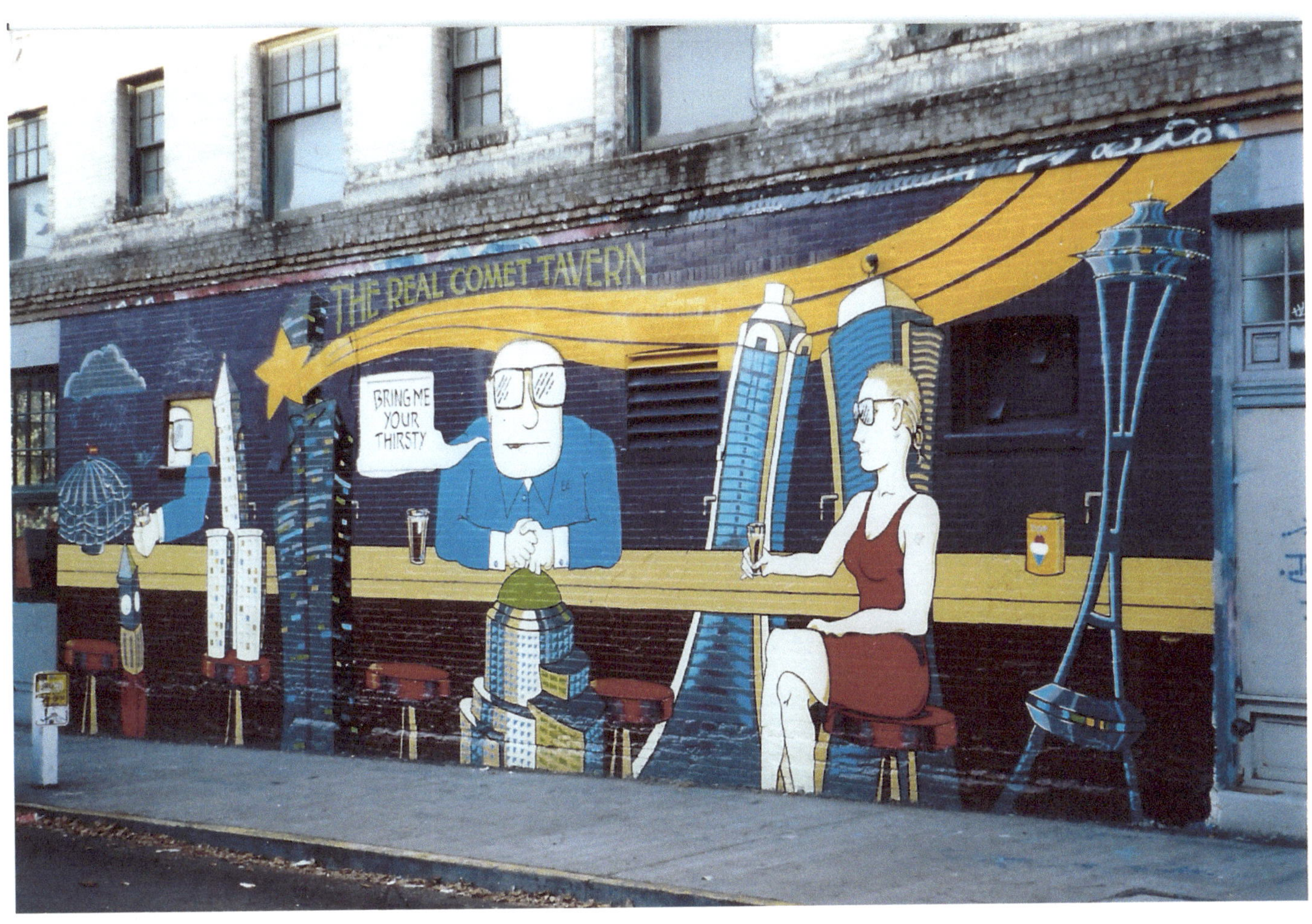
THE REAL COMET TAVERN
BRING ME
YOUR
THIRSTY

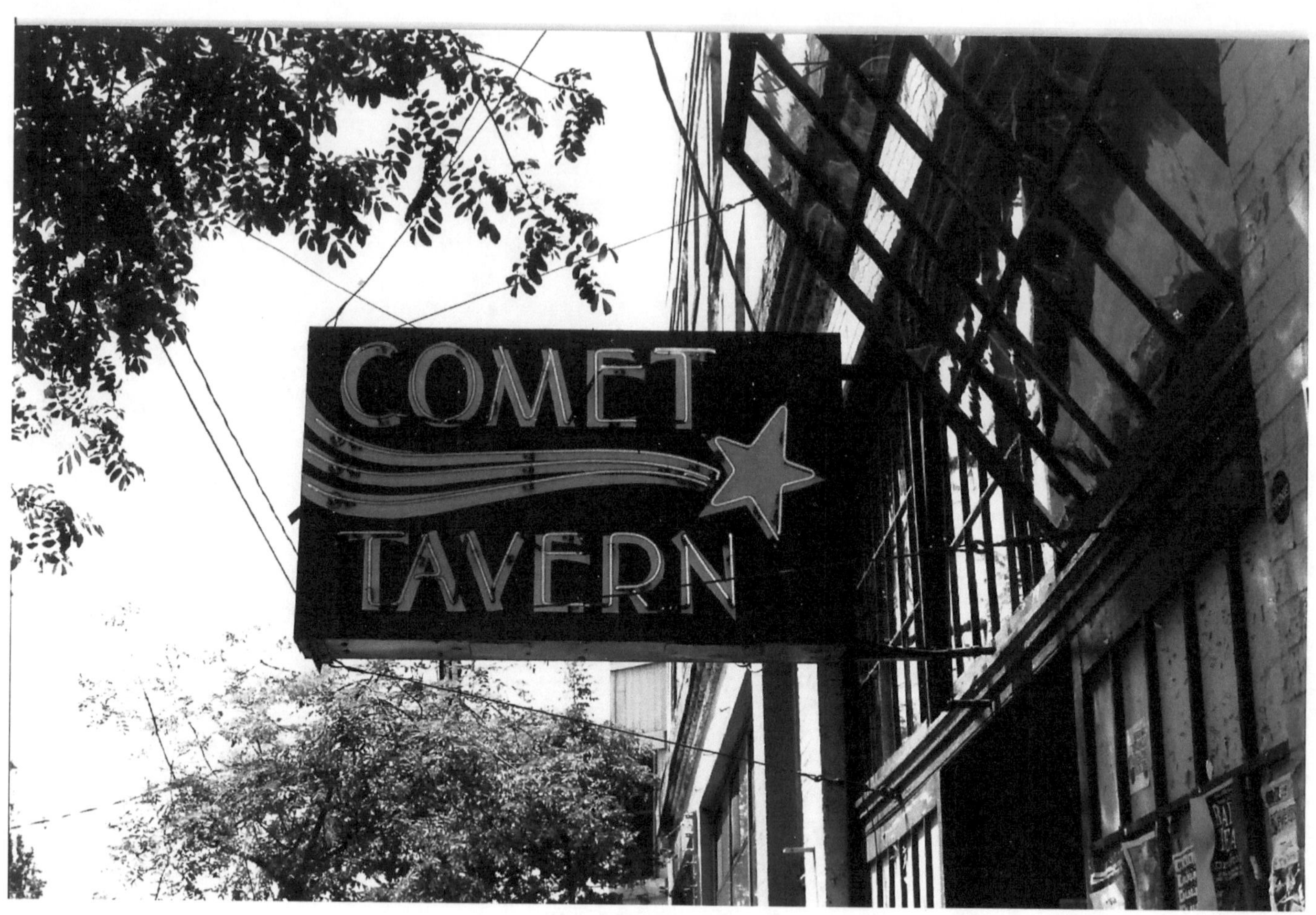
COMET
TAVERN

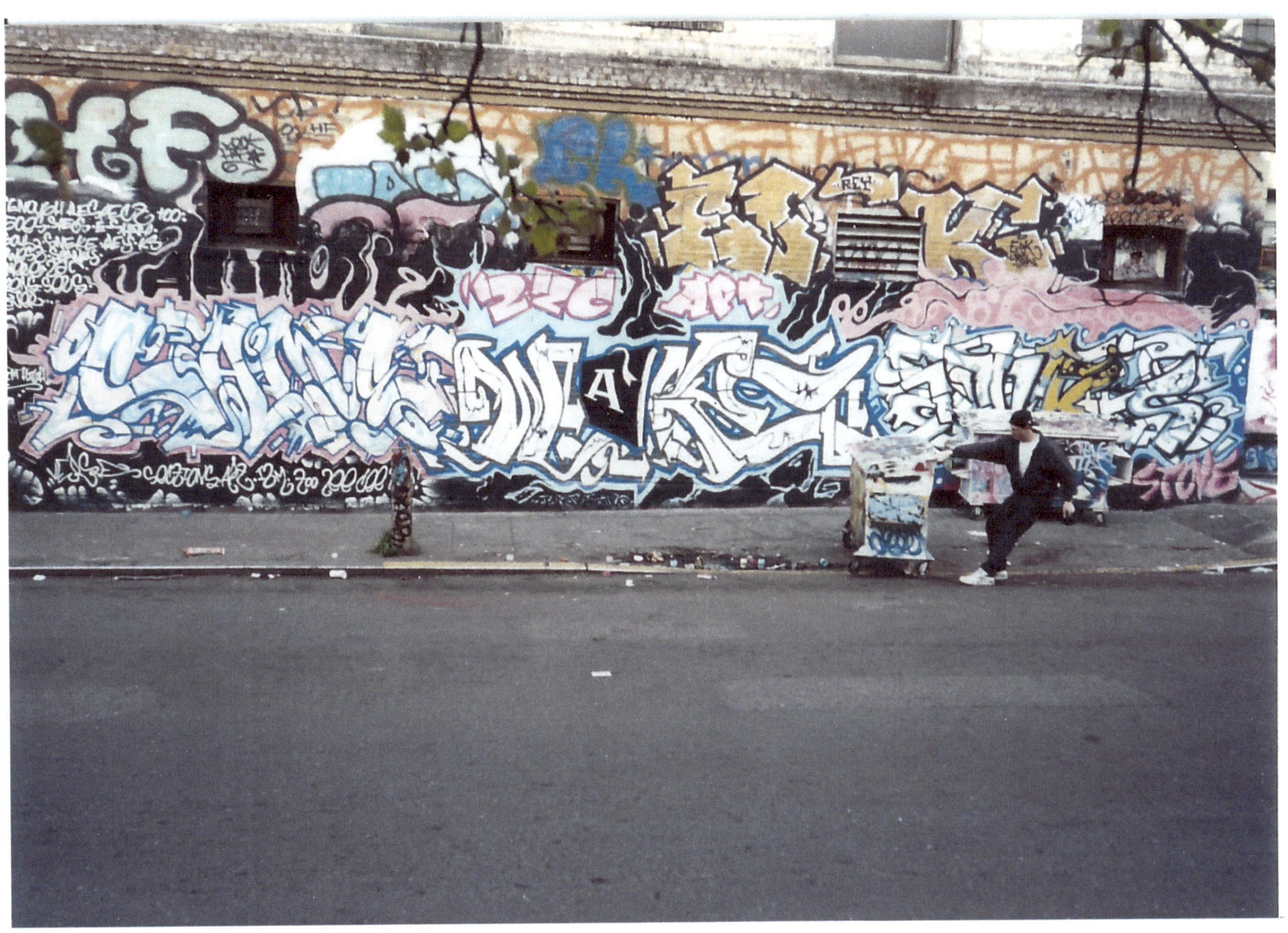

www.ingramcontent.com/pod-product-compliance
Lightning Source LLC
LaVergne TN
LVHW070118110826
845147LV00002B/145